1588

The Spanish Armada and the 24 Ships Lost on Ireland's Shores

MICHAEL B. BARRY

ANDALUS PRESS

Published by Andalus Press
Dublin, Ireland.

info@andalus.ie
www.andalus.ie

Irish edition, published as '1588, the Spanish Armada and the 24 Ships Lost on Ireland's Shores', ISBN: 978-1-8384859-3-1.

Spanish edition, published as '1588, the Surprising Survival of the Spanish Armada', ISBN: 978-1-8384859-4-8.

By the same author:
Across Deep Waters, Bridges of Ireland
Restoring a Victorian House
Through the Cities, the Revolution in Light Rail
Tales of the Permanent Way, Stories from the Heart of Ireland's Railways
Fifty Things to do in Dublin
*Dublin's Strangest Tales (*with Patrick Sammon*)*
Bridges of Dublin, the Remarkable Story of Dublin's Liffey Bridges (with Annette Black)
Victorian Dublin Revealed, the Remarkable Legacy of Nineteenth-Century Dublin
Courage Boys, We are Winning, an Illustrated History of the 1916 Rising
The Green Divide, an Illustrated History of the Irish Civil War
An Illustrated History of the Irish Revolution 1916-1923
Fake News and the Irish War of Independence
The Fight for Irish Freedom: an Illustrated History of the War of Independence
The Irish Civil War in Colour (with John O'Byrne)
A Nation is Born (with John O'Byrne)
The Emergency in Colour (with John O'Byrne)
Beyond the Chaos, the Remarkable Heritage of Syria
Homage to al-Andalus, the Rise and Fall of Islamic Spain
The Alhambra Revealed, the Remarkable Story of the Kingdom of Granada
Málaga, a Guide and Souvenir
Hispania, the Romans in Spain and Portugal

Jacket design by Anú Design
Back flap: author photograph, Veronica Barry
Book design by Michael B. Barry
Vignettes: Veronica Barry

Printed by Białostockie Zakłady Graficzne SA, Poland.

Contents

For Veronica Barry

At Streedagh Strand, Co Sligo, Ireland: a commemoration for the men of the Spanish Armada who lost their lives there.

Acknowledgements

This book benefitted from the help, insights and scholarship of many kind people. Thanks are due first and foremost to historian and author Antonio Luis Gómez Beltrán, who possesses an in-depth knowledge of the Armada and the events of 1588. I have been fortunate to get to know him. He unfailingly devoted considerable time to giving me fresh insights into the detailed history of the sixteenth century, particularly that of Spain. Special thanks are also due to the historian Pedro Luis Chinchilla, who maintains the essential and authoritative website on the Armada, www.armadainvencible.org. Pedro was generous with his time, encouragement and advice, as I went along my Armada journey. Of course, all errors that may occur in this book are my own.

Rubén López-Pulido, director of the Spanish Tourism Office in Dublin, has always been enthusiastic and encouraging to me in my writings on Spanish history. In the Spanish Embassy, Dublin, Ambassador Ion de la Riva and Cristian Font Calderón were helpful and supportive, as was the Defence Attaché to Britain and Ireland, Captain José Luis Nieto Fernández.

To help understand how sixteenth-century Spanish ships were constructed, I was privileged to get a tour of the museum of shipbuilding in the Basque Country, the Albaola Itsas Kultur Faktoria, Pasaia, by the director, Xabier Agote. Mikel Leoz courteously showed me around their 1545 full-size replica *nao*, currently reaching completion. Enara Novillo kindly furnished me with photographs. The Ulster Museum, Belfast, is fortunate to have the best display of Armada artefacts in the world. Greer Ramsey gave me an excellent exposition on the exhibits there and Stephen Weir kindly sent me a selection of images. Mark Kennedy, always helpful to me with my book endeavours, facilitated. Eddie O'Gorman, Chair of the Grange and Armada Development Association (Spanish Armada Ireland, www.spanisharmadaireland.com) and Committee member, Micheál Ó Domhnaill generously sent me the impressive aerial photograph of their 2023 Commemoration at Streedagh Strand.

I was lucky to get in touch with the Donegal-based artist Seán Ó Brógáin (seanobrogain@yahoo.ie), who sent me his drawings of de Cuéllar. Historian Joe McGowan was good enough to check my material on the Sligo events. Helene Brennan (www.helene-brennan.com) generously sent one of her series of excellent photographs from the Dingle Peninsula, in this case of Blasket Sound. The Tower Museum contains a trove of artefacts from the *Trinidad Valencera* and I am grateful to Ronan McConnell, and Roisin Doherty of the museum for sending me images. It was a privilege to meet Dave Atherton, author, and one of the City of Derry Sub Aqua Club team that discovered the *Trinidad Valencera* in 1971, a team that spent the next decade carefully recovering the remains.

The following were very helpful to me: Carlos Álvarez Nogal, Universidad Carlos III de Madrid; Caridad López Ibáñez of the Archives, Fundación Casa Medina Sidonia, Sanlúcar de Barrameda; Carolynn McCormack, Clark Art Institute; Ignacio Retuerto of Kronos Servicios de Restauración, Madrid; Kirsten MacLeod of Edinburgh Napier University; Beatrice Okoro, Royal Museums Greenwich; Catherine Sutherland, Special Collections Librarian, Magdalene College, Cambridge; Mar Vilalba; Paul Neilan, Gill Books; Michael Harpur, www.eoceanic.com; the staff of Sigüenza Cathedral – and Alasdair Goold-Verschoyle of www.books.ie, whose antecedents are from Co. Donegal, for the idea of the book.

Lastly, but most importantly, providing essential and, as always, much valued support: Veronica Barry and Patrick Sammon.

Key to the Armada squadrons

(As used in maps within)

Portugal		***Levant***	
Castile		***Urcas***	
Vizcaya		***Pataches & Zabras***	
Andalucia		***Galleasses***	
Guipúzcoa		***Galleys***	

Chronology

25 July 1554	Philip of Spain marries Queen Mary I at Winchester Cathedral. He is King of England until Mary dies in November 1558.
16 January 1556	Philip becomes King of Spain after his father Charles V abdicates.
15 January 1559	Elizabeth I crowned. She gradually re-establishes the English brand of Protestantism.
August 1559	Philip sails from Flanders to Spain, leaving his half-sister Margaret of Parma in charge.
August 1566	Uprising in the Netherlands: anti-clerical mobs smash Catholic churches.
August 1567	An army under the Duke of Alba arrives in Brussels, and proceeds to harshly suppress resistance.
May 1568	Mary, Queen of Scots, flees Scotland. Elizabeth orders that she be kept in protective custody.
November 1568	Spanish pay-ships shelter in an English harbour and the money is impounded. English property in Netherlands is seized as a result.
February 1570	The Pope excommunicates Elizabeth as a heretic.
April 1571	The Ridolfi plot is discovered in England. It includes plans to invade England and depose Elizabeth. The invasion concept thereafter becomes known as the 'Enterprise of England'.
October 1571	Victory by the Holy League over the Turks at the Battle of Lepanto. The balance of powers in the Mediterranean remains the same, but the Ottomans are soon diverted by the challenge from the Persians.
1572	Francis Drake plunders the Spanish Main, and continues in the years that follow to raid Spanish treasure fleets and settlements.
April 1572	Dutch privateers, the 'Sea Beggars', occupy the port of Brill.
4 November 1576	'The Spanish Fury', the pillage of Antwerp by unpaid Spanish troops. Don John of Austria, newly appointed, arrives too late to stop it.
December 1577	Francis Drake sets out on an expedition to the Pacific. After sailing round the globe, he arrives back in Plymouth in September 1580, his ship replete with captured treasure.
October 1578	Don John of Austria dies, and is replaced by Alexander Farnese (who becomes the Duke of Parma in September 1586).
January 1579	Rebels in the northern Dutch provinces form the Union of Utrecht.
February 1580	Philip II inherits the Kingdom of Portugal.
November 1580	A Papal force of Italian and Spanish volunteers is massacred by the Lord Deputy's forces after surrendering at Smerwick in Ireland.
August 1583	Following a great victory in the Azores, the Marquis of Santa Cruz urges Philip to make preparations for the invasion of England the following year.
August 1585	The Treaty of Nonsuch is signed, under which England agrees to send an army to support the Dutch rebels. Antwerp falls to Parma.
September 1585	On the orders of Elizabeth, Drake sails out of Plymouth to raid Spanish ports in the Old and New World. After the sack of Vigo and Baiona, Philip drops any hesitation he had for the Enterprise of England. At the end of December he requests his nephew, the Prince of Parma, to prepare plans for the invasion of England.
March 1586	Philip receives an invasion plan from the Marquis of Santa Cruz, which involves a fleet of 500 ships. Parma's plan arrives in June and sets out how his army would invade England from the Netherlands. Philip and his advisors continue with planning – over time several permutations are considered.
April 1586	The Marquis of Santa Cruz is ordered to go to Lisbon to begin assembling an armada. Towards the end of the year orders go out to Philip's domains to send men, ships and equipment.
1587	
8 February	Mary, Queen of Scots, is executed.
April	Drake sets sail to disrupt Armada preparations. He raids Cádiz and in June sets out for the Azores to intercept the treasure fleet. The Marquis of Santa Cruz is ordered to depart from Lisbon with ships to protect this.
April-August	Armada preparations continue in Lisbon.
End September	Santa Cruz and his ships return to Lisbon.
December	The Earl of Leicester, leader of the English expedition to the Netherlands, decides to return home.

1588

9 February	The Marquis of Santa Cruz dies. Days later a message is sent to the Duke of Medina Sidonia, appointing him in charge of the Armada expedition.
14 March	Medina Sidonia arrives in Lisbon. Preparations intensify.
29 May	The Armada begins to set sail from Lisbon.
19 June	After consistent bad weather and with victuals running short, the fleet is ordered to sail to Corunna.
22 July	The Armada departs Corunna.
30 July	Coast-watchers in south Cornwall behold a forest of sails hoving into view.
31 July	Part of the English fleet warps out of Plymouth harbour. The first battle occurs.
1 August	Drake takes the damaged *Nuestra Señora del Rosario* into his custody.
2 August	Battle off Portland Bill.
3-4 August	Battles off the Isle of Wight.
5-6 August	The English fleet, now in squadrons, follows the Armada as it heads towards Calais. Both fleets anchor off Calais in the late afternoon of 6 August.
7 August	Late at night, the English set fireships to sail towards the Armada.
8 August	In the morning, with the Armada dispersed, the English ships attack the flagship *San Martín* and other ships which form a rearguard. The bloody battle of Gravelines begins.
9 August	Medina Sidonia orders a council of war. The decision is that if the wind blew from the south, the Armada is to go around Scotland and Ireland and return to Spain.
10 August	The English fleet shadows the Armada as it sails north.
11 August	A captain is executed on the orders of Medina Sidonia.
12 August	The English fleet, tailing the Armada and now abeam of the Firth of Forth, being greatly short of food and water, breaks off and returns south.
18 August	The Armada turns west to sail through the Fair Isle Channel into the Atlantic.
19 August	Elizabeth makes her famous speech to her massed troops at Tilbury.
14 September	*Trinidad Valencera* strikes a rock off the beach at Kinnagoe Bay, Co. Donegal.
15 September	The *San Juan de Portugal*, accompanied by other ships, sails into Blasket Sound, Co. Kerry.
15 September	The *Nuestra Señora de Begoña* shelters in Blacksod Bay, Co. Mayo, but later manages to sail back to Spain. On 17 September *La Rata* also enters the bay – after it grounds the crew set it on fire. Its commander, de Leyva, leads survivors to the *Duquesa Santa Ana*, also in Blacksod Bay. It sails out and, on 29 September, is wrecked at Loughros More Bay, Co. Donegal.
15 September	A flotilla of ships take shelter in the Shannon Estuary. One, the *Anunciada,* is abandoned and set on fire.
15 September	The *Nuestra Señora del Socorro* sails into a bay near Tralee, Co Kerry. All the survivors are hanged.
21 September	The *Lavia, Juliana* and *Santa Maria de Visón* are blown by the Great Gale to ground just off Streedagh Strand.
21 September	*Santa María de la Rosa* strikes a rock and sinks in Blasket Sound. On 28 September de Recalde in his *San Juan de Portugal* departs the Sound and returns to Spain.
Mid- to late September	Other Armada ships are lost in Ireland, including: *San Nicolás Prodaneli, Gran Grín, Falcón Blanco Mediano, Santa Bárbara, San Esteban* and the *San Marcos*. Survivors are executed immediately or are taken into English custody. Around 330 survivors are executed in Galway at the beginning of October.
21 September	Medina Sidonia arrives in Santander in the *San Martín*. Other Armada ships return to ports in northern Spain.
21 October	Elizabeth commissions Francis Drake and John Norris to prepare a new assault on Spain. This, the 'English Armada', sails out at the end of April, 1589, only to have a disastrous outcome.
28 October	The *Girona*, sailing from Killybegs and laden with around 1,200 survivors (including de Leyva) is heading for Scotland. At midnight, she is swept onto the rocks of Lacada Point on the Antrim coast, and sinks. All but a few drown.
5 November	The *San Juan de Sicilia* blows up in Tobermory Bay, Scotland.
November	Spain's Council of State advises Philip that the best strategy is to continue war with England. The King orders the construction of a series of sophisticated galleons ('the Twelve Apostles').
Mid-December	Sir Richard Bingham writes to Queen Elizabeth, in reference to Armada survivors, to proudly inform her how in his province in Ireland, Connaught: '1,110 ... were put to the sword'.

The Iberian Peninsula in 1588

Notes

On shipwrecks in Ireland: the number of 24 wrecks is an approximate estimate. Given discrepancies in records of the time, it is difficult to establish a precise number. New evidence continues to appear and the number gets updated.

On dates: The dates used throughout this book are expressed as per the 'New Style' calendar that is in use today. This is the Gregorian calendar, introduced by Pope Gregory XIII in 1582. Most of Western Europe had adopted this New Style by 1588. However, for more than a century, the Julian 'Old Style' calendar, which ran ten days behind, continued to be used in England.

Introduction

Like most people, I was generally aware of the history of the Spanish Armada. I had been vaguely cognisant that some ships had been wrecked near Sligo in Ireland. As I delved into the history, I was surprised to see that Ireland's involvement in the Armada story was quite significant – that most of the losses were made up of the shipwrecks along Irish coasts. There were more surprising revelations, such as the merciless putting to death of a huge number of Spanish survivors in Ireland. As I proceeded with the book, I also found that, contrary to prevailing myths, the Armada was not utterly smashed – indeed a large proportion survived to fight another day.

Chapter 1 begins with the marriage of Prince Philip of Spain to Queen Mary of England in 1554, a time of friendship between Spain and England. Over the course of his brief reign as King of England, Philip offered some wise advice on improving the English navy, but probably did not pay much notice to the activities in Ireland, the colony next door where two plantations were put in place in both his and his wife's names. After Mary's death in 1558 a reluctant Philip made a desultory offer to marry her half-sister, an equally reluctant Elizabeth. In the meantime a heretical rebellion grew in the Spanish Netherlands. After Elizabeth ascended to the throne, she maintained the Protestantism of her father and, in 1570, an exasperated Pope excommunicated her. By 1580 relations between England and Spain were at a low ebb and after Philip inherited the Portuguese throne, Elizabeth supported the pretender Dom António. The Queen agreed in 1585 to send a large force to support the Dutch rebels. This was a step too far: Philip judged the Low Countries to be the jewel in the crown of his empire. Later that year Francis Drake began his attack on Northern Spain and went on to rampage across the Caribbean. In February 1587 Mary, Queen of Scots, was executed.

With relations between Spain and England in terminal decline, Chapter 2 tells how the journey to war was now inevitable. The constant English attacks on Spanish treasure fleets proved too much and the concept of 'The Enterprise of England', namely the invasion of England and sweeping Elizabeth from the throne, was being discussed. In 1585, a new, energetic Pope, Sixtus V, urged Philip to help eradicate heresy in England. English piracy was on the increase and Drake was to the fore. On the basis that it was more effective to strike at the heart of the English enemy than to set in place defensive forces across the vast Spanish Empire, Philip asked his advisors and commanders for plans. With English troops arriving in the Netherlands to help the rebels, preliminary work began in Lisbon on assembling a fleet, an army, and the equipment necessary for an invasion of England. In April 1587 Drake made an attack on Cádiz to forestall the preparations, which strengthened Philip's determination to proceed with the invasion. As England endeavoured to make ready its army, navy and coastal defences, the Duke of Parma was assembling his *tercios* on the Flanders coast. After the death of the Marquis of Santa Cruz in February 1588, his replacement, the Duke of Medina Sidonia, put more order on the Armada preparations in Lisbon.

Chapter 3 sees the Armada, essentially a large armed convoy, set sail at the end of May 1588, destination: the coast of Margate, to establish a beachhead, and to protect Parma's men in their invasion barges as they sailed from Flanders. Storms ensued, and with many provisions turned sour, the Armada had to stop at Corunna. On 22 July, the fleet of 128 ships, now reprovisioned, set out for the English Channel. As the Armada sailed along off the southern English coast there were a series of attacks by the English fleet but they did not manage to pierce the strong defensive formation ordered by Medina Sidonia. On 6 August, the Armada anchored at Calais – it was soon discovered that Parma was not ready with his invasion barges. When the English sent in fireships the following night, the fleet scattered. The following day, 8 August, the long and bloody Battle of Gravelines ensued. Medina Sidonia and a small number of galleons formed a rearguard, as the English ships swarmed in, blasting away repeatedly. Despite the expenditure of practically all their powder and shot, the English ships managed to directly sink just one ship. With the Armada back in its formation, it was decided after a council of war that if the wind continued from the south, the fleet would take the long journey north around Scotland and Ireland to return to Spain.

Chapter 4 tells of the long voyage into the Atlantic. Continuous storms beset them as they sailed west and then turned south. Many ships lost sight of the flagship and were driven towards the dangerous coasts of Scotland and Ireland. Finally on 21 September, the Armada flagship, leading a small number of ships, arrived off Santander. In the weeks that followed other Armada vessels returned to the ports of northern Spain.

Chapter 5 describes the shipwrecks caused by the exceptional stormy weather, mainly along the Atlantic coast of Ireland. It tells of what is perhaps the most painful and poignant fate of the whole Armada: the slaughter of around 1,500 survivors by the English authorities in Ireland, a dystopian setting where the Tudor regime was struggling to extend its control over the whole island.

Chapter 6 recounts the aftermath, principally the events of the English Armada of 1589. This large expedition had the intention of destroying surviving Armada ships and placing the Portuguese pretender, Dom António, on the throne, and being financed by plunder. It proved to be an utter disaster – more men and ships were lost than by the Spanish in the previous year's Armada. The Anglo-Spanish war continued, with conflict in France and Ireland. In 1595 there was a small Spanish landing and attack in Cornwall, and the following year, a large English raid on Cádiz. Months later, the Second Spanish Armada was mounted, only having to turn back due to severe storms. The war ended in 1604 with the signing of the Treaty of London.

Over the centuries that followed, in the Anglophone world, the Armada events were portrayed as the triumph of 'plucky' England (David) against the overwhelming foe, Spain (Goliath), with the underlying story that Drake and his ships had smashed the Armada to smithereens. This theme reached its peak in Victorian times (then with the British Empire at its height). In 1988, during the quatercentenary, there was literally an armada of books launched by British authors. By then the 'huge victory' theme had been toned down a lot, but the general picture was one of a totally defeated Spanish fleet, overcome by supposedly superior English naval tactics and ships. Most of these authors probably were unaware of the *Leyenda Negra* (the 'Black Legend', referring to the centuries-long denigration of Spain). By contrast, it is only in the last two decades that there have been many books published in Spain on the Armada events which give a refreshingly different perspective to the story, with many new facts. A significant step forward was the publication in 1989, by the Spanish Navy, of *La Batalla del Mar Océano*, the work of several eminent historians. Within its many large volumes, these experts brought together all the original documents (from Spain, England and other countries) which were written during the course of the Anglo-Spanish War, 1586-1604.

Yes, the Spanish Armada was a failure: it did not achieve its objective of sweeping away Elizabeth and her rule in England. However, it was a close call for England. The Armada formation had managed to sail up the English Channel and reach Calais, intact and unscathed. If the Duke of Parma had been ready and shaken off his temerity, he could have sailed to Margate, within the proven protective configuration of the warships of the Armada. If Parma's men, the best troops in Europe, had managed to set foot in England, they would surely have taken over that country in short order. And then on the night of 7 August 1588, the fireships were sent in and suddenly, the Armada was scattered and it lost its defensive formation. And thus the course of European history was changed. It was a victory for Elizabeth, particularly in view of the alternatives: losing both her throne and quite possibly her head. However the Armada was not defeated: the English ships had sunk just one ship by direct gunfire.

It may be a surprise to many but the Armada survived to fight another day – over two thirds of the ships made it back to Spain. Most of the ships that were lost were the more vulnerable merchant vessels – few warships were sunk. If the exceptional gales had not blown, most of the wrecks would not have occurred. As the historian Felipe Fernández-Armesto, referring to the fatal shipwrecks on the Irish coast and the extraordinary Great Gale of September 1588, noted: 'the Armada would ... have been reckoned a remarkably successful venture but for the work of the Irish siren'. In the event, Spain, with its deep resources, managed to shrug off the losses. In the aftermath, Philip II ordered the construction of a new, larger and more improved series of galleons, 'The Twelve Apostles'. As noted, the fable of the 'defeat' of the Spanish Armada still echoes around Britain, but what happened to the equally large English Armada of 1589, and its calamitous disasters, have never been really ventilated there.

And there is another myth, often repeated, about the 'Black Irish', the black-haired Irish supposedly descended from Armada survivors. Alas, it is not true – the survivors were slaughtered or, if they were lucky enough to evade capture, concentrated on trying to gain passage to Scotland.

The story of the Armada is still with us, helped by many institutions and associations who try to keep this memory alive. In Ireland the Portballintrae Heritage Society, Co. Antrim, remembers that great maritime disaster, one of the largest in Irish history, which was the sinking of the *Girona*. The shipwreck and march to Killybegs by survivors of the *Duquesa Santa Ana* have been commemorated in Donegal by the Donegal GAP Heritage and History Group. Most prominent of all is Spanish Armada Ireland, which has established an excellent Armada Visitor Centre at Grange in Sligo. Their well-patronised 'Remembering the Armada' event held at Streedagh every September is attended by Spanish Navy and Embassy representatives. The Underwater Archaeology Unit of the Irish National Monuments Service has recovered artefacts (being restored in the National Museum of Ireland) including cannon from the Streedagh wrecks. Not to forget the Ulster Museum in Belfast, whose display of artefacts from the *Girona*, including outstanding examples of jewels and gold, forms the best Armada exhibition in the world – it also has a large number of artefacts from *La Trinidad Valencera*. The main exhibition of material from the *Trinidad Valencera* is at the Tower Museum in Derry, with some also on display in the Inishowen Maritime Museum, Greencastle, Co. Donegal. Britain has the National Maritime Museum in Greenwich. To understand the solid construction of Spanish ships of the time, it is worth visiting the Albaola Itsas Kultur Faktoria Shipbuilding Museum at Pasaia (near San Sebastián, in Guipúzcoa). The Instituto de Historia y Cultura Naval Armada Española publishes scholarly articles on the events of 1588. The always interesting and authoritative *www.armadainvencible.org*, created in 2017 by the historian Pedro Luis Chinchilla, energetically keeps the Armada story alive in Spain.

There are monuments at some Armada locations in Ireland and Scotland. However, these are of variable quality and type. I suggest that a fitting commemoration of the events of 1588 would be the installation of a series of tastefully designed and consistent plaques near each wreck site in Ireland, Scotland, Norway, England, France and at those ports in northern Spain where the Armada ships returned.

In writing this volume, I have tried to take a dispassionate approach, telling the facts, while casting more light on the seminal events that took place in 1588. So here is my book aimed at the general reader, in which, using illustrations and many specially prepared maps, I tell the story of the Spanish Armada, from start to finish.

Michael B. Barry

Chapter 1

Context

A little over three decades before Spain and England burst into momentous conflict, there was peace and indeed harmony between the two countries. Marking a long period of friendly relations, the monarchies of Spain and England came together on 25 July, 1554 in a dazzling ceremony at Winchester Cathedral when Prince Philip of Spain, son of Charles V, the Holy Roman Emperor, married Queen Mary of England, daughter of Henry VIII. As the congregation awaited the wedding mass, a proclamation rang out declaring their titles: 'Philip and Mary by the Grace of God King and Queen of England, France, Naples, Jerusalem and Ireland; Defenders of the Faith; Princes of Spain and Sicily; Archdukes of Austria: Dukes of Milan, Burgundy and Brabant; Counts of Hapsburg, Flanders and Tyrol.' This represented a vast part of the civilised world. However, the ceremony would have taken much longer if the proclamation had included all the Spanish territories across the globe, which had grown at a dizzy pace since the first half of the sixteenth century. The Spanish had established their dominion over the West Indies and Central America for many decades. North America was being explored and, within a few years, to be settled in a few areas. In South America, most of Peru and Chile had been conquered by the 1540s. Years before in 1521, Magellan had discovered the great archipelago in the Pacific which was later called, after Philip, las Islas Filipinas.

Why would the most powerful nation in Europe, Spain, bother with an alliance with such a minor power? England (with Wales) represented less than one-third of the area of Iberian Spain, and at that time was not particularly powerful economically or militarily. However, England at that time enjoyed close commercial links with Spain. Charles V saw that the new union offered strategic advantages: it helped to neutralize Spain's long-time enemy and neighbour, France, then the most populated kingdom of Europe. With his health declining, Charles was in the process of succession-planning and was dividing up his Holy Roman Empire into more manageable parts. The eastern Hapsburg lands were to pass to the Austro-German branch – he was planning to abdicate there in favour of his brother Ferdinand. His Spanish domains were to be bequeathed to his son, Philip. The Netherlands, Charles' most valuable possession (and his birthplace), were to be within the Spanish domain. The marital alliance with England would provide an ally close to the Low Countries which would help guard against any French encroachments there. Furthermore, England could help protect the sea routes from Spain to the Netherlands. It represented a neat segmentation of Philip's inheritance into three coherent parts: Italy and Spain; England and the Netherlands, and the Americas.

In return, by marrying this Catholic prince, the pious Mary would fortify her precarious inheritance by renewing the dynastic link to the Spanish Monarchy. Indeed the Catholic Monarchs, Ferdinand and Isabella, had been her mother Catherine of Aragón's parents. Mary was a cousin of Charles V, but in the consanguineous world of European royalty that was disregarded. As with her mother's marriage, it offered an alliance with the most dominant royal family in Christendom. This alliance would help bring England closer to the centre of European power. It offered the arriviste Tudors (who had only seized power in 1485) an element of legitimacy and

Left: Philip of Spain and Mary of England were married at Winchester Cathedral on 25 July 1554.

prestige. Reigning alone, Mary was vulnerable as a woman. Simply by marrying, she, the first English Queen, would be strengthened – and the birth of an heir would copper fasten a new and powerful Catholic dynasty.

So what happened over the years leading up to 1588 when all was reversed and Philip sent out his great Armada on a mission to invade England, his erstwhile kingdom, now his principal enemy? As we shall see in this chapter, the road to the Armada, which came to be called the 'Enterprise of England', was to be complex, fraught with religious discord and much conflict on land and sea.

One consequence of her father's multi-marital and religious adventures was that Mary's claim to be queen had been contested. There had been the nine-day reign of Lady Jane Grey in July 1553. This had been quickly suppressed and Mary was able to accede to the throne. At the beginning of 1554, as the news emerged in England that she had decided to marry Philip, fear of domination by Catholic Spain resulted in a disorganised revolt. The rebellion petered out, followed by the usual executions. In the aftermath Mary's half-sister, Elizabeth (of a Protestant inclination and daughter of Ann Boleyn) came under suspicion. No links with the rebels could be proved and after some months in the Tower of London, Elizabeth was dispatched to a country house and kept under watch.

Philip and Mary's marriage started off well. It had been proclaimed before the marriage that the 'Queen should rule all things as she doth now; and there should be of the council no Spaniard.' Philip maintained a relatively low profile. He could not speak English, but was able to manage a few words of salutation. He did not bring any troops with him to England. However, his entourage of Spanish noblemen began to fret at the customs of the English court: 'There are no distractions here except eating and drinking … and they drink more than would fill the Valladolid River.' While Philip did not directly govern England, he freely gave suggestions to his wife and senior officials. Interestingly, he gave advice on naval matters. Philip advised the Privy Council that the realm's main defence against invasion 'depends on the navy being always ready … so it was right that the ships should not only be fit for sea, but instantly available'. Commenting on an official recommendation that Navy Royal ships should be brought to dockyards in the Thames for refurbishment, Philip helpfully recommended that 'the vessels ought to be stationed at Plymouth, from which they can more easily be brought into service.' This was advice, which as it turned out, was to impact the Armada fleet on 31 July 1588, sailing past Plymouth, after the English fleet warped out of the port to meet it.

Decades before, Mary's father, Henry VIII had separated from Rome and the 1534 Act of Supremacy, declared that he was the 'Supreme Head on earth of the Church of England.' It had been driven by Henry's immediate need to gain freedom to divorce his wife, Catherine of Aragón and marry Anne Boleyn. It was also a manifestation of the burgeoning sense of English exceptionalism, but unlike the events of the twenty-first century, where once again England disavowed perfidious rule from the Continent, Henry had found no need to call a referendum. Life was much simpler then; he merely had to look into his own heart. Mary, like her mother, Catherine

Left: a bronze siege cannon recovered from the 'Trinidad Valencera', which sank at Kinnagoe Bay, Co. Donegal, Ireland. The gun was cast by Remigy de Halut of Mechelen, near Antwerp, in 1556. Cast onto the barrel were the royal arms of Spain, quartered with those of England. At that time Philip II was married to the English queen, Mary Tudor.

and her grandmother Isabella, was a devout Catholic. She now concentrated on reversing her father's decrees on religion. With the support of Philip, she began the process of re-establishing the Catholic church of her childhood and reconciling England with Rome. However, this soon turned out to be a brutal process: anyone who denied papal supremacy was to meet a bloody end and at the beginning of 1555, a ruthless persecution got underway. In March 1556, Thomas Cranmer, the former Archbishop of Canterbury, was burnt at the stake. Protestants fled to the Continent and over the four-year Marian period around 300 'heretics' were killed. There is no evidence that Philip had been involved in the repression. However, in the popular mind the Catholic terror began to be associated with Spanish domination. Conversely Protestantism came to be seen as linked to the concept of the liberty of England.

Philip had an important responsibility to attend to. Although already a widower, Philip was eleven years younger than the thirty-seven-year-old Mary. One of Philip's courtiers had reported to Charles V's secretary: 'He treats the Queen very kindly, and well knows how to pass over the fact that she is no good from the point of fleshy sensuality'. Philip did his duty and by November 1554 it was widely believed that Mary was pregnant. In April, 1555, Elizabeth, the heir presumptive, had been summoned so that she might be present at the birth of the heir apparent. It was during this time that Philip met Elizabeth. The meeting of the pair, mortal enemies in decades to come, was reportedly a tender one. One account relates that Philip gave Elizabeth a diamond, and later requested Mary to forgive and forget the suspicions she held of her half-sister. As England prepared for the royal birth, *Te Deums* were sung in churches all over England. Mary had retired to Hampton Court, awaiting the birth. Eventually the truth dawned – there was no pregnancy. Philip had dutifully stayed in England during this time. However, his dalliance with England and its Queen had lost its promise. He could defer his imperial duties no longer – in particular as his care-worn father had decided to finalise his abdication. In early September 1555 Philip departed for the Netherlands, having spent more than a year in England. He assured Mary that he would return in a matter of weeks. To underline this he left most of his entourage behind.

Charles V continued with the complex abdication from his extensive empire. He relinquished his domains in Burgundy and the Netherlands to Philip in October 1555. The most important transfer, that of Spain, was made the following January. After this, Charles V left Flanders and retired to a monastery at Yuste at Extremadura in Spain. In March 1557, his son, Philip II, now the King of Spain, sailed back to England, to be greeted by joyful celebration. Philip now had a pressing need for military assistance, as war had broken out between Spain and its traditional enemy, France. Mary was keen to back her husband, but the Privy Council demurred. However, events intervened when, a month later, two French ships landed a small force of Protestant exiles at Scarborough, which captured the castle there. Their aim was to depose the 'unworthy Queen'. The mini-invasion was quickly suppressed. However, it proved to be a catalyst and on 7 June 1557 England declared war on France. Several weeks later, Philip left England to direct the Spanish armies in France. The royal couple parted, never to see each other again. An English army was sent across the Channel, which arrived just as the Spanish forces soundly defeated the French at St Quentin in Picardy in August 1557. On New Year's Day, 1558, the French came to take their revenge. A large army launched a surprise attack on the English enclave of Calais and its Pale. The castle there was captured within a week; the rest of the enclave over the subsequent weeks. The 5,000 residents of Calais were transported back to England. The loss of Calais was a severe blow to English pride. It had been their last toehold on the Continent – the last of the old Anglo-French kingdom. England was now an island kingdom.

Death passed close to Philip in the autumn of 1558. His father, Charles V died on 21 September at Yuste. His wife, Mary, Queen of England, who always endured uncertain health, became seriously ill. Her condition deteriorated and she died on 17 November. On hearing the news, Philip asked his trusted courier, the Duke of Feria, to represent him at the funeral rites. The union of England and Spain, always fragile and tentative was at an end. Philip directed that the title 'England, France and Ireland' be deleted from his seals.

The colony next door

The wedding proclamation of Philip and Mary in 1554 had included Ireland as part of their realm. Twelve years before this, an act of parliament had redesignated Ireland, previously considered a lordship, to be a separate crown of the English king. Ireland had probably been the most peripheral of Philip and Mary's European domains. Yet decades later, in 1588, the geography and climate of this distant island were to result in disastrous consequences for around a fifth of Philip's mighty Armada. Since the Anglo-Norman invasion of Ireland in 1169, the rulers of England had considered the country as being under their purview and continuously struggled to extend their dominance. England was a relatively small country in European terms. However, Ireland was smaller: little more than half the size of England and Wales. The island was England's backyard and became its first colony. Colonialism came with the usual disdain of the natives – one English administrator in Ireland in the sixteenth century expressed a view that legal and religious reform was useless: 'all is to no purpose to reform the wickedness of these stubborn, rude and most barbarous people'. His solution was the application of military force.

The island was lightly populated; estimates of the population during the sixteenth century range from 500,000 to 750,000. In Tudor eyes, Ireland was a patchwork of uncertain loyalty mixed with dangerous rebellion. This ranged from the Pale under royal control, to the independent magnates of Hiberno-Norman origin and to the largely independent Gaelic lords in the centre and the western extremities of the island. Starting with the first invasion of 1169, Norman lords (mainly from Wales) had seized most of Ireland. The fertile parts of the east coast had been shared out and densely settled. Called the 'Pale', It included the counties Louth, Meath, Dublin and Kildare, (taking a detour around the unreconstructed Gaelic Irish of the Wicklow Mountains) and a strip down to Wexford. Within, there were towns and villages populated by settlers from England. The terrain here became developed, with enclosed and drained estates, interspersed with roads and bridges. The Pale became in effect a 'little England' with the English language, culture and laws dominating (although over time there was an inward seepage of the Gaelic language).

In the century after their invasion the Normans expanded and seized large swathes of territory beyond the Pale, to the north, west and south. By 1450, the (by-now) Hiberno-Norman lords' territory had shrunk, but they still controlled most of the south and the south-west. They had become Hibernicised, having assimilated the Gaelic language, customs

Right: Irish people, from the sixteenth century book on historical and contemporary dress by Lucas de Heere, a Flemish painter.

and culture. Beyond these territories the native Gaelic lords ruled. Much of their lands were quite poor (the best land had been seized by the Normans), undrained and lay amidst ancient forests. There was some tillage, but, reflecting the low population density, stock raising was common. The native Irish were organised in an intensely local and fragmented system, in clans or extended family groups. Each clan had a chieftain, or lord who was usually known by the clan name, called after the common ancestor, like the *Ó Mathghamhna* (O'Mahony) after '*Mathghamhain*' (a king of Munster). The size of the lordships could vary and range from a large townland (in today's terms) to a large region, a significant proportion of a province. The larger lordships dominated their smaller neighbours, sometimes exacting fighting men or an annual tribute from them. There were threats of raids by other clans; sensibly, a chieftain would maintain a lightly armed unit of soldiers, called a kern. Of sterner mettle, with heavier weaponry, were the mercenary

Above: an Irish lord submits to the Lord Deputy. From a 1581 book by John Derrick 'The Image of Irelande'.

soldiers called galloglass (*gall óghlaigh* – foreign young men or warriors) originally from Scotland, who had settled in Ireland.

The Tudors planned to extend their control over this island of patchwork loyalties – fortunately for them there was no centralized, powerful Gaelic high kingship presiding over the whole of the country. In the early 1540s, Henry VIII's representative in Ireland, the Lord Deputy, began to implement the policy later called by historians as 'Surrender and Regrant'. The concept was that the Gaelic lord would go to the Lord Deputy and submit to the authority of the King. In return they would receive entitlement to their lands under royal charter and would be by given royal titles (lord etc.) appropriate to their status. This re-branding would offer a stability and certainty to the Gaelic lord. For the crown, it was a cost-effective way to achieve conquest by stealth, without the need to send expensive armies. In theory, these Irish, as one Palesman wrote, would now move 'from rudeness to knowledge … from savageness to civility'.

It was under the reign of Philip and Mary that the first plantation of Ireland was put in place (although it was likely that the royal couple would have nothing more than a vague knowledge of the happenings in this distant part of their domain). A scheme was initiated in the Irish midlands whereby English settlers would occupy lands confiscated from the rebellious Irish. In 1557 an act of parliament divided the midland territories of the O'Connors and the O'Mores into two shires. These clans, who regularly raided the Pale, had been seen as an irritant. As they were deemed to have rebelled, their lands were confiscated and it became crown property. The new shires were called the King's and Queen's Coun-

Above: plantations and the Pale. Ireland under the Tudors during the last half of the sixteenth century, with, indicated, the principal clan names.

ties, after Philip and Mary. The two garrison townships in the area were denoted as Philipstown (modern-day Daingean) and Maryborough (modern-day Portlaoise). In the event, the plantation was not a great success. The disinherited O'Connors and O'Mores retreated to the nearby bogs and hills, from whence they sallied forth to wage a guerrilla war on the settlers. As a result there were understandable difficulties in attracting new settlers. Those brave souls who did come to colonise set up close to the military settlements. It took over a decade to hunt down and neutralise the dispossessed clans.

Left: Queen Elizabeth I. Daughter of Ann Boleyn and Henry VIII, she was crowned queen on 15 January 1559.

The accession of Elizabeth

On Mary Tudor's death it was her half-sister Elizabeth's turn to ascend to power. Aged 26 years, she was crowned queen on 15 January 1559. Elizabeth, daughter of Ann Boleyn, had been brought up in the Protestant faith. Initially she chose to concentrate on stability and retained some of Mary's Catholic advisers, while appointing new men of a Protestant outlook. Slowly but surely, she rolled back Mary's unpopular laws that had enforced Catholicism. Over the following months laws were passed which restored the religion of her father. She styled herself 'Supreme Governor' of the Church of England (the services of which included Protestant evangelistic touches, while still retaining much of the Catholic ritual). One major threat to the legitimacy of her rule came from France, where King Henry II, after the death of Mary Tudor, had proclaimed Mary Stuart, Queen of Scots (his daughter-in-law) as the rightful ruler of England.

At the start of Elizabeth's reign, relations with Spain were amicable: soon after accession she sent a letter to Philip expressing her zeal 'to continue the old and perfect amity that ... hath been so friendly maintained.' However in Spain there was unease about the new Elizabethan regime, with its strong Protestant colouration and the danger of a possible marital alliance with France. The Duke of Feria, the Spanish ambassador, felt immediate action was necessary – he urged Philip to 'get a grip' and to 'take immediate steps to ensure both that the King of France does not gain a foothold here and that the vineyard that Your Majesty planted should not be ruined'. Philip, though twice a widower, once more rose to the challenge and sent a message via Feria, proposing marriage to Elizabeth – who, in what was to be her characteristic habit of dissembling, avoided giving a direct answer. Eventually, two months later, she informed Feria that she had no wish to marry.

In February 1559, representatives of France, England and Spain met at the chateau of Cateau-Cambrésis (in present-day northern France) to examine if there could be a new harmony in relations. There had been ineffectual negotiations the previous year but the desire for peace had increased, helped by the ruinous effect incessant warfare had on the French and Spanish treasuries. A treaty between the parties was signed in the spring and, for a time, peace broke out in Europe. Philip gained rights in Italy and importantly, made his hold on the Netherlands more secure. France made some gains: the most significant of which was that its control over the Calais enclave was recognised. In return, France agreed not to uphold Mary Queen of Scots' claim to the English throne.

Philip's inheritance: many challenges

Philip sailed south to Spain from Flanders in August 1559. From now on, he was never to leave the Iberian Peninsula. His permanency on the peninsula reflected what was to be a new, more Spanish-focused domain, as opposed to the central-European-focused empire of his father. We first examine Philip's empire, one of a size unprecedented in history. However, history has shown that empires of great size carry the seeds of over-extension and financial strain. Philip ruled over what was then the largest empire in the world, in terms of land mass. It included the kingdoms of Spain, Rouissilon-Cerdagne, Sardinia, Sicily, Naples and Milan. To the north were the Netherlands and the Franche-Comté of Burgundy. Importantly, there were the sprawling and expanding territories of the Americas. In 1565, the Philippines were added.

The great conquests in the New World since the voyages of Columbus had resulted in a new flow of riches. Many goods such as dyestuffs and sugar flowed back to Spain; however, the most important flow was that of the gold and silver of the Americas. The Crown got around 40 per cent of the bullion that landed at Seville, where the *Casa de la Contratación de las Indias* regulated the new territories and controlled the trade. By 1560, thanks to an improved technique of refining silver using mercury, there was an enormous increase in the flow of silver from the fabulous mines of Potosí (now in Bolivia). One estimate is that in the century and a half after 1503, the silver that flowed through Seville was enough to triple the European

supplies of that metal. The flow of gold was less – over the same period, Europe's gold stocks increased by a fifth. By the 1560s the bullion was transported back in convoys of ships which assembled at Havana in March for the voyage home. The fleet system provided protection from the increasing bands of privateers (of whom more later) who preyed on Spanish gold and silver. The new colonists needed supplies from home – in turn the ships left Seville, laden with goods like corn, oil, wine and textiles.

Above: the European inheritance of Philip II. Portugal was incorporated in 1580.

From time immemorial, much of any ruler's time has been spent in trying to raise revenue from every imaginable source, to pay for the ever-mounting expenses of state. So it was in the Spanish Empire where there were direct and indirect taxes, revenue from customs, income from licenc-

Right: a young Philip. He was inaugurated as King of Spain on 16 January 1556.

ing of monopolies and revenue from the wealthy church establishments. Added to this was the ever increasing income from the Americas. The task of raising money was to preoccupy Philip throughout his entire reign. Given the cost of maintaining his sprawling empire and fighting the constant wars that broke out, the Spanish state periodically ran out of funds. Philip was forever trying to squeeze money from his territories. Great efforts were made to raise taxation from all over, both from civil and religious sources. Given the diverse arrangements for organisation of Spain, this was not easy. It was a complex decentralised system and Philip was frequently involved in negotiations with the Cortes to raise more revenue. In eastern Spain, the states of the Crown of Aragón maintained their power and independence – and resisted any large increase in taxes. The main burden of revenue collection fell on Castile, where there was direct royal control. This in turn damaged Castile's economy. The agriculture sector could not produce enough for the local population or their compatriots in the New World. The influx of cheap silver from the Indies had increased the money supply. Prices rose. Cheaper and better-quality foreign goods entered the market.

Philip's domains spanned many continents, but in reality his empire was frequently under financial pressure. On many occasions there were extraordinary variations and imbalances, both in revenue and expenditure. A system of public debt had developed over preceding centuries. This allowed a central administration to borrow when there was unexpected expenditure not covered by tax revenue. In Spain most of this was made up of long term debt, *juros*, which were administered by the cities that regulated taxes. There were also short-term debts, *asientos,* held with foreign bankers, mostly from Genoa. There were four financial adjustments during Philip's reign: in 1557, 1560, 1575 and 1596, when the Crown suspended payments on the *asientos* to foreign bankers. These have been mistakenly called bankruptcies (an inability to pay your debts). However, these were not caused by a crisis in liquidity, but as the consequence of negotiations that were taking place in the Cortes between the Crown and the cities of Castile. All of these were settled after lengthy discussions with the Cortes, with tax increases and interest rate reduction, facilitated by switching some *asientos* to *juros*.

Another challenge to the new king's empire was heresy. The devout Philip II came from a line of monarchs who functioned within the strict orthodoxy of traditional Catholicism. In 1492, his great-grandparents, Ferdinand and Isabella, the Catholic Monarchs, had succeeded in ending the last vestiges of Islamic rule in the Iberian Peninsula (as well as expelling the Jews in the same year.) His father, Charles V's Holy Roman Empire had been rocked by the rise of Lutheranism, although by the time of Philip's accession, equilibrium of a kind had developed in the section of the empire that included the German princely states. However, by the 1550s, a more assertive form of Protestantism, that of Calvinism, had grown and became dominant in Geneva. In due course Calvinist exiles returned to their native France and the Low Countries where they gained many converts among the educated classes. By 1562, in France, serious conflict between Catholics and Protestants of the Calvinist tradition (commonly referred to as Huguenots) had broken out – tensions that were to lead to a recurring series of civil wars over the following decades. For Philip, while this brought some alleviation of pressure from the traditional enemy, now weakened, it brought the danger of heresy close to his northern frontiers.

The challenge in the Netherlands

The most serious challenge for Spain in the Low Countries was the rise of Calvinism there. Charles V (born in Ghent), had inherited the northern Burgundian estates from his father as part of the Hapsburg Holy Roman Empire. Over the course of his reign, he added to these lands to mould a new entity, the Spanish Netherlands (formed of seventeen provinces that later were to form modern Belgium, Netherlands, Luxembourg, and a northern sliver of France). All of these seventeen provinces came under the rule of Philip when in 1555, his father, Charles, made his abdication from rule of the Netherlands. This was one of the most advanced and valuable parts of Philip's inheritance. With many ports and a large mercantile fleet, merchants from the Netherlands had developed extensive trading networks around Europe. It was a rich land, highly urbanised with towns populated by businessmen, bankers and productive artisans. The textile industry was advanced and there was intense agricultural production as well as well-developed herring fisheries. It was a place of culture, with a literate population who enjoyed a good level of education.

As we have seen, Philip had left the Netherlands for Spain in August 1559. On his departure, he left in charge, advised by a Council of State, his half-sister, Margaret (who had been born in Flanders), wife of Ottavio Farnese, the Duke of Parma. However, the local nobility had been used to a royal presence and did not take to being ruled by the inexperienced Margaret. They became resentful at being directed by what was, in effect, a form of remote control by Philip in far-away Spain. Furthermore, a last-minute instruction to Margaret from Philip as he departed immediately caused problems. He had directed her to carry out a radical reorganisation of the number of the bishoprics in the Netherlands. This ousted many from lucrative sinecures, raised hackles and caused an immediate backlash. The widespread opposition resulted in paralysis of Margaret's fledgling administration. Another difficulty that arose was unsurprisingly, that of religion. Up to now, heresy had been kept at bay in the Netherlands by the Inquisition. However, a consensus had grown up against the excesses of the heresy laws. Margaret's council of advisors recommended that executions of heretics, the cause of much resentment, should cease. Philip, distracted by attacks by the Turks in the Mediterranean, did not bend and replied with directives insisting that convicted heretics must continue to be executed. However, the nobility of the Netherlands persisted and the weak Margaret bent to

Below: the 'iconoclastic fury' of August 1566, as manifested in Antwerp. All across the Netherlands anti-clerical mobs smashed up Catholic churches, looting the gold and silver within and destroying images and statues.

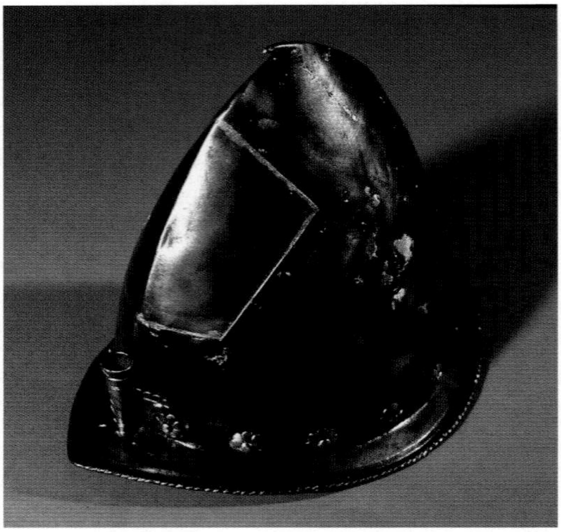

Left: a morion, a type of combat helmet, that was generally worn by the 'tercios', the Spanish elite military units. After the unrest in the Netherlands in 1566, the tercios were put on standby in Milan, with the intention that they would march north after the Alpine winter snows had abated.

their will. On 9 April 1566 she issued an order that magistrates exercise more leniency towards heretics. In an atypical move, Margaret now asserted herself and stood up to her brother: she wrote to him, stating that, with the Netherlands on the brink of rebellion, he had two choices, either lead the war in person against the heretics or authorise her concessionary approach – Philip accepted the concessions.

Pandora's Box was now opened: the pause in persecution allowed Calvinist ministers to emerge from the shadows. Their doctrine proved attractive to all classes and there were widespread meetings and many new converts. The year 1566 coincided with an economic downturn in the Low Countries. Against a background of unemployment and poverty, the populace heard the preachers eloquently rising to apocalyptic heights, preaching against idolatry and the riches of the Catholic Church. At the end of June one eyewitness in Antwerp noted that 30,000 people had attended Calvinist gatherings there and, a harbinger of the future, that they were armed. In August the dam burst: the 'iconoclastic fury' began and flashed across the Netherlands – anti-clerical mobs smashed up Catholic churches, looting the gold and silver within and destroying images and statues, in line with the Calvinist belief that these were idolatrous.

Philip heard the news in September and reacted immediately. He was determined that the incendiary strains of Protestantism that had arrived in France and Scotland were not going to be allowed in his domains. His authority had to be reasserted – the rebellious heretics were going to meet a firm hand and an army was to be sent. (It helped that the treasure fleet from the Americas had just landed a record amount of silver at Seville). As the direct sea passage via the Strait of Dover had become dangerous due to the menace of privateers, the army would have to travel by land through what were predominantly Philip's domains. A new military way was mapped out and commissaries made preparations. Dubbed the 'Spanish Road', this ran from Genoa to Milan, then through the Franche-Comté, and north to Luxembourg. Arrangements were made to place the 8,000 soldiers at Milan on standby. These were the *tercios*, the elite Spanish military units, each amounting to around 3,000 experienced and professional soldiers. The most

Right: Fernando Álvarez de Toledo, the Duke of Alba. This distinguished veteran of many battles was chosen by Philip II to lead the tercios and reassert royal authority in the Netherlands.

effective troops in Europe, they were made up of arquebusiers, pikemen and swordsmen. *Tercios* were recruited from Spain, but also from Germany and Philip's possessions in Italy. Philip selected his most experienced commander to be Captain-General of the new army: Fernando Álvarez de Toledo, the Duke of Alba, distinguished veteran of many battles including the conquest of Tunis in 1535.

The Spanish army wintered in Milan, waiting for the Alpine winter snows to abate. However, Margaret of Parma had not dallied in the meantime. In the months following the August revolt she had levied new troops and had taken steps to restore order. The Calvinist rebellion had collapsed as rebel towns and cities surrendered and accepted government garrisons. As Alba was setting out for Milan at the end of April 1567, an emissary from Margaret arrived at the royal court with a message informing that Spanish troops were not now required; their presence would only harm the resolution that had been just arrived at. The king held firm, and the *tercios* set out on the long march north, arriving in Brussels in August 1567.

The Duke of Alba immediately began to deploy his troops, billeting them in principal towns and cities. The 'Council of Troubles', along with subordinate regional tribunals, was established to try those accused of heresy or rebellion. As the arrests began, Margaret of Parma (who nominally exercised civil power) was offended by Alba's brusque manner and she decided to resign at the end of 1567, swearing in the Duke as her successor as Governor General. And so, across the Netherlands, Alba's reign of terror got underway. Over the next six years, there were around 1,000 executions (which included prominent members of the local nobility). To avoid the fate of his noble colleagues, the most influential aristocrat in the Low Countries, William I, Prince of Orange fled abroad. In 1568, from exile, William rallied armies to attack Alba's forces at different points, including an invasion in the south with support from the French Huguenots. The rebels initially enjoyed some success. However, by the end of 1568, William's revolt came to an end – it had been defeated in battle and also had failed to garner widespread support. And so it appeared that the Duke of Alba had prevailed and now the Netherlands came back under rigid Spanish control.

Secluded in the Escorial

Philip II was a man of high moral values, conscious of his duty to God, and also to his subjects. Inheriting vast domains from his father, Philip moved his new capital to their centre of gravity in the centre of Spain, and specifically, to the centre of Castile. In 1561 the peripatetic Spanish court was finally settled in Madrid. Two years later Philip ordered the construction of a vast new building around 40km to the north-east of Madrid. This, the Escorial, monumental in scale, was to be partly a monastery and partly his royal residence. The famous victory over the French at St Quentin in 1557 had occurred on the Feast of St Lawrence, a martyr roasted on a gridiron. Philip had been in overall command of the battle, and the story runs that he ordered that the Escorial be built in the shape of a gridiron, as thanks for the saint's intervention at the victory. The battle obviously proved a seminal event for Philip – scenes from the victory at St Quentin take up a wall of the grand Hall of Battles at the Escorial.

Classical, in cold granite, proportioned with strict lines, but with a powerful intensity, rarely has a building better articulated the personality of its occupant. Here Philip was able to seclude himself with the state papers, documents and dispatches from all over his realms. No detail was too small. Every issue, whether it be in the Americas, Netherlands, Italy or the Iberian kingdoms, was fastidiously considered and each document suitably noted. The royal postal service was excellent: a dense network of couriers, by horse and ship, would carry the important dispatches to all corners of Philip's domains, and bring back yet more for his urgent attention. As he put in long days with his papers, Philip led a lonely life, marred by family tragedy. Some of this misfortune was contributed to by the European royal custom of consanguinity (intermarriage amongst close relatives), thus increasing the danger of genetic defects. This was illustrated in the case of Philip's son and heir, Don Carlos, who had started to manifest odd behaviour (his parents Philip and Maria Manuela of Portugal were double first cousins – in other

Above: the Escorial, located around 40km north-east of Madrid. This monumental building was partly a monastery and partly Philip's royal residence.

words, they shared all four grandparents). In January 1568, Philip, with immense reluctance, was forced to place the 22-year-old Carlos in detention – the young prince died around six months later.

Carlos' mother, Maria Manuela had died days after Carlos's birth in 1545. As we seen, Philip's second wife, Mary Tudor died in 1558. Needing an heir Philip married yet again: Elizabeth of Valois (daughter of Henry II of France, thus achieving another dynastic union). She died in 1568. Next Philip married Anne of Austria (his niece) who lived until 1580. This constant sequence of loss and death forced Philip to retreat somewhat from the wider world. Propelled also by a sense of duty, he sought succour in his chamber, immersed amongst documents, charting out the daily destiny of his domains. After his arrival in Spain in 1559 Philip made just a few visits to his Spanish kingdoms and never again travelled outside Spain, with one exception – he spent a few years in Portugal after inheriting its crown, leaving Lisbon in March 1583. His Castile-centric rule did not help increase the links with the monarchy's outlying nations – we have already seen how the lack of a direct royal presence was one of the underlying reasons for the revolt in the Netherlands.

Threats within Spain and across the Mediterranean

As Philip saw it, heresy from the north was threatening his border with France as well as the Spanish Netherlands. There was another more imminent peril: to the south and east, the powerful adherents of Islam, the Ottomans, were encroaching along the Mediterranean. Philip, the great-grandchild of the Catholic Monarchs, who had defeated the last Muslim ruler in Iberia, was acutely aware of the danger. In March 1560, he authorised a large expedition (in alliance with the Italian states) to attack Tripoli

Left: a fine tiled plaque by M. Guillén, in the village of Genalguacil, set in the folds of the Sierra Bermeja in Andalucia. After the revolt of the Moriscos, which began in 1569, Christian soldiers sent here had behaved harshly. In the midst of skirmishes, the Moriscos set the village church on fire, with the Christian soldiers within.
The Morisco revolt had been an existential threat to Spain, but was eventually suppressed by Don John of Austria and his forces in 1570.

in Ottoman-held North Africa. Encountering a storm, the Christian forces turned back and then seized the island of Djerba, (in present-day Tunisia). However, the Ottoman Navy sailed from Istanbul to the island and in May 1560 bloodily defeated the Christian forces.

In 1569 an existential challenge suddenly materialised within Spain itself – a revolt in the Alpujarras. Back in 1499 after a minor revolt, the Catholic Monarchs had decreed that all the Muslims of the recently subjugated Kingdom of Granada be forcibly baptised. These now came to be known as *Moriscos*, or Muslims who had been forced to convert to Christianity. The *Moriscos* settled down to an uneasy existence in what was becoming an exclusively Catholic Spain. In January 1567, restrictions on *Morisco* dress and culture were implemented. This proved to be the last straw and at the beginning of January 1569 a revolt flared up in the Alpujarras (the mountainous region south of Granada) which spread rapidly. The initial Government response was swift. The Spanish armies ranged deep into the territory. Many of their troops behaved harshly and the uprising gained new strength. In March 1569 Philip turned to his half-brother, Don John of Austria, to lead the suppression of the rebellion. The Spanish forces were now greatly reinforced and were made up of a mix of seasoned veterans. Don John's army ranged through the Alpujarras and in the nearby regions, including the Sierra Bermeja. In October 1569 Philip decreed the waging of total war. Don John demonstrated this amply when he took the town of Galera in February 1570 where thousands of *Moriscos* were killed as a result. Resistance reduced rapidly and by November 1570, the war was effectively over. The way was clear to complete the expulsion of all the *Moriscos* (an estimated 80,000) from the Kingdom of Granada to the rest of Spain.

In 1570 Pope Pius V urged Philip to participate with him in a Holy League (with Venice and other Italian states) to attack the Ottomans – the immediate reason was that the Turks had seized most of Cyprus from the Venetians. Philip agreed immediately to participate, with Spain contributing half of the costs, ships and soldiers. Don John, fresh from his suppression of the Alpujarras revolt, was appointed supreme commander. A vast fleet of around 200 ships and 65,000 soldiers and crew, was assembled at Messina, located by the toe of Italy. In mid-September 1571 the naval force sailed across the Adriatic to the Greek coast. On arrival, they found that the Turkish fleet was in the Gulf of Corinth, anchored off Lepanto. They set out and on 7 October 1571, crucifixes were raised and prayers rang out as the Christian fleet attacked the massed ships of the Turks. Cannon mounted high on the galleys of the Christian side badly damaged the Turkish ships. As the ships collided, the Christians boarded. After bloody battle, the Holy League prevailed. Over one third of the Turkish fleet was destroyed or captured – suffering around 25,000 men killed, including their admiral. In reality the great victory at Lepanto didn't result in any significant change in the balance of powers in the Mediterranean. However, over the following years, the Ottomans were diverted by the threat from the Persians to the east. This allowed Philip to concentrate on the challenges in northern Europe.

Below: the line up at the Battle of Lepanto where the combined Christian naval forces of Spain, Venice, and the Papacy defeated the Turkish fleet in 1571. In the foreground is an allegorical representation of the three Christian powers. The artist Giorgio Vasari was commissioned by Pope Pius to commemorate the event in the Sala Regia in the Vatican.

In terminal decline: relations with England

Why did relations between Spain and England deteriorate from the friendship of Mary Tudor's time – or indeed from early 1599 when Philip had made an offer of marriage to Elizabeth? The decline was gradual during the first few years, but then gained in intensity. The root causes were religion along with England's interest in strategic self-preservation – the balancing of the two European superpowers of France and Spain. Added to this was the English resentment at being excluded from the *El Dorado* that was the Americas. The protagonist of all this was Elizabeth. Raised as a Protestant, after her coronation in 1559, she started to reinstate the English brand of Protestantism. She was generally pushing on an open door as Mary Tudor's bloody mini-Inquisition had discredited Roman Catholicism. Elizabeth re-established the independence of England from the papacy, as originally proclaimed by her father, Henry. Her Protestantism was a hybrid form, and was not aligned with the stricter impositions of Calvinism. While the Church in England inherited many of the beliefs and ceremonies from the Roman Catholic Church, the ceremonies were simpler and there was less decoration in churches. The Catholic concepts of transubstantiation and the Marian dogmas of the Immaculate Conception and Assumption were discarded.

Henry's original Act of Supremacy 1534 had been repealed by his daughter, Mary. Now in 1559 parliament passed a new act which confirmed Elizabeth as Supreme Governor of the Church of England. It was also made an offence to proclaim the authority of any foreign prince, or prelate – in other words, this reaffirmed that England was to be free of any Papal authority. During the early years of Elizabeth's reign, Philip had been supportive of her, his sister-in-law, not because he particularly agreed with her actions, but because he wanted to maintain the Anglo-Spanish relationship. He even interceded with the Pope to dissuade him from excommunicating Elizabeth. Philip feared that it would exacerbate the situation for Catholics in England, and also worsen his difficulties in the Netherlands. However, as time passed, it became difficult for Philip to maintain this attitude. Gradually things changed – as the years rolled on legislation was passed in England which imposed restrictions on Catholics. At the beginning of 1566 Pius V was elected Pope in Rome. He was a strong proponent of orthodoxy and, alarmed by the spread of Protestantism, he adopted a harsher attitude towards Elizabeth.

The year 1568 proved to be one where relations between England and Spain went into severe decline. The first event was a relatively minor spat. In April of that year the English ambassador to Spain, John Man, a married clergyman, was reported as fulminating in private conversations against the King and Pope. Philip made him *persona non grata* at the Court and banished him to a suburb of Madrid. Finding it an insult to her honour, Elizabeth recalled him and from then onwards there were no more English ambassadors sent to Philip's court – thus reducing even further the opportunities to resolve disputes by diplomatic means. Yet, at this stage Philip hadn't given up. He dispatched a new ambassador to the English court, Don Guerau de Espés. His instructions were to 'serve and gratify Elizabeth on every possible occasion ... trying to keep her on good terms and assuring her from me that I will always return her friendship as a good neighbour and brother'.

The next dispute between England and Spain in 1568 had its roots in events of many decades before. Soon after Columbus's discovery of the Americas, Pope Alexander VI (Rodrigo de Borja, born in Valencia) had, in May 1493, decreed that all lands west of a pole-to-pole line, 100 leagues west of the Azores, belonged to the Catholic Monarchs of Castile and Aragón. (The Papacy had form in arbitrarily allocating other people's lands: in a decree of 1155 an English-born Pope granted King Henry II of England the right to invade and govern Ireland.) In the following year, the two great seafaring nations of the time, Spain and Portugal, divided the new world between them – under the Treaty of Tordesillas of 1494 they agreed that lands to the west of a line west of the Cape Verde islands would belong to Spain (the Crown of Castile); those to the east of the line would belong to Portugal. Resentment at this monopoly in the newly-discovered lands led

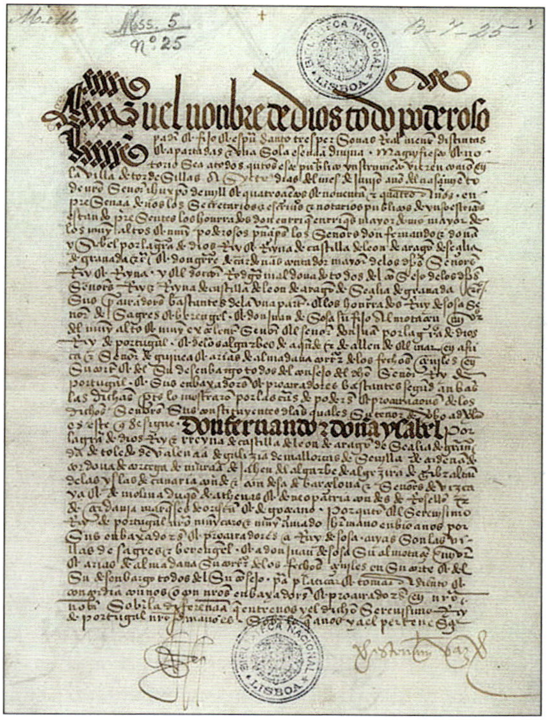

Right: the first page of the Treaty of Tordesillas, 1494. Under this all lands to the west of a line to the west of the Cape Verde islands would belong to Spain; those to the east of the line would belong to Portugal. One of the fundamental reasons for the eventual outbreak of hostilities was English resentment at being excluded from what was, in essence, a monopoly.

to attempts by the English to circumvent the rules set down by the Spanish. For Elizabeth the authorisation of privateers was a useful method in getting access to the riches of the Americas. Matters came to a head in 1568 when John Hawkins, a slave trader and privateer, with a fleet of six armed merchantmen, sailed to the Caribbean and engaged in what might be called 'armed trade' – forcing Spanish colonial settlements in the Indies to trade with him. In September, Hawkins' fleet had been battered by storms and he anchored at San Juan de Ulúa on the Mexican coast, securing what he thought was a temporary truce while he made repairs. Nevertheless the English ships were attacked by Spanish galleons, and Hawkins barely managed to make his escape. The Spanish had taken what they considered prudent action to smite piracy, but the English were resentful at what they considered the breaking of a truce.

The following month there was another flare up, this time closer to home and involving vast sums of money. A flotilla of Spanish ships en route to the Netherlands had experienced storms in the Bay of Biscay and then, spotting some Huguenot privateers, had headed for the safety of English waters. There it was discovered that amidst the general cargo, there were 155 chests of money. It turned out that these contained 130,000 ducats, dispatched by Genoese bankers as pay for the Duke of Alba's troops. The money-chests were soon transported to the Tower of London – for 'safe-keeping'. The affair of the pay ships and the impounded funds dragged on. Elizabeth had several reasons to hold onto the ducats: it would handicap Alba in driving on his army to suppress the Dutch Protestant rebels, and primarily, she needed money, a commodity her state was always short of. As

Left: Spanish troops. Elizabeth's diversion of a consignment of large sums of money destined to pay the Spanish tercios in the Netherlands became a cause for bitter dispute.

the English continued to equivocate, the Duke of Alba decided to retaliate at the end of 1568. He peremptorily ordered the seizure of English property in the Netherlands. This forced Elizabeth's hand, and in response she announced the seizure of all Spanish property in England. Alba realised that he had been too precipitate: the Spanish property seized in England was worth far more than the English equivalent in the Netherlands. He also realised the dangers of adding England as an enemy – this would add to the perils on the crucial (and privateer-infested) sea route to the Netherlands. Negotiations on the fate of the seized funds dragged on into 1574: a calculation was made of the value of goods seized on both sides and a balance of £22,000 was paid to the Spanish. The dispute petered out, but left a sour taste, laying down another strand of enmity with England, one of the reasons for a future war.

In May 1568, the Catholic Mary Queen of Scots, a claimant to the English Crown, had fled to England. Even by the often curious standards of monarchy, Mary Stuart had led an unusually tangled and complicated life. Daughter of James V of Scotland, she was born in December 1542. Six days later the infant acceded to the Scottish throne after the death of her father. A marriage agreement to marry the French Dauphin was made and Mary was sent as at the age of five to France. In 1558 Mary and the Dauphin, Francis, were wed. After the death of Henry II of France in July 1559, Mary and Francis became Queen and King of France. It was a brief reign as Francis died at the end of the following year. Mary returned to Scotland in mid-1561. Scotland was in ferment, split between competing Catholic and Protestant groups. The widow cast her eye on Lord Darnley, a Catholic, and married him in 1565. This led to open rebellion by Protestant lords. A son was born in 1566. In February 1567 Darnley was found dead, suspected of being assassinated. In a bizarre move, Mary married Lord Bothwell (suspected of murdering Darnley) the following May. Uproar continued and an army was raised against Mary. She was captured and imprisoned in a castle

Right: Mary, Queen of Scots. In May 1568, this Catholic Queen, a claimant to the English Crown, fled to England. Elizabeth immediately ordered that Mary be kept under protective custody.

at Loch Leven. In July 1567 she was forced to abdicate in favour of her infant son, James (who was to become James I of England on Elizabeth's death in 1603). Mary, managing to escape from the castle, fled south and reached England. Elizabeth immediately ordered that Mary be kept under protective custody. Mary's arrival posed a major threat to Elizabeth, who was regarded by Catholics as illegitimate – as the legitimate great-granddaughter of the Tudor King Henry VII, Mary had a claim to the English throne. She now entered many years of confinement, moving between various English castles and estates, always under strict observation by a legion of spies.

Frustration at the Elizabethan regime was made manifest in November 1569, when Catholic grandees in the north of England rose in rebellion, with the objective of deposing Elizabeth and replacing her with Mary. The nobles assembled an army of 6,000 and marched southwards. They were defeated by a larger force, loyal to Elizabeth. The rebels retreated and some

Left: Sir Francis Walsingham. Elizabeth's principal secretary and spymaster. He was instrumental in the collapsing of the so-called Ridolfi plot, whose conspirators hoped to replace Elizabeth with the Mary, Queen of Scots.

fled to Scotland. The rebellion lasted scarcely more than two months, but it was a reminder to Elizabeth of the dangerous fissures at the heart of her realm.

By February 1570, Rome finally lost patience with the Protestant Queen: Pope Pius V issued the papal bull, '*Regnans in Excelsis*' which declared Elizabeth to be a heretic, excommunicated her and called on loyal Catholics to depose her. This gave impetus to many conspiracies to assassinate Elizabeth. One of the most famous was the so-called Ridolfi plot. The Florentine banker, Roberto Ridolfi, a fervent Catholic, had settled in London, where he circulated freely among high society. His zeal to depose Elizabeth had led to involvement in planning the Northern Rebellion. Its failure led Ridolfi to believe that the solution now was foreign military intervention. His co-conspirators included a group of peers led by the Duke of Norfolk (a second-cousin of Elizabeth), as well as the Spanish Ambassador, Don Guerau de Espés. The latter (who, on appointment, as we have seen had been instructed by Philip to keep Elizabeth on good terms) was now actively scheming to have her overthrown. De Espés had helped elaborate a plan where the Duke of Alba and his army of the Netherlands, would invade England, depose Elizabeth and place Mary Queen of Scots on the throne. (It was from this time that this invasion idea became known as the 'Enterprise of England'). In early July 1571 Ridolfi managed to secure an audience with Philip, who gave the proposition his support.

Fortunately for Elizabeth, she had in place a widespread spy network. At the beginning of 1571 de Espés was expelled. In April, acting on intelligence, a courier was arrested carrying letters from Ridolfi. Liberal use of torture allowed the messages to be decoded. As the investigation rolled on, the Duke of Norfolk was sent to the Tower in September and, in June 1572, was beheaded. Ridolfi, who was on the Continent, never returned to England. The Ridolfi plot was not the end of the conspiracies – there were many more over the years, but all were detected and neutralised by the efficient English spy system, run by Sir Francis Walsingham.

Revolt breaks out once more in the Netherlands

We have seen how the heavy hand of the Duke of Alba had suppressed the revolt in the Netherlands. However, this meant that his large army had to be garrisoned within the country and along the frontiers. Philip (who had other wars to fund) made it clear to Alba that he was not going to finance this standing army – it had to be funded by the Dutch themselves. In March 1569 Alba convened the estates of the Dutch provinces and requested consent to apply a series of taxes: some were approved but the proposal for a 'tenth penny' tax (akin to a sales tax of ten per cent) met with strong objections. In July 1571, a frustrated Alba decided to force through the measure. In response there was uproar, tax strikes, and the troops had to be sent in. As shopkeepers and merchants ceased to trade, refusing to pay the tax, the economy went into recession.

Below: the capture of the port of Brill in the Netherlands by the 'Sea Beggars'.

Amidst this uproar, the 'Sea Beggars' enter the story. In 1569 William of Orange (the leading Dutch rebel, now in exile in France) had given a motley group of Calvinists and the unemployed of the Brabant and Flanders

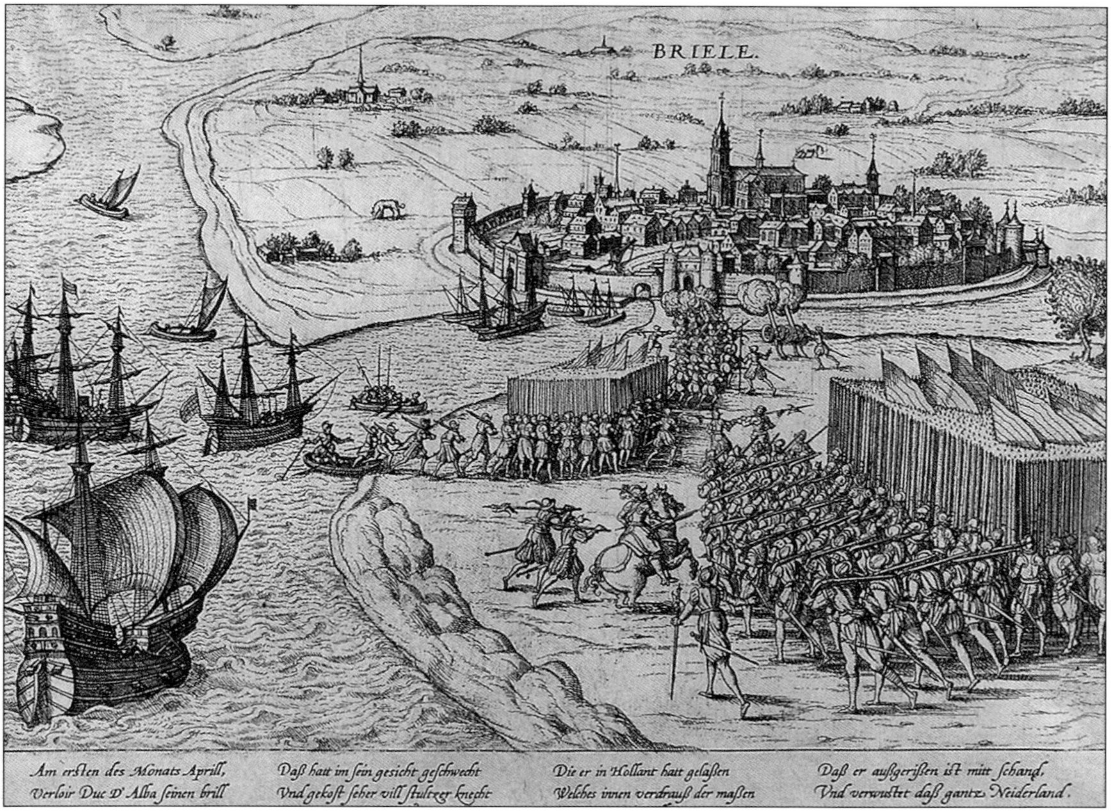

coasts letters of marque authorising them to attack enemy ships. These, who became known as the *Gueux de Mer*, or 'Sea Beggars', now energetically set out to attack Spanish ships en route to the Netherlands. In time their fleet grew to over 80 small ships. Initially they were allowed to shelter in English ports. Elizabeth soon grew exasperated with them as they had attacked neutral shipping. She instructed that the freebooters leave English ports on 1 March 1572. A month later, after some indecisive wanderings along the Channel, the corsairs seized and occupied the port of Brill (now Den Briel) near Rotterdam, an easy capture, as the Spanish garrison had previously vacated it. In turn, the Sea Beggars rapidly seized other neighbouring towns. The flames of revolt were now fanned by resentment of foreign rule, the presence of the Spanish *tercios* and the imposition of high taxes. Other rebel bands advanced from Germany and France. Many towns now declared for William of Orange. In May, a rebel force, with the assistance of French Huguenots, seized Mons in the south. French Catholics were displeased by this intervention and this added to the tensions which precipitated the St Bartholomew's Day massacre of Protestants in late August 1572 in Paris. The result was that the French had not now any relieving force available from the south and the Duke of Alba was able to oust them from Mons. He moved on to recapture other strategic towns under rebel control, using brutal methods *pour encourager les autres*. Spanish control was duly reinstated across most of the Low Countries but a large part of the western coastal provinces of Holland and Zeeland still remained in rebel hands. The pace of war slowed and Alba continued, operating amidst the difficult and watery Dutch terrain, with the challenging task of laying siege to a series of well-fortified towns.

However, Philip II had become frustrated by the expensive and lengthy war. He desired peace and decided to relieve Alba. His replacement, the Catalan, Luis de Requessens, (a veteran of the Alpujarras war and Lepanto) arrived in November 1573. After the years of Alba's terror, moderation was the new policy – de Requessens introduced new measures (including abolition of the hated 'tenth' tax) in an attempt at reconciliation. However, a financial crisis now erupted – with huge expenses racked up from the war against the Turks in the Mediterranean as well as in the Netherlands; Spain put a pause on its debt repayments in September, 1575. The bankers who were supposed to pay the troops refused, until their claim against Philip II was settled. In the midst of these difficulties, de Requessens died of ill health in March 1576 and there was an immediate vacuum in Spanish rule. As the months rolled on with no pay, the leaderless army mutinied once again and ran amok. On 4 November 1576 they began the bloody sack of the great mercantile city of Antwerp. The days of terror and pillage became known in history as the 'Spanish Fury'. Amidst the destruction, an estimated 8,000 citizens were killed. It was unfortunate that the atrocities happened just one day after the arrival in the Low Countries of Philip's half-brother, Don John of Austria, who had been appointed to replace de Requessens. If he had arrived some weeks before, this stern military commander might have been able to defuse or quell the mutiny.

Above: on 4 November 1576, Spanish troops, who had not received their pay, began the sack of the great mercantile city of Antwerp. The days of terror became known in history as the 'Spanish Fury', as depicted here in an old print.

Don John had accepted his appointment on the basis that he could have a free hand to seek solutions to the Netherlands crisis. In addition, the concept had been floated, that in the event of a successful invasion of England that would place Mary Queen of Scot on the throne, Don John would marry Mary and be King of England – a prospect hugely important to the ambitious 29 year-old Don John. The concept of an invasion of England ('The Enterprise of England') had by now gained many adherents. English and Irish Catholic exiles in Rome had persuaded the Pope of its merits, assuring him that landing of an expeditionary force would induce a rising by English Catholics, to replace Elizabeth with Mary on the English throne. Philip was now very much in favour, but first, peace had to be achieved in the Netherlands.

In the preceding months, delegates of the States-General (the assembly representing all the provinces of the Netherlands) had been working on negotiating a peace agreement between loyalists and rebels, which provided for freedom of worship and the departure of Spanish troops. As news of the outrage at Antwerp resonated across the Netherlands it helped to galvanise minds and propel the States-General to ratify the peace settlement (called the Pacification of Ghent) on 8 November 1576. Delegates presented the pacification document to Don John soon after he arrived in Luxembourg. Don John was not enamoured of many of the conditions, particularly the core demand that required withdrawal of the Spanish army. However, he was keen for peace, one which would give also him freedom to make prepa-

Left: in this allegorical nineteenth-century Dutch painting, Philip II is shown at his departure from the Netherlands in 1559. Here, he is depicted as encountering William of Orange, accusing him of personally leading the resistance by the nobility against Spanish rule.

rations for an invasion of England. He signed what was called a Perpetual Edict in February 1577, which accepted the terms of the States-General. The *tercios* were withdrawn to Italy two months later.

Nevertheless, the peace quickly started to fall apart. William of Orange claimed he had not been consulted during the final negotiations: he rejected the Perpetual Edict on the basis it did not bring the necessary religious and political freedoms. The provinces of the Netherlands split once more into factions and unrest spread. In turn, Don John was in essence a man of war and not a conciliator in civil matters – in August 1577 he ordered the *tercios* to return. Don John was not to rule for long. He was struck down by typhus and died on 1 October, 1578, near Namur, aged only 31. Before he died he bequeathed command of the Army in Flanders to his, and Philip's, nephew, the Italian-born Alexander Farnese son of Margaret of Parma, the Prince of Parma (who in 1586 became Duke, after his father's death). Farnese, a veteran of the Battle of Lepanto, was also appointed governor general, and soon began to demonstrate his skill in the art of diplomacy.

Diplomacy or no, the rebel group under William of Orange (who had converted to Calvinism in 1573) had no interest in reconciliation with Spain or in tolerating the Catholic faith in their jurisdictions. These, the northern, more Calvinist dominated, provinces met to discuss matters of self-defence and mutual interest. In January 1579 they signed the Union of Utrecht, an act of alliance between Holland, Zeeland and several other northern provinces.

This uncompromising accord did not reflect the more moderate attitude prevailing amongst the States-General. In May 1579 the southern Catholic nobles concluded a separate agreement, the 'Treaty of Arras' (considered as being the foundation-stone of modern-day Belgium), in which they agreed to respect the sovereignty of the Spanish king. Farnese tried to negotiate with the other provinces, represented by the States-General. The dialogue was not helped by Farnese's troops taking Maastricht and Mechelen in the summer of 1579. The peace talks proved abortive and in July 1581 the States-General issued the 'Act of Abjuration' which rejected Philip's sovereignty over their lands. The Dutch had sourced a replacement sovereign: the unprepossessing Duke of Anjou (son of Henry II of France and Catherine of Medici), was now declared 'prince and lord of the Netherlands'. This, of course constituted a heinous insult to Philip, offering the sovereignty of the Low Countries, lands he had inherited and his by established law, to another. Anjou arrived in August 1581, but left for England a few months later on an ill-fated mission to secure the hand of Elizabeth in marriage. He returned at the beginning of 1582, but as the months rolled on his authority declined. In an attempt to boost his fraying credibility, in January 1583 he mounted an assault on Antwerp with the aid of 3,500 French troops. They were heavily defeated – and the Dutch dalliance with the French prince began to draw to an end after Anjou's departure in mid-1583.

In the meantime Farnese had built up his forces. It was fortuitous that there had been an increase in the flow of silver from the New World, allowing Philip to send reinforcements to the Netherlands. Minding his logistics, Farnese also upgraded the 'Spanish Road' that ran from Genoa north to the Netherlands, protected at intervals by a line of forts. This gave him security of supplies, independent of the sea route, then infested by Protestant privateers. By the summer of 1582 his Army of Flanders had grown to around 60,000 soldiers. Using this, the most professional army in Europe, Farnese proceeded to methodically extend Spanish control. By the end of 1584 he had made significant gains, including control of much of the Flemish coast.

Privateering and Drake's circumnavigation

Piracy on the high seas has been around for millennia. Privateering is a more sophisticated variety of piracy: here the sovereign or designated authority sanctions private vessels to attack and seize enemy ships. In effect it was a privatisation of the state's monopoly on violence, and it had the promise to prove profitable for the ruler as well as for the privateer (or corsair). The sixteenth and seventeenth centuries became a golden era for privateering. From the 1520s onwards, in France, then engaged in intermittent war with Spain, French privateers began to plunder Spanish vessels sailing from the

West Indies. As Calvinism spread in France, the local adherents, known as Huguenots, began to increasingly participate in privateering. Over the following decades, they expanded their activities to raid Spanish colonies along the Caribbean. It was lucrative, and also offered the chance to attack the traditional enemy – as well as strike a blow at Catholicism. One estimate is that by 1574 there were over 60 privateering vessels, large and small, operating out of French waters. We already encountered the Dutch privateers, the Sea Beggars, who successfully seized Brill in 1572, and extended their control over the neighbouring region, thus posing a major challenge to Spanish rule in the Netherlands (and who had earlier operated from the Huguenot base of La Rochelle).

Up to the 1570s, privateer attacks on Spanish ships had been mainly carried out by the Protestant French and Dutch. Before this there had been little English participation. England was a relatively small country, an island nation which enjoyed a healthy sea trade in northern European waters. At the beginning of the Tudor era it only possessed limited sea-power. After Henry VIII came to power and in the face of challenges from the French, it became policy to improve naval power. The kingdom promoted the construction of a fleet of private ships which, in times of strife, could be incorporated into the Navy Royal (a permanent fleet, established by Henry in 1546). To encourage the building of larger ships, for every ton over a hundred tons, a payment of five shillings was disbursed by the crown. The advent of a fleet of private ships, larger and more numerous, meant that these had to earn their keep in times of peace. And so it turned out, the English state began to take a liberal view of the difference between conventional legitimate trade and what might be termed 'armed trading', privateering or even pure piracy. Over the years a band of English commanders came to the fore, ready to take advantage of the great opportunities now manifesting across the oceans. Many sprang from a local coastal gentry where there had always been tolerance of (if not participation in) piracy. Agile, amoral, daring and opportunistic, this new breed of adventurers was to gain, not just plunder, but also to obtain valuable sea-going experience which was to underpin English naval strength. The defeat of John Hawkins at San Juan de Ulúa in 1568 (and subsequent harsh treatment of the survivors), due to, as perceived by the English, Spanish perfidy, had added to the bitterness. From the 1580s onwards, as hostility between the two nations became more manifest, English privateers, armed with letters of marque, came to the fore. With rich returns to be had, fleets of privateers were mustered in English harbours, financed by an alliance of adventurers, London merchant companies and the nobility (frequently including the Queen.) The emergence of these privateers, with Spain in their sights, was a harbinger that Philip II's struggle with Protestantism in the north, then principally made up of campaigns on land, was also to be fought at sea.

Francis Drake was the ultimate sea-adventurer of the Elizabethan era. The young Drake, from Devon, had commenced his naval career sailing on a barque, and subsequently graduated to a slave trading voyage to the West African coast led by his second-cousin, John Hawkins. Drake served on several expeditions with Hawkins, the last being the ill-fated one which ended at San Juan de Ulúa. When the attack by the Spanish galleons occurred, Drake (ruthless and always one to look after his own interests) abandoned Hawkins in the harbour and sailed for home in the 50-ton *Judith*. He subsequently denied Hawkins's accusations of desertion. After this incident Drake harboured hatred for the rest of his life for the Spanish and their Catholicism. Over the following years, Drake was able to indulge this aversion, sailing to the West Indies and the Americas to attack Spanish treasure ships and coastal settlements.

Drake did not operate just in warmer oceanic waters. Back in Plymouth from a series of expeditions, he and his ships were subcontracted in 1575 for duties in Ireland, by Walter Devereux, the 1st Earl of Essex. Some years before Essex had been authorised by Elizabeth to conduct a campaign (at his own expense) to subdue the Irish clans the north east and colonise Antrim. Drake's mission was to assist in an attack on the stronghold of the dominant clan, the MacDonnells (of Scottish origin) on Rathlin Island. Drake's flotilla of three ships transported John Norris and his soldiers to the island. At the end of July, following four days siege of the castle there, the defenders surrendered. All 600 inhabitants of the island (including women and children) were slaughtered.

Right: Francis Drake, adventurer and pirate. After bringing plundered treasure back to fill Elizabeth's coffers, he become one of her favourites.

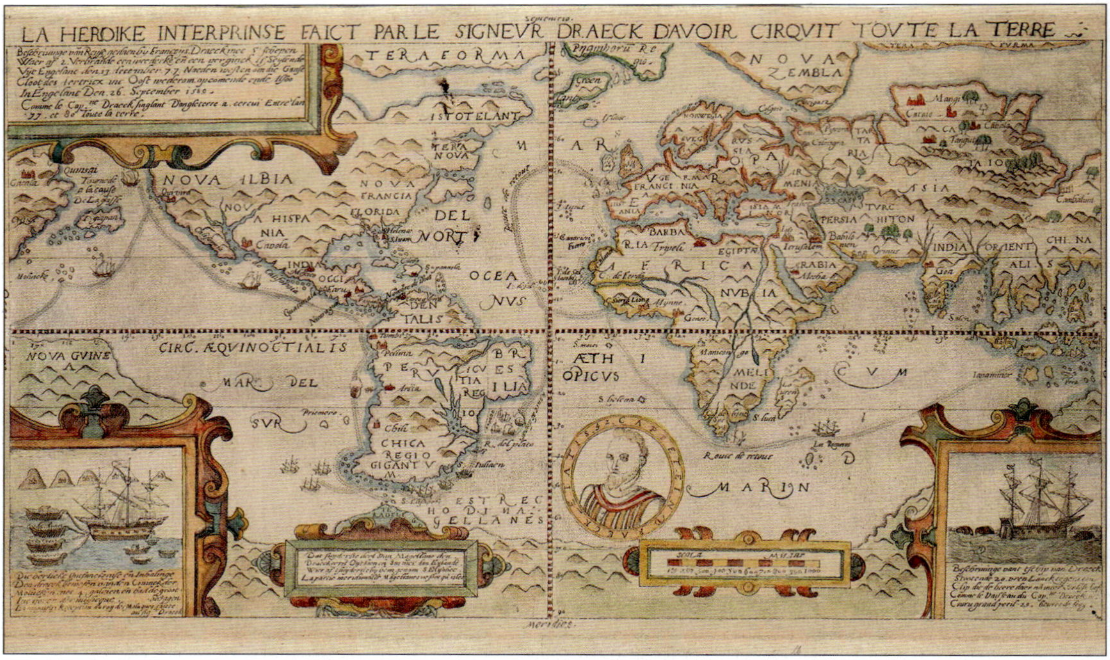

Above: map of Drake's circumnavigation of the world, 1577-1580.

Alas, there were no riches to be had in the chilly waters to the north of Ireland – Drake did not cover his expenses in the Rathlin expedition. For glory and wealth, it was time to turn once again to the Spanish Main, and Drake began to promote the idea of another expedition amongst Elizabeth's advisors. According to Drake, Elizabeth sent for him and said: 'Drake, so it is that I would gladly be revenged on the King of Spain for divers injuries that I have received'. Over the autumn of 1577, Drake duly assembled a small fleet of heavily armed ships in Plymouth harbour. The expedition was authorised by Elizabeth and funded by her together with a consortium of investors. With Spanish agents about, secrecy was tight and it was put about that the forthcoming voyage was merely a trading one to North African ports and Constantinople. Drake set out in December 1577 on a voyage, one much more ambitious and long distance than any previous. The ultimate target was the Spanish colonies on the South American Pacific coast, up to now undisturbed by any raids from pirates. Drake's ships headed towards the South American Atlantic coast and continued southwards. Sailing through the Strait of Magellan at the end of August 1578, Drake's small fleet was beset by storms. By the time he was able to make course north to Peru, Drake was left with only one ship, his own flagship, the *Golden Hinde*. Many shore raids and capture of treasure ships later; Drake headed further north and, according to some reports, reached Lower California. Next he sailed west across the Pacific, and, after rounding the Cape of Good Hope, he arrived back in Plymouth in September 1580, laden with treasure. Elizabeth had many reasons to be delighted. The epic voyage was a tribute to English seamanship and endurance. More prosaically, but very importantly, she received her half-share of the bounty, which exceeded the Crown's revenue for that year.

Rebellion and massacres in Ireland

At the time of Elizabeth's coronation in 1559, her knowledge of Ireland, her second realm, was fairly limited. This was unsurprising – by the standards of the time, it was a faraway land, difficult to get to, separated by a sea. An absentee monarch (and it was to be so for her entire reign) she had control of less than half the territory; the rest of the country, even more remote and with rudimentary communications, was ruled by Gaelic chieftains. She would have inherited the colonial prejudice that their culture and language was inferior, wild and primitive. However she was curious about this exotic part of her realm and in 1562 requested the preparation of a primer in the Gaelic language. Her initial fear was that the French would gain a foothold here (perhaps via Scotland) and pose a major threat to England. As the years rolled on the threat changed to one of a Spanish invasion in what was in effect, her Irish backyard.

Elizabeth left much of the detail of governing the island to her Lord Deputies. Tudor rule in Ireland emanated from Dublin, then an overwhelmingly English city. It was not large by European or even English standards, with a population approaching 10,000. Enclosed by city walls, it sat on the south side of the River Liffey, connected to small suburbs to the north by one bridge over the river. Within the walls were tightly packed houses (unsurprisingly, plagues occurred frequently), two cathedrals and, at the centre, Dublin Castle, where the Lord Deputy lived and governed.

The general mission of a Lord Deputy was, as well as maintaining order, to conquer and assimilate further territory, preferably at little or no cost to the exchequer. Henry VIII's policy of gradual absorption, employing the 'Surrender and Regrant' system had enjoyed some success. However, by the time of Elizabeth's accession this process had begun to falter. In time an initiative was devised that successively managed to extend control deep into Gaelic Ireland. This was the establishment of presidencies, or regional councils – one was set up in Connacht (called Connaught by the English) in 1569 and another some years later in Munster. The president was, in effect, a local governor with full authority, supported by the military. Another useful method devised to establish control in a particular locale was the declaration of martial law. A commission of martial law was granted to a representative of the Crown (an officer or a gentleman). The commissioner could proceed to the area of dissent, and impose order. Suspected traitors could be summarily executed without trial. It was very cost effective –the commissioners and their band of followers were paid by the confiscation of the goods of those they put to death. One historian (who called the system 'state terrorism') has calculated that around 260 commissions were issued in the 20 years after Elizabeth came to power.

Elizabeth's instinct was generally one of delay, always hesitant to incur the substantial expenses generated by war. However, events intervened and on occasion she was forced to get involved in the conflicts that bubbled all over Ireland. In 1565 there was conflict between the rival families of the Earl of Desmond (the FitzGeralds, or Geraldines) and the Earl of Ormond (the Butlers). In Munster, the local clan leaders were suspicious of the English government and their plan for what later emerged as the presidency. Amidst the uncertainty, James FitzMaurice FitzGerald, captain general of the FitzGeralds managed to garner the support of the local lords, who particularly feared land confiscations. In 1569 he led the Desmond army to revolt and rebellion flared up all over Munster. The English reacted in strength and their troops suppressed the rebellion with much bloodshed and using scorched-earth tactics. With the rebel cause lost, FitzMaurice submitted in early 1572. Three years later he travelled to the continent, and on arrival, he found that the religious and political landscape in Europe had become a fertile ground to gather opposition to Elizabeth's rule. We have seen how in 1570 the Pope had excommunicated the English queen. Philip II had decided that the Protestant Elizabeth and her reign posed a major threat to Spain's interests. France was also concerned about Mary Queen of Scots, now held in custody in England. To fan the flames there was an ever-growing number of English and Irish Catholic émigrés in Rome and Spain who ardently urged action to depose Elizabeth. Amidst this febrile atmosphere, James FitzMaurice FitzGerald was able to paint the struggle against the Tudor regime in Ireland in the colours of both a national and religious struggle. In Paris, he had interviews with Catherine of Medici, the powerful Queen Mother, and offered to her son, Henry III, the kingship of Ireland, if France supported the overthrow of English rule there. Catherine granted the Irish rebel a pension, but, as she had enough problems with the ongoing religious strife in France, declined to assist with an invasion. The persistent and charismatic FitzMaurice set off for Rome. Pope Gregory XIII proved enthusiastic in the cause of dethroning Elizabeth and agreed to fund an expedition where FitzMaurice and an English adventurer, Thomas Stukeley (who had managed to re-invent himself as a champion of the Catholic cause), would sail to Ireland and lead a rebellion there. FitzMaurice journeyed to Spain in 1577. Once more, Fitzmaurice offered the kingship of Ireland, in exchange for Spanish intervention – this time it would be given to Don John of Austria. Philip II declined, as Spain was embroiled in the war in the Netherlands and he was doubtful about mounting a major expedition to Ireland. This prompted Dr Nicholas Sander, an English priest in exile in Madrid, to write to his fellow English prelate, William (later, Cardinal) Allen 'to take hould of the Pope: for the King of Spaine is as fearefull of warre as a child of fyer ... The Pope will geve two thousand ... The state of Christendome dependethe uppon the stowte assailinge of Englande'. In February 1578 Stukeley, provided with 700 men and a ship by the Pope, sailed from Italy, destination, Ireland. However, en route his ship turned out to be unseaworthy and he had to call into Lisbon for repairs. There, the mercurial adventurer was diverted to join another crusade, this time the expedition to Morocco, planned by the young Portuguese King Sebastian. The invasion proved disastrous and in August 1578 Stukeley was killed in the Battle of Ksar el-Kebir.

By the end of 1578 FitzMaurice had made his way to northern Spain, making the final preparations for an expedition to Ireland. While the expedition did not receive direct Spanish support, Philip II, irritated by ongoing English annoyances such as Drake's circumnavigation voyage had decided to allow FitzMaurice to covertly assemble a force in Galicia. In June 1579

Right: a map (compiled in the aftermath for the Master General of the Ordnance) depicting the events at Smerwick, Dingle Peninsula, Co. Kerry, Ireland, in November 1580. It shows the assault on the Papal expeditionary force, ensconced behind their fortifications. The imaginative and totally out-of-scale map shows the ships of the Navy Royal in Smerwick harbour, as English soldiers march out of their so-called Castell More, heading to the fray.

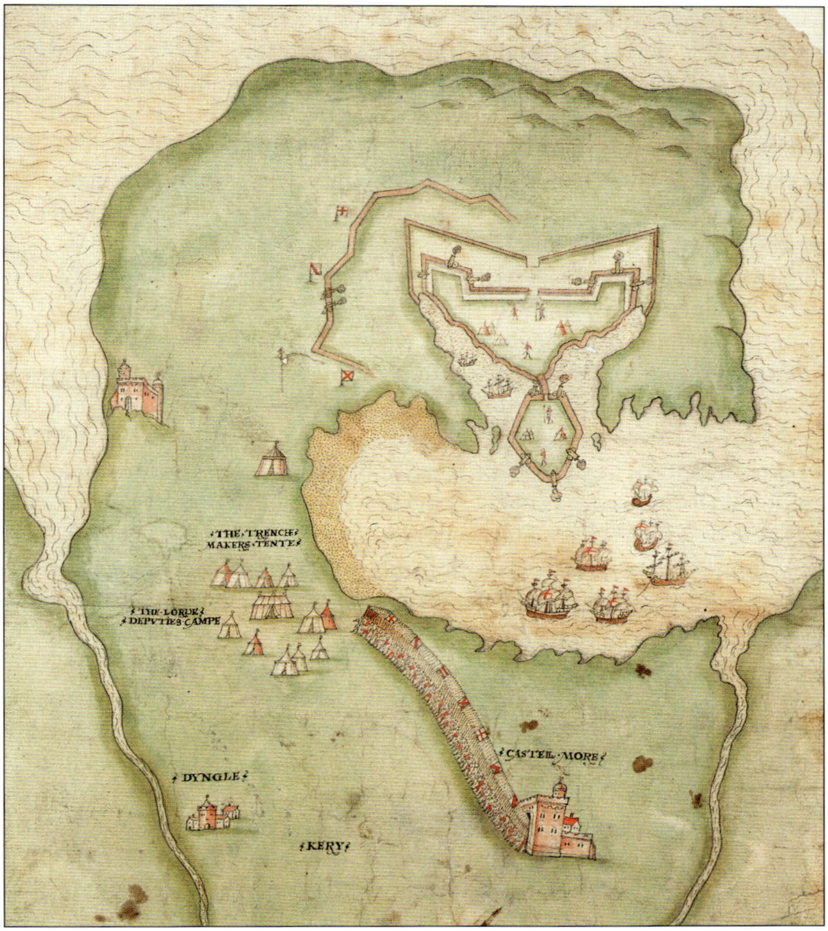

the Irish rebel leader sailed from Ferrol, with four ships and a motley force of around 60. It comprised Italians, soldiers recruited in Galicia and several Irish and English Catholic exiles, including Nicholas Sander who was the Pope's representative. FitzMaurice's flotilla (augmented by two English ships that were captured on the way) sailed to southwest Ireland and on 18 July 1579 landed at Smerwick harbour, at the tip of the Dingle Peninsula.

Hoisting the papal standard, they proclaimed that they were engaged in a holy war against a heretic queen. The small force set up in the ruins of an Iron Age fort called Dún an Óir ('Fort of Gold', located on a small promontory) and proceeded to fortify it. (The name probably had ancient origins, but there is an intriguing story that the name derived from a ship laden with ore, mistakenly thought to have contained gold, from the Canadian Arctic Circle, which was wrecked there just a year previously. The ship had been part of the expedition led by the privateer-adventurer Martin Frobisher in search of the Northwest Passage. Frobisher was to feature in later naval actions, both here at Smerwick and, famously, leading his squadron against the Armada).

The initial response to the Smerwick landing from the Munster nobles was low-key. However, as news spread of the small invasion, an uprising flared up across the Geraldine domains in Munster, which has been called the Second Desmond Rebellion. The flames of rebellion had been fanned by the ongoing English encroachment and the introduction of the requirement to pay taxes to the Crown. FitzMaurice set out to spread the revolt, but in mid-August he met a banal end – he was killed in a clash with the Burke clan of Limerick over stolen horses. The English had been caught by surprise at the uprising – they only had 1,200 soldiers in Ireland at that time. By the end of the rebellion, they had, at great cost, increased the numbers fourfold. Nicholas Malby, President of Connaught, who had form in brutal repression, was swiftly drafted in as governor of Munster to deal with the rebellion. Malby enlisted the aid of the Earl of Ormond and they directed the assault on Geraldine strongholds. Artillery, sometimes delivered by sea, was particularly effective. Next came brutal sweeps through the rebel lands. It was sixteenth-century 'shock and awe': tenants were killed; crops were burnt and cattle seized. In the midst of this another rebellion broke out in mid-1580, dangerously near the heart of the Pale, led by James Eustace, Viscount Baltinglass. The newly–appointed Lord Deputy, Baron Grey de Wilton (veteran of the Calais campaign in 1558, and one of the more dogmatic Protestants amongst Elizabeth's courtiers – and later to be one of the commissioners who condemned Mary Queen of Scots), led his troops into the wild terrain of the Wicklow Mountains. On 25 August 1580, Fiach MacHugh O'Byrne (clan leader, allied with Baltinglass through marriage), routed the English force at the valley of Glenmalure.

The Papal representative, Nicholas Sander, had been travelling around Ireland endeavouring to stimulate revolt, at the same time sending letters to the continent requesting more help from the Pope and Philip II. On hearing that reinforcements had arrived at Smerwick in mid-September 1580, he hurried back. However, he was disappointed at the small number of soldiers, insufficient to make a difference to the rebellion. Over 700 Spanish and Italian soldiers, commanded by the Italian, Sebastiano di San Guiseppe, along with a substantial amount of victuals and arms to equip a large army, had been transported to Smerwick by six Spanish ships. The new arrivals proceeded to strengthen the earthworks of the rudimentary fort and mount artillery. The ships were under the command of the experienced naval commander Don Juan Martínez de Recalde. The expedition to Smerwick afforded him an opportunity, before he returned to Spain, to examine the south-western Irish coast. This knowledge, as we shall see later, proved invaluable when de Recalde, then second-in-command of the Armada, sailed in his vice-flagship, the *San Juan de Portugal*, into the shelter of Blasket Sound on 15 September, 1588.

By mid-October 1580 Baron Grey de Wilton had received substantial reinforcements from England. He left some of these to deal with the rebellion near the Pale, and eager to redeem his reputation after the disaster at Glenmalure, he set out rapidly for the south west to deal with the invaders. He was accompanied by his secretary, Edmund Spenser, and his army was officered by a contingent of captain-adventurers. A flotilla of the Tudor navy, commanded by Admiral Sir William Wynter, was also dispatched post haste from England. On 5 November Wynter sailed his dozen war-

Right: Dún an Óir, originally an Iron Age fort, at Smerwick today. The defensive outer earthworks can still be seen in the photograph.

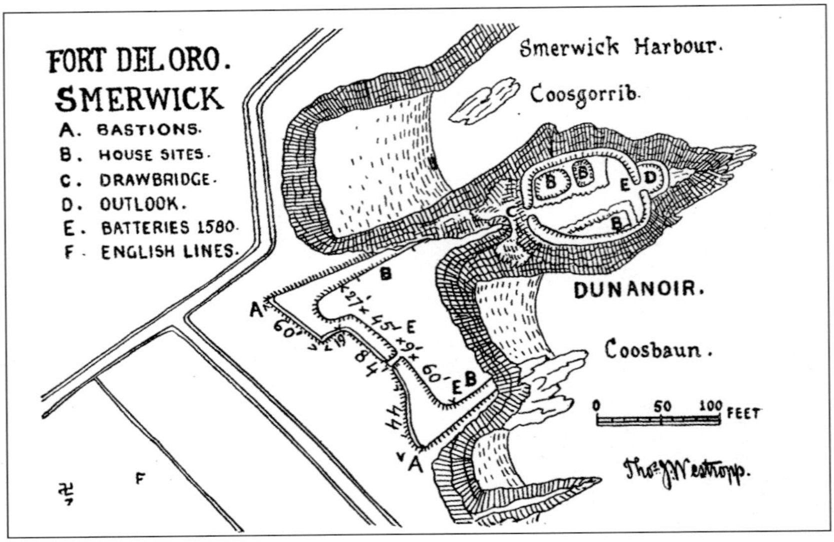

Left: a map, dating from 1910, by the antiquarian Thomas Johnson Westropp, showing the engagement at Smerwick. It sets out the buildings as well as the bastions and batteries.

ships into Smerwick harbour (several of the larger ones, including the *Swiftsure* and *Revenge*, were to feature prominently in the 1588 exchanges with the Armada). He landed artillery pieces as Grey, who had been joined by the Earl of Ormond and his soldiers, advanced from Dingle to begin the siege of the enemy, entrenched in Dún an Óir. Some of the defenders are thought to have returned to the continent, but the garrison had possibly been augmented by supporters of FitzMaurice. On 8 November, a ferocious exchange of artillery began.

Under cover of darkness, the English managed to advance their trench to within 100m of the defender's forward lines. After some accurate English fire an Italian camp-master came out on 10 November and asked that they might surrender and be permitted to leave. Grey grimly asked: who had sent them? He presumed that was not the King of Spain, who was in amity with the English Queen. The reply was that the Pope had sent them for the protection of the Catholic faith. This was likely to induce a violent reaction from a zealot like Grey who regarded Catholicism and the Pope as the heretical enemy. He responded that the Pope was a vile commander and an 'Antichrist'. During the sixteenth century in Europe the concept of honourable surrender (based on medieval chivalry) was observed – on occasion. An enemy who yielded in combat normally would expect to receive reasonable treatment. However, at the time the right to wage war was, in theory, the sole prerogative of a sovereign. Cruelty rather than reasonableness was the norm in Tudor Ireland and Grey obviously did not regard the Pope as a legitimate sovereign. Irish accounts say that, to secure surrender, Grey promised mercy and a free departure from Ireland, but in Grey's version, no promise was given that the defenders' lives would be spared.

Whatever was the agreed premise, on 10 November, the fort's commander and his men emerged, trailing their rolled flags. Grey tells in his account 'then I put in certain bands who straight fell to execution. There were 600 slain'. Vice-Admiral, Richard Bingham, commander of the *Swiftsure*, who was present, wrote that the soldiers who did the killing were under the

Right: many heads. A memorial at Smerwick to the 600 slain there in November 1580.

command of the ward master Captain Edward Denny (a cousin of Walter Raleigh) – and that these were soon joined by sailors. Other accounts say that Captain Walter Raleigh, (then in his 20s, later to become the famous colonist, explorer and writer), was amongst those who directed the carnage. The bloodshed did not end with the slaughter of the Italian and Spanish soldiers. Three men (a priest, an Irish interpreter and an English servant of Nicholas Sander) were hauled off to the local blacksmiths. Their bones were smashed on the anvil and then they were hanged. Finally, the bodies were shot to pieces by the soldiers, using them as target practice. Around 20 of the Spanish and Italian officers were ransomed. Thus, by the end of 1580, all traces of Papal (and Spanish) forces had been extirpated from Elizabeth's kingdoms. Baron Grey de Wilton's name has gone down in Irish history: the term 'Grey's word' signifies the breaking of a promise.

Smerwick gave a fillip to the careers of the captain adventurers who were present. Richard Bingham later became governor of Connaught, and in 1588 was to enthusiastically direct the round up and killing of Armada survivors. Edward Denny, a one-time privateer, was later knighted and granted a huge swathe of confiscated Desmond land in Kerry – and with his wife was to instigate the execution of Spanish sailors who came ashore at Tralee.

With overwhelming force and persistence, the revolts in Leinster and in Munster were gradually suppressed. By 1583 the Second Desmond Rebellion was finally put down. In Tudor eyes, plantation was to be the effective answer to end the twin scourges of popery and disorder. The plantation of Munster now got under way. Undertakers, in return for paying rent to the Crown and with obligations to develop new and fortified towns, were granted swathes of confiscated land. These undertakers (usually men of wealth) duly imported tenants from England and Wales to work the land. The Gaelic Irish on the former Desmond estates were now displaced by settlers, English speaking and Protestant.

Philip's new realm: Portugal

We turn now to another Atlantic nation, well over 1,000km to the south. Although scarcely larger than Ireland, Portugal had developed an illustrious sea-going tradition. Along with Spain, Portugal was the other European nation which dominated the oceans during the sixteenth century. Its empire extended in the Atlantic to Africa on the west and Brazil on the east. Furthermore, the Portuguese had travelled south around the Cabo da Boa Esperança, or Cape of Good Hope, across the Pacific to India and the East where they had established forts and trading posts.

Portugal, possessing several enclaves in North Africa, had pretensions to take control there. The twenty-four year old King Sebastian, worried about the Ottoman threat in the Mediterranean, had impetuously decided to back the cause of the Sultan in Morocco, who had just been deposed. Stretching the resources of his country, he assembled a large army and fleet which in August 1578 attacked the forces of the new Sultan, at Ksar el-Kebir, in northern Morocco. It ended in disaster with huge loss of life. Sebastian was killed and his body disappeared. The cream of Portuguese nobility was either dead or captured for ransom. Among those who lost their lives, as we have seen, was the colourful English Catholic adventurer Thomas Stukeley who, having set out with a papal force to invade Ireland, had instead quixotically decided to participate in the Moroccan expedition.

Sebastian had no children, so there now followed a confused period of claims to the succession. Sebastian's great-uncle, the elderly Cardinal Henry (and son of Manuel I, King of Portugal), now became king of the shattered kingdom, then in the course of being beggared by ransom demands for the many noble captives held in Morocco. Henry lived for less than two years until January 1580, and left a council of regents in charge. Of the many claimants to the throne, one of the two frontrunners was Dom António, the wealthy Prior of Crato – a grandson of King Manuel (but of illegitimate birth). Dom António had been among those taken prisoner at the battle of Ksar el-Kebir, but, pleading poverty, had cannily secured his release in return for a small ransom. The other aspirant, with an even stronger claim, was King Philip II of Spain. The practice of dynastic marriages of that era had resulted in Philip being the closest legitimate relative. Philip's mother had been the Portuguese princess Isabella, and thus he too was grandson to Manuel, nephew to Cardinal Henry and uncle to the recently deceased Sebastian. Dom António enjoyed some support in Portugal. However, Philip's emissaries began to build up a network of influential Portuguese sympathisers to his cause, including those merchants who wished to participate in the wealthy Atlantic trade that presently passed through Seville. During the intermission afforded by Henry's brief reign, Philip had built up his forces in Andalusia, ostensibly as preparations for an invasion of Morocco. In the months that followed Cardinal Henry's death, Spanish troops were moved to Extremadura, on the Portuguese border. To lead them, the Duke of Alba was called out of retirement. On 27 June 1580, the Spanish army, massed at Badajoz, crossed the Portuguese border. In a coordinated move, the Marquis of Santa Cruz, who had assembled a large fleet at Cádiz, sailed out for Portugal. On the way the fleet assisted the Duke of Medina Sidonia, foremost nobleman of Andalucia, in subduing the Algarve, and then continued north towards Lisbon. Towards the end of July Dom António proclaimed himself King of Portugal in the historic town of Santarém (north of Lisbon). Various battles followed where the Spanish vanquished the prelate's followers. In August 1580, the Duke of Alba reached Lisbon, and, assisted by Santa Cruz's fleet, took the city and the Portuguese navy. Dom António tried to organise a resistance movement but it proved fruitless and he fled abroad at the end of 1580. The aspirant to the throne reached England, via France, where Elizabeth received him warmly.

Philip hastened to assure the Portuguese that he would respect their liberties and laws and in April 1581 the Portuguese Cortes at Tomar recognised him as King Philip I of Portugal. Now, all of the Iberian Peninsula came under his sway. He had gained a vast new overseas territory, and as the historian Garret Mattingly, noted 'Nobody since the beginning of history had ever ruled so much of the earth's surface as Philip II.' On a strategic level Philip had gained many skilled seamen, harbours and dockyards. Lisbon, with its outstanding harbour, and facing the Atlantic, was to prove an excellent naval base. A great prize were the ten heavy ocean-proven warships in Lisbon harbour. These, able to carry large cannons, were a valuable addition to Spanish sea-power. Now Philip had acquired more naval strength and capability which was to allow him to build on and credibly proceed with plans for the Enterprise of England.

However, the war of the Portuguese succession had not gone away: Dom António continued to energetically campaign to recover what he regarded as his inheritance. While the Indies and Brazil had accepted Spanish rule, all the islands of the Azores (save São Miguel, the largest one) had declared for the prelate. In early 1581 he offered an intriguing proposition to the English – if they helped him consolidate his control over the Azores, he would allow them to set up a base there. For Philip, the Azores, lying around 1,600km west of Lisbon, were hugely important: they provided a stopping over and provisioning point on the trade routes for the returning Spanish treasure fleets, as well as for the Portuguese ships returning from the East Indies, laden with spice. If these islands were in enemy hands they would offer an ideal location to intercept the treasure fleet, as well as offering a springboard to make attacks on Spanish settlements along the Caribbean. The offer of a base was tempting to Elizabeth, but she was fearful of the Spanish reaction – as reinforced by threats from Don Bernardino de Mendoza, the Spanish Ambassador.

Left: Dom António, Prior of Crato and pretender to the Portuguese Crown.

There were three distinct acts to the conflict as it evolved in the Azores from 1581 onwards. The first played out in June 1581, when a small squadron under the command of Don Pedro de Valdés set out for the Azores. His orders were to await another squadron, due from Lisbon, and jointly escort the returning fleets that were expected from the Americas and the East Indies. On arrival at the island of São Miguel (loyal to Philip), de Valdés heard that French corsairs were in harbour at Terceira, the principal island in the archipelago of those which had declared for Dom António, and that the islanders there were poorly armed. De Valdés impulsively headed for Terceira with his squadron. At the end of July, with his peace overtures brusquely rebuffed , de Valdés sent his men to land on the island, with his son Captain Diego Valdés at their head. The islanders gathered reinforcements (in one account, they included soldiers from the French corsair ships) and battle ensued. Suffering 200 dead, including de Valdés's son, the Spanish had to make an ignominious retreat in the face of superior numbers. In due course the expected Spanish squadron of 12 ships arrived and the joint force escorted the treasure fleets back to safe harbour. On his return to Lisbon, in disgrace, de Valdés was imprisoned by order of the king.

Dom António left England for France in October 1581. He was warmly received and installed in the Louvre by the French regent, Catherine de Medici. She was supportive of anything that would reduce the danger of Spanish hegemony. She also had a remote claim to the throne of Portugal, being a distant relative of a Portuguese king. One account says when she met Dom António, she agreed to withdraw her rather shaky claim– and in return for her assistance, he agreed that he would cede Brazil to her. With Catherine's blessing, a large fleet of French privateers was assembled, under the direction of the Italian Filippo Strozzi, a kinsman of Catherine and an experienced Colonel-General of the French infantry. Amongst the 58 ships of privateers were 11 small English vessels. In June 1582, the fleet set out from Belle-Isle in Brittany, heading for the Azores. Flying the Portuguese flag and with Dom António on board, the expedition had the objective of defeating Philip's supporters and reinforcing the prelate's control over the archipelago. The prospect of capturing Spanish treasure ships arriving from the Indies was an additional incentive for the privateers. Back at Lisbon the Marquis of Santa Cruz had earlier been ordered by Philip II to subdue the rebel islands in the Azores – and, referring to de Valdés' debacle in 1581, instructed 'to get the job done this time'. The Marquis began preparations in the spring of 1582, gathering ships from all over to augment the Atlantic-capable galleons of the Portuguese navy, now under his control.

A powerful Spanish fleet of 28 warships plus support vessels, under the command of the Marquis, in his flagship, the *San Martín*, previously the *São Martinho* of the Portuguese navy, sailed out from Lisbon to intercept the French expedition. At the end of July 1582 the opposing fleets met in deep water near the island of São Miguel in the Azores. After initial skirmishing, a major battle (sometimes called the Battle of Ponta Delgada) began on the 24 July. This was the second key event in the struggle for control over the Azores. The corsair fleet had the wind at the start and attacked the Spanish rear-guard. Spanish tactics were the traditional one of closing with an enemy ship, firing a broadside and then overcoming the enemy ship by boarding it. The French, with their lower and smaller ships, were able to sail in nimbly around the less numerous, but larger Spanish ships and pound them at some distance with their guns, inflicting serious damage. The following day continued with variable wind and there was ineffectual skirmishing. On 26 July, as the wind rose, Strozzi spotted an opportunity when the galleon *San Mateo* became isolated from its formation and reverted to the traditional tactic of ramming and boarding. At the head of a line of ships, he came near the *San Mateo*, with heavy exchange of guns by both sides. Strozzi crashed into the now heavily damaged galleon, and with support from three other of his ships, led a charge aboard. The 250 men aboard the *San Mateo* resisted strongly. Santa Cruz ordered his ships to the rescue and the Spanish rear-guard, led by Miguel de Oquendo, came up, and sent a broadside into Strozzi's ship, causing it to sink. Strozzi was badly wounded by a harquebus shot and died shortly afterwards. After five hours of hard combat, the Spanish won decisively.

Before he sailed for the Azores, Santa Cruz had received instructions from Philip, that he mete out exemplary punishment to those that opposed him. A trial of the several hundred French prisoners was soon held. They were judged as having sailed under instructions of the Queen Mother and not the King of France, (there was the added sin of sailing under the pretender's Portuguese flag). Thus they had not been in the service of a legitimate sovereign and, deemed to be corsairs, they were sentenced to death. On the first of August the noblemen were beheaded and the lesser ranks hanged. One Spanish historian, in comparing this very hard '*castigo*' with the massacre at Smerwick in Ireland in 1580, argues that the execution of the prisoners here was done in accordance with the orders of the King,

Left: the illustrious Spanish naval commander Álvaro de Bazán, the Marquis of Santa Cruz.

as well as conforming to 'reason and justice'. The difference, he argues, is that those at Smerwick had surrendered to Baron Grey de Wilton, on the promise that their life would be spared.

It was a famous victory for Santa Cruz and his fleet. Suffering just over 200 dead, they had not lost any ships, although some were badly damaged. Of the French fleet, estimates of their losses range from 1,200 upwards killed in battle, with ten ships lost (two burnt, four sunk and the remaining four captured.) As historian Felipe Fernández-Armesto has noted 'The Spaniards actually sank more enemy ships at Terceira than the English did in the whole Armada campaign [of 1588]'.

The Marquis of Santa Cruz returned in triumph to Lisbon, to be welcomed there by civic and religious celebrations. The Marquis now commenced planning for the third and final act of the Azores drama: an amphibious landing on the islands of such force that would suppress Dom António's rule there once and for all. In what was to presage the preparations for the later Armada, missives were dispatched to all corners of Philip's realms, and the great bureaucratic machine creaked into action. In time the

Right: as depicted in the Hall of Battles at the Escorial, the landing of the tercios at Terceira in the Azores in July 1583.

quays of Lisbon became crowded with the enormous quantities of food and supplies needed for the great endeavour. A large fleet of around 100 ships was gathered. At its fighting core were five Atlantic galleons, along with 12 galleys, two galleasses and assorted *pataches*. To transport three *tercios*, over 30 large merchant ships were mustered. These were supplemented by a flotilla of flat-bottomed landing craft, which had to be towed to the Azores. Santa Cruz's large fleet arrived at Terceira at the end of July 1583. The 30-km long island was well fortified and the defenders had been reinforced the previous month by French soldiers. The Marquis had astutely identified a small cove that was lightly defended as the landing point. The galleys went in, towing, as the nineteenth-century Spanish historian Fernández Duro noted, 'a rosary of barges'. The *tercios* landed and assembled into their square formations, effective in overcoming enemy soldiers. The *tercios* rolled on, silencing, one by one, the forts and positions of the defenders. After hard fighting, the Spanish prevailed, and at last, the Azores were fully under Philip's control. Dom António (who had escaped to France after the 1582 sea battle and had returned in June once again to Terceira) managed to escape once again. In 1585 he made his way to England, where he was welcomed at the Tudor court. Based here, he continued over the following decade to press his claim to Portugal.

Back in Spain, there was much celebration after the great triumph in the Azores. Trophies, including captured French and Portuguese flags, were put on display. Philip ordered frescoes to be painted in the Hall of Battles at the Escorial to celebrate the victorious battles. A gilded bronze medal was minted in 1583, with Philip's head on one side, with the inscription, 'King of Spain and the New World' and on the obverse, the globe with the motto '*Non sufficit Orbis*' (previously used by the Roman poet Juvenal in reference to Alexander the Great) or, 'the world is not enough'. As we will see in Chapter 2, the victory had also spurred Santa Cruz in August 1583 to write to Philip from Terceira urging the invasion of England.

Left: nephew of Philip II, Alexander Farnese, Prince of Parma, who was mandated by the King to suppress the Dutch rebellion.

The Dutch Revolt rolls on

Meanwhile, far away to the north, the Dutch revolt continued. As we have seen, in July 1581, the States-General had issued an 'Act of Abjuration', rejecting the authority of Philip II. Nevertheless, Alexander Farnese, Prince of Parma, and his fearsome army continued with methodically crushing the revolt. By early 1584, with most of Flanders captured, Farnese carried on to advance through Brabant. It was good news for the Spanish cause in July, hen the principal leader of the Dutch Revolt, William, Prince of Orange, was assassinated in Delft by a Catholic from the Franche-Comté (inspired by a proclamation by Philip which had put a price on William's head). A month later, Farnese began the siege of prosperous Antwerp, then the focal point of the revolt. The besiegers constructed a long pontoon bridge of boats over the River Scheldt, with the intent of cutting off access from the sea to the city. The siege dragged on and in April 1585, the defenders launched a flotilla of fireships towards the bridge. Two of these (known in history as the 'hellburners') had been specially devised by the Italian military

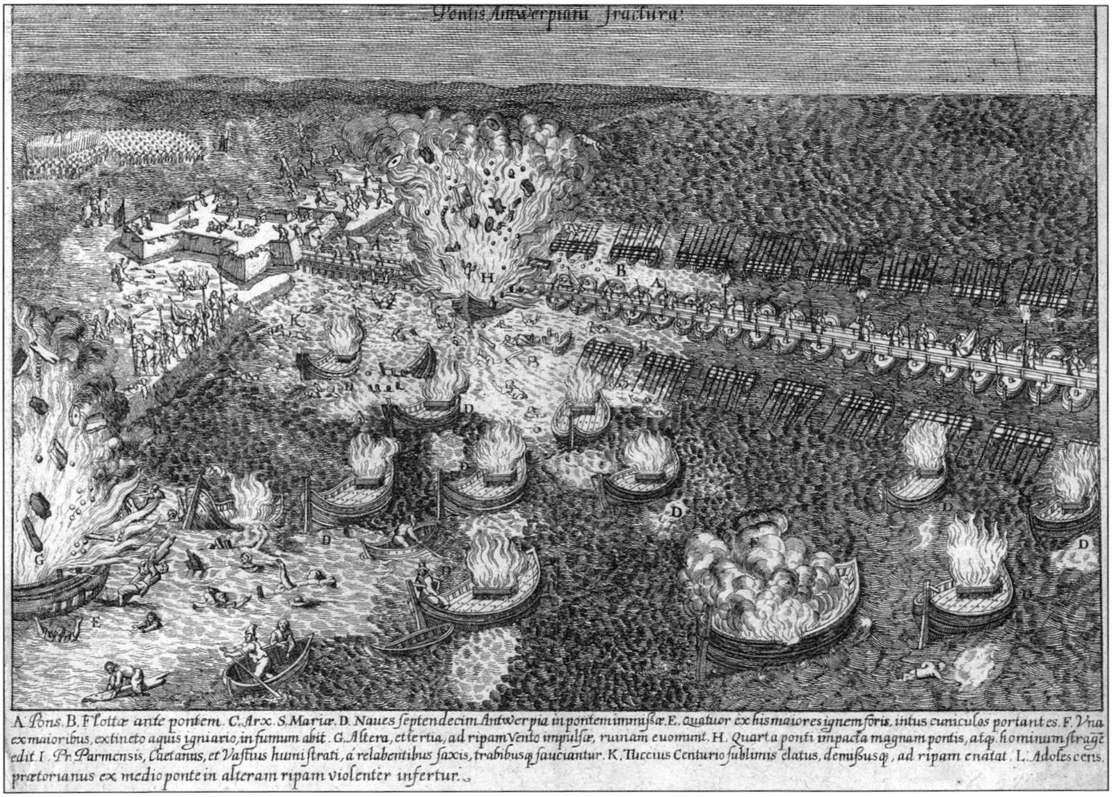

Above: as a flotilla of other fireships approach, a 'hellburner' explodes, in April 1585, at the pontoon bridge constructed by the Prince of Parma's forces during the siege of Antwerp.

engineer, Federigo Giambelli: ships laden with gunpowder, to be set off by timers made by an Antwerp clockmaker. One of the 'hellburners' blew up at the bridge, killing a reported 800 Spanish troops. Parma himself was flung to the ground by the force of the explosion. Nevertheless, the siege continued and in August 1585 the city capitulated to the Spanish. Under the direction of Parma, demonstrably an outstanding commander of land armies, Spain was regaining its ascendancy in the Netherlands. In reality, it was enjoying a new *Reconquista*.

As the Spanish were enjoying success in the Netherlands, factions in England (notably led by her favourite, Robert Dudley, the Earl of Leicester, and Sir Francis Walsingham, her principal secretary) pressed the more cautious Elizabeth towards a more 'Protestant' foreign policy. They urged active support for French Huguenots (then under pressure from King, Henry III, who had turned on them) and for the Dutch rebels. Tension escalated when in May 1585, urged by Parma to target clandestine Dutch Protestant trade with Spain, Philip II ordered the seizure of all northern European ships (except those of the French) in Spanish and Portuguese ports.

Thus in June 1585, when the Dutch rebels sent a delegation to England, requesting assistance, Elizabeth was in a receptive mood. Against the background of the ongoing siege of Antwerp, they offered her sovereignty over the Low Countries. She was astute enough to decline, realising that to agree would be to commit England to provide unlimited support towards what promised to be an interminable conflict. Elizabeth was playing a delicate

Left: Robert Dudley, the 1st Earl of Leicester, confidante of Queen Elizabeth. His appointment as commander of the English troops in the Netherlands did not fare well and he returned to England in December 1587.

game. She did not wish to see Parma and his Army of Flanders reconquer the Low Countries. At the same time she did not want a vacuum to be created, with the danger of a takeover by the French. As a compromise, she agreed to what she hoped would be a quick intervention and consented to send troops to assist the States-General of the United Provinces. On 20 August 1585 (coincidentally, at around the same time as Antwerp was on the verge of surrendering), a Treaty was signed at Nonsuch, a Tudor palace in Surrey. The treaty stipulated that an army of '4000 foot and 500 horse' was to be provided immediately – with a promise of more. As part of the agreement, England would be given control of the ports of Flushing and Brill, as surety until the Queen's outlay on the Dutch war had been repaid. Elizabeth was nothing if not a great dissembler, always seeking an exit strategy from the consequences of her actions. Just after signing the treaty, she wrote to Parma, explaining that she saw this as opening the way to possible reconciliation and accord with the Spanish.

By the end of August, an English force, under the command of John Norris, had landed on the Dutch coast. He had recently left Ireland, where in mid-1584 he had been appointed President of Munster, with the Plantation of Munster on his agenda. We had last seen Norris in Ireland, ten years before, directing the massacre at Rathlin Island. Of the many captain-adventurers of that era, he enjoyed one of the most colourful careers, seeing service in practically every Tudor theatre of war. He had fought for the Huguenots in France and was experienced in the Low Countries, having led an earlier group of English volunteers fighting for the States-General in 1577. Another detachment was sent to garrison Flushing and Brill and the build-up of English troops continued. Elizabeth's confidante, the Earl of Leicester, was appointed as overall commander of the expedition. Having mortgaged his estate to help finance the expedition, he arrived in December 1585 with additional troops. Leicester was initially well-received by the Dutch and the following January he was offered the position of governor-general of the United Provinces by the States-General. He accepted, much to the subsequent fury of Elizabeth, who was outraged by her favourite getting above his station. As it turned out, Leicester's interventions in government there were clumsy. His attempt to introduce a ban on Dutch trade with Spain annoyed the Dutch merchants.

The campaign of the small and inexperienced English forces against the formidable Spanish army did not fare well. In some areas, the English soldier's reputation for undisciplined behaviour resulted in them being refused billets by the Dutch population. Elizabeth had declared that the English intervention was a limited one, to protect the Dutch towns from attack. This constrained Leicester, and he had to restrain from engaging in any major battle with the forces of Alexander Farnese, who in September 1586 become the Duke of Parma, after the death of his father. As Parma's army continued its onslaught and captured rebel towns, the cost of maintaining her overseas army began to weigh heavily on Elizabeth's already strained exchequer. In the following months the English army did not receive their pay or rations. (The situation was not helped by the practice by captains of corruptly skimming the troop's wages). Leicester tried to raise credit on his own behalf to pay the troops. The Sack of Antwerp by unpaid *tercios* in 1576 had demonstrated that neglecting to pay the troops was a dangerous practice. As the expense of the shambolic English expeditionary force mounted, Elizabeth began to consider the cheaper option of making peace. In December 1587, Leicester, heavily weighed down by personal debt, went home. Elizabeth had earlier ordered contacts be made with Parma regarding a ceasefire. Despite Dutch misgivings, in early 1587 English delegates were sent to Ostend to conduct negotiations. Nothing much was resolved, but the negotiations allowed the Spanish (then in full-bore preparation for the Armada expedition) to obscure their real intentions. However, it did give the English negotiators in the Netherlands the opportunity to observe some of Parma's build-up for the coming invasion of England.

We have seen that in May 1585, Philip ordered the seizure of northern European ships in Iberian ports. As it turned out, the actual intention had been to target Dutch vessels – all other ships were subsequently released. Elizabeth's reaction at the time had been one of fury. In addition to her decision to dispatch troops to the Netherlands, she had decided that it was

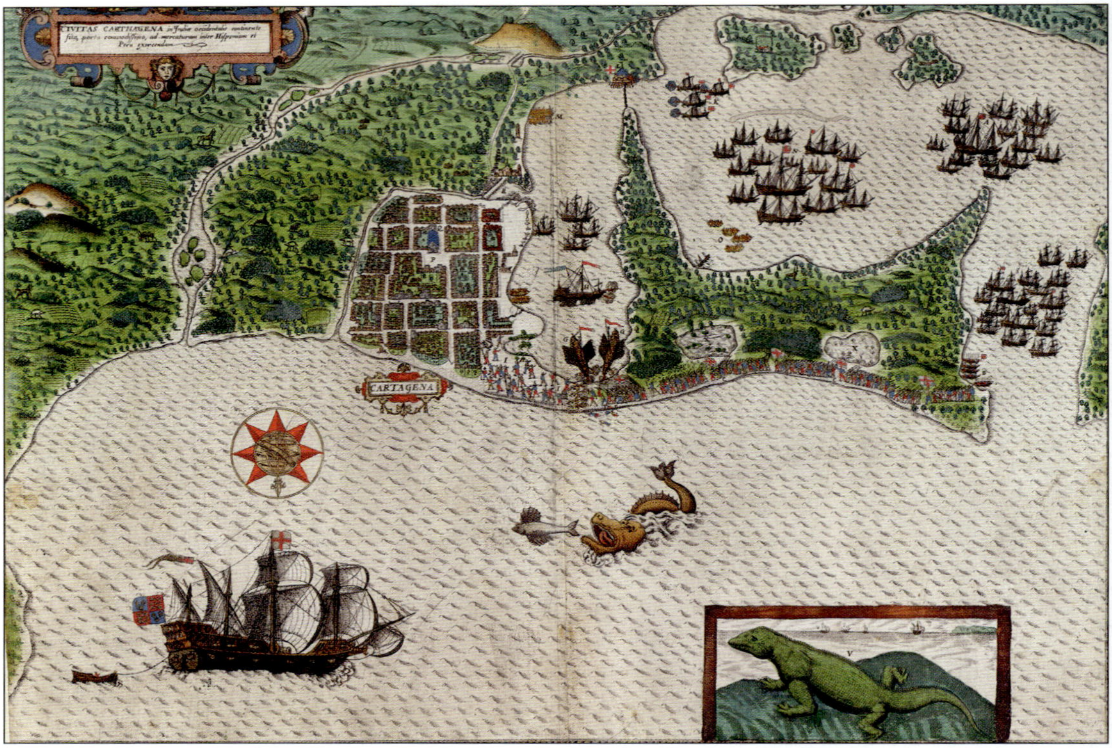

Above: a depiction of Drake's takeover of the rich and important port of Cartagena de Indias (in present-day Colombia) in February 1586.

time to intensify attacks on the Spanish shipping. Letters of marque were issued to any who had suffered from the sequestrations, which empowered them to seize any ships sailing under the Spanish flag, an initiative that gave impetus for English financiers to invest in a new fleet of armed merchant ships (thus adding to overall English naval strength). The Queen ordered a flotilla of ships to head immediately to the Newfoundland fishing grounds and attack the Spanish fishing fleet there. Fortuitously for her cause, at this time Sir Francis Drake had already been engaged in the assembly of a large fleet (privately funded, half-financed by the Queen) for a new voyage of plunder. As the news came of the fall of Antwerp, Elizabeth ordered Drake to sail out. Drake was ordered to make a display of English power in Spanish waters and obtain the release of the confiscated English ships and crews. In reality her intent was to inflict as much damage as possible on Spain and its possessions and to secure booty to help contribute towards the enormous cost of the English army in the Netherlands. Drake left Plymouth in September 1585 with 25 ships with around 2,300 soldiers and sailors. Arriving off the north-western coast of Spain, the expedition settled into a leisurely looting of Baiona and Vigo (in Galicia), interspersed with desecration of churches. Next, having been re-victualled, the fleet sailed south towards the Canary Islands. Failing to encounter the Spanish treasure fleet there, the expedition continued south and attacked the Cape Verde islands. Drake then sailed west, where despite an outbreak of fever amongst his men, the fleet proceeded to raid across the Spanish Caribbean. In February 1586, following the usual burning and looting of Spanish colonies, the raiders arrived at the rich and important port of Cartagena de Indias (in present-day

Colombia). Drake captured it with ease and then set up in the city. His fleet needed some succour, as the expedition had been depleted by disease. Two months later, after negotiating a substantial ransom from the local notables, it was time for Drake's flotilla to leave. It sailed onwards to strike at Spanish Florida and then continued northwards to arrive in April 1586 at the English colony at Roanoke (an island off present-day North Carolina). The colony had been established the summer before under a charter granted by Elizabeth to Sir Walter Raleigh: the objective had been the English colonization of North America, as well as to secure a base from where English privateers could venture out to raid Spanish treasure. The colony had not been a success and, short of supplies, most of the Roanoke settlers sailed away with Drake. Drake headed for England and arrived back in Plymouth in July 1586. Unlike Drake's previous circumnavigation expedition, there was little booty and the investors incurred a loss of around a quarter of their investment. Nevertheless, Drake's incursions along the coasts of the Old and New World were a visible manifestation of England's new maritime reach and power – and clearly demonstrated to Philip how it posed a mortal threat to his domains.

Execution of Mary Queen of Scots

To Spanish eyes, the detention of the Catholic Mary, Queen of Scots, had been yet another offence against the true faith, committed by the heretical Elizabeth. As the 1570s rolled into the 1580s the Scottish Queen had been kept in strict seclusion in England, at inland locations, away from the sea, secure from any rescue expedition. Her very existence was a permanent threat to Elizabeth's inheritance of the Crown and her movements and messages had been closely observed by many spying eyes. Sir Francis Walsingham, Elizabeth's efficient spymaster, had full grasp of the plots that bubbled around Tudor England. He became aware, in the summer of 1586, of a conspiracy, led by one Anthony Babington, to murder Elizabeth and her senior courtiers. As usual, the plotters were rounded up and executed, enduring the usual barbarous death. However, as the plot had been running its course, Walsingham had set up what would be called in today's terms a 'sting' operation. He had arranged a way for Mary's letters to be smuggled out from her place of detention at Chartley Manor, in Staffordshire – and these were then deciphered. In due course, papers were seized at Chartley, including some allegedly connected with the Babington conspiracy. In September 1586 Mary was moved to Fotheringay Castle, in Northamptonshire and put on trial for treason before a special commission. During this, she denied having written to Babington. The outcome was a forgone conclusion – Mary was duly sentenced to death. Elizabeth ascended the heights of indecision about killing a sister queen and hesitated to sanction the execution. As her courtiers urged her on, she eventually signed the death warrant and handed it to her secretary, William Davison, on its way to have it sealed by the Lord Chancellor. As Davison was leaving she called him back and asked him his opinion: would it be better to arrange for Mary to be assassinated rather than executed, as this would allow the death to be presented as due to natural causes, thus lessening any negative reaction in Scotland and France.

Above: an illustration of the execution of Mary Queen of Scots on the morning of 8 February 1587 at Fotheringay Castle.

To put this in context, assassination was a neat solution for many a crowned head in that era (and continues up to today): as we have seen, William of Orange was assassinated in 1584; Philip II had a troublesome courtier, Juan de Escobedo, assassinated in 1578. Elizabeth requested Davison discuss the possibility of assassination with Mary's gaoler as well as with Walsingham. Davison courageously replied that they would not assent to such killing. The execution warrant was duly brought to the Lord Chancellor who affixed the royal seal. The next day Davison received a letter from Elizabeth: it instructed him not to give the warrant to the Lord Chancellor. But it was too late; the order had filtered through the Crown administrative system and had been sent without delay to Fotheringay Castle, where Mary was in captivity. On the morning of 8 February 1587 Mary was beheaded. Arising from the confusion at the time of her signing the death warrant, Elizabeth tried to evade responsibility: claiming innocence and that she was not guilty for Mary's execution. She wrote to Mary's son, the Scottish King James VI, referring to the 'miserable accident which (far contrary to my meaning) hath befallen'. She need not have worried: James, a Protestant, had been estranged from his Catholic mother. Previously he had pleaded with Elizabeth to spare her life. However, in the event, he made few protests about her fate as he did not wish to prejudice his claim to the English succession – in a letter to Elizabeth after the execution he merely referred to it as an 'unhappy fact'. Davison, set up as the scapegoat, felt Elizabeth's wrath and was sent to the Tower, where he spent over a year. Preparations for the Enterprise of England were well underway when the news of Mary's execution reached Philip in Spain. It served to reinforce the wisdom of the decision he had taken to depose the heretic queen.

Chapter 2
The Decision to Invade

The decision to develop, plan and carry out an invasion of England was not inevitable. The whole concept arose due to a multitude of reasons, mixed in with an amount of muddled judgement. Philip II has been known as the prudent king. Ruling over a vast, and far-flung empire, this diligent, austere and introverted monarch had assiduously avoided war, if at all possible. His large domain incorporated distant lands, with long borders. There was a multiplicity of neighbours, many hostile, and thus he was vulnerable on many fronts. His empire was immensely rich and he endeavoured to extract revenue from all over, but the tax harvest was uneven, resulting in a disproportionate burden on Castile, the heartland of his domains. The costs of running this gigantic realm were equally as vast as its geographic spread. What Philip needed was a long period of peace to allow him to rearrange the finances of his exchequer. In the event, the various wars that erupted throughout his reign meant that he was never able to achieve this.

Elizabeth, testing Spanish tolerance

Elizabeth I, after coming to the throne, had no desire to bring her small and indebted England to war with anyone. However, many will look back at the continuing series of English provocations over the years, and wonder whatever had this intelligent and well-educated woman been thinking of? How did she indulge in a form of 'magical thinking', that she could keep prodding the Spanish lion, and not expect retribution? Like Philip, Elizabeth was also cautious, and was a past master of putting at difficult decisions. At the beginning of her reign relations with Spain were cordial. After her coronation in 1559, aged 25, she had received an offer of marriage from none other than Philip. He was her brother-in-law, at the time favourably disposed towards England, as well as being its ex-King. He was Europe's most eligible royal bachelor, heir to a vast kingdom and, despite being twice a widower, not too worn-out at 31. This was no hot-blooded pursuit of a fair maiden: a markedly unenthusiastic Philip was prepared to 'sacrifice my private inclination' and marry her, seeing it as in the interest of maintaining Catholicism in England. Elizabeth kept her cool and declined the offer.

Elizabeth was firm in her Protestant beliefs, but initially refrained from coercing her Catholic subjects, who made up around half of the population. However, she had to keep her Protestant ruling elite appeased, many of who were zealous in the establishment and dissemination of their faith. In time plots and uprisings by English Catholics led to increasing repression. The plethora of plots against her in the 1570s and 1580s were clearly aimed at her demise; understandably she found this hugely disturbing and inflammatory – it hardened her attitude to Catholicism and Spain. The Pope excommunicated her, and the conflict was painted in England as a battle of Protestantism and liberty versus Popery and repressive Catholicism. Always afraid of the danger of hegemony in Europe by either France or Spain, by 1585, Elizabeth felt particularly threatened by the presence of Parma's large and effective army in the Low Countries, a short and direct sea voyage, just over the horizon. She harboured resentment at the unilaterally-declared Luso-Castilian monopoly of the burgeoning and lucrative trade of the Americas. Then there was cupidity. The English Queen, always broke, had become addicted to the easy riches that arose from her unleashing of English privateers on the Spanish treasure fleets – a policy that brought together the great benefits of patriotism, plunder and Protestantism.

The 'Enterprise of England' begins to take shape

The expression 'The Enterprise of England' is thought to have been first coined in 1569 by Don Guerau de Espés, Spanish Ambassador to England, who occupied the office at a time of worsening relations between the two countries. De Espés turned to disaffected Catholics who were conspiring against the Queen. He was expelled two years later, after discovery of the Ridolfi plot. This concept was in essence the plan to overthrow Elizabeth and replace her with Mary Queen of Scots. The concept was bruited that Don John of Austria (Philip's half-brother) would then marry her. After his arrival to the Spanish Netherlands in November 1576, Don John considered the possibility that Spanish troops would depart from there to invade England – but death claimed him in October 1578.

As English piracy grew and Elizabeth's support for Dutch rebels became more flagrant, Philip periodically reviewed the possibility of taking firm action against England. Nevertheless, being perennially cautious, the King refrained from doing anything decisive on that front. However, the great Spanish victories in the Azores in 1582 raised Spanish confidence and morale. As we have seen, in July of that year, Don Álvaro de Bazán, Marquis of Santa Cruz, in the great naval battle off São Miguel, had conclusively smashed a French fleet of privateers (who were supporting the pretender to the Portuguese throne, Dom António). A year later, an amphibious operation, where the *tercios* successfully landed and took the island of Terceira demonstrated the capabilities of the Spanish army. This provided a template for a possible landing in England.

Right: a bronze statue of Admiral Álvaro de Bazán, Marquis of Santa Cruz, at the Plaza de la Villa, Madrid. Fittingly, he is standing on the banners of defeated enemies. In August 1583, just after his great victory at Terceira, he wrote to Philip urging him to begin preparations for an invasion of England.

On 9 August 1583, just after his great victory at Terceira, the Marquis of Santa Cruz, flushed with his success, wrote to Philip, advising that 'victories so absolute as the one God has been pleased to grant Your Majesty in these islands usually rouse princes to other enterprises … [Your Majesty] should follow this victory by making the necessary preparations for [the invasion of] England next year … It is not right that while Your Majesty is in this world a heretical woman who has done so much harm to [your] kingdom should live and reign'.

Again the King maintained his steady caution and did not directly pursue the idea, making a note on the margin of Santa Cruz's letter: 'the time has not come to discuss this'. However, in his reply to the Marquis he did say that he had requested the provision of biscuit from Italy and instructed the acceleration of galleon construction in Vizcaya. In addition he wrote to his nephew, the Prince of Parma to get his views on an invasion of England. Parma, in reply, was generally in favour of an attack by the Army of Flanders across the Channel, but fearful of French assistance to the rebels, he asked to be first allowed complete the reconquest of the

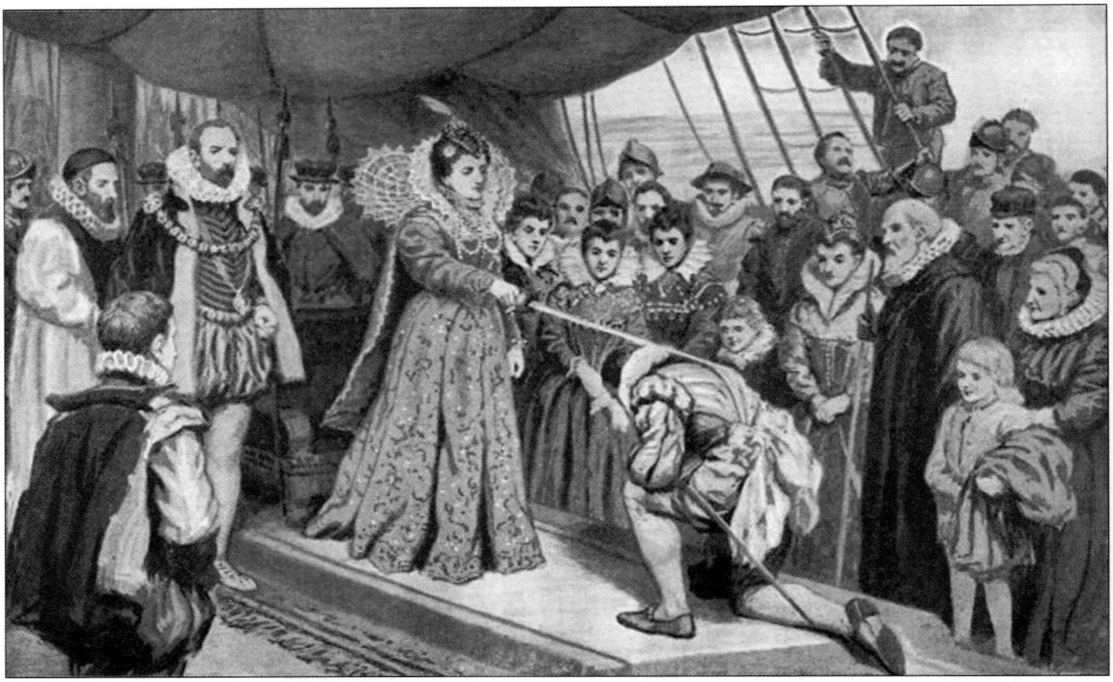

Above: an illustration of Francis Drake being knighted by Queen Elizabeth after his circumnavigation voyage. This depiction of the Queen and Drake is a patriotic fiction which dates from Victorian times. In reality, to dissimulate, she arranged for the French Ambassador to do the dubbing during the ceremony at Greenwich.

Netherlands. Rumours of a possible strike against England buzzed around Europe, and Philip was pestered with a variety of proposals, but still he held firm. It must be remembered that England was only one of the problems that faced Philip. He had to keep a wary eye on the other large power in Europe, his neighbour France, which as we have seen, was riven by conflict between Catholics and Huguenots. Philip had achieved a great success in 1580 when he annexed Portugal – but the pretender, Dom António had not gone away. He was still asserting his claim from his sanctuary in England, while continually endeavouring to assemble an expedition which would sail to Portugal and win him the throne.

An early and continuous provocation to Philip were the repeated attacks on Spanish shipping. Elizabethan society harboured a strong adventurer-ethic, where an individual could make money and rise in status by sometimes doubtful methods. A notable example of this was where English privateers, sponsored by the state, swooped on Spanish settlements in the Spanish Main and on the treasure fleets. Initially Elizabeth was able to maintain a certain level of deniability. However, Crown involvement and approval became more blatant. After Francis Drake's voyage of circumnavigation and his triumphant arrival back in September 1580, laden with Spanish booty, the Spanish Ambassador, Bernardino de Mendoza, in an audience with Elizabeth, requested that he be punished. Instead she arranged that the French Ambassador knighted Drake at Greenwich. As we have seen, attracted by the riches she was reaping, Elizabeth continued to encourage privateering. The harrying of the treasure from the Indies, and the resulting constriction of one of Philip's most important financial arteries plainly could not be allowed to continue.

Above: Pope Sixtus V, as painted by Filippo Bellini. Elected in April 1585, this energetic man wanted to defeat enemies of the faith and advocated an expedition against Queen Elizabeth.

As the army commander, Don Diego de Mendoza y Pimentel, told his Dutch captors in 1588 (after his Armada ship, the *San Mateo*, had been captured in the aftermath of the Gravelines battle, after drifting close to shore), it was better to capture or suppress England rather than that the king should 'continually keep such an army for to keep free the passage of the Indies … that it was not convenient, that one Drake, with two or three rotten ships, should come always and at his pleasure, to spoil the havens of Spain … and so to hinder the business of the Indies'. Thus, rather than establish a huge and costly defensive fleet that would have to be on permanent station, cruising all over the Spanish Main on the look-out for English privateers, it made sense to root the disease out at its English core, where it was harboured, victualled, planned and controlled.

The Pope: enthusiastic champion of the faith

In April 1585, a new energetic pope, Sixtus V, was elected. However, the relationship that emerged between himself and Philip, the most powerful king of the Catholic world, was a mistrustful one. Philip, who had powers to select bishops in his realms, had always had a difficult relationship with the papacy. He came from a line of pious kings; his father had been Holy Roman Emperor. Philip had belief in his own close connection with God, and felt that he could interpret the Deity's interests better than any prelate.

Four years before, after a spat with the Papacy, he had said: 'I am the only ruler who truly respects the Holy See, and yet instead of showing gratitude to me as they should, the popes take advantage of it to try to arrogate the authority that is so necessary … to the service of God'. Sixtus, in turn, was wary of the dangers of Spanish hegemony and distrusted Philip and was also exasperated by his slowness to act. Paradoxically, he also harboured a strange fascination with Queen Elizabeth. He said to the Venetian ambassador: 'Were she only Catholic, she would be without her match, and we would esteem her highly', adding: '… look how well she governs; she is only a woman, only mistress of half an island, and yet she makes herself feared by Spain, by France, by the Empire, by all'.

From the very beginning of his papacy, Sixtus passionately advocated that there would be a 'spectacular' – a significant expedition against an enemy of the faith. There was the ongoing Ottoman threat in the Mediterranean the Pope sent a proposal to Philip that he invade Algeria. There were other candidates: the heretical concentrations across northern Europe, such as the Calvinists of Geneva or the Huguenots in France. Notwithstanding Sixtus' appreciation of Elizabeth's qualities, there was also the possibility of an invasion of Protestant England. The multiplicity of targets caused some puzzlement to Philip, and he was annoyed that, what to him was the most pressing threat, was not included: the rebellion in the Spanish Netherlands. He angrily noted on a letter from his ambassador: 'Doesn't the [recapture of] Flanders seem outstanding to them? And they don't even consider how much it costs. There is little foundation to the English idea; one should keep away from such distant things.' Philip asked for a contribution from the Pope to help ensure quicker success in the Low Countries.

In August 1585, the Pope, a tenacious man, returned to the idea of a campaign against England and again called on an unenthusiastic Philip to act. Nonetheless, word arrived in September of the previous month's Treaty of Nonsuch where Elizabeth agreed to openly provide troops and finance for the Dutch Protestant rebels. This was a step too far – of all of Philip's possessions, for him, the Low Countries were the jewel in the crown. Suppression of the Dutch rebellion was vitally important to him – and the revolt continued to be a colossal drain on his perennially challenged exchequer. The provocations continued – in October the news arrived of Drake's brutal attack on northern Spain and occupation of Vigo and Baiona. Philip's father, Charles, had advised him in his youth: 'Avoid being angry and never do anything in anger'. However, in the face of the many aggravations this systematic and considered king could forbear no longer. He had no alternative but to set in place plans for the Enterprise of England. At the end of October Philip wrote to the Pope, declaring that he was now in agreement with his proposal for an invasion of England. The King also requested a contribution as the Pope had earlier intimated that he would provide financial backing. Philip pointed out that he was over-extended in the Netherlands, and with the proposed invasion estimated as costing over three million ducats, he could only cover one third to a half of the cost. (In reality, as it transpired, the Enterprise of England went the way of all grand projects and the actual cost turned out to more than the original estimate).

Right: Sir Francis Drake, with his hand on a globe, poses in his finery. This is in oil on panel as depicted by an unknown artist c.1581. In September 1585 Drake set out from Plymouth to raid the Caribbean. On the way, Drake stopped off to occupy and pillage Vigo and Baiona in Galicia. As news arrived of this direct attack on Spanish soil, it was one more thing which helped propel Philip II to put in place concrete preparations for the invasion of England.

Planning begins

Philip now initiated the meticulous planning for his great enterprise. First, he needed to identify and appreciate the big picture. He duly entrusted his trusted advisor on foreign affairs, the experienced Don Juan de Zúñiga, to review the global dangers to his realm and prioritise future strategy. In his painstaking manner, de Zúñiga accordingly listed the threats from traditional foes, demonstrating how many of these had lessened. Across the Mediterranean, the Ottomans were distracted by conflict with the Persians. Felicitously for Spain, its traditional rival on the northern border, France, had been neutralised by recurring internal sectarian strife. The threat of French heresy reigning supreme had become imminent after Francois, Duke of Anjou (seen in Chapter 1 accepting sovereignty from the Dutch rebels in the early 1580s) died in June 1584 and the Huguenot Henry of Navarre became heir to the throne. In December 1584 Philip intervened and signed a secret treaty with the Duke of Guise. A monthly subvention of 50,000 escudos was promised, with Guise pledging to deny Navarre's ascension to the throne and that the Duke's Catholic Holy League would work for the elimination of Protestantism in France. This treaty had the added benefit of putting an end to the direct risk of Huguenot support for the Dutch rebels.

By contrast, de Zúñiga noted that the menace from England was growing. Elizabeth was now actively inflaming what was for Philip a festering sore, the Dutch revolt – and of course English privateers (with Drake to the fore) were rampaging across the high seas of the Hispanic world. It was obvious that this English menace was a large threat to the fundamentals of Philip's monarchy. De Zúñiga concluded that a purely defensive war to repel the English threat would incur permanent expense across his domains, from Spain to the Indies; better (and more cost-effective) to mount an amphibious operation of devastating strength, to the heart of the problem.

As the weeks rolled on, reports of Drake's continuing rampage streamed back: passing by the Canaries, the English adventurer had sailed south to raid the Cape Verde islands in November – and he was now heading for the Caribbean. The news, which arrived on 24 November, that English troops had actually set foot in the Spanish Netherlands proved to be the final straw. It was time to move from theory to concrete plans. On 29 December 1585 Philip asked his nephew Alexander Farnese, the Prince of Parma (then enjoying success in his Netherlands campaign) to devise a strategy for the Enterprise of England. The Marquis of Santa Cruz, enthusiastic for an invasion, was asked at the end of January to prepare a plan. Santa Cruz did not tarry – he reported back on 22 March 1586 with a detailed scheme, entitled, with characteristic precision: 'The fleet and army that it would seem necessary to assemble for the conquest of England'. Like any sensible planner or project manager, he asked for more than he could expect to receive. Accordingly, he did not stint on resources – his plan was to mount an expedition of overwhelming strength. In many ways, it was going to be a rerun of the successful Terceira campaign – albeit on a much grander scale. He proposed an invasion fleet of 510 ships, made up of galleons, transports, and smaller auxiliary craft. There would be around 17,000 seamen. The fleet would transport around 57,000 soldiers, including cavalry. The artillery would include a siege train comprised of four batteries. He estimated that the expedition, which he had itemised to the minutest extent, would cost nearly four million ducats. This proposal raised obvious difficulties for Philip: the projected cost was large, and to assemble this number of ships would strain Spanish resources – many would have to be sourced from afar.

A huge cost perhaps, but for this cautious king, his tolerance of English excesses was at an end – he unequivocally had decided to undertake an invasion. Philip held meetings with his advisors but there are no written records of the strategy that they were considering, such as whether there was going to be a direct landing in England, or an indirect attack, with an initial landing on the south coast of Ireland. It was not surprising that Ireland featured in these plans. The country, despite its relatively small size, has through the millennia possessed a huge strategic importance, because of its location at the western end of the Atlantic, and particularly relevant in this case, it offered a means to strike at the soft underbelly of England. For the Spanish a landing in Ireland (with a large force, considerably greater than that employed in the debacle at Smerwick) would provide an ideal staging post for an attack on western England. The country was not unknown: there had been connections between Spain and Ireland in trade and fishing for centuries. Most of the population, Catholic, was judged to be friendly. The King was continuously being urged by the many Irish Catholic émigrés, present in Spain and the Continent, to liberate their country from the English Protestant yoke.

The die was now cast – there would be a major operation against Elizabethan England, even though the precise detail was still to be established. Philip decided to lay the groundwork and on 2 April 1586 issued instructions to three of his most dependable men: the Marquis of Santa Cruz was to go to Lisbon and begin assembling a fleet; the Duke of Medina Sidonia, experienced in assembling the treasure fleets for their annual voyage to the Indies, was to levy troops and gather supply vessels in Andalucia and the highly experienced Don Juan Martínez de Recalde (last seen in charge of the flotilla that had deposited Papal soldiers at Smerwick), was to form a new squadron in the north (a task given a head start by the embargoing of ships in Cantabrian ports).

In the middle of all these considerations, reports continued to filter back of Drake's ongoing depredations in the Caribbean. After sacking Santo Domingo, he had now taken over Cartagena de Indias. Indeed, the news had grown legs on its way back over the Atlantic – one account claimed that Drake's expedition consisted of 20,000 men. Philip's response was immediate: Santa Cruz was to join with the transatlantic escort galleons, sail for the Caribbean, there to find and eliminate Drake and his pestilential flotilla. Santa Cruz demurred, saying he needed more ships. In the event, Philip sent the escort ships across the Atlantic, while the Marquis dispatched six galleons to the Azores, to await the treasure fleets returning from the Indies .

Parma's proposal

Options for the invasion continued to be discussed in the Escorial. After some time, the Prince of Parma dispatched his proposal on 20 April 1586. The delay was compounded by the unusually long time it took for the document to reach Spain – Philip only received the plan in the second half of June. Notwithstanding the time Parma had taken in preparing it, the proposal was brief and to the point – it amounted to a memorandum of a mere 28 pages. The plan was of a different hue to that of Santa Cruz: the invasion of England was to be swift and simple – and Parma's army was to have the starring role. He proposed to send 30,000 soldiers, with 500 cavalry across the Channel in flat-bottomed barges. The journey would take eight to twelve hours. October was the best time. He added that it was

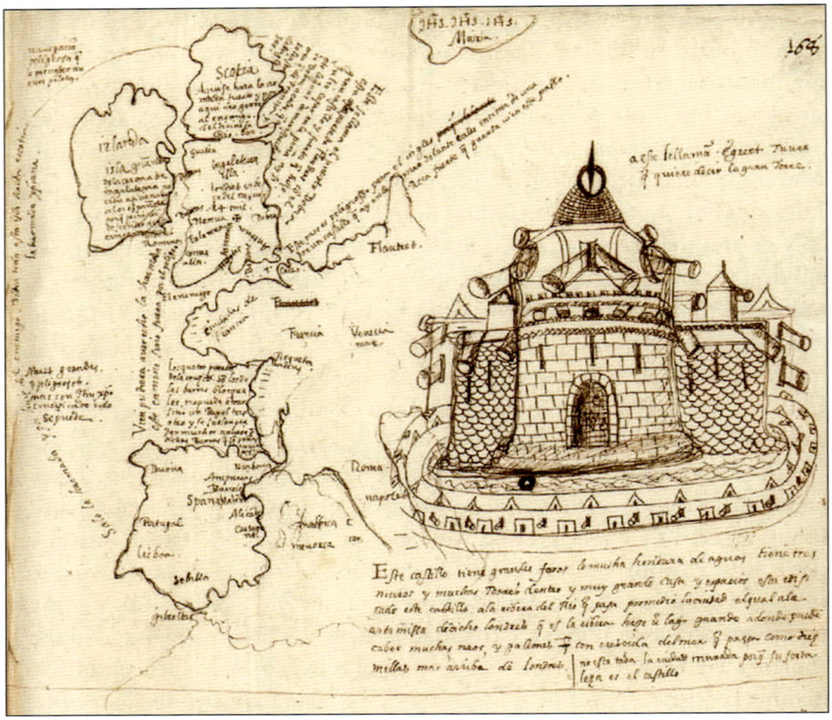

Left: a sketch map prepared in June 1586, by Bernardino de Escalante, one of Philip's advisors. De Escalante had reviewed both Santa Cruz and Parma's proposals for the invasion. Here he shows possibilities for the conquest of England: an invasion of Ireland (or Wales), while, with Elizabeth's forces being diverted by this, the Army of Flanders would cross the Channel, destination London.

essential that there be no interference from the French and enough troops were to be left behind to contain the Dutch rebels. Sensibly, he stated that the Spanish should depend on their own resources and not place any reliance on help from allies, particularly from English Catholics. Ever a general of land forces, Parma relegated the navy to a minor role. Naval protection was needed if secrecy was breached and the English knew of the invasion – and in that case, the Spanish ships would be on station to keep the seaway from Flanders open, or to act in diverting Elizabeth's navy away from the invasion fleet. A possible landing area, he suggested, was on the coast between Dover and Margate – its closeness would help towards the rapid capture of London. He put the cost at 300,000 escudos a month. Lamenting that invasion plans were currently being openly discussed by ordinary people in Flanders, he said that the success of his invasion would depend on it remaining a secret. Philip's initial reaction to this requirement for complete privacy during the assembly of an enormous invasion army was understandably sceptical – he scribbled on the document 'hardly possible!'. Interestingly, Philip's advisor Juan de Zúñiga, who, in his recent strategic review had advocated the invasion and then the overthrow of Elizabeth and her regime, now turned out not to be in favour of annexing England, because 'of the cost of defending it' – better to set a friendly Catholic ruler on the throne.

The King and his advisors (with Juan de Zúñiga and Bernardino de Escalante, strategist and expert in navigation, to the fore) continued with their analyses. As is the way of committees, the plans were multi-stranded and waxed and waned in complexity. They included the permutations of diversionary invasions of, variously, Scotland, Wales and Ireland. The planning was facilitated by the knowledge of England that Philip had acquired during his time as husband of Mary Tudor. Over the period 1554-57 he had gotten to know London and the royal court and was acquainted with some principal ports – he had sailed to Southampton, and departed twice from Dover.

A strategy emerges

Over the following weeks the strategy took more shape and on 26 July 1586 a master plan (thought to have been mainly based on a paper by Bernardino de Escalante) was sent to Parma and Santa Cruz, Curiously, there were no requests to these two military leaders, the main protagonists, to comment on this – their orders now were to simply execute it. There were to be two onslaughts on Elizabeth's realm. A large fleet, laden with troops and an artillery siege train, would sail from Lisbon to Ireland (most likely the port of Waterford). It would land there and establish a beachhead. This, it was hoped, would entice the English Navy to a fight in Irish waters, well away from Parma's preparations. Two months later, the Armada would depart from Ireland, destination the English Channel. While the main Armada fleet gained control of the Strait of Dover and the Thames estuary, Parma would proceed with his invasion barges and land 30,000 seasoned troops at Margate. The troops and artillery siege train transported in the Armada would land and join Parma as he prepared to march on London, the centre of English power – there, with luck, he would capture the Virgin Queen and her ministers. The scattered and poorly trained English militias were not foreseen as posing any threat to the battle-hardened Army of Flanders. The invasion would be launched in a year's time, envisaged around August or September 1587.

This was a provisional plan – much detail remained to be finalised. Philip and his advisors began to flesh it out. Unsurprisingly, the most difficult element was the raising of the necessary finance. Luckily, over recent years, the flow of bullion from the Indies had increased. However, much more was needed. Philip sent out orders across his domains to raise more taxes and he had to dig deeper into his coffers. State bonds and land were sold to the nobility which generated immediate funds, but of course this resulted in the forgoing of future income. There were cut backs in expenditure on most other things. Within the Portuguese empire that Philip had inherited, the plan for construction of a fortress at Mombasa was deferred, as was a proposed expedition against the expansionist Sultan of Aceh in Sumatra.

Detailed preparations begin

Santa Cruz was in Lisbon, beginning the momentous task of assembling ships for an Armada fleet, what Philip had described as 'the navy for the protection of my realm, and for the destruction and punishment of the pirates who menace my coast'. Everything was needed for the enterprise: ships, guns, powder, cannon balls and a whole range of military and naval supplies. As well as seamen to man the ships, regiments of soldiers had to be assembled. Training was necessary in every area, from artillery to navigation. A miracle of logistics was required. Philip's empire was enormous and

Philip II did not lack for learned and experienced advisers. Below: a treatise, dating from 1577, one of many written by Bernardino de Escalante, in this instance on the Portuguese voyages to the Orient. Escalante had been a cleric and a mariner. He had knowledge of English waters, having accompanied Philip on his voyage to England in 1554, to marry Mary Tudor.

DISCVRSO
ELA NAVEGACION QVE
Portuguefes hazen à los Reinos y Pro-
ıcias del Oriente, y de la noticia q̃ fe tiene
delas grandezas del Reino dela China.
VTOR BERNARDINO DE
fcalante Clerigo, Comiffario del Santo oficio
en la Inquificion del Reino de Galizia, y
Beneficiado en la villa de Laredo.
IRIGIDO AL ILVSTRISSIMO
feñor Don Chriftoual de Rojas y Sandoual
Arçobifpo de Seuilla.
Con Licencia.

Left: the busy quays of Lisbon. As preparations got underway for the Armada, supplies arrived from all over Spain and the Mediterranean.

the bureaucratic sinews needed to administer such dispersed territories had developed over time. Instructions were sent from Madrid to all parts of Philip's empire. His officials, whether Spanish, Portuguese, Italian or Dutch, set the massive administrative machine into motion.

It is worthwhile looking at how this operated at micro level. In Seville, a military veteran, one Miguel de Cervantes, (later to pen the classic novel, *Don Quixote*), was engaged as one of the commissioners of supplies in Andalucia – a territory that was (and is) a rich source of wheat, olive oil and wine. He travelled up and down the dusty roads of the region seeking out the necessary commodities. He had to overcome the widespread reluctance of the rural communities (occasionally issuing fines and seizing goods). Such was his zeal in seizing supplies from clerical sources that he was excommunicated twice (then a common hazard when dealing with clerical authorities). Cervantes had to adjudicate costs and arrange for payment, and finally arrange for the storage and dispatch of the supplies to Lisbon. Cervantes' labours were duplicated by numerous others across the Iberian Peninsula. And so the oxcarts rolled their dusty way from the towns and cities of central Spain to Lisbon. Provisions from the more distant regions were transported by sea. The enormous quantities were duly noted and accounted for in great ledgers. The list of provisions on board amounted to 98 folio pages, in the fleet of around 90 assorted ships which arrived in Lisbon at the beginning of August 1587 (assembled at Cádiz by the Andalucian magnate, the Duke of Medina Sidonia, of whom much more later). The economy of the Iberian Peninsula was stretched to provide the vast amount of victuals needed to sustain the tens of thousands of men for this expedition which would last many months. Bushels of biscuits were provided from the ovens of Burgos and rice came from Valencia and the Levante. Galicia

Above: a sixteenth century view of a brewery – filling barrels with beer. In the English navy sailors were provided with beer; in the Armada, the men received wine. In that era, the technology of storing foodstuffs and liquids in barrels was still at an imperfect stage. Mariners on long voyages frequently found that the produce in barrels had turned putrid.

provided produce from the sea – salted fish, sardines and anchovies. Salted meat arrived from the central regions of Spain. Such was the quantity of food required, that the call had to go out across Europe. As the months passed, large quantities of cheese were shipped from the Baltic and rice from Milan. A vital part of a soldier's diet, chick-peas and beans, were sourced in Sicily. And then there were the containers needed to safely store the victuals. Smoke rose in the air as the potteries of Lisbon and Seville laboured to produce the huge amounts of clay vessels to store food. Equally importantly, the coopers of Iberia sprang into action to make the wooden barrels that were essential to transport the water, wine and such as salted meat, fish and other provisions for the voyage. The Armada's needs encompassed much more than food and sustenance: a mountain of equipment had to be sourced, from weapons to shoes, clothes, armour and tents.

As Cádiz, the northern ports and Lisbon hummed with activity, the resources of the Mediterranean were also expected to provide for the Armada. Instructions were dispatched to the Viceroys in Sicily and Naples to send ships, troops and artillery. All over the Mediterranean merchant vessels were embargoed – they came from the principal ports: Venice, Genoa, Naples, Sicily and the Dalmatian republic of Ragusa. Slowly at first, ships began to arrive in the harbour at Lisbon, adding to the fleet of powerful Atlantic galleons, formerly the Portuguese navy, already there.

The Pope reluctantly supports the Armada

As 1587 dawned, Philip had no reason to doubt that the invasion of England was necessary. The severe threat that was the Dutch Protestant revolt, now directly supported by English troops, persisted. There was Elizabeth's harbouring of Dom António, still pressing his claim to the Portuguese throne. English privateers continued to prey on Spanish ships, with the added indignity that some of this booty was being used to defray Elizabeth's expenditure in support of the Dutch rebels. And then, on 8 February 1587, Mary Queen of Scots was executed. A principal cause for her execution was her claim to the English throne which posed a serious threat to Elizabeth's legitimacy. Her presence had also been a continuous inducement to English Catholics to rise up and depose the Protestant Queen. The previous May, Mary had sent a letter to the Spanish ambassador in Paris, Bernardino de Mendoza, stating that she intended to disinherit her son, James VI of Scotland, if he did not return to Catholicism, and that she would make a will which would bequeath to Philip her rights to the English throne (in the event, no such will was found after her execution). This could be seen as a further incentive for Philip to conquer England, but in any case he had another claim to the throne due to his descent from John of Gaunt (an English royal prince of the fourteenth century, ancestor of English kings). In the event, the execution of Mary, and the consequent outrage across Catholic Europe, gave further impetus to the Enterprise of England, but it also removed an underlying danger for Philip, that Mary, perceived as pro-French, could have ascended the English throne.

It is worth pausing here to consider Philip's overall intentions with regard to England. Many hold the mistaken perception that he wanted to annex the country and add it to his empire. In reality it would have been impossible for Philip, a monarch with domains spanning the globe, to personally rule there. There was also the peril that such an occupation could result in a revolt by English Protestants, adding another headache for him like the ongoing rebellion in the Netherlands. Ultimately Philip's strategic interest was to neutralise England, to stop its annoyances and interventions in Spanish affairs – and of course he fervently believed in the re-Catholicisation of England, an aspiration which also garnered useful support from the Pope. An Armada that fomented an English Catholic insurrection would be useful in helping to depose Elizabeth. With her demise, a Catholic ruler accommodating to Spanish interests could be installed. Over the previous decade many possibilities had been discussed by Philip and his advisors as to who might be a suitable candidate for the English throne: Mary Queen of Scots had been the primary contender — in one scenario, she would have been married off to the King's brother, Don John of Austria.

The Enterprise of England was taking its final shape, and now with the news of Mary's execution, it was necessary to consider afresh who would rule England after the hoped-for conquest. Just after the execution he sent a dispatch to his ambassador to the papal court, Enrique de Guzmán, the Count of Olivares. He was to 'cautiously approach' the Pope and brief him regarding Philip's claim to the English crown that: 'my [right] … rests on my descent from the House of Lancaster and upon the will made by the Queen of Scotland …'. He should impress on the Pope that he did not intend to undertake a war in England which would result in placing upon that throne a young heretic like the King of Scotland (James VI, Mary's son). As noted, Philip could not conceivably have governed England personally and in any case he had to tone down this claim: if the French heard of the possibility of Spanish direct rule of England, utterly changing the strategic balance in Europe, they would have been spurred to intervene. In turn, the Pope was also wary of Spanish hegemony in Europe. Philip took an indirect route: he advanced the candidacy of his daughter Isabella for the English throne. In continuation, Philip told Olivares that the Pope must be assured: 'I have no intention of adding England to my own dominions but to settle the crown upon my daughter, the Infanta'. Negotiations with the Pope continued. Philip kept his eye on the succession issue: a draft prepared for submission by Olivares to the Pope in June noted that as Philip 'cannot go thither [to England] to reside, it is highly important, since the country is so over-run with heresy, that a Catholic King or Queen should be on the spot to lead it back to perfection again'. By mid-summer 1587, it was agreed that Philip would nominate a ruler who was pledged to reinstate and maintain Catholicism in England – all subject to ratification by the Pontiff. However, it was understood that Philip's daughter would be nominated, as Olivares noted that in the agreement 'the clause was so worded that your Majesty might appoint … the Infanta'. Until a suitable ruler could be nominated and crowned, they agreed that Parma, when he achieved victory in England, would hand over to an interim administration run by the English cleric William Allen (superior of the English College in Douai, made a cardinal by Sixtus in August 1587, and leader of English exiles against the 'heretic and usurper', Elizabeth).

Financial support for the Armada was an important part of the negotiations. The Ambassador had been pessimistic: 'when it comes to getting money out of [the Pope] it is like squeezing his life blood'. However the execution of Mary Queen of Scots propelled a reluctant Pope to make a more concrete manifestation of support for the Enterprise of England. In July 1587, he signed a convention with Olivares that he would provide one million gold ducats towards an invasion – the funds were duly placed in an escrow account with Roman bankers. It was to be payment-by-results, half to be paid when a notary certified that troops had landed in England; the other half when the mission was complete. As well as the agreement to place a Catholic ruler on the throne, there were other terms and conditions: the invasion force had to sail before year's end and church property and rights would be duly restored in England.

Drake's attack on Cádiz

The English intelligence system, efficiently directed by Sir Francis Walsingham, Secretary of State, enjoyed the services of many secret informants across the Continent. Over the years there had been rumours about Spanish preparations for an invasion. Information flowed in great quantity from a variety of sources. There was the observational information, from such as captured Spanish mariners and merchants. Much of this was not particularly high-grade – what was lacking was direct information on what the decision makers, (the King and his senior advisors) were thinking. The diplomatic world had the potential to occasionally bear fruit – ambassadors in Madrid and other capitals spent their time gathering news and gossip which they relayed back home, an information channel that the English found easy to tap. The Papal court in Rome was a particularly leaky vessel. Pope Sixtus V, having offered to part-finance the Armada, was now (using modern parlance) a stakeholder and thus had to be kept up to date by Philip. In turn the Pope briefed his cardinals and inner circle. Intelligence gold for the English was struck in the Netherlands in December 1587 when a Dutch raiding party captured a junior officer of the Army of Flanders, who happened to be nephew of one of the cardinals. Through interrogation, they obtained details of the plans for the Armada – which they promptly relayed to the English.

It is one thing to gather intelligence. The next and more difficult task is to analyse it and sift out what was true or false. Such was the volume of contradictory noise and chatter flowing back that it resulted in confusion. Where were the hard facts within this mass of information? Rumours abounded on possible destinations for the Spanish: Ireland, Scotland, and the Isle of Wight, even Algiers or Larache in Morocco. In many cases these conflicting reports reflect the various permutations in strategy that was were being discussed by Philip and his advisors. The fundamental problem for the English was that there was no clear-cut information on where and when this great new fleet was going to strike. Gossip, sometimes verging on the fantastical, increased jitters in England, and there were many false sightings of invasion fleets. Nevertheless, in early 1587, solid news was arriving from merchants and spies: details of the ships, men and supplies being assembled in Lisbon. In February 1587, the Treasurer of the Navy, John Hawkins, proposed sending out six warships to the Iberian coast to ascertain what was happening and to mount a blockade.

Sir Francis Drake, with his characteristic vigour, had been arguing for months for a pre-emptive strike – it would buy time for England to build up her defences. After some indecision, Elizabeth agreed and a Royal Commission was signed on 25 March 1587. It directed Drake to 'impeach the purpose of the Spanish fleet and stop their meeting at Lisbon'. In the usual manner, to ensure that the expedition was self-financing and profitable, it gave him full rein to sail the oceans and seize prizes. (The English Ambassador in Paris, Sir Edward Stafford, who in return for money, had passed on secrets to Spain, reported on Drake's planned attack).

The expedition was intended to be a sharp blow, to demonstrate to Philip the strength of the English navy; to deter him from attacking England and all the better to force him to the negotiating table. The fleet that was being assembled was a mixture of state and private vessels. The core of Drake's fleet was made up of several of Elizabeth's royal galleons. There were 20 armed merchant ships, provided by individuals or syndicates. Booty was high on the agenda – anything captured was to be shared out by a mathematical formula which took note of tonnage and manpower involved. The crown had provided just four ships, but these were large in relation to the smaller private ships and this assured her of a good share, over 40 per cent. As the fleet was being gathered, the southern ports were temporarily closed, to ensure secrecy about Drake's expedition. As Drake finalised his preparations in Plymouth, he had to deal with the embarrassing problem of a shortage of sailors. When news of the destination had leaked out, there were desertions by crew members, men who would have been attracted by the prospect of treasure on the Spanish Main, but not by the dangers inherent in attacking a harbour such as Lisbon, with its shore batteries and armed galleons. The shortfall had to be quickly made up by soldiers co-opted as mariners. On 12 April the fleet set off from Plymouth, led by Drake in his flagship, the *Elizabeth Bonaventure,* just under 600 tons. Good progress was made and, three days later, the flotilla reached the coast of Galicia. However, a violent storm soon blew up off Finisterre – it raged for five days and the ships were widely dispersed.

Elizabeth had received false reports from Ambassador Stafford that Philip had changed his mind about the invasion. In addition peace overtures had been received from the Duke of Parma. With her customary indecision, she tried to have it both ways. She wrote orders for Drake: 'you shall forbear to enter forcibly into any of the said King's ports or havens'. However, the desire to solve the problems of her depleted exchequer, by seizing Spanish silver and gold still ruled: 'you should do your best endeavour… to get into your possession … such shipping of the said King's … as you shall find at sea'. The order was sent by a pinnace which sailed on 19 April, but this was blown back by contrary winds and it never reached Drake. Making his way south, Drake heard from some Dutch ships that a large fleet was gather-

Right: a section of a map showing Drake's attack on Cádiz in April 1587.

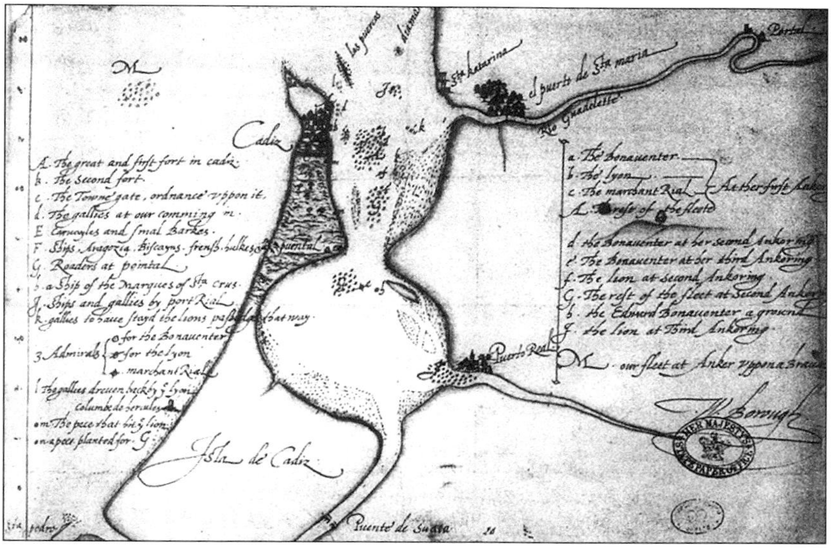

ing at Cádiz, in preparation to joining the main Armada fleet at Lisbon. This offered a better prospect to Drake – although it had forts and artillery, Cádiz, with its wide, more open, harbour was an easier target than the heavily fortified Lisbon, with its difficult narrow harbour approaches.

At around 6 p.m. on 29 April, flying no flags, Drake's fleet entered Cádiz harbour, taking the defenders by surprise. The harbour was packed with ships, around 60 in total, many of these merchant vessels. Eight galleys were in port (recently arrived from patrol near Gibraltar), and as soon as they realised the hostile intent of the newly-arrived ships, rowed out to attack. The leading galley was raked by English cannon fire, and as it withdrew, the others retreated. Shore batteries opened up, but with little result. The smaller merchant ships at anchorage fled to the shallower waters of the inner harbour, but the larger vessels were at the mercy of Drake's ships. Only one of the vessels, a heavily armed large Genoese *nao,* attempted to defend itself. After heavy exchanges the *nao* sank. The Duke of Medina Sidonia, (whose ducal seat was at nearby Sanlúcar de Barrameda) arrived with thousands of militiamen to conduct a defence. He fortified positions around the harbour. The presence of the militia ensured that the raid continued as a naval, not a land action. The English continued their marauding and ranged through the ranks of ships anchored in the harbour, which were mostly unmanned. On the third day the English withdrew at dawn, laden with plunder seized from the Spanish vessels, many now on fire or sunk. Drake claimed that 37 ships were sunk, burned or captured – the Spanish reported a loss of 24 ships. As the English withdrew, they were pursued by the galleys, firing with their guns.

The English flotilla sailed west, as Drake sought to intercept Juan Martínez de Recalde and his Vizcayan squadron which had been reported due in Cádiz. After around a week, Drake broke off the search and landed a force at Lagos, on the Algarve but this was repelled by large local forces that had assembled. Then it was a short sail to Sagres near Cape St Vincent where they seized the fortresses there. Next the flotilla cruised north along the Portuguese coast and anchored off Cascais, the strategic town to the north of the mouth of the Tagus Estuary and which dominated the approach to Lisbon harbour. Drake assessed the strong harbour defences and decided not to attack, and he returned south. As his ships cruised off the southern coast of Portugal he captured a multitude of small vessels, some carrying supplies for the Armada. Drake cheerfully reported that he had captured 'forts, barques, caravels and divers other vessels'. Amongst these was one with an essential cargo – barrel staves and hoops, destined for the Armada at Lisbon. Drake declared that these amounted to 1,700 tons, an unlikely figure. It has been claimed that this was one of the underlying reasons for the failure of the Armada in 1588 – it supposedly forced the use of unseasoned wood for barrels, which led to the spoiling of the fleet's food supplies. In fact, a convoy that was being prepared to send staves to Lisbon, was immediately cancelled, after news of Drake's attack on Cádiz. The distinguished naval historian Nicholas Rodger has noted that while there was a general shortage of casks there is no direct evidence in Spanish documents to indicate that this was caused by Drake's destruction. In any case, there was no money to be had in capturing barrel staves. The actions at Cádiz and the Algarve did not impede logistics or directly delay the preparations for the Enterprise of England, as the order to assemble ships for the Armada from the Indies fleet was only made on 8 May – and the ships from Sicily and Naples arrived at Cádiz in mid-June.

Drake had gleaned intelligence about a rich prize that was expected off the Azores. This was the Portuguese *nao*, the *São Filipe*, returning home from Goa in the east. Having wintered in Mozambique, the arrival of this ship was imminently expected, on a route sailing out from the African coast on the north-east trades. Drake set off in the direction of the Azores. It proved a sweet ending to his raiding enterprise when, on 18 June, with seven ships (most merchant ships had been dispersed in a storm and returned to England) he captured the *São Filipe*, laden as it was with an array of veritable treasure: from precious stones to gold, from spices to silk (valued at around €50 million in today's values – three times the value of all that had been seized at Cádiz). And so, with bulging holds, the victorious flotilla arrived back in Plymouth on 7 July 1587. The protracted raid had enriched Elizabeth, Drake and the syndicates. After Drake's return, in an effort to safeguard the impending peace negotiations with Parma, Elizabeth characteristically dissembled and claimed that, because of the revised orders that had been issued at the start, she had been 'unwitting, yea unwilling' to approve Drake's actions and was 'greatly offended with him'.

After Cádiz, Spanish preparations continue

The Cádiz raid had been wounding. A later book by the philosopher and aphorist Sir Francis Bacon, dubbed the event as 'the singeing of the King of Spain's beard'. However, the seeming success at Cádiz rebounded on the English: rather than causing Philip to have second thoughts, it solidified more than ever his determination to stamp out the English threat. After the raid, and as Drake disappeared over the Atlantic horizon, the Council of War unanimously counselled Philip to take action. Juan de Idiáquez,

Philip's Secretary of State and his most trusted advisor, noted the sovereign's response to Drake's raids: 'Defensive measures will no longer suffice. He [the King] must set fire to their house …'.

As we have seen, ships were gathered once again, destination Lisbon – but first the safety of the treasure fleet had to be assured. At the end of June, Santa Cruz was ordered to prepare a fleet and head for the Azores, eliminate English corsairs and escort the *flota* back from the Indies. In mid-July Santa Cruz left Lisbon with a substantial fleet: 37 ships in total, including 22 galleons, and carrying around 6,000 troops. One of the most impressive warships among Santa Cruz's Azores fleet was the large *San Francisco de Florencia*. It had originally been built for the Duke of Tuscany's navy, its only galleon. In 1585, the Grand Duke, intending that his duchy would be the new spice entrepot, replacing Antwerp after the fall of that city, had dispatched the ship to Lisbon to bring spices back to Florence. This ship, armed with splendid brass cannon to fend off corsairs from stealing the spices, had the misfortune to be spotted by the Marquis of Santa Cruz at the Lisbon quays. He admired the Tuscan ship, noting that it was better than anything he had. As the months passed, it so happened that many problems seemed to arise in effecting delivery of the spices. In November 1586 the captain realised what was happening and gave orders to sail, whereupon the *San Francisco* was prevented from leaving the harbour. For months afterwards the Tuscan ambassador tried in vain to get the ship released. In July 1587, it was pressed into service by Santa Cruz, when the call came to head for the Azores.

Santa Cruz's fleet reached the Azores on 19 August. Just a week later, the treasure fleet (carrying 12m ducats, a welcome addition to Philip's treasury) had arrived from the Caribbean. The combined fleet set off for home, but on the way encountered a fierce Atlantic storm. As they reached home waters and with the treasure fleet heading towards Sanlúcar de Barrameda and Seville, the escort fleet was able to return to Lisbon at the end of September.

Drake's adventures in Cádiz and the Azores had the indirect effect that Santa Cruz was forced to divert and spend nearly three months sailing the Atlantic. Only now was he able to get back to the main business. In addition to ordering repairs to his recently-returned and storm-damaged galleons, the Marquis had to address the shortages that were apparent in every field: military and naval supplies, as well as victuals (which had been seriously depleted by the voyage to the Azores). Constant irritations were the missives from Philip, who instructed that Santa Cruz immediately 'sail in God's name for the English Channel'. The King was understandably impatient, as he was spending a huge amount of money on the Armada, inactive in harbour (in addition to funding Parma's army that was being assembled in Flanders). Philip, whose health had deteriorated during this period, repeated his demands all through October and November that the Armada sail. Nonetheless, with the onset of winter and associated poor weather conditions and the short days, it became clear that the Armada could not sail until the following year. By that time, after persuasion by Parma, the strategy for the attack on England had been simplified, and the concept of a landing in Ireland or Scotland had been dropped. The plan was now that the Armada would sail directly for the English Channel, where the Marquis of Santa Cruz would secure his position off Margate and advise Parma of his arrival. Under escort by the Armada ships, Parma would land his troops in England, and be reinforced by the soldiers aboard the Armada. The delays had done nothing to improve Parma's mood. By now he had lost any enthusiasm he may have had for the whole enterprise. He had built up his forces and they had reached their peak of readiness by the autumn of 1587. He fretted at the continual delay: in his letters to Philip he pointed out that his troops were restless, suffering exposure to the winter rain and snow and the ranks were being thinned by desertions, disease and poor food. He also stated the obvious: the preparations for the Armada were widely known across Europe and secrecy had been lost.

As 1588 dawned the Marquis of Santa Cruz continued in Lisbon with the preparations, toiling manfully to bring the muster of ships, men, materials and victuals up to what was required. However, his health was failing, and, frustrated and burdened by the myriad logistical problems and the complaints of an impatient King, he took to his bed, gravely ill with typhus. On 9 February 1588, Santa Cruz, the most senior admiral of Spain, died, aged 61, ending an illustrious career during which he had commanded most major Spanish naval victories of the past decades.

The Duke of Medina Sidonia reluctantly takes up the mantle

The King, who had heard in early February that Santa Cruz was dying, had already decided to pass the Armada command to Don Alonso Pérez de Guzmán el Bueno, the Duke of Medina Sidonia. The Duke must have been foremost in Philip's mind when on 8 January he had approved his appointment as Captain General of the Coast of Andalucia, a position the Duke had long sought. In mid-February a courier arrived at the ducal seat at Sanlúcar de Barrameda with a letter from the king's secretary and advisor, Juan de Idiáquez informing him that the King 'had put his eyes on you' and was appointing him in charge of the Armada expedition, as Captain General of the Ocean Sea.

Medina Sidonia was not even lukewarm about his new elevation; he was totally set against accepting what seemed to him as a poisoned chalice. In an obvious state of shock, he immediately dashed off an impassioned and eloquent reply to de Idiáquez, 'I first kiss the royal feet and hands of His Majesty for entrusting me with such a great task, to fulfil which I would wish to have the abilities and resources necessary for the same service; however, my Lord, I find myself in poor health to embark, as I have experienced from the little time I have spent at sea, which almost kills me due to my many rheumatisms'. Then the Duke, one of the richest men in Spain (owner of vast estates in Andalucía, and enjoying the royal privilege of the right to fish the southern coast for the *almadraba*, the rich tuna fisheries), tried to employ, what would be called in Ireland, the 'poor mouth': 'Moreover Your Grace knows that I am in such necessity that I have to go to Madrid to borrow … thus I do not have a real to spend in the king's service'. He explained how unqualified he was: 'it is not right that the command of so … important an enterprise be taken by one who has neither experience of the sea nor of war'.

Right: a rare portrait of Alonso Pérez de Guzmán el Bueno, 7th Duke of Medina Sidonia – depicting him in his 50s. The Duke was 37 years of age when he was appointed by Philip to take charge of the Armada.

Also: 'I feel that I shall give a bad account of myself, going thus blindly, being obliged to rely on the experience and opinion of others, knowing neither what is good nor what is bad'. He begged that the position be given to someone more qualified. Philip, on reading the letter, brushed off Medina Sidonia's refusal as 'modesty'. Two days later the Duke sent off a second letter to the king, explaining that he did not think the Armada expedition would be successful. However, the councillors of state were so appalled by this disturbing message that they withheld the letter from the king – and they replied to the Duke telling him 'it is important that you step forward with the determination expected of Your Lordship'. Philip's will prevailed and on 27 February, Medina Sidonia left Sanlúcar de Barrameda for Lisbon, under orders to make haste as the Armada was waiting to depart.

The Duke has been much pilloried ever since as being responsible for the failure of the Armada, by many historians – along with puzzlement as to why he was selected. Questions have been raised about the Duke's role in directing the Armada during the combat along the English Channel,

but there is no doubt that he was the right man for the immediate task of sorting out the disarray that reigned at Lisbon. Indeed there was wisdom in selecting this 'prince of many parts' as the Venetian ambassador to Philip's court wrote at the time. The Duke is, he continued 'prudent and brave', although 'one might desire in him a wider experience of the sea'. Philip had many good reasons for this appointment. Medina Sidonia was the premier grandee of Spain, and thus able to command and bind the various competing naval and military factions that had developed in Lisbon.

Left: a difficult place to leave. An interior view of the palace of the Dukes of Medina Sidonia at Sanlúcar de Barrameda.

Philip had deep confidence in the Duke: as a reward for his leadership during the annexation of Portugal, he had also been offered the Governor Generalship of Milan, but a lukewarm Medina Sidonia always seemed to have more pressing matters and he never travelled to Italy. In 1581, he had appointed him to command an expedition to capture Larache in Morocco (intended to give a toehold, to better defend the shipping routes to the Indies – in the event, the expedition did not take place). The closest the Duke had come to real battle was in leading the local forces to relieve Cádiz during Drake's recent raid. Even though the discipline had not been invented in 1588, he would have been what would today be called a good project manager – or in military terms a quartermaster-general. Since 1581 Medina Sidonia had been responsible for the fitting out and provisioning of the Indies fleets and he had demonstrated this ability once again with his recent marshalling of the ships and supplies at Cádiz that were destined for the Armada. Philip trusted the Duke to be prudent with expenditure – this was extremely important, given the large amount of ducats currently flooding out of the treasury for the Armada preparations. As events turned out, he was the right man for the task of improving matters at Lisbon. During the Armada voyage, when strategic decisions had to be taken, he took these in a sound and solid manner – but at times he lacked the spark of a great military commander.

Despite Medina Sidonia's belief that the Armada being assembled was inadequate to the task, this trusted and proven administrator immediately got down to work after his arrival in Lisbon on 14 March. The Duke examined the scene. On falling ill the Marques of Santa Cruz had assigned the squadron commanders to continue with preparations. Bad weather had delayed preparations and with nobody around to take decisions, problems had abounded. Some ships had too much ordinance, much of it unsuitable, others had too little. There was a shortage of food – the assembled mariners and soldiers, stuck on their ships in harbour, were consuming the victuals that had been laboriously transported to Lisbon. The Duke took a firm grip and proceeded to put things in order. He studied the documentation that had been prepared under Santa Cruz, and then met with the senior officials who were present. Next he evaluated what had been assembled: around 90 ships (made up of a mix of warships, merchant ships and smaller vessels). Clearly many more vessels were required. Gradually things began to improve: some of the men were allowed ashore. More ships sailed for Lisbon. There was an attempt to rearrange the medley of mismatched artillery that had been sourced from all over. Cannon and shot were redistributed amongst the ships. More and bigger guns were put on order, and the gun foundries ramped up production. Using his noble connections, Medina Sidonia sent out his requests across Spain to the Dukes, Counts and Marquises. They in turn did their duty, mustering thousands of soldiers, who over the next weeks were dispatched to Lisbon.

In Santa Cruz's time it was known that there was a shortage of seamen and Medina Sidonia implemented the plan for a forced levy of around foreign 750 sailors who had been on embargoed merchant ships. Even more critically, there was a severe shortage of skilled pilots for the Armada. There were many pilots experienced in navigating across the Atlantic to the Indies, but apart from some pilots of the *urcas*, there were few with experience of northern waters. To improve knowledge of northern navigation and prepare for the voyage, six of the most experienced pilots were assigned to spend days at Juan Martínez de Recalde's quarters, reviewing the planned route and preparing customised maps. The efficient Duke arranged for a printer, experienced in producing nautical charts, to travel from Seville to Lisbon. There, at the end of March he printed out a rutter, a set of guidelines to the northern waters entitled: 'Route of the coasts of Brittany, Normandy, Picardy to Flanders and that of England, the Bristol and St George's Channels, and part of the coast of Ireland', which were distributed to the ships. (As it turned out, knowledge of the coast of Ireland proved to be important, and one account tells that eight Irish pilots sailed with the Armada. However, the section relating to Ireland was fairly brief, mainly giving sailing instructions related to distances and bearings from Cape Clear.)

The preparations continued, with carpenters swarming over the ships in the harbour, making last minute repairs. Recognising the need for more ships, Philip agreed to release the prized galleons of the Indian guard, from their duties escorting the treasure fleets and these, under the command of Don Diego Flóres de Valdés, arrived from Sanlúcar at the end of March 1588 to form the Squadron of Castile .

Earlier in the year, two ships, both from Venice, the *Lavia* (later to founder on a Sligo beach) and the *Regazona*, had been unlucky enough to be engaged in delivering cargoes of sugar to Portugal – they were embargoed in Lisbon harbour. They were regarded as an excellent addition to the fleet, one of the King's officials reported that they 'were so powerful that they could give battle to ten or twelve English [ships]'.

There was a strong representation of Ragusan ships in the Armada. The maritime Republic of Ragusa (now Dubrovnik in Croatia) was renowned for the quality of ships produced in its shipyards. These traders of the Mediterranean also had a long tradition of hiring their merchant vessels to other states. The Ragusans were Catholics and there were extensive trading ties with Spain. Ragusan ships had been chartered for previous Spanish naval adventures: they were part of the Marquis of Santa Cruz's fleet during his takeover of Lisbon in 1580 and several years later also participated in the Azores campaigns. The habitual presence of Ragusan ships in Spanish naval operations indicates that the Ragusan ships, skilfully crewed, were eminently suitable for the task and, that for the owners, Spanish service was seen as a lucrative hire. When it came to preparations for the Armada, Ragusa took care to avoid being seen as openly providing assistance, for fear of offending the Ottoman big brother next door. While in reality the Ragusans were happy to hire out their ships, they had to conceal this from the Turks, foes of Philip II. Their ambassador in Istanbul duly made it known that the ships for the Armada had been forcefully commandeered. Four Ragusan ships were engaged for the Armada. One had been hired at Palermo, supposedly embargoed by the Viceroy there. Other Ragusan ships were requisitioned at Alicante and Valencia. To add to the subterfuge, the Ragusan ships were given Italian or Spanish names, all the better to hide their origin. The Ottoman Sultan was always interested in making headway against the threat from his rival in the Mediterranean, Spain. However, he was reluctant to engage in open war, and when the Armada preparations were well underway, he declined requests from Elizabeth's ambassador in Istanbul to initiate diversionary attacks against Spanish domains.

When Philip ordered Medina Sidonia to Lisbon, he had instructed that the Armada would depart at the beginning of March at the latest. As it turned out, the Duke only arrived in Lisbon in mid-March. However, Philip was in a highly anxious state. This was understandable, with the preparations costing him hundreds of thousands ducats per month. To keep solvent he cast around his domains for new taxation sources and also tried to raise loans from Italian bankers. The Duke of Olivares, Philip's envoy in Rome, raised the possibility with Pope Sixtus that he might pay an advance of the promised 1,000,000 gold ducats, in effect the success fee to be paid on the overthrow of Elizabeth and her Protestant regime. Sixtus was having none of it. Indeed, Olivares reported that when the Pope heard that the Armada was on the cusp of departure, the prospect of actually having to pay out the enormous sum perturbed Sixtus, so much that he claimed he could not sleep at night.

Invasion Preparations in the Netherlands

Back at the planned springboard for the direct assault on England, the Netherlands, the Duke of Parma was also worried about lack of money. As he continued with the invasion preparations he needed more finance to pay the troops he had gathered and for their provisions. However, he was in a good strategic position in the Netherlands, as over the previous years, he had enjoyed a run of successes. In late 1586 there had been clashes across eastern Netherlands. In a heavy battle, Parma managed to repel an Anglo-Dutch attempt on loyalist Zutphen. In the course of the encounter, the English commander, Sir William Stanley, seized nearby Deventer. (Stanley had fought in many campaigns in Ireland and had been Sheriff of Cork – he had been knighted for his services in suppressing the Second Desmond Rebellion). In January 1587, Stanley, who had Catholic sympathies, decided to change sides. He and his regiment of nearly 1,000 Irish soldiers, officered by English Catholics, defected to the Spanish side, handing over Deventer. Stanley carried on as governor of Deventer, still in charge of his regiment, now incorporated into Parma's army. The loss of these two strategic points posed a serious reverse for the Dutch rebels, as it left the province of Holland, the heartland of the revolt, open to assault.

Parma was in control of most of the county of Flanders, all save Ostend and Sluys along the northern coast. Parma's men made a reconnaissance of Ostend (occupied by English troops) but its defences appeared too formidable. Sluys looked more promising and in mid-June 1587, the Army of Flanders began assembling for a siege there. The town, once a great port, was now silting up, but had a commanding position in relation to neighbouring ports and was also at the heart of a network of canals. Parma advanced in

Right: the siege of Sluys by Parma's forces, in mid-1587.

three columns amidst the watery landscape and set up his headquarters on a nearby barren sandy island. Barges set out with reinforcements for Parma, and despite artillery exchanges with small Zeeland warships, they managed to deposit their troops along with siege cannon. In the weeks that followed, the defenders fought bravely as Parma's soldiers and siege guns advanced closer to the town. The Earl of Leicester (assigned by Elizabeth to lead the English forces supporting the Dutch rebels) set out to relieve the siege by the Spanish, who now amounted to around 5,000 men. At the end of July, a great fleet of transports carrying 3,000 English soldiers, escorted by English and Dutch warships, arrived at the besieged town. There followed a series of operations directed by Leicester, so useless that the historian Garrett Mattingly has written: 'the chief effect of this fortnight of imbecile manoeuvres was on the morale of the beleaguered garrison'. Nevertheless, the Sluys garrison continued their strong resistance. Finally the position was captured on 5 August, with Parma (who had lost 700 men in the action), accepting the town's surrender on honourable terms. Flushing, with its large harbour, next came into Parma's sights. It was just to the north, on the island of Walcheren, across the River Scheldt; capturing this could provide a safe harbour for the deep-draughted ships of the Armada. Parma was now on its doorstep and began mustering his forces in Sluys and Antwerp. The rebel provinces of Zeeland and Holland were now vulnerable. However, demonstrating the dangers of micro-management and control from far away, Philip II ordered Parma to cease campaigning, to remain in Flanders and to begin assembling his forces in anticipation of the invasion of England. As it turned out, the States-General had a narrow escape. If it hadn't been for the Armada, Parma would most likely have rolled on to re-establish Spanish control in the Low Countries. Instead he now went to concentrate on drawing together the various elements of an invasion force. In Parma's proposal for the Enterprise of England that he had sent to the King in April 1586, his plan had been

Left: the port of Flushing. After the taking of Sluys, this came next into Parma's sights and he began mustering his forces in Sluys and Antwerp. Capturing this could provide a safe harbour for the deep-draughted ships of the Armada. However, Philip II ordered Parma to cease campaigning, to remain in Flanders and to begin assembling his forces in anticipation of the invasion of England.

Above: the situation in the Netherlands around 1588.

for a force of 30,000 infantry and 500 cavalry, making up the major part of the Army of Flanders (with a smaller element left behind to guard the Netherlands).

Parma now set to energetically, and over the following months he travelled continuously to the designated departure ports and their hinterland, supervising preparations. More troops were recruited, given impetus by substantial funds sent by the King. To secure his territory he had also to assign a strong garrison for Flanders and, as well, arrange for the French border to be fortified. By the end of 1587 his invasion army had reached its peak numbers and were billeted near the invasion ports. However, with the invasion date continually being put back due to delays in Lisbon, Parma fretted:

Left; Justin of Nassau (son of William of Orange), since 1585, lieutenant-admiral of Zeeland. The Dutch navy had been on station along the coast of Flanders, posing a threat to Parma's plans for sailing out with his forces to invade England – however the Dutch withdrew to shallower waters on the advent of the Spanish Armada.

his forces were suffering from the bad weather and were being reduced by disease, the perennial scourge of massed armies of those times. There was also hunger. The blockade by the Dutch navy had cut off the flow of grain from the Baltic. After the failure of harvests in the southern provinces there was famine. As well as devastating the local population, Parma's army was reduced as well. Nevertheless, Parma concentrated on the logistics: victuals and munitions were stored in coastal Flanders; magazines were constructed near Dunkirk and Nieuport to store gunpowder. The cost of providing for his waiting army mounted as the Armada's departure continued to be delayed. One account tells how Parma took out personal loans to help pay for this.

By June 1588 he had amassed around 27,000 men for the expedition. Spanish troops had made the laborious journey to the Netherlands, first by sea to Genoa, then the long trek northwards over the Alps, and finally via the Spanish Road. These were in the minority, making up around 20 per cent of the total. Philip's domains in Italy and Burgundy contributed 4,000 men. The largest contingent was made up of Walloon and German troops, amounting to 15,000. There were around 1,000 Irish (together with a few Scottish) soldiers, who had followed Sir William Stanley when he had defected at Deventer. Such was the perceived ferocity of these Irish troops that an English intelligence report noted that the Spanish called them '*los salvages perdidos*'.

Right: a view of a flyboat at Amsterdam Harbour. The Dutch navy used these small shallow-draught vessels to patrol the waters in and around the Netherlands.

The ports of embarkation were to be Dunkirk and Nieuport on the Flanders coast. Many invasion barges were sourced, including those which had been used during the siege of Antwerp. In 1588, Parma had sought additional vessels in Denmark, but this failed due to English diplomatic intervention. A programme for building additional barges was begun but suffered from problems as green wood was used for the hulls. By July 1588, with Medina Sidonia now on the high seas, over 170 vessels had been assembled, divided into three squadrons. The fleet was made up of flat-bottomed craft including *pleitas*, which were around 20m long and 6m wide, with a capacity for 200 men. There were also some *huyas*, which were shorter and wider. To escort these, there were over 30 armed vessels, including around 20 flyboats, small shallow-draught ships.

While Parma's army had dominance on land, the Dutch navy was patrolling the estuaries, inlets and shoals along the Flanders coast. Each state of the United Provinces had its own admiralty which received a sizeable part of its income from escorting merchantmen Despite efforts to centralise the command structure, each provincial admiralty tended to operate in their own local interest. Dutch squadrons had been used to blockade the approach waterways during the siege of Antwerp (1584) and recently, at the siege of Sluys. The consolidated navy amounted to around 200 ships. All had the shallow draught needed to ply the waters in and around the Netherlands. Most were small coastal protection vessels – the biggest were 200-ton flyboats, carrying over a dozen small to medium size guns. It did not pose a problem to source merchantmen for the navy, given that the Dutch merchant fleet was then one of the world's largest, with an estimated 2,700 vessels varying in size from 25 to 100 tons. A perennial problem was lack of finance – between January and November of 1588, sailors in Holland and Zeeland did not receive their wages. Some of the Dutch navy vessels were in poor shape: the squadron of 23 ships sent to aid England in July 1588 (to counter the Armada threat, in accordance with the Treaty of Nonsuch) were judged to be in such poor condition that they were sent back to the Netherlands. Undeterred, they re-joined their comrades from Zeeland who were patrolling the coast of Flanders, under the command of Justin of Nassau (illegitimate son of William, Prince of Orange), lieutenant-admiral of Zeeland. As a further precaution to confuse hostile Spanish forces, the Dutch had removed all signs and navigation aids along the labyrinthine waters of the coast.

We have already seen how the Earl of Leicester and his English expeditionary force had failed in their efforts to push back Spanish power in the Netherlands. Elizabeth, by now acutely conscious of the money and soldiers she had poured into the Dutch abyss, reacted with fury to a request for more assistance from the rebels there, responding 'she does not believe such ungrateful people … live upon the earth'. Against the background of the reports of Armada preparations in Lisbon, she announced her intention to open negotiations with Parma, and invited the Dutch to send delegates. Despite the fact that the other provinces which had borne the brunt of the fighting were in favour, the States-General declined to participate. In February 1588, formal talks began between English and Spanish representatives at Bourbourg (just inland from Gravelines, in Spanish-ruled territory, today part of northern France). Elizabeth's commissioners had two principal objectives: the removal of all foreign troops from the Netherlands, and toleration for Protestants there. This was immaterial to Philip; the Armada die was cast for him after Drake's attack on Cádiz. It suited him to string out the talks, hiding from the English his true intentions. The talks also had the potential to cause further disharmony amongst Dutch ranks, while casting doubt on England's commitment to their cause.

England prepares

As rumours of invasion spread through England, it was time to make urgent preparations there. However, England's military capability was hobbled by lack of funds. One historian has noted that the Elizabethan regime was 'not good at raising the two fundamental resources needed for war – money and troops'. Elizabeth was always short of money. Her father, Henry VIII had died leaving the coffers empty. Elizabeth, ruling a small country, could not count on anything like the same volume of taxes that Philip was able to harvest. In addition to the wealth flowing from the Americas, Philip also could count on a healthy flow of taxes from the church. Henry VIII had taken a one-time profit when he seized the monasteries – there was no more tax to be levied on these. The situation was precarious in 1588, as the English economy had been in depression over the previous two years. 'The whole country is without trade and knows not how to recover it' exulted a Spanish spy in a report from London. Trade had been interrupted by such Spanish actions as the seizure of northern European ships in 1585. Wool was the principal English export commodity and the trade of this with Germany had been disrupted by the conflict in the Netherlands. The expenditure to aid the Dutch rebels had turned out to be much more costly than planned. The unfortunate fact was that, in that year of mortal peril, 1588, Elizabeth's finances were at their lowest. In addition, she could not procure a foreign loan then – given the looming threat of the Armada, no financier believed she was going to be in a position to pay it back.

Right: John Hawkins. This veteran privateer and slave trader was made Treasurer of the English navy in 1578. He presided over many reforms and entered into a contract with the Crown to maintain and refurbish the fleet.

However, despite the poor financial outlook, the Navy Royal was in relative good stead. Elizabeth's father Henry VIII had spent much money in developing a permanent navy. By the end of his reign, it had grown to 53 ships, and importantly, a basic administrative and logistical structure had also been put in place. The navy was developed into a force that was capable of opposing what was then the main strategic threat across the Channel: France. The lack of money on Henry's death resulted that the annual expenditure on the navy was static, and the fleet was rationalised. However, during Mary and Philip's reign, three warships of 500 tons were laid down (which ironically, three decades later were to sail against the Armada). After Elizabeth took the throne and the cold war with Spain grew, it was obvious that the English fleet needed to be improved. By contrast in Spain, there had been continuous improvements in naval matters. In 1563 Philip had appointed Cristóbal de Barros to superintend and promote shipbuilding in the north of Spain. De Barros presided over the building of several series of advanced galleons, suitable for oceanic duty. As a result of Spanish experience in sailing the Atlantic, there were well-developed naval practice in place, such as naval doctrines for defence and battle, and as well schools and treatises on navigation and artillery.

Thus, it was fortuitous for England's defence that in 1578 John Hawkins, veteran privateer and slave trader, was appointed Treasurer of the navy. This experienced seaman made reforms that helped make the English navy a more effective force. Hawkins established a system of naval stores and restructured the dockyards. Advance bases for the navy were assigned in such ports as Weymouth, Falmouth and Plymouth. He cracked down on existing inefficiencies and corruption, as one admiring biographer noted 'with Spartan severity' – although in an Elizabethan age noted for adventurers out for self-enrichment, it is not surprising that enemies accused Hawkins of financial irregularities. He had a broad vision that a navy was more than docks, ships and guns: he was conscious of the need to avoid disease among the crews and was an advocate of cleanliness on board. He did not neglect the sailors. In a measure intended to improve conditions and as well, recruit better quality crew, Hawkins managed to get their monthly pay increased from around seven to ten shillings, no mean achievement in the prevailing era of Tudor parsimony.

Anticipating war with Spain, a fresh shipbuilding programme got underway. In October 1579, Hawkins negotiated a contract with the Queen: for £2,200 per year he would carry out repairs of the fleet using his own shipwrights. English shipwrights, assimilating a general trend (a Spanish book of 1575 had laid down new ideas on construction of ships, based on sailing the Atlantic), had already prepared warship designs that were more streamlined and long in relation to the beam. The traditional high fighting castles at front and back were being reduced in height. Together with improved arrangements of masts and rigging, this resulted in increased speed and manoeuvrability. In addition to the building of new ships, Hawkins arranged for many of the older navy ships to be reconstructed.

With rumours of an impending Armada threat increasing over 1587, the Navy Royal was mobilised at the end of November. As Elizabeth was painfully aware, this was a heavy burden on her exchequer, and two months later it was put in reverse – the ships were reduced to half crews. When the ships assembling in the southern ports were being provisioned, the parsimony continued, and only limited supplies of powder and ball were put on board.

In comparison to the protracted and difficult Armada preparations in Lisbon, it proved easier and faster to assemble the English fleet – only taking a matter of months. One of the reasons was that England was not a big country: the small number of adjacent ports resulted in short distances and communications lines. The small circles of courtiers, naval commanders, privateers and financiers mostly knew each other. Against the background of the perennial shortage of money by the Crown, the practice of mixing royal and private ownership enabled the assembly of a great number of ships for the English fleet on an economical basis.

In general, the English fleet was made up of a small number of large ships plus a myriad of medium to small vessels. There were 34 navy warships, many of which were new or had been rebuilt since 1577. Seven were over 600 tons, the largest was the *Triumph*, at 988 tons, with nine being in the 400-600 ton range. (Note that tonnage in those times was calculated using differing methods, and such listings for English ships vary widely). In addition the state engaged armed merchantmen to form the bulk of the fleet – around 80 private vessels of 100 tons upwards were hired (or volunteered) during the Armada engagements. All of this was supported by around 75 smaller ships in the under 100-ton range.

Charles Howard, Lord Effingham, was appointed as Lord High Admiral at the end of 1587 (with the designation 'Commander-in-Chief of the navy prepared to the seas against Spain'). The first vice-admiral to be appointed was Lord Henry Seymour, who was in command of the squadron guarding the Narrow Seas (the Strait of Dover, and its junction with the North Sea) – a vice-admiralship important for English defence over the centuries. As 1588 dawned, Seymour and his squadron were on watch for any sign of invasion by the Army of Flanders. We shall see later Sir Francis Drake being made vice-admiral in June, and how Howard made more command appointments amidst the heat of the Armada battles.

Right: a sixteenth-century view of an English halberdier in royal livery, along with a gentleman, member of a guild. In reality, England had neglected its land army.

Left: Sir John Norris, He had one of the most extensive Elizabethan military careers. He served in Ireland on four occasions, including when in July 1575, he presided over the massacre of the inhabitants of Rathlin Island. After leading units of the English expedition to the Netherlands, Norris was called on to survey the southern English maritime counties and prepare plans on how to repel a Spanish invasion. In 1589, along with Sir Francis Drake, he led the unsuccessful expedition that attacked Corunna and later attempted to place the pretender Dom António on the throne of Portugal.

The limitations of the land forces

As the rumours of invasion hardened into fact in 1588, the conundrum for Elizabeth and her advisors was that while they knew that there was going to be an invasion, they did not know when and where. Much of the southern coast was regarded as vulnerable, and it was also feared that the enemy would force its way up the River Thames to London. A fundamental problem was that England had neglected its land army – it did not possess a standing force of fully armed and trained soldiers. There were part-time soldiers called the 'Trained Bands', the responsibility of each county. These ranks were stiffened by a small body of seasoned veterans of the Netherlands war, who also were invaluable in supervising training. The quality of this militia, commanded by local nobles and gentlemen, was variable. Some counties and towns were reluctant to pay and provide soldiers. There was a general shortage of weapons and equipment. There was also provision for a general muster, the augmentation of the 'Trained Bands' by a large auxiliary force (with luck, these levies would be able-bodied and possess some basic training).

The counties also had responsibility for a chain of warning beacons. It was an ancient practice and the Lord Lieutenants of the different counties were now reminded to look to the beacons and maintain the vigil, as the threat of a Spanish invasion grew. The beacons, with attendant watchers, were positioned on prominent coastal hilltops and headlands to provide an early warning system. The experienced soldier, Sir John Norris, was sent to the southern maritime counties to assess the most likely places where landings might be made and prepare plans on how to repel the invasion. Despite the shortage of money, efforts were made to install rudimentary defences and upgrade the previous coastal defence system established by Henry VIII. Ramparts and ditches were installed on beaches judged vulnerable to invasion. Efforts were made to block off potential anchorages for Spanish ships by creating booms across harbour entrances. The most exotic of these was a boom deigned in 1588 by Federigo Giambelli, the military engineer who had created the 'infernal machines' or 'hellburners' which destroyed

Right: a view of English soldiers on the march, this time in Ireland.

Parma's bridge during the siege of Antwerp in 1584. This elaborate boom was installed at Gravesend across the Thames. It consisted of an iron chain, supported by 120 floating ship's masts. Alas, the boom broke at the first flood tide.

There were two schools of thought on how to muster the soldiers to best resist the Spanish invaders. The traditional view was that it was advantageous to spread the defensive forces along the coasts. The other was to have the forces concentrated at central rallying points, from which they could sally forth in strength and smite the invader. The strategy that evolved was an amalgam of these ideas: the militia in the maritime counties would attempt to delay the invasion host, and in any retreat, to adopt a scorched-earth policy. This would give the main force time to arrive and mount a counter-attack. The main army was to be divided into two groups. The first, under the command of the Earl of Leicester with a planned strength of 27,000 infantry and 2,500 cavalry, was intended to be the principal force to attack the invaders. The second group was a core unit entrusted with guarding London and the Queen herself, with a strength, at least on paper, of 29,000 infantry and over 4,000 cavalry. As we have seen, Elizabeth had cooled on the Netherlands expedition. It was a time to re-prioritise and in May 1588, English troops in the Netherlands, to the discomfiture of the Dutch, were ordered back to defend the homeland.

Medina Sidonia gets his orders

Back at Lisbon, the preparations were reaching finalisation. On 1 April 1588, Philip dispatched his final orders to Medina Sidonia for command of the Armada expedition. These were comprehensive and written with care. They commenced with a reference to God's will (in that era, all sides, both Catholic Spain and Protestant England, had a deep belief in the role of Divine Providence and God was frequently invoked.) The instructions ran: 'All victories are the gifts of God … You are going to fight for the cause of our Lord … His forces will be added to your own'. The instruction was that 'you will sail with the whole of the Armada, and go straight to the English Channel, which you will ascend as far as Cape Margate, where you will join hands with the Duke of Parma ... and hold the passage for his crossing'. At

Margate, after consultations with Parma, he was to place the 'troops with which you are to furnish him, and you will act accordingly. It is my desire that when these troops land they shall be under the command of my Commander-in-Chief of the Light Cavalry of Milan, Don Alonso de Leyva, until [Parma] takes them over'. Thus, with de Leyva establishing a beachhead, he should not be deflected from his course and only do battle with the English fleet if forced to do so. The king advised Medina Sidonia to keep his ships together and reminded him that the English in combat refused to close with their ships, preferring to fight by broadside from a distance. Cooperation with Parma was important, Philip stressed. When Parma had safely landed in England, the king advised, the Armada should anchor in the Thames Estuary and guard the passage to Flanders. He was to wait there until the undertaking was successfully settled. He then added: '... you may then return, calling in and settling matters in Ireland' – if he and Parma were to jointly agree on this.

We should remember that Philip's ultimate goal was not the annexation of England and its incorporation within his empire. In his ideal world, Elizabeth would be overthrown and a friendly Catholic ruler drafted in (and as a bonus, it would result in a friendly Catholic-ruled Ireland as well). However, the bottom line was that he wanted to neutralize England and stop its provocations.

In a supplementary secret instruction to Medina Sidonia, Philip outlined the alternative if the main plan failed. He directed that 'if for our sins', God does not grant success, and Parma 'should be unable to cross to England ... you will, after communication with him, consider whether you cannot seize the Isle of Wight ... This will provide you with a safe port for shelter' – and from there come to an understanding with Parma on how best to proceed in relaunching the operation.

Medina Sidonia also received a sealed document, to be handed to Parma only in the event he should land in England. Within, the king spelt out the most important and minimal points to secure in negotiations with the English, in the event, as he noted, that the 'result be not so prosperous'. Firstly, the free exercise of their faith should be permitted to all Catholics. Secondly, the English should hand over all parts of the Netherlands that they control, and thirdly, that they pay reparations for the injury they have done to him and his domains (a demand, which if it had been made, would have been strongly resisted by Elizabeth, always acutely conscious of the state of her precarious treasury).

The Armada takes final shape

As April 1588 dawned, the Armada took its definitive shape, with the large array of vessels moored along and off the Tagus shoreline. There were now 130 ships (supplemented by a number of minute *carabelas* and *falúas*, which acted as tenders). On board were 19,000 soldiers, 8,000 sailors and 2,000 rowers of the galleys and galleasses. An enormous variety of ships were anchored in the harbour and moored along the quays of Lisbon. Intended to play a leading role in the front-line were the squadrons of Castile and Portugal, with their strong galleons. The Squadron of Portugal was made up

Above: a nineteenth-century print portraying the Armada at Lisbon in May 1588.

of nine galleons, all but one former Portuguese navy ships, eminently suited to Atlantic warfare. It included the 1,000 ton flagship, the *San Martín*, which had played a prominent part in the Azores battles of 1582 and 1583. The *San Mateo* (built in Portuguese Goa) was there, now repaired after the damage it endured during its valiant fight in the Battle of São Miguel in the Azores in 1582. This grouping was completed by two large *zabra*s of around 170 tons. The Portuguese Squadron was to form the leading edge of the Armada, assigned to protect the core of transport ships.

Equally, the Squadron of Castile was assigned to play a protective role. Its backbone was the ten galleons (all built in Cantabria and, with one exception, not more than five years old) fresh from their duties of escorting the treasure fleets of the Indies. Also intended for front-line protective duties was the squadron of four galleasses from Naples. These 500 tonners were heavily armed front and aft. These were hybrid ships, employing a fusion of wind and oar power. They were intended to fight and manoeuvre rapidly and, in unfavourable wind, to reach those areas where other ships could not sail. The galleasses could tow invasion barges as close to shore as their draught would allow. However, with even shallower draught, the four galleys of the fleet had the potential to tow barges even closer to the beachhead – and for the Enterprise of England would have the potential to sail some distance up the Thames and blast the shore defences with their forward heavy guns. However, the heavy storms in the Bay of Biscay were to deny these greyhounds of the Mediterranean from playing any part in the Armada battles. Forming the second line were the squadrons of Vizcaya, Guipúzcoa (the region around San Sebastián) and Andalucia, made up of heavily armed *naos*, or merchant ships. These were generally large vessels, mainly in the range of 500-900 tons. At the core of the Armada formations were the squadrons of the Levant and of the *urcas*. These were intended to primarily act in a transport rather than a combat role. The Levant Squadron was comprised of merchant ships, including grain carriers, sourced from around the Mediterranean. Many had been built in Italy in such places as Venice and Genoa. Four were from Ragusa, all of which had seen action in the Azores battles of 1582 and 1583. Three other ships of the Levant Squadron, the *Lavia*, the *Santa María de Visón*, and the *Trinidad Valencera* were also veterans of the Azores. At 1,100 tons, the *Trinidad Valencera* was one of the larger ships, a size exceeded in the same Levant Squadron by its flagship, the *Regazona* –which at nearly 1,300 tons was the largest vessel of the entire Armada. The large holds of the Levant ships were ideal to convey the men, supplies and heavy artillery train needed for an invasion force. There was no boarding attempt made on these ships during the subsequent Armada battles off the English coast, but if an enemy ship had attempted to do so, they would have received a shock: these ships were well armed and carried a large compliment of troops who could have overcome the enemy vessel. Incongruous amongst these large merchant ships of the Squadron of the Levant was another vessel, a large galleon. This was the heavily armed and soundly-constructed *San Francisco de Florencia* which had been sequestered from the Duke of Tuscany's one-ship navy – we last encountered it in 1587 sailing with Santa Cruz to the Azores to fend off corsairs and escort the treasure fleet. It was included in the squadron presumably because like the other ships, it was crewed mainly by sailors from the Levant, Italy in this case.

Perhaps the most workaday role in the Armada was that assigned to the Squadron of the *Urcas* (or hulks). Like those of the Levant, these were to transport the heavy matériel for the expedition. The 23 vessels of the squadron came mainly from the Netherlands, Germany and the Baltic. Generally more lightly armed, these slow, broad-beamed and capacious ships had dutifully carried cargo through northern waters over the previous two decades – one, the *Esayas*, had been constructed in Germany as far back as 1542. Several *urcas* carried the around 300 mules and horses detailed to support the invasion army when landed. Finally came the small workhorses of the fleet, the estimated 23 vessels of the Squadron of *Pataches* and *Zabras*. The use of a special squadron for command and communications duties had been a tactical innovation introduced by the Marquis of Santa Cruz. He had envisaged that these small vessels would transmit orders more swiftly, and also act in a scouting role. Mostly built at Castro-Urdiales, near Bilbao, these nimble craft, used as attendants to the main fleet, were mainly in the 50-60 ton range. A few were over 100 tons, and the squadron flagship, the 305-ton *Nuestra Señora del Pilar de Zaragoza*, was a *nao*.

Thus, by the end of April 1588, it had taken two years to gather men, ships and supplies from all over the Spanish Empire and beyond. The length of time it had taken to assemble such a varied fleet reflected the difficulties of sourcing material and manpower, from such a vast and far-flung empire. However, the task was underpinned by the strong sinews of the all-encompassing imperial bureaucracy. The large costs incurred were possible solely due to the deep pockets of Philip II and his exchequer. Most of the time he adroitly negotiated timely loans from his Genoese and other bankers, while all the time, awaiting news of the next treasure fleet. There were many compelling reasons which had driven Philip to go to this enormous effort and expense: the primary one was to force the English to withdraw their support of the Dutch rebels; another was to eliminate the scourge of English privateering across the Spanish Main. For the devout Philip, there was also the prospect of the defeat of heresy in England and the relief of Catholicism there.

Chapter 3
Sailing to Gravelines

The feast of St Mark the Evangelist, 15 April 1588, was the occasion for the full forces of the Spanish Crown and Church to congregate in Lisbon Cathedral and wrap God's mantle around the Enterprise of England. In the presence of the king's viceroy (Philip's nephew, the Cardinal Archduke Albert), the Archbishop of Lisbon solemnly consecrated the standard of the Armada, which was handed over to the Duke of Medina Sidonia. The banner had been woven by the 'ladies of Portugal' and displayed the arms of Spain along with Christ crucified and Our Lady. It proclaimed '*Exurge, Domine et vindica causam tuam*' (O Lord, arise and vindicate your cause). As the procession emerged from the cathedral, a volley of arquebuses was answered by the thunder of the gun salute of the Armada at anchor. The banner was then paraded all the way to the harbour, between the colourful ranks of soldiers, their armour and helmets glittering in the sun.

The senior command

Down at the waterfront, preparations were reaching a crescendo. The roads leading into Lisbon were crowded by squadrons of men marching, in between the supply-trains, carrying last-minute victuals, supplies and equipment. The Duke of Medina Sidonia had worked wonders since his arrival in mid-March. Despite the continuous stream of missives from the Escorial urging him to proceed, the Duke had professionally orchestrated the final preparations and in a matter of weeks had achieved a triumph of logistics. While it was not in as perfect a state as he might have wished, the Armada was now reaching a critical mass, one sufficient for it to carry out its mission. The fleet might still be short of victuals but an impatient Medina Sidonia decided to depart – these could be dispatched later by a supply flotilla. In addition to his work in recent weeks, acting in effect as Quartermaster supreme, the Duke had to consider his overall command duties as 'Captain General of the Ocean Sea'. This gave him control over the entire Armada, but he also had direct charge of the Squadron of Portugal. His flagship was the huge 1,000-ton *San Martín*, built in the 1570s and, like the other vessels in this squadron, one of the Atlantic-proven warships inherited when Philip became King of Portugal in 1580.

Medina Sidonia may have lacked much direct military experience, but he was backed by a strong team, all widely experienced in military and naval campaigns across the sprawling Spanish Empire. Key among Medina Sidonia's senior leadership and the most experienced in naval matters was Don Juan Martínez de Recalde, Admiral General and second-in-command of the entire Armada. Sailing in the vice-flagship, the *San Juan de Portugal*, he also directed the Squadron of Vizcaya. Salt was in his blood – he came from a distinguished family of Bilbao ship-owners. By sixteenth-century standards, he was quite old at 62. He had started his career in the Army of Flanders but soon switched to the navy, leading flotillas against the Dutch rebels along the coasts and waterways there. Next came naval service in the Atlantic. In September 1580 he had commanded the flotilla of ships which transported from Spain the second contingent of the Pope's troops to land at Smerwick on the southwestern Irish coast (thus gaining what later turned out to be useful knowledge of these waters). In addition, during the 1570s he had scouted out the ports and waterways along the English Channel. He had served under the Marquis of Santa Cruz in the Terceira battle. Following this the King made him a knight of the Order of Santiago. His marriage in 1585 to the niece of Don Juan de Idiáquez, Philip's Secretary of State, did his career no harm.

The fleet was divided into various squadrons, commanded by veteran commanders, many with experience of the northern sea route to Flanders. Like de Recalde, several were from Spain's northern coast, with its long and outstanding maritime legacy. Commanding the Squadron of Guipúzcoa was Don Miguel de Oquendo, from San Sebastián, from a family of five generations of seafarers. At an early stage, he made several voyages to the Americas in the merchant service. His service to the Crown began when he led a flotilla at Oran in North Africa in 1575. Two years later he was honoured with the position of Mayor of San Sebastián. He performed valiantly during the Azores campaign, leading a fleet of Guipúzcoan ships at Terceira. Another veteran seaman was Don Martín de Bertendona, in charge of the Squadron of the Levant, formed by Italian and Ragusan merchant ships tasked with transporting the troops and equipment. A native of Bilbao, he came from a Basque seafaring family and had taken part in many campaigns, including that in Flanders. After the annexation of Portugal, the King had entrusted him with the command of the naval defence of Portuguese waters.

Another from the north coast of Spain (Asturias) was Don Pedro de Valdés, in charge of the Squadron of Andalucia. This prickly and impulsive man had made his career serving in many significant naval encounters across Philip's empire. We last saw him during his unsuccessful attempt to capture the island of Terceira in July 1581, in disobedience of his orders . This had been disastrous for Pedro de Valdés – he had lost his son in battle and was subsequently imprisoned in Lisbon by order of the King. However, he was later released due to the influence of the Marquis of Santa Cruz and the Duke of Alba. His appointment to lead the Andalucian Squadron, in effect his rehabilitation, arose from the need for experienced commanders. He was a cousin of Don Diego Flóres de Valdés (commander of the Squadron of Castile). In his mid-50s, and a member of the prestigious Order of Santiago, Diego Flóres de Valdés had enjoyed a long naval career, with senior commands of fleets in the Americas and had been Admiral of the Indies fleet. Both of the de Valdés cousins were highly opinionated and there was no love lost between them.

Don Hugo de Moncada, who came from a titled family, led the small squadron of four galleasses. In a background, but essential, role for the functioning of the Armada were the squadrons that were primarily non-combatant. The supply vessels, the Squadron of *Urcas* was commanded by Don Juan Gómez de Medina. Essential for communications and close supply, the Squadron of *Pataches* and *Zabras* was led by the experienced Agustín de Ojeda.

A man of great importance in the Armada leadership was Don Alonso Martínez de Leyva, Captain General of the Cavalry of Milan who had been designated to lead 6,000 troops when they landed in England and establish a beachhead for Parma's invasion army. Although the youngest of the commanders, only in his mid-thirties, this tall, slim son of the Viceroy of Naples and member of the Order of Santiago had enjoyed a distinguished career. As a youth he had taken part in the war against the *Moriscos* in the Alpujarras. He had commanded the galleys of Sicily and had served in Portugal. De Leyva was highly regarded by Philip, so much so that the king had given a secret document to Admiral General de Recalde, only to be opened in the event of the Duke of Medina Sidonia's death. This stated, that in such an occurrence, de Leyva was to take command of the Armada. De Leyva's charisma was so great that a group of young nobles, eager for the chance of glory and honour in the invasion of England, had elected to travel with him on his ship, the 820-ton *Santa María Encoronada*, otherwise known as *La Rata,* so-named after its first captain, the Genoese, Giovanni Ratti.

Setting sail

At last, it was time to sail and on 11 May 1588 the first of the assembled vessels began to sail down the Tagus and gather at the mouth of the harbour at Belém. As the ships assembled, a strong wind howled up the harbour, as

Right: the great harbour of Lisbon. A view from 1572, by the Flemish engraver and map maker, Frans Hogenberg.

Left: the Belém Tower, a fortification dating from 1519 at the entrance to the River Tagus. At the end of May 1588, squadron by squadron, the ships of the Armada sailed past here: destination England.

Medina Sidonia recounted, with '*tanta furia*', halting operations. This was a harbinger of what was to come for the rest of the Armada expedition – a run of unseasonably harsh weather. That night a small vessel, under Captain Francisco Moresín, arrived in Lisbon harbour carrying a dispatch from the Duke of Parma, in which he related, to the disappointment of Medina Sidonia, who had expected a greater force, that he did not expect to gather more than 17,000 men, 1,000 cavalry and 300 small boats.

As the contrary wind blew, the Armada had to remain sheltered within harbour. Finally, on 28 May as the weather improved somewhat, Medina Sidonia wrote to the king that he hoped to leave the following morning. As the Armada finally set sail, it was an impressive sight: it took a considerable time to sail past the Belém Tower until finally, by 30 May the full fleet had reached the open sea.

The weather was still poor, and as the Armada attempted to head north into opposing winds, the variable qualities of ships making up the Armada soon became evident. The *urcas*, the requisitioned hulks laden with supplies and troops, with their stout lines, floundered in the waves. The slow progress frustrated Medina Sidonia – he had to order the galleons to shorten sail. As the winds shifted around the compass, the ships attempted to sail against the wind, tacking from side to side. Nevertheless, a northerly wind blew the fleet as far south as Cape St Vincent. It took two hard weeks to beat up the coast and reach the north-western tip of the Iberian Peninsula, Cape Finisterre. Captain Moresín had been dispatched back to Parma in Flanders in a fast *zabra*, with news of the fleet's departure. In addition Medina Sidonia said that he would advise of his position when he reached the English coast, so that Parma could then bring out his fleet. The Duke also declared his wish for a safe port capable of sheltering 'so great a fleet as this'. Medina Sidonia, after setting sail from Lisbon, had convened a meeting of pilots to determine which ports or assembly points would be suitable to shelter in the event of a storm, within reasonable distance from Parma and his forces. While the Armada's final destination predetermined, i.e. to arrive off Margate, Medina Sidonia's request regarding ports indicated his continuing desire to mitigate risks to the fleet from bad weather.

The haven of Corunna

As the Armada made its laborious way northwards there was a setback: it soon emerged that much of the stored food (on board for over six months, as a result of the delayed departure at Lisbon) had turned putrid and some had to be thrown overboard. One of the underlying problems during the sixteenth century was that the preservation techniques available were rudimentary compared to modern processes. Methods such as salting, smoking, pickling and drying were used to some extent, but these were not always successful for long-term storage, especially on lengthy sea journeys. Barrels for food storage represented one of the more practical options available, but these frequently proved ineffective. The problem of food spoiling affected the Armada during its long time at sea, but it also affected the English ships during the events of August 1588, after they had reached the Firth of Forth, even though they only had made a relatively short sea voyage.

With the additional time wasted beating down and then up the Portuguese coast, the Armada was beginning to run short of provisions. The fleet waited off the Cape Finisterre coast for the supply tenders that had been prearranged. These had earlier set out from Galicia to await the Armada, but with no sign of the fleet, the tenders had returned to port. After days awaiting the relieving tenders, and short of water, on 19 June, Medina Sidonia had no choice but to give the signal to sail into Corunna for resupply and repairs. As the first of the ships sailed into Corunna, a fierce gale sprang up during the night, and many of the fleet were scattered, with some driven to ports along the northern Spanish coast – a few were blown as far north as the Scilly Islands. With nearly 30 ships (including many of the best) missing, Medina Sidonia fell into despair. On 24 June, he wrote to the King, pouring out his misgivings. In his tale of woe, he told of the weather, as bad as had ever been seen by anyone. He listed the missing ships, the damage suffered and all he lacked. He pointed out the deficiencies of the *urcas*. In addition many on board had fallen sick due to the putrid food. Given the state of the Armada and the fact that the Duke of Parma was only able to raise an insufficient force, he proposed that the King discontinue the enterprise and offer honourable terms to the English. This despairing *cri de coeur* from his most senior commander must have been a major shock for Philip. However, he was having none of this despondency. He replied immediately and firmly, rejecting the Duke's misgivings. He accepted that bringing these matters to his attention arose solely from Medina Sidonia's 'ardour to serve me and a wish to succeed in your command'. He told how the English forces were inferior, and concluded that the Duke was to continue with his mission. In a subsequent letter the King instructed Medina Sidonia to gather his forces: 'The men and stores are to be kept intact, by feeding the men on fresh provisions. The ships are to be united in Corunna, or, at least, so many of them that those missing shall not be of importance'. The King, always able to focus on minutiae, dismissed Medina Sidonia's complaint about ships: the *urcas* frequently sailed to England and were perfectly capa-

ble of navigating the English Channel. Finally, he ordered Medina Sidonia to get into a state of readiness to sail no later than 12 July.

Medina Sidonia now assigned Diego Flóres de Valdés, commander of the Squadron of Castile to serve on board his flagship as his senior naval advisor. Philip had doubts about Flóres de Valdés, who had more experience of convoys than of battle. He let the appointment stand, but as a counterbalance, the King assigned Don Francisco Arias de Bobadilla (commander of the land army) to be military advisor. Brother-in-law of Alonso Martínez de Leyva and aged 50 years, he had earned a reputation for being one of the most prestigious of the *Maestres de Campo.* He had commanded *tercios* (units of around 3,000 soldiers) during the Flanders campaigns of the Duke of Alba. He had fought with such valour in the siege of Mons in 1572 that Alba assigned de Bobadilla to personally carry the news of the victory to Philip II. After further service under Parma he had distinguished himself, holding high command in the Portugal and Terceira campaigns.

In Corunna, recovery and recuperation proceeded apace. *Pataches* were sent out to scout for stragglers and slowly the missing ships from other ports appeared and rejoined the fleet. There was much to be done after the pounding off the Portuguese coast: replacing missing masts and cordage, as well as caulking leaking vessels. The rudder of the galleass *Girona* required strengthening, a perennial Achilles heel of that type of vessel. The north of Spain was scoured for supplies and the fleet was revictualed. Hundreds of additional soldiers were distributed among the various commands. It was a triumph of logistics: the authorities in Corunna and its hinterland responded promptly to the unexpected challenge of repairing ships and providing supplies and men for an enormous fleet. It showed that Philip's *dirigiste* sys-

Above: the Torre de Hercules (originally Roman) at Corunna, with the great harbour in the background. On 19 June 1588, Medina Sidonia, with the Armada beset by shortages and battered by storms, was forced to sail for the port. Much repair and revictualling later, the fleet was able to depart on 22 July. Before it left, tents were set up on the island of San Antón in the harbour and more than 8,000 men of the Armada confessed there and received communion.

tem could function well when put to the test. The health of the Armada soldiers and sailors had improved due to the provision of fresh food, as well as the establishment of a hospital in the port. Spiritual health was not forgotten: the Duke ordered the setting up of tents and altars on the island of San Antón in the harbour – more than 8,000 men confessed there and received communion from the priests who accompanied the Armada. On 19 July, as the fleet came close to readiness, the Duke assembled his senior officers for a council of war. As well as other senior officers, most of the squadron leaders were there (but not those of the *urcas*, *pataches* or galleys, who were further down the pecking order of the Armada command). After a discussion of the weather, all voted to leave on the next suitable tide. At dawn on Friday 22 July, the fleet weighed anchor, trumpets sounding and banners flying. And so, with some minor readjustments to the fleet since Lisbon, 128 ships of the Armada, great and small, with those on board amounting to almost 28,600 souls, set off on the great Enterprise of England. Favourable winds allowed the fleet to make good headway, and on 25 July the Duke sent a fast *patache* (commanded by Don Rodrigo Tello) to advise Parma of their progress.

However, two days before, the squadron of galleys, displaying their Mediterranean pedigree, had begun to show that they were unsuitable for the conditions of the Bay of Biscay. On 23 July the galley *Diana* fired a cannon and sent a message via a *patache* to the squadron commander, Diego de Medrano (on board his flagship galley, thought to have been called the *La Esphera*) that having lost its caulking due to the force of the waves, it was taking in water As it was still close to the north coast of Spain, it headed for shelter and managed to reach Viveiro. Like all the galleys and galleasses, it was manned by rowers (in this case, 169 convicts and 24 slaves). On 25 July, the feast day of Santiago (St James), the rowers took advantage of the fact that the captain was attending Mass – they mutinied with the intention of taking over the vessel and sailing to France. The revolt was soon put down and the ringleader killed.

Below: a depiction in the Trachtenbuch of Christoph Weiditz of a slave rower carrying barrels of water on board a Spanish vessel. Normal manning for a galleass was around 275 rowers (made up of convicts, slaves and voluntary, or paid rowers). A galley had around 200 rowers.

Back at the main fleet, on 26 July Diego de Medrano reported to Medina Sidonia on the absence of the *Diana* and added that he considered the sea too rough for the three remaining galleys – if the weather forced him, he would have to head for France. The Duke ordered him to do his best to stay with the fleet and assigned two *pataches* to assist with communications. The weather got worse and by 10 a.m. on the 27th, with the storm intensifying, the three galleys (accompanied by the *patache Nuestra Senora de Gracia)* were forced to seek safe haven. At dawn of 28 July Medrano had lost sight of the *Princesa* and the captain of the *Bazana* informed him that with his vessel flooding, he had to head for land. Medrano decided to head for Spain, with the *Bazana* in tow. He dispatched the *patache* to search for the *Princesa,* which unsuccessful, returned the following day. A severe squall on 30 July separated the three vessels, and the *patache was* blown back to the northern Spanish coast. Medrano in his *La Esphera* sighted the south-western French coast at dawn the next day. They came across the *Bazana* which had run aground at a bar at the entrance to Bayonne harbour. Most of the crew had abandoned the ship. The rowers had then revolted and fled

– it is probable that one of these was the convict David Gwynn, who later showed up in Kerry in Ireland during the Armada events there, as we shall see in Chapter 5. The *La Esphera* continued upriver to dock in Bayonne harbour. The governor of the city tried to seize the vessel on behalf of the King of France. However, following negotiations, the flagship galley was released and reached Fuenterrabía in northern Spain. The last of the galleys, the *Princesa*, managed to secure shelter in a harbour in Brittany. After making repairs, it returned to Spain, arriving in Pasaia on 20 August.

Above: chains used to secure convict and slave rowers on galleys and galleasses. The entire squadron of four galleys, Mediterranean craft, had to retire from the Armada due to their unsuitability for the conditions in the Bay of Biscay. In the case of two of these vessels, there were mutinies by the rowers when they reached harbour.

In the afternoon of 26 July, the flagship of the Squadron of Vizcaya, the 798-ton *nao*, *Santa Ana* (not to be confused with the similarly-named but much larger flagship of the Squadron of Guipúzcoa), had become lost in fog. Separated from the fleet, bad weather forced the *Santa Ana* to seek shelter in the bay of La Hogue on the Cherbourg Peninsula. Continuing bad weather obliged the ship to transfer to the more sheltered harbour of Le Havre, where it remained for the duration of the Armada campaign. Luckily Juan Martínez de Recalde, commander of the squadron, who was to play a leading part in the Armada battles, was not aboard the flagship. (A postscript on the *Santa Ana*: in September 1588, four English warships sailed into Le Havre harbour, intending to destroy the Spanish ship, but they were driven off by shore batteries).

As weather conditions improved, news came that the galleass flagship, the *San Lorenzo*, had broken its rudder (the weak point of all galleasses). There was worse to come: as the visibility improved, Medina Sidonia, now around 400km south of the Scilly Isles, realised that he was missing 40 vessels. He launched a search operation, sending off *pataches*, including one assigned to scout out the Lizard Point, off Cornwall, the southernmost tip of England. As Friday 29 July dawned, clear and bright, at last there was some good news – the *pataches* had located the missing ships. However, the galleys and the *Santa Ana* remained a lost cause. In addition, the stragglers hadn't sustained any significant storm damage, and repairs had been completed on the *San Lorenzo*. The following day, the Armada, under full sail, got its first sight of enemy shores: Lizard Point. The Duke was filled with optimism and, thankful to God, ordered the firing of three cannon and the raising of a banner emblazoned with images of a crucifix, Our Lady and Mary Magdalene.

It was time for a council of war. When the senior commanders had assembled, Alonso Martínez de Leyva (supported by Juan Martínez de Recalde) proposed that they attack the port of Plymouth, around 50km distant. The western arm of the English fleet was anchored there: a foray by 20 galleons would provide an opportunity to sink them at their moorings. Medina Sidonia calmly rebutted the proposal. It was contrary to the King's orders which were strictly to proceed to rendezvous with Parma and not to be diverted by an improvised attack on a southern English port. Furthermore, the port entrance was narrow and well defended by coastal batteries. (There also was a lack of up-to-date intelligence – the fact that Howard's fleet had joined Drake's in the port was unknown to them). After more discussion, the assembled council voted unanimously to continue onwards.

Right: the difficult journey of the Armada, from Lisbon to the English Channel.

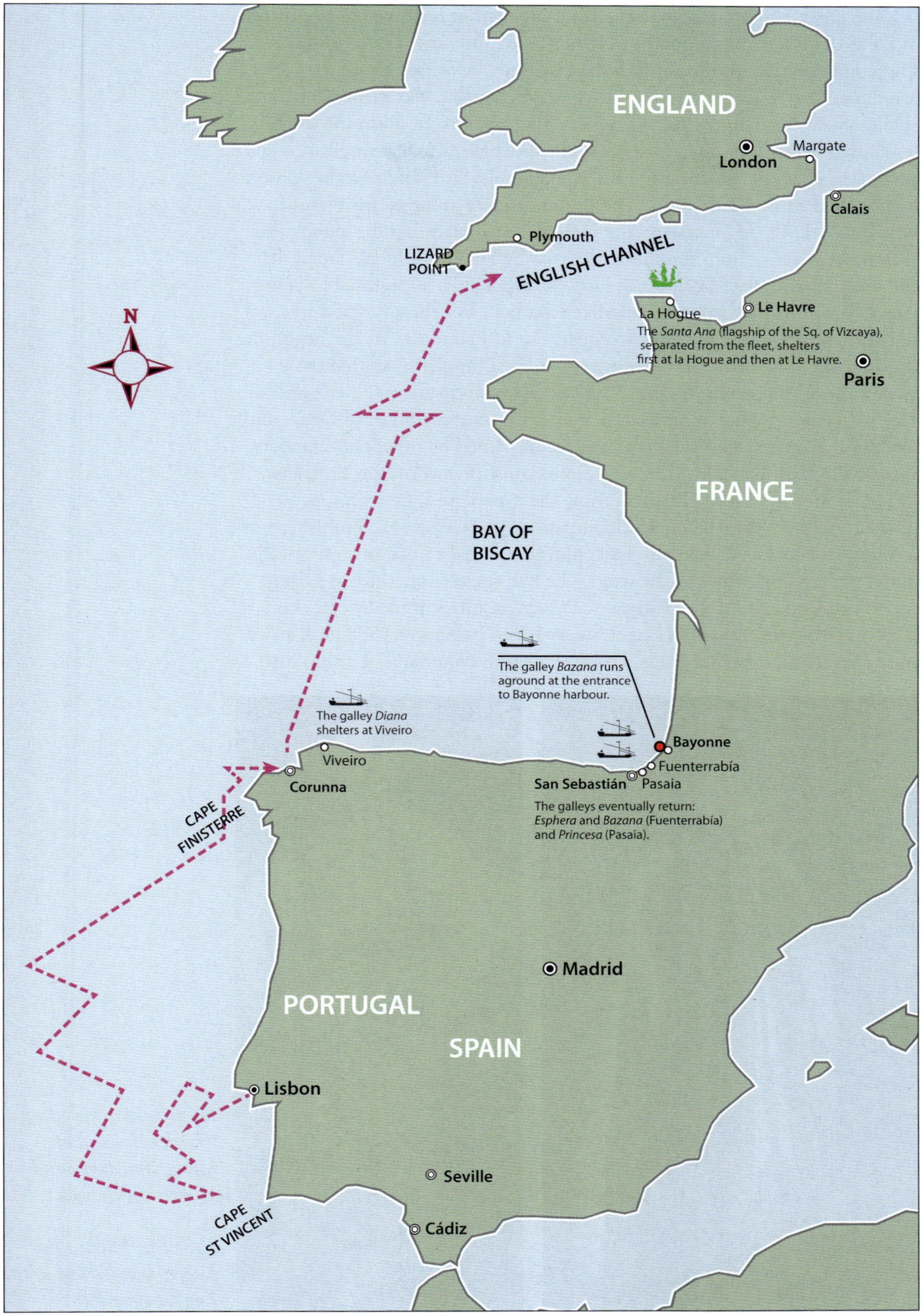
ENGLAND
London
Margate
Calais
Plymouth
LIZARD POINT
ENGLISH CHANNEL
La Hogue
Le Havre
The Santa Ana (flagship of the Sq. of Vizcaya), separated from the fleet, shelters first at la Hogue and then at Le Havre.
Paris
N
FRANCE
BAY OF BISCAY
The galley Bazana runs aground at the entrance to Bayonne harbour.
The galley Diana shelters at Viveiro
Viveiro
Corunna
Bayonne
Fuenterrabía
Pasaia
San Sebastián
The galleys eventually return: Esphera and Bazana (Fuenterrabía) and Princesa (Pasaia).
CAPE FINISTERRE
Madrid
PORTUGAL
SPAIN
Lisbon
Seville
Cádiz
CAPE ST VINCENT

The Duke sent a message to the King saying that he intended to proceed as far as the Isle of Wight, and to shelter there until news came from the Duke of Parma. With the constant bad weather, he fretted about the lack of a suitable deep-water port along the coast of Flanders, where the fleet could shelter given the danger that 'our vessels might be driven on to the shoals'.

Earlier in the year, there had been much debate amongst English naval commanders about the intentions of the Spanish. Sir Francis Drake, who by now had garnered an almost mythical notoriety amongst the Spanish, who dubbed him *El Draque* or 'the Dragon', predicted that the enemy fleet was likely to arrive from the south and pass by Portsmouth. He urged that the main English fleet be based as far west as possible, as opposed to being concentrated further along the English Channel. In February 1588 he led a flotilla, which became the western squadron, to Plymouth. At the beginning of June, the Lord Admiral, Charles Howard of Effingham, arrived there with most of the remaining fleet – all save a small squadron under Lord Henry Seymour which remained on guard, cruising the Strait of Dover and along the Flanders coast. Howard was accompanied by other commanders, principally John Hawkins (Drake's second cousin), and Martin Frobisher. We have already seen in Chapter 2 how the experienced Hawkins, as Treasurer of the Navy, had helped reorganise the Navy Royal. Frobisher was a rough-hewed adventurer who had enjoyed a varied career, metaphorically and literally sailing close to the wind – he had spent some time in prison. His expedition to find the Northwest Passage resulted in the legend about a returning ship that was wrecked at Smerwick in Ireland in 1578 and, as we have seen, two years afterwards, Frobisher was in command of a ship dur-

Far left: Lord Admiral, Charles Howard of Effingham, commander of the English fleet.

Near left: Martin Frobisher, who led one of the English squadrons.

ing the bloody siege there. He had served as second-in-command to Drake during the wide-ranging expedition against Spain and its colonies in the Americas in 1585. Frobisher subsequently harboured a dislike for Drake, resenting his arrogant manner.

Just after his arrival at Plymouth, on 2 June, Lord Admiral Howard elevated Drake to the rank of Vice-Admiral. The fleet, now at anchor in the port, was the characteristic mix of Crown-owned and private ships: it was made up of a core of Elizabeth's larger warships, with the addition of a multitude of smaller armed merchantmen, hired to act as ships of war. Bad weather (the same that had dispersed the Armada sailing from Lisbon) kept the fleet in Plymouth, with Drake straining at the leash to do what he had done before, head south, dart into a Spanish harbour and smite the enemy. Elizabeth, by contrast, preferred to have her navy on standby, ready to rapidly move to whatever point the Armada might be sighted at off the English coast. Victualling the English fleet proved a problem, and at the beginning of July Howard was warning that men had fallen sick and thousands wanted to leave the service. However, just in time, supply vessels sailed into harbour. As news came back of sightings of Spanish ships and that the Armada had put in at Corunna, the Queen reluctantly agreed that an expedition could set forth to forestall the Spanish.

Howard sailed out with a fleet of over 90 ships and headed south. The weather turned inclement and a southerly wind pushed them back. Conscious that the same wind could be propelling the Armada onwards to England, they decided to turn back. Five days later on 22 July, they arrived in Plymouth Sound (just as the Armada was setting out from Corunna). While the royal ships had survived the bad weather and were generally in good shape, the private merchantmen had suffered badly and needed caulking, cordage and spars. As normal in the Tudor navy, always dependent on minimal state funds, food on board had been in short supply during the recent foray and crews were put on short rations. Sickness broke out in some ships and anyone with a contagious disease was now placed ashore.

The Armada is sighted

On the afternoon of 29 July, the tiny 50-ton scout *Golden Hind* raced into Plymouth with the news of sighting the Armada near the Scilly Isles. The legend of Drake and his uninterrupted game of bowls supposedly occurred at this moment: the story featured in a biography of Walter Raleigh written in 1730 and is false, but it helps reinforce the English self-image of *sang-froid*. In any case, the English fleet made its preparations but there was little wind and they were unable to get underway immediately. That evening they employed the only way to get out of harbour on an ebb tide, using the awkward manoeuvre of warping (using a small boat to drop an anchor forward and pulling on the cable). Much hard effort later, they succeeded and by the next morning, most of the larger ships had made it to the shelter of Rame Head, around 10km southwest of the harbour.

On Saturday 30 July, the Armada was now sailing north-eastwards along the Cornwall coast. As the forest of sails came into view, the coast-watchers in Cornwall, on the nearest headland, lit the first beacon. Immediately

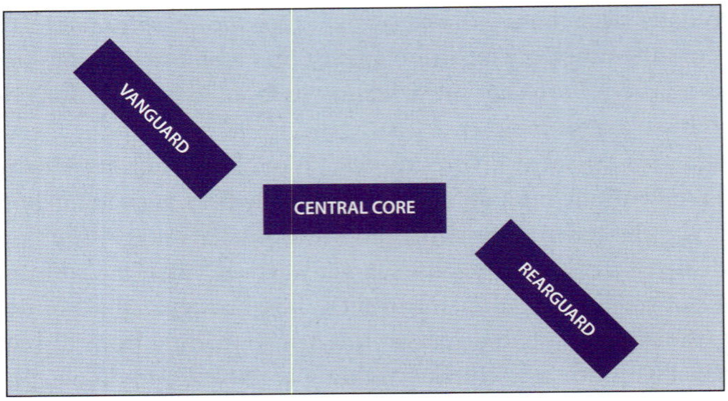

The final battle formation for the Armada, as ordered by Medina Sidonia at the beginning of the Channel battles, was based on Spanish naval doctrine for combat in the Atlantic. (The plan is as elaborated by the historian Antonio Luis Gómez Beltran in his book 'La Invencible y su Leyenda Negra').
This was a flexible formation, ready to adapt to whatever challenges the enemy presented.
In one of the early battles along the Channel, in the course of combat, the shape had temporarily altered to a pincer shape and it looked like a crescent. In the aftermath of the battles, Lord Admiral Howard commissioned a series of tapestries to tell his version of the events, which were subsequently installed in the English House of Lords. Howard incorrectly assumed that the Armada had always been in a crescent formation. Hence this misapprehension featured in these tapestries and in the subsequent engravings made by John Pine in 1739.

the chain of beacons flared, in turn, along the south coast and then to the north, signalling: 'the Spanish fleet are on the sea!'. Late that night, a fishing smack from Falmouth was captured by a Spanish *patache*. The crew of four were later interrogated by an English-speaking officer, revealing news that the English fleet had left Plymouth earlier under the command of Howard and Drake and the ships were standing out to sea.

The First Battle

Next morning, Sunday 31 July, with the wind to the west-north-west, the English fleet was sighted. By now Howard was well clear of Plymouth Harbour with all ships and had divided his fleet of over 100 vessels into two, with the intention that they would gain position windward of the Armada. Howard had led the main force of around 80 ships to pass south in front of the Armada, and then to turn west. The other smaller squadron under Drake had later sailed west, hugging the coast and to the north of the Spanish fleet. The English had by now managed to gain the weather gauge, the advantageous position relative to the Armada.

With the enemy in sight, the Duke of Medina Sidonia ordered the hoisting of the royal standard in his flagship, the *San Martín*. In practised and disciplined manner, the Armada took up its battle formation, each ship slacking or making sail to manoeuvre into place. Essentially an armed convoy, this was an impressive sight, the might of Spain now spread out into distinctive sections. In the centre core, or *batalla*, were the front-line ships, the squadrons of Portugal and Castile, all directed by Medina Sidonia. On the left wing, the four advance ships of the vanguard were led by Alonso de Leyva. The rearguard (on the right wing) was under the control of Juan Martínez de Recalde. A galleass was posted to each wing, leaving two to be assigned as necessary. All these fighting elements formed a protective cordon around the vessels in the middle, the *pataches, zabras* and wallowing *urcas*.

Battle was commenced by Lord Admiral Howard. With his ships now holding the advantageous windward position, in an echo of ancient knightly contest, he sent his personal barque, the 80-ton *Disdain*, to make a symbolic challenge to the Spanish. Impudently, it fired a shot into the massed array, and then retired. Just after 9 a.m., the action began when Howard (in the *Ark Royal*) led his ships in a pack from the southwest, following the wind. Medina Sidonia had ordered his ships to turn around, and they were now roughly in a westerly direction, facing the wind. The English ships began the attack trading shots with their enemy at a distance, commencing with the Spanish vanguard, on the left wing, led by de Leyva (on the landward side). They pressed on with their assault, to reach de Recalde's right wing, on the seaward side. In this and all the following engagements, unlike the Spanish, the English ships did not manifest any tactical doctrine, and in effect made it up as they went along. They sailed past the Spanish ranks, blasting away as an enemy ship came into sight. The right wing now also came under attack by Drake (in the *Revenge*) and the following ships to the north. De Recalde in his *San Juan de Portugal*, and the vice-flagship, the *Gran Grín*, took the brunt of the fire.

The *San Juan de Portugal* became separated and the English ships came closer. De Recalde shortened sail to close, intending to use the favoured Spanish tactic, that of grappling and then boarding the enemy. However the English held their distance and at around 300m bombarded the *San Juan* with their guns. Observing this, the other Spanish galleons decided to come to the rescue. As they turned, the wind was against them and they too had to shorten sail but in due course managed to relieve the pressure on de Recalde. The action continued until around one in the afternoon when the English suddenly withdrew. De Recalde's ship had sustained the pounding of eight English ships for hours and suffered 20 casualties. The foremast was pierced by a shot and the rigging was damaged. Nevertheless, the ship was still sound, demonstrating that Spanish (and Portuguese) galleons were of solid construction and could sustain a lot of cannon fire. It was an inconclusive but instructive engagement for both fleets, each side now better able to understand the characteristics of the enemy that faced them.

In the mid-afternoon two serious accidents occurred. One was when, as the ships were manoeuvring to reform their battle formation, the vast flagship of the Andalucian Squadron, the 1,150-ton *nao*, *Nuestra Señora del Rosario*, one of the most powerful ships in the Armada and under the command of Pedro de Valdés, collided with a *nao* of the Vizcayan Squadron. The collision damaged the bowsprit of the *Nuestra Señora del Rosario*. Sometime later, in a separate incident, a Spanish ship blew up. There was an explosion in the gunpowder stored in barrels in the *San Salvador* (vice-flagship of the Guipúzcoan Squadron), a large *nao* of 958 tons, which had the important role of transporting the paymaster of the Armada, Juan de Huerta. In addition to being a payship, the vessel had been carrying munitions. The explosion of such large quantities of gunpowder destroyed much of the sterncastle and aft upper decks, and hundreds were killed. There has been much speculation as to the cause, including a story that a disgruntled Flemish gunner on board had deliberately set a line of powder to the magazine, ignited it and jumped into the sea. Medina Sidonia in the *San Martín* sailed up to supervise the rescue, ordering *pataches* and *zabras* to close in to aid the burning ship. Survivors were rescued, many with severe burns. As the fires were extinguished, supplies and most of the treasure aboard were taken off along with the paymaster, de Huerta. The wrecked *San Salvador* was put in tow by two galleasses.

Meanwhile, the *Nuestra Señora del Rosario*, which had lost steerage, collided with another ship, further breaking the bowsprit and damaging

Above: one of a series of engravings made by John Pine in 1739 of the House of Lords Armada tapestries. It depicts the opposing fleets at the beginning of the Channel engagements. It erroneously shows the Armada in a crescent formation. The 'San Salvador' is portrayed exploding in the lower foreground.

the foremast sail. While this was being repaired, amidst the rough seas, the foremast crashed down, falling on the mainmast which collapsed. Coming to the rescue once again, the *San Martín* drew close and took the stricken vessel in tow. However, in the increasing wind and rising sea, the towline parted. The weather continued to worsen and Medina Sidonia pondered on how to help the ship, now lagging behind the fleet. The Duke's naval advisor Diego Flóres de Valdés (with no love lost for his cousin, the commander of the *Nuestra Señora del Rosario*, Pedro de Valdés) noted that the fleet was dispersed far ahead in danger of losing its formation, and that the enemy fleet was close by. As he did not want to lose sight of the main Armada, Diego Flóres urged the Duke not to stop, but to let the stricken ship fall behind. As darkness fell, Medina Sidonia took the painful decision to abandon the *Nuestra Señora del Rosario*. Two *pataches* were sent to the stricken ship, but Pedro de Valdés refused to abandon his vessel. As the *San Martín* departed to resume its position at the front of the Armada, the Duke left Agustín de Ojeda, in his small flagship, along with some *pataches*, to shepherd the *Nuestra Señora del Rosario*. However, in the choppy seas the auxiliary vessels failed to secure the stricken ship or evacuate the crew. The decision by Medina Sidonia to leave the *Nuestra Señora del Rosario* behind was the correct tactical choice, but it dampened morale amongst the men of the Armada.

As night fell and with his fleet standing off, Lord Admiral Howard held a council of war on the *Ark Royal*. He puzzled over the real intentions of the Spanish: he still did not know the enemy plan, whether it was to attempt to capture a port, or make an attempt to land. He decided to continue to windward, and follow the Armada, keeping a close eye on the enemy . He assigned Sir Francis Drake to lead the fleet and instructed him to light the large poop lantern as a guide through the darkness. Howard sent a dispatch to Walsingham, telling how 'we gave them fight' and of the bravery of his captains. He added a strong plea for more shot and powder.

Right: a highly romanticised and inaccurate nineteenth-century depiction of Don Pedro de Valdés on board his 'Nuestra Señora del Rosario', surrendering to Sir Francis Drake. In reality de Valdés capitulated after coming aboard the 'Revenge'.

While the main English fleet trailed the Armada, the small privateer *Margaret and John* came upon the *Nuestra Señora del Rosario* late in the evening. It was showing neither illumination nor any indication of life. Sniffing a prize, the 200-ton privateer edged closer. Those on board later claimed that they had seen off the escorting *pataches*. Impudently, the English fired off muskets at the stern of the *Nuestra Señora del Rosario*, nearly six times its size. Two large cannons responded and the *Margaret and John* wisely stood off. Around midnight, it left to rejoin the main fleet, which was still shadowing the Armada.

As the English fleet ploughed onwards, Lord Admiral Howard, in the *Ark Royal*, continued to follow the light that he assumed was of Drake's ship. He steadily closed the distance, until at dawn, he saw that the lantern light was that of a Spanish ship, and realised that he was almost within the enemy formation. There was no trace of Drake's ship. Howard fell back to create some distance from the Armada, as it continued its stately progress eastwards, parallel with the English coast.

Drake and his Prize

The next day, Monday 1 August, Drake, in the *Revenge*, rejoined the fleet, which, lacking a directional point in the darkness, had fallen into slight disarray as dawn broke. The wily sea fox had a complex tale to tell. He recounted that on the previous night he was sailing along, accompanied by the 300-ton privateer *Roebuck* and two pinnaces. He spotted some unknown sails in the darkness and fearing that it was a Spanish manoeuvre, he extinguished his lantern and went to investigate. These turned out to be merely some German merchant vessels, so he headed back to reassume his position. As dawn broke, *mirabile dictu*, to his surprise, he came across the *Nuestra Señora del Rosario*, floundering helplessly. Those on board initially refused to surrender. However, after a parley on board the *Revenge*, Pedro de Valdés surrendered. Questions have been raised as to why de Valdés capitulated so easily without a fight, given that he had more guns and men than the *Revenge* and its accompanying privateer combined – one suggestion has

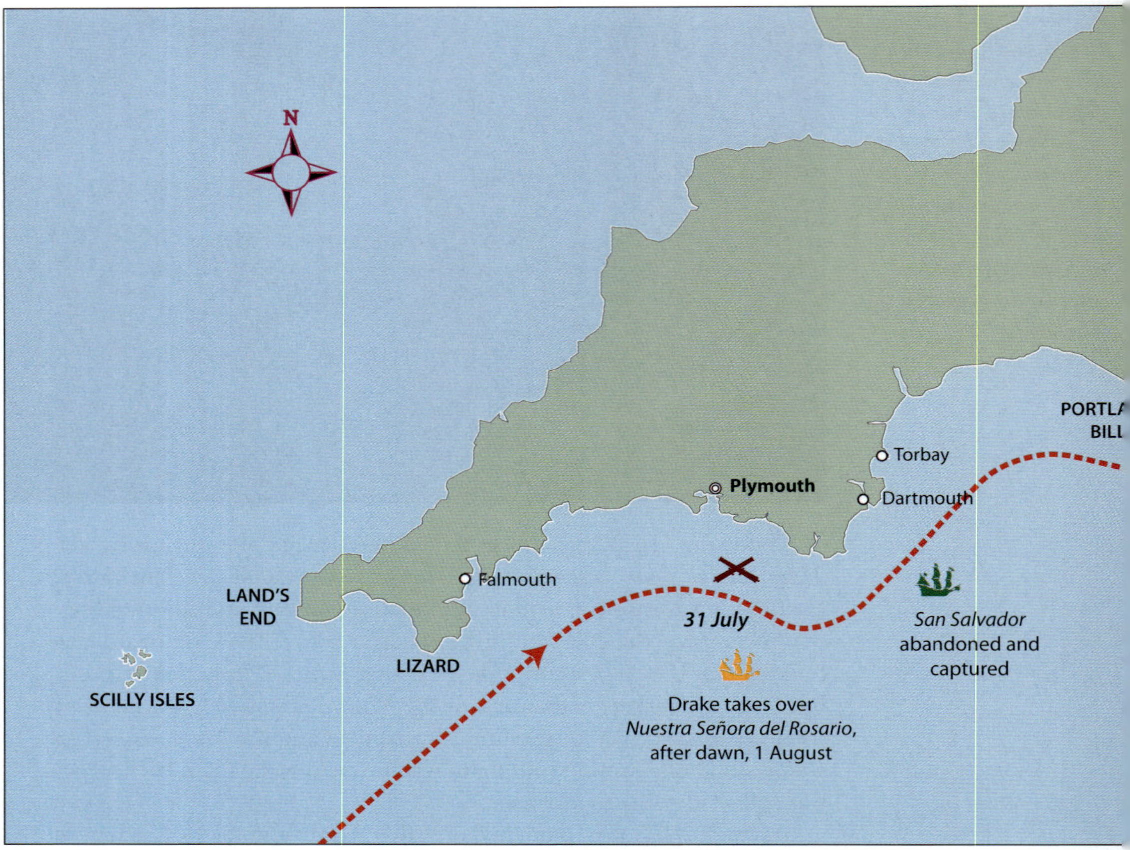

Above: the battles along the English Channel.

been that he, understandably was disgruntled at having been abandoned by the Armada. Avoiding what would be an appalling fate, five English Catholics out of the seven who had been sailing on board the *Rosario* had prudently slipped away by boat the previous night. As they searched the Spanish ship, Drake's men found a felicitous bonanza: as well as the 46 large cannons, copious quantities of powder and shot and the substantial personal jewellery of the ship's officers, there were 50,000 gold ducats on board, part of the general Armada funds. These were rapidly transferred in canvas sacks to the *Revenge.* In the event, less than half of this money reached Elizabeth's treasury and, unsurprisingly, historians name Drake as the prime suspect for the larceny. As he returned to his station, Drake brought de Valdés with him, to present to the Lord Admiral. The *Nuestra Señora del Rosario* was dispatched to Torbay as a prize, escorted by the *Roebuck*, where the ordinance, gunpowder and supplies were unloaded and the around 400 men on board were sent to captivity. The two ill-starred English Catholics still left on the *Nuestra Señora del Rosario* were dispatched to the Tower of London, to await torture and worse.

Strangely, Drake's story seems to have been accepted. The grave dereliction of duty, by dousing his lantern, leaving his assigned station and leaving the fleet directionless at a time of heightened conflict, appears to have been overlooked without any sanction from Lord Admiral Howard. Nevertheless,

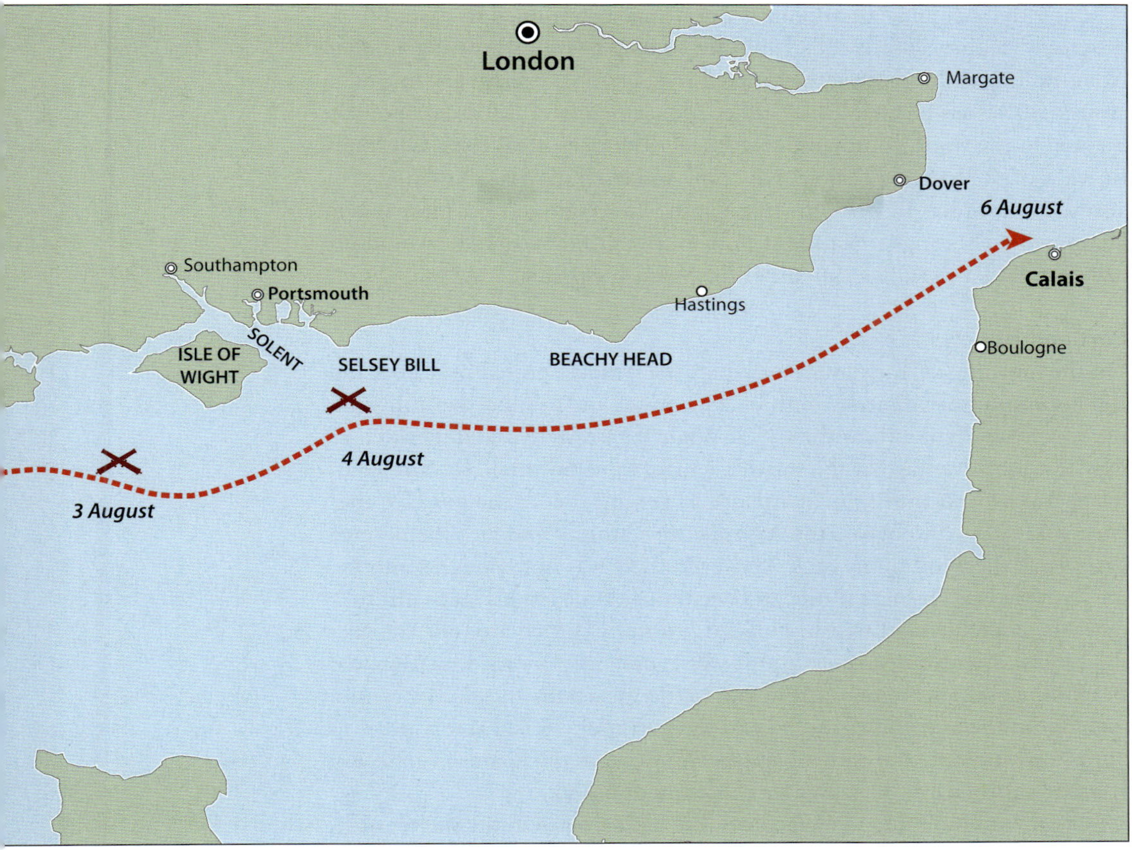

fellow commander and privateer, Martin Frobisher, who loathed Drake, was having none of this fanciful story. Knowing how a privateer would react, he accused Drake of having spotted the *Nuestra Señora del Rosario*, that he had trailed her all night, 'because he would have the spoil'. This incident reflected the disparity between the two navies: the tight command and control structure of Medina Sidonia within the Spanish navy and by contrast, the more adaptive and looser configuration of the English fleet, with its mix of Navy Royal and large numbers of privateers, for whom personal gain and seizing a prize were regarded as highly desirable.

The bad news continued for the Spanish that Monday: the *San Salvador*, severely damaged by the explosion the previous day, was in dire straits. As dead bodies lay among the splintered decks, it was taking on water, too much for the pumps. Medina Sidonia ordered that the survivors abandon ship and that the wreck be cast off. Later on, the English fleet came upon the wallowing wreck. The Lord Admiral ordered Lord Thomas Howard (his cousin) in *Lion* and John Hawkins in *Victory* to secure the *San Salvador*. The captains went on board to inspect but the stench of the corpses was too much and they promptly withdrew. The burnt hulk was dispatched under tow to Weymouth, where the hugely welcome powder and shot were taken off and later shipped out to the English fleet.

Later that Monday afternoon, as the Armada continued its easterly progress, Medina Sidonia called another council of war. Expecting an attack from the English to the rear, he ordered that a stronger rearguard line of around 40 vessels be established under Alonso de Leyva. Medina Sidonia remained in the front, commanding a smaller number of galleons. Ominously (in view of the hanging that actually took place ten days later) the Duke also sent out orders in writing: any captain whose ship left her place would be immediately hanged. Stating the obvious – Sir Francis Drake would not have survived a week as a captain of the Spanish Armada.

Portland Bill

On the morning of Tuesday 2 August, as the Armada passed near Portland Bill (a promontory directly south of Weymouth and around two-thirds of the way from Plymouth to the Isle of Wight), an easterly wind blew. Having now lost the advantage of the weather gauge, Lord Admiral Howard led his fleet north-northeast, in an attempt to get inshore, to the north of the enemy. He hoped to bypass the Armada, turn around and face them, once again with the wind to his back. However, there was not enough room as the Armada was too near shore, and Medina Sidonia led his ships out to meet the approaching English. Howard promptly turned around. While the English fleet headed south-south-west, some ships headed by Martín de Bertendona set out to intercept it, and battle was commenced. The cannons roared out, the arquebuses rattled and the gunsmoke rolled across the sea as both sides attempted to gain advantage. Sometimes the Spanish came close, attempting to board, but never succeeded in doing so.

Another, more minor, engagement was taking place in the shelter of Portland Bill. Martin Frobisher's 988-ton *Triumph* (the largest ship in the English fleet), with the wind calmed, had anchored there. The galleass squadron darted to intercept what seemed to be a tempting target. However, between the galleasses and the *Triumph*, which was accompanied by five medium-sized ships, lay the treacherous Shambles, a shallow sandbank with a strong tidal race. The tide was going out and the four galleasses struggled to get into position as the strong current began to rage. In an exchange of fire, the galleasses managed to damage the rudder of the *Triumph*. Then, as the wind rose, the *Triumph's* boats managed to tow her out of danger.

Medina Sidonia now saw that de Recalde (who had just completed repairs to his *San Juan de Portugal*) had become isolated and the enemy ships were heading to the attack. The Duke set out to the rescue, and was spotted by Lord Admiral Howard, who called his ships to follow him. The *San Martín* now had to endure the calvary of heavy and sustained fire. Howard's *Ark Royal* let off a broadside as it passed by, followed by the rest of his ships, arrayed in a flock. No end was in sight, as the English turned around and repeated the process. For over an hour the *San Martín* sustained repeated pounding by English cannonballs. Its resilience is not just a tribute to Medina Sidonia and his officers, but also to the inherent design of the galleon. The beleaguered galleon replied strongly with its guns, and the English ships increased their distance from what was proving to be a tough and dangerous

Right: a detail from 'The Spanish Armada sails off the English coast', by the Dutch painter Cornelis Claesz van Wieringen.

foe. Eventually a group of Spanish galleons came to the rescue and the day's battle ended.

Isle of Wight

On the morning of Wednesday 3 August, as the Armada continued eastwards, it became apparent that one of the Spanish ships on the southern flank had lost formation. It was the 650-ton *Gran Grifón* (from Rostock, flagship of the Squadron of *Urcas*), under the command of Juan Gómez de Medina. It had been difficult for the unwieldy *urca* to keep its position. The laggard was soon spotted by English ships, which put on sail to intercept it. As the *Gran Grifón* with its blunt prow attempted to regain station, the English ships, led by Drake in the *Revenge*, passed close by, unleashing a broadside at close range. The *Gran Grifón* responded doggedly with salvos from its 38 guns (most were of low calibre, characteristic armament of a merchant ship, but she had been provisioned at Lisbon with four medium bronze culverins, effective in battle). The ship was pounded repeatedly, suffering casualties and, according to Gómez de Medina, was hit by 20 cannonballs. Medina Sidonia set out in the *San Martín* and ordered assistance: the galleass squadron, followed by de Recalde in the *San Juan de Portugal,* also came to the rescue. Amidst a fierce exchange of fire a galleass secured a hit on one of the English ships, possibly the *Revenge*, and damaged its spars. By midday, after several hours of gunfire, the battle came to an end. The *Gran Grifón* reached the safety of the Spanish formation, towed by a galleass. As the wind dropped the English fleet drew back and maintained their distance and the Armada drifted eastwards in the current. As it reached just south of the Isle of Wight, the designated destination near Margate lay approximately 250km to the east, several days' sail away.

In the aftermath of these exchanges, the English ships, whose artillery tactic was to blast at will, were running out of munitions and several pinnaces were sent off to get more powder and shot. They returned with new supplies from the nearby home ports. However, there was still barely enough due to the all-prevailing low stocks of naval supplies – the powder taken off the recently captured *Nuestra Señora del Rosario* and *San Salvador* proved fortuitous. Lord Admiral Howard called a council of war that Wednesday evening. As he took stock of the situation, matters became clearer. He now had a better idea of his opponents: he knew their formation and tactics, as well as the numbers and types of ships making up the Armada, which had by now sailed along half the southern English coast. Thus he was able to discount the danger of landings at the ports it had passed. As noted, his fleet was now short of munitions. Recognising the discipline of the Spanish ships within their tripartite formation, in the face of the scattered attack by English ships, Howard decided to tighten up command. His fleet was redistributed into four equal squadrons, each commanded by himself, Drake, Hawkins and Frobisher.

Past the Solent

Like a pack of lions or hyenas, tracking a herd of wildebeest on the lookout for stragglers, the English kept a watchful eye on the Armada. As dawn broke on Thursday 4 August the 900-ton *urca*, *Duquesa Santa Ana* (of the Andalucian Squadron) and the 830-ton galleon *San Luis* (of the Portuguese Squadron) fell astern. One suggestion has been that it was a trap: that Medina Sidonia had prearranged this, positioning the stragglers as bait and arranging for de Recalde and de Leyva and their ships to be on the alert. As the wind had died down, John Hawkins and his squadron, who were nearest, lowered their ships' boats to row them closer to the laggard vessels. In turn, three galleasses were dispatched to the attack, towing de Leyva, in his 820-ton *nao*, *La Rata*. With their concentrated rowing power, the galleasses could now come into their own when there was little wind. As the English guns opened up, they inflicted superficial damage on the galleasses. Nevertheless, these were able to tow the two stragglers away from the swarm of attackers and back to the Armada formation. A south-westerly breeze blew the jumble of ships eastwards.

As the Armada slowly sailed towards the eastern approach to the Solent (the sheltered strait between the Isle of Wight and the English mainland), Lord Admiral Howard was keenly aware of the danger that the Spanish would stop there – in the previous day's council of war he had made it clear that his ships would have to prevent the Spanish from entering the Solent or trying to land. Later on that Thursday morning as the Armada approached, Martin Frobisher and his squadron positioned themselves to the east of the Isle of Wight, close to shore. Medina Sidonia in the *San Martín*, headed out, leading his ships to meet the opposing squadron. The English ships began to engage with the *San Martín*, which had now become separated and was beginning to sustain heavy fire. Other galleons soon rallied to their Captain General's assistance and provided a shield. Most of the English ships managed to slip away as the Spanish appeared. However, as the Spanish bore down, Frobisher in his *Triumph* was caught, becalmed to leeward. He ordered his boats to tow him away from danger and others from his squadron came to his aid. Soon the longboats had the *Triumph* in tow and next it was able to hoist its sails, catch the wind and escape from danger. In the meantime there was a sudden attack on the other flank of the Armada, to seaward. Medina Sidonia fired a signal gun for the Armada to regroup. As evening fell he sent off a dispatch to Parma, informing him that he had been off the Isle of Wight. He added: 'I expect to be on the Flemish coast very soon'. The battles had continued 'from dawn to dark' and he had tried unsuccessfully to induce the enemy fleet to come close and grapple. As his stores were running short, he asked Parma to at once send ships with a great quantity of powder and ball. The following day, in another message to Parma, asked for the dispatch 40 or 50 flyboats.

At the council of war held earlier, on 29 July, as Medina Sidonia had informed the King, he had intended to travel as far as the Isle of Wight and make a decision, if he had no word from Parma, whether to secure an anchorage there. The Duke indeed had not heard any fresh news from Parma. His decision then, to sail on was most likely driven by the King's overriding imperative to make haste and join with Parma. De Recalde who, in his *San Juan de Portugal*, had been active during the engagement with Frobisher, later wrote how bitterly disappointed he was to have been recalled by the signal gun, and also complained (it must be remembered, with the benefit of hindsight) about the decision to sail on. He continued: 'Nor was it wise to sail with our fleet beyond that anchorage … near to the Isle of Wight, until we heard from the Prince of Parma, because it was the best anchorage in the whole Channel for every eventuality'.

Right: one of the charts of the Armada battles made in 1590 by Augustine Ryther (after Robert Adams) in his 'Expeditionis Hispanorum in Angliam'. These accompanied a brief history of the events by Petruccio Ubaldini, based on Lord Admiral Howard's own account. Here, we see the formations during the relatively uneventful voyage to Calais on 4-6 August – again the Armada is erroneously shown as a crescent. The English fleet has now been formed into four squadrons.

Sailing East

The next two days were a period of relative peace. The Spanish continued their steady easterly progress, with the English maintaining a watchful distance. Not having had a lot of supplies to start with, and after their high rate of fire, the English ships were once again short of powder and shot. Howard decided to conserve this, as his battle diary noted 'it was not good ... to assail them any more until their coming near unto Dover ... and in the meantime, better store of munition might be provided from the shore'. On Friday 5 August, the wind died down. In the calm, small vessels shuttled to the English fleet with munitions. Minor repairs were also made. The tranquil period gave Lord Admiral Howard time to knight Martin Frobisher, John Hawkins and several other commanders. For Howard the knighting ceremony reflected an element of, 'so far so good' and he could take comfort in knowing that the Spanish were now unlikely to attempt a landing on England's south coast.

To Calais

As dawn broke on Saturday 6 August the Armada was approaching the entrance to the Dover Strait, only 35km in width. At around 10 a.m., Boulogne was sighted and they turned north-east, sailing past the offshore shoals and the low coastline towards Calais. In the late afternoon, they arrived at the Calais Roads and dropped anchor, around 6km off the port. In a council of war, opinion was generally in favour of moving on, but the pilots warned the Duke about the danger that, further on, the currents would force the Armada into the North Sea. Given that the exposed anchorage at Calais was the least worst mooring that Medina Sidonia could find while he awaited news of the elusive rendezvous with Parma, he decided to remain there. At the same time, their watchful foes stood off, anchored in view of the cliffs of Calais, just out of long-distance cannon range from the Armada.

In the meantime, the English fleet was being reinforced by the 35 ships of Lord Henry Seymour's squadron (increasing the total English strength to around 140 ships). Seymour had been on station, patrolling the Dover Strait and the Flanders coast, keeping a lookout for Parma's army. Further up the coast, independently of the English (and harbouring some distrust of them), Lieutenant-admiral of Zeeland, Justin of Nassau, and his fleet of armed flyboats of the Dutch navy (most in the range 100 to 150 tons) had been on station, with the mission of bottling up Parma and his barges and preventing them from exiting the canals and harbours of Flanders – although it has been suggested that Justin and his navy of small ships, with the Armada galleons now over the horizon, had withdrawn to the mouth of the River Scheldt. In addition, all signs and markers providing help to navigate the channels along the Dutch coast, had been removed. In all of this the United Provinces had the very real incentive of knowing that if the Spanish subdued England, then Parma would be able to return and smite them with new energy and resources.

After dropping anchor, Medina Sidonia, now having arrived to within less than a day's sail from a possible rendezvous point, was in the impossible situation of not knowing precisely where, when or how this was to take place. He immediately sent a *patache* with a message to his fellow duke. His frustration was obvious, telling how he had constantly written '... giving information as to my whereabouts ... and not only have I received no reply to my letters but no acknowledgement of their receipt ...'. He explained his location and how the enemy fleet was on his flank 'and able to bombard me'. The Captain General once again requested Parma to send out his flyboats, adding, 'with this aid, I shall be able to resist the enemy's fleet until your Excellency can come out with the rest, and we can go together and take some port where this Armada may enter in safety'.

Over the second half of 1587, in anticipation of the planned invasion of England, Parma had moved most of his Army of Flanders close to the Flemish coast. By August 1588, there were 26,000 soldiers stationed around Nieuport and Dunkirk. His battle-hardened force was the best in Europe, however it was a land army. Parma's naval assets were limited, and he considered that he needed much more if he was to venture out across the Channel to England. The capture of Sluys in August 1587 and the construction of a canal allowed Parma's barges to travel to Dunkirk without having to venture into open sea. He had amassed a substantial fleet of unarmed canal barges. These amounted to 173 vessels of various types, arranged in three squadrons. Many were the *pleitas*, around 20m long and capable of transporting 200 men. These were shallow-bottomed, capable of transporting troops in fair weather. There was a shortage of mariners to crew these vessels, and some had been recruited from Denmark and Germany. However, these small craft would need to be defended. Parma had set in place a programme to build flyboats – small, shallow-draughted fast warships that would be able to counter those of the Dutch navy which had the task of blockading the harbours and inlets of Flanders.

The Dutch navy did not play a direct role in the attacks on the Armada. The reality was that they prudently stayed inshore in August 1588, avoiding contact with the Spanish galleons, which with their deep draught were unable to sail inshore to destroy these small ships. Parma had left his shipbuilding programme late. One source says that he had 32 shallow-draughted warships in Dunkirk and Sluys – with dozens more in (blockaded) Antwerp. Parma was a highly effective general of land forces, but with no experience of naval warfare. The Dutch navy, such as it was, had withdrawn to coastal waters. Medina Sidonia's *pataches* carrying dispatches seemed to have reached harbours in Flanders without apparent difficulty.

Below: a late-sixteenth-century view of Calais.

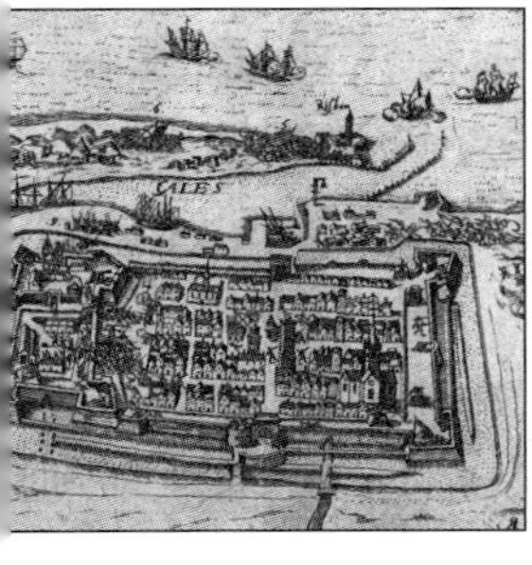

As Medina Sidonia and his ships lay moored at Calais Roads, the lack of a secure anchorage in the vicinity was obvious. Parma had possession of Dunkirk, but the larger ships of the Armada with their deep draught could only navigate to within several kilometres of that port. It was a sour memory that during the autumn of 1587 Philip had refused to allow Parma to continue with his project of capturing the deep-water port of Flushing, and instead ordered him to concentrate on preparing an army for the invasion of England.

One must understand the difficulty posed for Philip II in trying to direct the complicated three-dimensional panoply of the Enterprise of England from his tiny room in the Escorial, around 1,300km distant from where the invasion was to take place. Philip got many things right – he was able to effectively muster the resources of his vast empire in preparation for the Armada. However, despite having good knowledge of the Low Countries (having spent many years there) he neglected the last but essential detail. He did indeed instruct his galleons to beware of the shoals of Flanders, but missed out on how to solve the problem of the final few kilometres – how to get Parma's barges out of the Flanders inlets to deep water under the close protection of the Armada fleet. Another difficulty which complicated the Enterprise of England, particularly in view of Parma's tardiness in his final preparations, was the poor communications between the principal protagonists, the two dukes (particularly after the Armada had set out). Some of this was due to purely physical circumstances – the bad weather and the difficulties of dispatching small ships along long distances, particularly through stretches of waters patrolled by the enemy. Naturally, after the Armada arrived at Calais, their proximity resulted in quicker messaging. Late on Saturday evening, 6 August, a message arrived at Calais from Parma (written a mere three days before). The note informed Medina Sidonia that it would take until Friday 12 August before he, Parma, could sail out with his force. All the Captain General could do in reply was to ask Parma to hasten and come out, as the Calais anchorage was poor and the Armada could be swept away anytime by bad weather. He added: 'The general opinion is that it will be very unadvisable for the Armada to go beyond this place, as your Excellency may judge'. He reminded Parma how large were the Spanish ships – imparting the obvious fact that, with the largest galleons drawing over eight metres, there was no suitable deep-water anchorage along the Flanders coast available for the Armada.

Don Rodrigo Tello, who had brought Parma's message to Medina Sidonia, was not optimistic about the timescale presented by Parma. The vessels he saw at the embarkation ports of Dunkirk and Nieuport were unready: they had no masts or spars and stores were not loaded. Parma, who had been in Bruges, on hearing of the Armada at Calais, left on 8 August for Nieuport to order the embarkation to begin. The following day he headed to Dunkirk where he planned to go on board himself. Parma, who should have been in place much earlier, encountered a very unpromising situation: some canal barges were leaking and not suitable to sail across the strait. One wonders what would have happened if Medina Sidonia had, by some miracle, been assigned to the Netherlands by Philip six months before – and the Duke had been free to apply his project management expertise in supervising the preparations there for the invasion.

Parma's unreadiness

Back at Calais Roads, on the Sunday morning of 7 August, Medina Sidonia had to face the unpalatable truth about the poor readiness of Parma's army. Nevertheless he endeavoured to continue his mission, hoping against hope that Parma would be able to emerge from the Flanders embarkation ports. The Duke had sent a messenger requesting to see the Governor of Calais, the 79-year-old Giraud de Mauléon, seigneur of Gourdan (a Catholic, who had lost his leg during the capture of Calais from the English just 30 years before), to assure him of the Armada's friendly intentions. De Mauléon turned out to be remarkably hospitable, and sent his nephew with a present of refreshments to Medina Sidonia. A delegation was sent to buy supplies (the prices immediately multiplied) and over the Sunday the harbour hummed with activity as French boats ferried out fresh water and as much victuals as the Calais region could provide. However the Governor did not provide the munitions that had been requested.

De Mauléon reminded Medina Sidonia of the obvious – that the anchorage at Calais Roads with strong tidal currents, was dangerous. This exposed location certainly was not a place to linger for nearly a week awaiting Parma. The Duke sent Jorge Manrique, Inspector-General of the fleet, by road, to see Parma and to emphasise the Armada's perilous situation and ask him to provide a suitable port. As Parma later pointed out to the King in a letter of 10 August, 'I have always supposed that the Duke would have managed this [securing a port] as speedily as possible on his way up, and I am therefore not at all surprised at his anxiety, and his request that we here should go and help him to obtain a port'. He added that he would only emerge 'in fine settled weather, and with the Channel clear of enemies'. He claimed that his troops at Nieuport and Dunkirk had been practically ready to depart on the evening of 8 August. He continued: 'how badly informed the Duke must be as to the character of our small, weak boats, entirely unfit for fighting, or even to live in any heavy sea or high wind. The enemy's ships are, moreover, on this coast to prevent them from going out'.

A close call

The mere implied presence of the Dutch fleet had induced fear in Parma and ensured that the Dutch, without firing a shot, managed to kill off the crucial element of the Armada plan, that of sailing on to invade England. At this juncture, it is worth launching an armada of 'what ifs'. What if there had been a weather window and Parma (overcoming his temerity on maritime matters), with a experienced naval commander at his side, had ventured forth in accordance with established Spanish protective naval doctrine, with the aim of rendezvousing with Medina Sidonia's fleet, in position offshore?. What if he had sailed out of Dunkirk and Nieuport, under protection of his own armed flyboats, and possibly under the initial protection of his coastal artillery positioned at the harbour entrances?. If Medina Sidonia had assigned the shallower-draughted and well-gunned vessels, namely the galleasses, smaller galleons, *naos* and larger *pataches*, to sail as close to the harbour approaches as possible, it would have been unlikely that the Dutch navy would have been able to dart along the coast and interdict, through Parma's protective screen of flyboats, the barges as they were towed the first few kilometres to reach deeper water. Once Parma's barges had managed to get corralled within the lines of the iron-disciplined Armada, then they all could have made sail for Margate – all of this is, of course, predicated on there being clement weather. The Armada could have continued with its assigned role: a convoy of troops and equipment, protected by a strong escort of fighting ships. The strength of the Spanish formation system had been demonstrated, with Spanish naval doctrine proving it's worth

Left: what might have been. A Dutch painting from around 1618, depicts a metaphorical engagement between a Spanish galleon (left) and a smaller Dutch warship.
It is not a scene from an actual battle, but it could illustrate what might have happened if Parma had ventured out of the Flemish harbours, with his flyboats and barges – and the Duke of Medina Sidonia had sent those of his smaller, more shallow-draughted, armed vessels as close to shore as possible to meet them.
In reality the flyboats of the Dutch navy had sensibly stayed close to shore at a distance from the might of the Armada. In this 'what-might-have-been' scenario the Dutch could possibly have continued with their common-sense attitude and would have declined to engage with Parma's defensive flyboats, when augmented by dozens of smaller Armada ships. Once within the Spanish fleet's defensive formation the Army of Flanders could have sailed on to Margate.

– the Armada had sailed along the English Channel, under sustained attack for around 250km of it, while managing to remain intact and undamaged. In a similar manner, the Armada, employing the same protective tactics would have been able to escort, within its ranks, Parma's barges along the 70km distance from the Flanders coast to Margate. De Leyva could, without difficulty have, as instructed and planned, been able to establish a beachhead on Kentish soil, to the south of the River Thames. With the English forces concentrated to the north of the river, the *tercios* of the Army of Flanders could have made a successful amphibious landing (as Spanish forces had successfully done at the island of Terceira, under opposing fire, five years before). Once landed, it is likely that these, the most feared and professional army in Europe, would have cut through any opposing English forces with little difficulty and made rapid progress to London.

However, this scenario has to remain hypothetical, because, with the advent of the fireships and the resulting shattering of the Armada formation, this fireship manoeuvre on the night of 7 August became the pivotal moment after which the Enterprise of England was to meet failure. As it turned out, it had been a close call for England.

Fireships

Lord Admiral Howard on his *Ark Royal*, with the ranks of the Armada ships clearly in sight to his north-east, called a council of war that Sunday morning. Earlier, Sir William Wynter, captain of the *Vanguard* (veteran of many expeditions including that at Smerwick in 1580, see Chapter 1) had proposed the tactic of using fireships against the tightly-packed Armada – a stratagem which could burn and sink even the greatest of warships. As the current was running towards the Armada and Howard's fleet was windward, the manoeuvre was an obvious one and it was immediately adopted. The danger was obvious to Medina Sidonia too and that evening he ordered that a series of ships' boats and *pataches*, fully manned with oarsmen, be positioned as a protective screen around the perimeter of his fleet, ready to throw a grapnel and tow any fireship away to burn out harmlessly.

There was no time for the English to get suitable vessels from Dover or other ports, so eight small ships were selected from the fleet. At sizes ranging from 90 tons upwards these were larger than the normal type of fireship – there were several of 200 tons, including the *Thomas Drake,* owned by Drake himself. The ships were prepared in the usual manner: with guns double-shotted; stuffed with firewood and the sails and every surface smeared with tar and pitch. There was no time to prepare the 'hell burners'

Above: 'Launch of Fire-ships against the Spanish Armada', by the Netherlandish School, c.1590. On the night of 7 August 1588 the English sent in eight fireships against the Spanish fleet at Calais.

packed with explosives and used with devastating effect against Parma's great pontoon bridge at the siege of Antwerp in 1585. (These had been devised by the Italian engineer Federigo Giambelli, who was at Gravesend, engaged in preparing a defensive boom across the River Thames.)

Just around midnight of that Sunday all was ready. The eight ships were driven by the favourable tide and wind towards the crowded Spanish lines. The men on board lit the fires, scrambled into the attendant small boats and made their escape. As smoke and flames billowed from the rigging and masts of the fireships, the screening line of Spanish boats sprang into action. Two of the fireships were intercepted and towed clear. However, it proved impossible for the ranks of rowers in the small boats to intercept and tow the other burning ships, which were larger than usual. Their task became too hazardous as the pre-loaded guns began to discharge over their heads. The men were also fearful that these were the notorious 'hellburners'. The remaining six fireships, now burning furiously, drifted closer to the Spanish fleet. Characteristically, Medina Sidonia kept his cool. After observing the trajectory of the fireships he sent out the Prince of Ascoli in a small boat, with the message that ships in danger were to slip and buoy their cables and move away to a safe location – and return afterwards to their former anchorage. (Ascoli was left behind, and was able to make his way to Spanish Flanders – and not, as we shall see in Chapter 5, to the Dingle Peninsula!). Aware of the awful consequences of their wooden vessels going on fire, the Spanish commanders took immediate action. In most cases there was no time to winch up the anchor. The majority of captains ordered that an axe be used on the anchor cable and each ship made for safety and ran with the wind. Despite the alarm and the darkness, most ships managed to get underway in a seamanlike manner, with only one collision among the massed fleet, between the galleasses, with consequences that we shall shortly see. Nevertheless, the well-ordered Armada had now metamorphosed into an array of uncoordinated vessels. One report relates that five of the *pataches* remained off Calais and later returned to Spain.

Left: a galleass, built in Italy. Like the rest of the four-strong Galleass Squadron, the 500-ton flagship 'San Lorenzo' had been built in the Naples shipyards. It was well armed, including two pairs of cañon de batir, *in the prow and the stern. The vessel had been damaged in the melee of the night of 7 August and, driven by wind, ran aground just off the ramparts of Calais Castle.*

Discipline prevailed on the *San Martín* and a nearby group of galleons. The Duke ordered that the *San Martín*'s anchor cable be let go with a buoy at the end and then dropping a sheet anchor. In the dawn light of Monday 8 August, the *San Martín* was around 10km to the north of Calais. Most of the fleet was out of sight and scattered in a northeasterly line in the general direction of Gravelines, around 20km from Calais. There were just a few ships nearby, and the first to join the flagship was the *San Marcos* of the Squadron of Portugal. The English fleet now spotted the magnificent opportunity posed by this isolated group and hoisted sail. Once more, Medina Sidonia prepared to face the foe and protect his scattered fleet. As he dispatched *pataches* to round up his flock, the Duke and his small band of warships turned to meet the enemy.

In the meantime, Lord Admiral Howard had been distracted by the sight of a tempting target. He diverted with his squadron, leaving the other three squadrons to continue towards Medina Sidonia's grouping. The flagship of the galleass squadron, the *San Lorenzo* (500 tons, 50 guns, Don Hugo de Moncada in charge), was in trouble. It had collided another vessel during the melee of the night before, damaging the rudder and mainmast. The rudder had previously been damaged during the storm in the Bay of Biscay at the end of July. As the crippled galleass was being driven by the strong tide and wind, the oarsmen frantically tried to regain control. It ran aground just off the ramparts of Calais Castle and the galleass heeled over, presenting its hull to seaward, leaving its guns now impotent. Many of the crew and rowers jumped overboard. The English warships, with their deeper draught, could not come close. The small privateer *Margaret and John* (previously seen encountering the stricken *Nuestra Señora del Rosario* after the first Armada battle of 31 July) sailed closer but got stuck on a reef, only being released later on by the rising tide. Howard sent out his longboat with around 60 men to the attack. These were joined by other small boats and a pinnace launched from the grounded *Margaret and John*. As the English

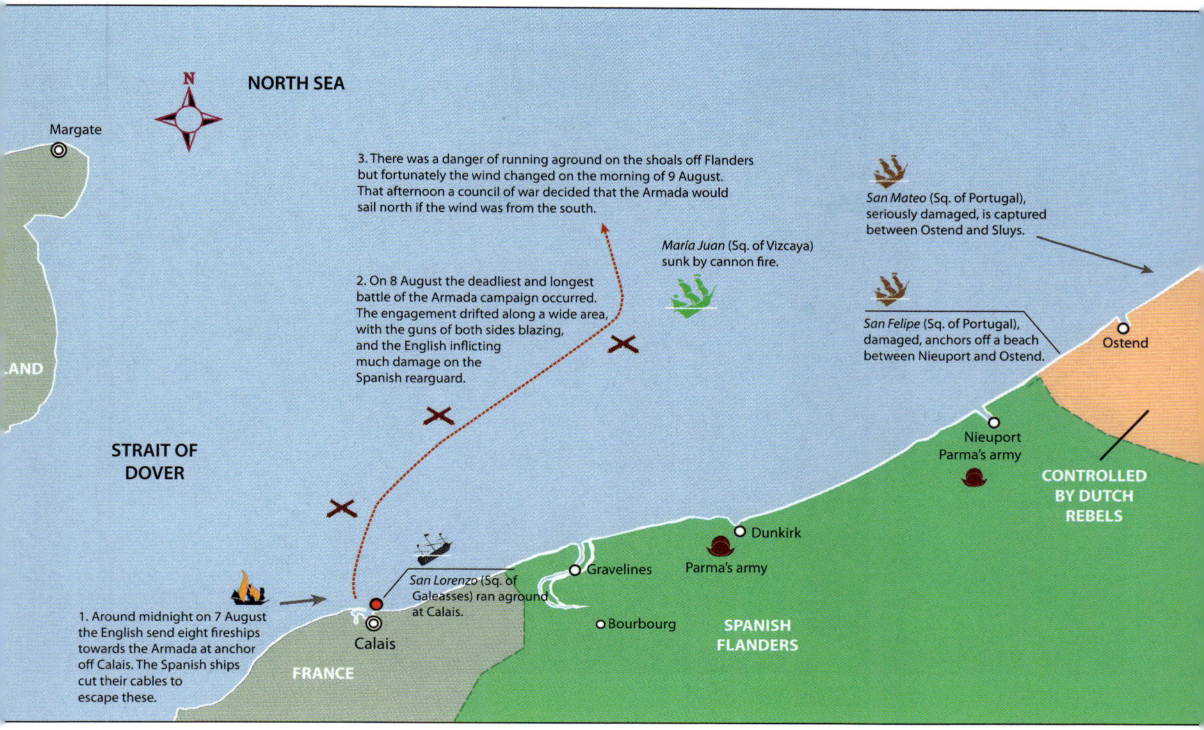

Above: from fireships to a great battle – the events at Calais and Gravelines.

sailors came up to the beached galleass, they found it difficult to assault it, due to the hull looming high above them. The 50 remaining crew of the galleass, led by the commander, Hugo de Moncada, laid down a hail of small-arms fire on the English sailors clustered in their small open boats. As the firing continued, de Moncada was fatally struck in the head by a musket ball. The galleass crew now abandoned the *San Lorenzo*, some swimming ashore through the surf, others drowning. The English proceeded to pillage the wreck, filling their boats with what they could carry. The haul included a reported 22,000 ducats as well as trunks of other valuables. However, envious eyes were watching from the shore. Governor de Mauléon dispatched two noblemen in a boat with a message that he did not dispute the right of the English to pillage the *San Lorenzo*, but as the vessel was on French territory, under the rules of war the ship and cannon aboard were his, the governor's. This did not go down well with a privateering audience. After being told by an officer of the *Margaret and John* that they would have to negotiate with Lord Admiral Howard on the matter, the sailors, as later reported, 'fell to spoiling the Frenchmen, seizing their rings and jewels'. After the return of his messengers, the Governor ordered the guns of the castle to open fire, whereupon the English beat a hasty retreat. Some of the fleeing sailors drowned as they tried to regain their boats. With casualties of around 50 killed on each side, one estimation is that more Englishmen died in this single engagement with the galleass than in all the other Armada battles. De Mauléon later allowed the *San Lorenzo* survivors to salvage the guns and ammunition aboard. In due course the survivors, as well as their salvaged material, were sent to Flanders.

Above: a Dutch engraving showing the great battle off Calais and Gravelines, with a galleon sinking in the foreground amidst the gunsmoke. What looks like fireships are in the background.
In the aftermath of the Armada, the Dutch were adept at anti-Spanish propaganda, producing drawings, pamphlets and medals which promulgated the supposed defeat of their Catholic enemy.

Gravelines

On that Monday morning, the great day-long battle of Gravelines commenced. Medina Sidonia, along with four other galleons, were situated between the English fleet and his scattered fleet. The Duke was fighting a rearguard action, hoping to buy time for the Armada while it tried to regain formation, in spite of the prevailing east-south-east wind. In time other ships arrived and the Spanish rearguard increased to 16 ships. As well as the flagship and the *San Mateo*, these included the *San Luis*, *San Felipe*, the *Santiago*, and the *San Cristóbal*. De Recalde was there in his *San Juan de Portugal*, as well as de Leyva in *La Rata*. They were vastly outnumbered by the English, who now, squadron by squadron, went on to assault the Spanish ships. Though well gunned, their ships were generally smaller, and because they carried minimal victuals and supplies, were higher on the water, thus able to sail faster than the Spanish ships laden down with material for a long voyage and the planned invasion. Lacking any tactical doctrine, the English captains adopted an instinctive manoeuvre. This involved picking out an enemy vessel and swarming around it, with agility. As they passed close by to around 100m range, they let off a broadside. They were 'volleying', firing their cannons rapidly and without time to aim precisely. As the English ship wheeled around and returned to the fray, their gunners had time to let their cannon cool down. However, the gunners in the particular Spanish ship, at the centre of the fray, did not have the luxury of an interval, and were limited by the time necessary to allow the guns cool. Hence, as witnesses attested, the Spanish rate of fire was less.

By around midday Howard and his ships had returned from his foray with the *San Lorenzo* and joined the fight. The wind had changed to the south-south-east direction, and as the battle raged on, both fleets were slowly drifting north-north-east. Unlike the previous battles along the Channel, the closeness of range and the English superiority in numbers resulted that real damage was being inflicted on the Spanish ships at the centre of the maelstrom. However, the Spanish responded with their measured and targeted cannon fire The battle continued at close range; unfortunately for the Spanish, it was not close enough to grapple and swamp the enemy. The *San Felipe* (800 tons, galleon of the Portuguese Squadron, completed in 1583 and named in honour of Philip, newly installed as the King of Portugal) was in the thick of the running battle. In his account, the Accountant-General of the fleet, Coco Calderón, told how, as the enemy came closer, the *Maestre de Campo* aboard, Don Francisco de Toledo 'ordered the grappling hooks to be got out, and shouted to the enemy to come to close many quarters. They replied, summoning him to surrender in fair fight; and one Englishman, standing in the maintop with his sword and buckler, called out "Good soldiers that ye are, surrender to the fair terms we offer ye". But the only answer he got was a gunshot, which brought him down in sight of everyone, and [de Toledo] then ordered the muskets and arquebuses to be brought into action. The enemy thereupon retired, whilst our men shouted out to them that they were cowards, and with opprobrious words reproached them for their want of spirit, calling them Lutheran hens, and daring them to return to the fight'.

Below: the battle flag of the 'San Mateo', now held in the Museum de Lakenhal at Leiden. Badly damaged in the battle at Gravelines, the galleon had drifted close to the Dutch coast where on 10 August it was attacked by Dutch and English ships. Towed to Flushing, it sank at the approaches to the port.

The battle raged on, as a great cloud of gunsmoke formed over the mass of ships. During the afternoon the sea began to calm, but larger galleons such as the *San Martín* had to take care as they drifted towards shallower depths. Nevertheless, as Captain Alonso Vanegas, onboard the flagship, recounted, it continued to dash in to the rescue: 'The enemy had the galleon *San Felipe* heavily engaged within their fleet ... The ship suffered significant damage as it was targeted by numerous enemy vessels. The Royal flagship and the galleon *San Luis* ... turned to provide assistance, with the galleon *San Mateo* and *San Juan de Sicilia* also joining the fray, becoming heavily entangled near our fleet. Our flagship, facing enemy fire, turned to aid them, but the enemy vessels that were about to board *San Mateo* and *San Juan* retreated'.

At around four in the afternoon a sudden squall with drizzle interrupted the action and the fighting came to an end. It was due to the exhaustion of the crews and, as a result of their scatter-shot discharges, the shortage of powder and shot in the English fleet, which now stood off. Onboard the *San Martín*, with a north-westerly wind blowing and, aware of the danger of being blown them towards the treacherous banks of Flanders, an 80km series of shoals and sands, the pilots advised the Duke that it was advisable to head for the more open waters of the North Sea.

As it turned out, despite the day-long heavy pounding of the Armada off Gravelines, only one Spanish ship actually sank that day. This was the 665-ton *nao* of the Squadron of Vizcaya, *María Juan,* with a Corunna muster of 93 seamen and 213 soldiers onboard. During the morning of the battle it had become separated and English ships promptly came up and blasted away. Rudderless and with its mizzen mast brought down it was badly

Left: a Dutch depiction of the aftermath of the take-over of the 'San Mateo' on 10 August. Note the captured battle flag being borne away.

damaged. As darkness fell, at around 9 p.m. the *nao* capsized – only one boatload of those on board managed to escape.

As we have seen, two galleons of the frontline Portuguese Squadron, the *San Felipe* and the *San Mateo,* had fearlessly fought in the defensive line. These were now in trouble, having been surrounded by English ships on several occasions, and enduring the repeated gun fire. The *San Felipe* had been assaulted by an estimated 12 to 16 enemy ships at close range. It had been so badly pummelled that around 100 men had been killed and it was in such a state that it had now to be abandoned. Around 300 survivors were transferred to the *urca, Doncella,* and another 18 to the galleon *Ascención*. The *Maestre de Campo*, Francisco de Toledo, brave and defiant as ever, chose to remain on board with the captain and around two dozen others. With no masts, the *San Felipe* drifted to anchor on 9 August off a beach between Nieuport and Ostend. De Toledo and other notables managed to escape in a small boat and reach the safety of Parma's territory at Nieuport. The remaining men (around 25) also managed to get to land, and were taken into captivity, to be eventually ransomed and liberated. The following day, English seamen garrisoned in Flanders arrived and took over the ship. The Dutch navy, under Justin of Nassau, seized the vessel but it sank as she was being towed to Flushing.

The *San Mateo* was an older ship, having being constructed in Portuguese Goa in the early 1570s. Nevertheless its age did not stop the galleon playing a prominent part in the rearguard in the battle of 8 August. For several hours, at musket shot range, it had fought over ten English ships, responding with such intensity that it ran out of powder and shot. After the battle, the ship was damaged and the pumps were unable to counter the leaks. Seeing the ship in distress, Medina Sidonia dispatched several ships to its assistance. However the aristocratic Don Diego de Mendoza y Pimentel (Count of Priego, Marquis of Gelves, *Maestre de Campo* of the *tercio* of Sicily) who was in command, refused to abandon ship and asked for a diver to help. The diver was sent, but by nightfall the vessel was borne by the wind and current towards the Flanders coast between Ostend and Sluys. On 10 August two Dutch flyboats, supported by three English ships stationed at Flushing, attacked the *San Mateo* and, after two hours of intense combat, overpowered the crew. Amidst the fury, the Dutch threw some of the crew overboard. As later reported from Flushing: 'the best sort were saved; and the rest were cast overboard …'. Around 40 died, according to a Dutch account. The battered ship was towed towards Flushing, where it sank at the entrance to the harbour. Around 300 prisoners were taken. All were liberated in 1590 on payment of a ransom, save six men of rank (including Don Diego de Mendoza y Pimentel) whose deliverance proved more complicated – these were set free after a prisoner exchange and payment in April 1591. The aristocratic Don Diego went on to enjoy a stellar career, becoming Viceroy of Aragon in 1614 and Viceroy of Nueva España (with its capital in Mexico City) in 1621.

The smallest of the casualties of the Gravelines battle was the tiny *patache*, *San António de Padua*, (75 tons, assigned in a support role to the Squadron of Castile) which came to grief off the coast of Flanders. It was captured by the Dutch near Ostend, and was burnt after taking the 21 men on board prisoner.

In a later report, Sir Henry Killigrew, one of the two English Councillors on the Dutch Council of State (appointed under the Treaty of Nonsuch), writing from Holland, noted that though the Dutchmen had not given much active help, 'these Hollanders have lighted upon those argosies which we did distress, and have received great spoil thereof'.

Reverberations of the Battle

In the early hours of Tuesday 9 August, a strong west-north-westerly wind blew. With the leadsmen in the bows closely counting the decreasing depth, Medina Sidonia in the *San Martín* tacked against the wind, trying to avoid the banks of Flanders – and fired two shots to signal most of the fleet, downwind, to do the same. Providentially, at around 11 a.m., the wind changed to west-south-west and the Armada was able to head out to towards the salvation of deep water.

With the English fleet standing off, there was time for both fleets to take stock of the damage and casualties after the previous day's great battle. Up to then, the damage borne by the Armada in the previous Channel battles, more-long range, had been generally minor. On that Monday the Spanish ships sustained real damage in the battle off Gravelines where, with the Armada scattered, their rearguard had been outnumbered ten to one during the initial hours. With the Spanish battle formation no longer in place, the English ships were able to close on the few individual ships and pepper them at close range. There was a somewhat greater number of heavier guns in English service, and, as we have seen, by their wheeling in and out, they were able to sustain a high rate of fire. However, much of this fire was wasted, due to what might be called, a scatter-shot approach.

Practically all of the front-line Spanish ships were holed and some leaking, not least the *San Martín*, calculated to have suffered over 100 hits. One English iron cannonball was found which weighed 50 pounds (23kg). As one witness wrote: 'Despite this being a galleon with seven layers [of timber], the balls … pierced it from one side to another'. Divers and carpenters diligently worked at placing lead plates over the holes.

Spanish sources have been open about the losses at Gravelines. It had indeed been a sanguinary day: one estimate of Spanish casualties there was

Below: the aristocrat Don Diego de Mendoza y Pimental. This 'Maestre de Campo' had been in command of the 'San Mateo' during the great battle at Gravelines. In the aftermath he had refused to abandon ship and was taken prisoner after the galleon was captured by the Dutch. Don Diego was ransomed and later gained a reputation as a reforming administrator. In 1621 he was appointed Viceroy of Nueva España.

of 600 deaths and 800 injured. However, given that only one ship was sunk directly, it is a tribute to the shipwrights of Lisbon, the northern Cantabrian coast and other parts of Philip's domain that the great vessels of the Armada could absorb the repeated impact of cannonballs.

English sources at the time are generally silent on the damage caused to their fleet. The English fleet did receive its share of Spanish cannonballs. An account by the English writer, Richard Hakluyt says that the English losses were 'about one hundredth of their people'. He recounted that 'Sir Francis Drakes shippe was pierced with shot about forty times, and his very cabben was twise shot thorow, and about the conclusion of the fight, the bedde of a certaine gentleman lying weary thereupon, was taken quite from under him with the force of a bullet'.

That afternoon, Medina Sidonia called a council of war. When de Recalde and de Leyva arrived, a discussion was already underway which, according to de Leyva, dealt with options for surrender – another account tells that Medina Sidonia was against surrender, he would 'rather to die like a knight'. De Recalde and de Leyva vehemently advocated continuing the fight, and that they should turn back and 'complete … there what our King commanded' – returning to the Flanders coast to link up with Parma. The possibility of wintering in Norway (then ruled by the King of Denmark) was considered and immediately shot down – there was no appetite for trusting their fortunes to the hostile Protestant powers of northern Europe. Another equally unappealing option was that the battered fleet should sail northwards, make the turn westwards into the Atlantic around the apex of Britain and Ireland, and then make the long southward return to Spain. They took note that all of these choices would have to take consideration of the shifting and variable fortune afforded by the wind. Coco Calderón (Accountant-General of the fleet, who later wrote a comprehensive account of the Armada events) advised that such a voyage around Scotland, Ireland, and 750 leagues through unknown seas would be arduous – and that food and water would be lacking. After some discussion, the council came to a unanimous decision: if the wind was from the north, they would return and attempt to combine with Parma and the invasion army; alternatively if the south wind continued they would continue north of Britain and Ireland, and then west through Atlantic waters to sail south to Spain. As it turned out, the wind continued from the south-west – and accordingly the Armada sailed into the North Sea.

It was also time for a brief council of war on the English flagship, the *Ark Royal*. The squadron commanders reported that there was little damage to the fleet, but they were practically out of victuals, water, powder and shot. Recognising the danger the Armada still posed, they resolved to follow the Spanish 'until we have cleared our own coast and brought the Firth [of Forth] west of us'. Howard ordered Lord Henry Seymour to return to take up position in the Channel and watch out for the activities of Parma's army in Flanders. Days later, as the Armada passed the Firth of Forth on 12 August, Howard and his squadron broke off the chase and headed for home – having no choice, as by now they were desperately short of food and water.

Guns and Ships: relative strengths and tactics

The traditional Spanish doctrine was for a warship to carry an overwhelming force of soldiers. As it came near an enemy ship, it fired an initial salvo at close range with the intention of dismasting and immobilizing the enemy. Then it grappled with the enemy vessel. Up to that moment the troops would be sheltered in the stern and forecastles, discharging their arquebuses. Next they would board, using their superiority in numbers to prevail. The one thing the Spanish ships had was superiority in soldiers, but in these sea-battles along the Channel and at Gravelines they never got a chance to board and overcome the English vessels in the traditional manner.

During the initial exchanges in the early days along the Channel, the English had launched broadsides generally from a distance. However, as the historian Dr I.A.A. Thompson, in his analysis of the guns of both fleets put it, 'The Spaniards had succeeded in parading along the whole coastline of southern England to anchor in Calais Roads largely unscathed by enemy action'. It was the Gravelines battle where the Armada suffered real damage, as on that Monday 8 August, because of the fireships, it had lost its protective formation. The ships had been scattered and the English ships instinctively took up the chase and swarmed in packs on the small number of ships that formed a protective rearguard. With odds of ten to one, they clustered around individual Spanish ships and let off their broadsides. As explained in Appendix B, (which gives more detail on guns and ships) the fact that the Spanish had longer gun carriages did not make any significant difference to the rate of fire. The gunner on any Spanish ship at the centre of the vortex could only discharge at a measured rate, due to concerns about heating of the gun. The gunners amidst the English ships, adopting their whirling dervish tactics, had the convenience of an interval, before their ship lined up gain. The corollary to the pounding that the Armada ships received is that the Spanish warships were well built and able to absorb considerable punishment. Timber such as oak from the Cantabrian Mountains, well-developed designs, along with excellent shipwrights, resulted in robust Spanish vessels – the galleons and *naos* were in effect, floating bastions. As demonstrated in all the Armada battles, despite much expenditure of powder and shot, the English found it difficult to directly sink a Spanish ship.

Most English ships were smaller and had less cargo space. Carrying little victuals and shot, they were lighter in the water and were able to manoeuvre nimbly at Gravelines. The English had the added motivation that they were defending their country. The leaders of the squadrons had seafaring experience (mainly gained by privateering) but many of the captains of the private ships were inexperienced. In the early Channel battles they were unable to break through the Spanish defensive position. Under the stern leadership of Medina Sidonia the Armada had managed to stay together. Showing impressive discipline and seamanship, the Spanish ships maintained their station within their specified formation, despite the vagaries of weather and enemy attack – all up to the fateful battle off Gravelines on 8 August, when all was to change after the Armada ships scattered in the face of the fireship attack of the night before.

Left: a section of 'The Defeat of the Armada: Elizabeth I at Tilbury' from the Parish Church of St Faith, Gaywood in Norfolk, England. This seventeenth-century oil-on-panel painting depicts Elizabeth's visit to Tilbury.

Spectacle at Tilbury

On the morning of Thursday 18 August, led by Lord Admiral Howard, most of the English fleet hove into Margate, at the mouth of the Thames estuary – Hawkins had led over 30 vessels to Harwich. Over the preceding days the rumours across England had hardened into fact: the Armada had been last seen in the far north and the Spanish peril had receded. In addition, that other threat to England, Parma's Army of Flanders, remained there, bottled up due to the implied threat of the Dutch navy.

It was a coincidence that on the same Thursday, around 70km away from Margate, at Tilbury, north of the River Thames in Essex, a grand ceremony of the land army was being held, presided over by none other than Queen Elizabeth. In the months preceding the Armada events, the English leadership had concluded that the Tilbury area was the most likely target for an invasion landing. A warning had been issued to the deputy lieutenants of counties that 'the enemy will attempt to land in some part of Essex'. (In the event, Philip had issued orders for his forces to land at Margate in eastern Kent, to the south of the Thames estuary). A Henry VIII-era fort at Tilbury had been hurriedly strengthened, and the location had been designated to be one of the main muster points for England's soldiers. Robert Dudley, the Earl of Leicester, had duly set up at Tilbury with his entourage. It took until the first week of August for 4,000 men of the Essex militia to arrive there and there was logistical chaos resulting in a great scarcity of food.

Two weeks later, Leicester, despite continuing supply problems, had managed to gather 16,000 infantry and 2,000 cavalry. On 15 August he wrote to the Queen, after hearing that she planned to visit him, assuring her that her lodging was prepared and the men were now ready 'to die for her'. It was indeed time for Elizabeth to go forth and proclaim a famous victory. On Thursday morning 18 August, the same day as the starving mariners of her navy were stepping on shore, Elizabeth set out from her London palace and boarded her royal barge at the quay in Whitehall. With trumpets sounding and escorted by her costumed courtiers and plumed solders, she made a queenly progress downriver through London, as church bells rang. Awaiting her at the palisaded Tilbury encampment, set on a rise above the

Right: Elizabeth I triumphant. This, the 'Armada' portrait, painted in the aftermath of the Armada events, is high-octane propaganda. The Queen (adorned by pearls, symbol of virginity) has her hand on a globe, a symbol of her new international power, an aspiration buttressed by the imperial crown sitting to her right. One panel shows English ships gathered, facing the crescent-shaped Spanish fleet in the background. The other panel shows an enemy vessel being wrecked on a wave-swept and rocky coastline.

river, was the Earl of Leicester, her Captain General, and his soldiers. The grey-haired Earl was now past his prime, having once been the Queen's favourite. (It turned out to be the Earl's last hurrah – he died unexpectedly a few weeks afterwards, to the intense distress of the Queen).

With Leicester on one side, and her new favourite, the 23-year-old Robert Devereux, Earl of Essex, on the other, Elizabeth reviewed her soldiers who were drawn up in colourful troops of foot and horse. As the Queen, clad in white velvet and wearing a shining silver cuirass, passed through the ranks, the soldiers cheered. The finery and precise rows masked the fact that these troops were untried and had not fought any battle, still less confronted the best soldiers in Europe, Parma's Army of Flanders, even now still gathered just less than 150km away across the water.

Elizabeth spent the night at a gentleman's manor house nearby and returned the next day for a further review of the troops. Many consider that the concept of monarchy is a myth that must be underpinned by illusion and spectacle. This was very evident when, in front of her massed soldiers, Elizabeth seized the moment of sweet victory (or at least the avoidance of defeat and her escape from being bloodily deposed) and, mounted on a white horse, she began her famous speech. None of the notes taken on the occasion of the speech coincide with the words revealed later. However, there were more wordsmiths in England at that time than just Shakespeare: an English clergyman published a version of the speech sometime after 1624. It is likely that the great speech was rewritten and burnished to reach new inspirational heights for a wider audience in the pamphlets that were distributed far and wide.

A stirring message was imparted: 'My loving people … let tyrants fear! I have always so behaved myself that, under God, I have placed my chiefest strength and safeguard in the loyal hearts and good will of my subjects. Therefore I am come amongst you as you see … being resolved, in the midst and heat of the battle to live or die amongst you all and to lay down, for my God and for my kingdom and for my people, my honour and my blood … I know I have the body of a weak and feeble woman but I have the heart and stomach of a king and of a king of England too …'. Elizabeth added: 'I myself will be your general, judge, and rewarder of every one of your virtues in the field. I know already, for your forwardness you deserve rewards and crowns; and We do assure you, in the word of a prince, they shall be duly paid.' This rousing rhetoric garnered loud cheers across the massed ranks.

There was some alarm nevertheless when, shortly afterwards, news arrived to Leicester and Elizabeth that 'The Prince of Parma has in readiness 30,000 or 40,000 men and intends with the next … tide to put out his forces for England'. Despite this, two days after Elizabeth's speech, orders were issued that the army in the south-east area be reduced in size: immediately to 6,000 and to 1,500 by the end of the month. After they had fallen out and dispersed, some of the impecunious soldiers had to resort to selling their arms and armour. Further, the gun foundries in the Forest of Dean and the Weald were ordered to cease production. Any fears of the risks of this demobilisation were soothed when intelligence reports arrived over the following weeks, informing them that firstly, Parma was not going to sail and, then that he had retired to Bruges and his invasion fleet had been decommissioned.

In the days that followed, Elizabeth received reports from the commanders of her navy, the men who had sailed valiantly to deflect the Armada from her shores. Despite their success in resisting the Armada, they were in a cautionary mood. Lord Admiral Howard, having arrived safely at Margate Roads, noted the lack of provisions, and recommended that the fleet should not be discharged at once, as the Spaniards might return after refitting somewhere. Walsingham, Elizabeth's principal secretary, having analysed several reports, had picked up on the theme of work still to be done, and wrote: 'So our half-doing doth breed dishonour and leaves the disease uncured'. Drake wrote to the Queen, advising that although the Armada was so far north and unlikely to return he advised her not to 'diminish any of her forces'. He added that 'God hath and will hear her prayers, she putting her hand to the plough for defence of His truth'.

Most of the English fleet were privateers and for them, there had been minimal opportunity during the entire enterprise for plunder and prizes. For some, it was time to get back to making real money, and at the beginning of September Sir Francis Drake was informed by Howard of the Queen's desire to send a force to intercept the Spanish treasure fleet from the Indies. At the same time Drake also had to give an account of the money and *matériel* taken from the captured *Nuestra Señora del Rosario*. As already noted over half of the 50,000 ducats found onboard had disappeared. Drake recounted that 'I did take now … 3,000 pistolets … for, by

Jesus, I had not three shillings left in the world … But I will repay it within days after my coming home'. Sir Martin Frobisher, who heartily disliked him, was having none of Drake's duplicity. In a speech at Harwich he said: 'Sir Francis Drake reporteth that no man hath done any good service but he … He thinketh to cozen us of our shares of fifteen thousand ducats; but we will have our shares, or I will make him spend the best blood in his belly; for he hath enough of those cozening cheats already'.

By the end of August, information came of the Armada's movements: 'a very great fleet of monstrous great ships … about 100 in number… whereby their course was to run betwixt Orkneys and Fair Island'. During the second half of September more welcome news arrived, this time from Ireland. Elizabeth had initially been fearful that there would be a Spanish invasion of Ireland, but the reports from her officials showed that there was no danger of a Spanish takeover – her Lord Deputy and his officials had taken care that the survivors of the many Armada shipwrecks on the Atlantic coast were promptly rounded up and systematically killed.

The Spanish Armada had been fended off, but now the bills had to be paid by Elizabeth's Treasury. A torrent of bills surged in from all quarters: charges for powder, cordage, victuals and all the supplies needed to keep a large fleet in fettle. In addition, the various merchants were demanding recompense for the hire of their ships and payment of their seamen. It soon became ever more important to reduce the outflow of money from the stretched royal coffers. The army had been rapidly reduced in size. It was now the navy's turn. In the weeks that followed, the fleet was immediately demobilised. The hired private ships were discharged, and others were laid up. By mid-September, the number of ships and men to the Queen's charge fell precipitously to 34 vessels and around 1,500 seamen, a fraction of the muster employed to fend off the Armada, of 197 ships and nearly 16,000 men. Despite this reduction, by the end of the month the Queen still could express her displeasure with Burghley (Lord High Treasurer) for sending her 'so great a list of the captains and officers remaining in Her Majesty's pay'.

Below: an illustration of Lord Burghley, careful husbander of Elizabeth's treasury. Such was his desire to balance the books that he responded to requests to help the destitute and sick English sailors, in dire straits after the Armada , by saying: 'by death, by discharging of sick men and such like, there may be spared something in the general pay'.

At the time of breaking off their pursuit of the Armada at the Firth of Forth, the English fleet, while it had suffered little material damage, had been in a sorry condition. A report from the Duke of Cumberland had noted that they 'left the pursuit of the Spanish fleet for want of powder and victuals; and driven to such extremity that the Lord Admiral had been obliged to eat beans, and many of the men had to drink their own water [urine].' As the ships dispersed to their home ports, the sailors were starving, many ridden with typhus and dysentery. During the second half of August Lord Admiral Howard sent a heartfelt message to Burghley: 'Sickness and mortality begins wonderfully to grow amongst us; and it is a pitiful sight to see, here at Margate, how the men having no place to receive them into here, die in the streets'. He told of the *Elizabeth Jonas* (one of the Queen's galleons): of the original 500 crew only 200 survived and how 'Infection will grow throughout the most part of our fleet. The men have been so long at sea and have so little clothes'. He appealed to the Lord High Treasurer: 'My Lord, I would think a marvellous good way that there was a thousand pounds worth … of hose doublets, shirts, shoes and the like sent down … for else in very short time I look to see most of the mariners go naked'. At the beginning of September, matters had disimproved and Howard spelt it out clearly in a letter to the Queen. With 'great grief' he informed her of the state in which he found her fleet. 'The infection has grown very great … and those that come in fresh are soonest infected; they sicken one day and die the next.' Fatalities had been remarkably light during the Armada battles, but now there was a high mortality rate. One estimate is that over around one third of the soldiers and sailors in the English fleet died in the aftermath.

Burghley had been doing his utmost to navigate Elizabeth's leaky ship of state away from the rocks of bankruptcy. Accordingly he responded negatively to any requests for money for the seamen. Coldheartedly recognising the fiscal advantages of death and disease, his response was: 'by death, by discharging of sick men and such like, there may be spared something in the general pay'. Howard, Drake, Hawkins and the other commanders paid out of their own pockets (in Howard's case, his share from the capture of the *Nuestra Señora del Rosario*) for the support of their sailors. Over the following months, the streets of English seaports were full of starving cripples and beggars, the former sailors of the victorious English fleet. The Crown responded sternly with an order to 'soldiers and mariners upon pain of imprisonment … Her Majesty commands them to repair out of hand to the counties and places where they were last abiding and there to employ themselves in dutiful sort according to their several vocations and callings'. Fending off the invasion had been achieved by England at relative low cost, helped by the efficient method of hiring in a substantial amount of the fleet. As we have seen, there was little state support for distressed seamen. The amount paid out by the government as 'rewards to the injured' was £180.

One estimate is that the navy, over the year up to the end of October 1588 (including the period of Armada events), cost Elizabeth's exchequer £393,000, excluding the cost of mobilising the army. This was an enormous sum for England and its relatively modest economy, but it was less than what Philip had expended. The King told the Cortes of Castile in December 1588 that the Armada had cost him ten million ducats, or approximately £2,500,000. However, it is thought that Philip had exaggerated the total cost as part of a negotiating ploy, as the King wished to get the Cortes to levy more taxes – and that the real cost was much less than this. Whatever the figure, the big difference was that Philip enjoyed the substantial resources of a vast empire. The Anglo-Spanish War was not over. As we shall see in Chapter 6, Philip possessed sufficient resources to soon lay down a fleet of new, improved galleons and was able to mount an even bigger Armada expedition in 1596.

However, thanks to a lot of luck and the efforts of the relatively low-cost English fleet, fortune had smiled on Queen Elizabeth and her reign: the coiled power represented by the *tercios* on board the Spanish fleet, as well as that of the Army of Flanders, was not to be unleashed against her. By contrast, for the Armada, misfortune had not ended: as we shall see in the next chapter, the Spanish ships were about to endure a fearful purgatory of great winds, waves and savage reefs.

Chapter 4

The Long Voyage Back to Spain

On the evening of Tuesday 9 October, the Armada, now reduced to around 110 vessels, sailed on. The decision taken by that afternoon's council of war had been to obey the weather and sail in the direction dictated by the wind. This continued from the south-west, thus, fickle (or was it God's?) fortune brought it about that they were to sail north. The Armada was now headed towards Scotland, at the beginning of an itinerary that would amount to around 3,500km, a distance three times that of the alternative – to return by the route by which they had come. There were continuing tensions between the Duke of Medina Sidonia and the experienced naval commanders of the fleet, who had wanted to return to the seas off Flanders and join with the Duke of Parma. An angry Don Juan Martínez de Recalde sent a note to Medina Sidonia, saying 'certainly we made a dreadful decision' – and received a sharp reply from the Duke reminding him that 'we could not have done anything else, for the reasons discussed at the council, that you yourself attended'. As the Dover Strait and the coast of Flanders receded far behind, Lord Admiral Howard's ships continued to track the Armada. In the late afternoon of 10 August, Medina Sidonia ordered his fleet to reduce sail and slow down. He positioned a rearguard of twelve warships along with the three remaining galleasses, to face the enemy. However, the English ships held back and did not engage. And so, the two fleets continued their journey northwards.

The Duke now turned to a matter which had greatly annoyed him. Some days before, on the morning of Tuesday 9 August, with the English fleet approaching and the banks of Flanders drawing near, the Duke, in his *San Martín* had fired two shots, commanding his scattered fleet to rally. Several ships had ignored the order and captains of the offending ships were summoned to the *San Martín* to a court-martial. Medina Sidonia (suffering from a lack of sleep and understandably in a foul humour, after the failure of his 'Enterprise of England') decreed swift retribution, with an order to hang them

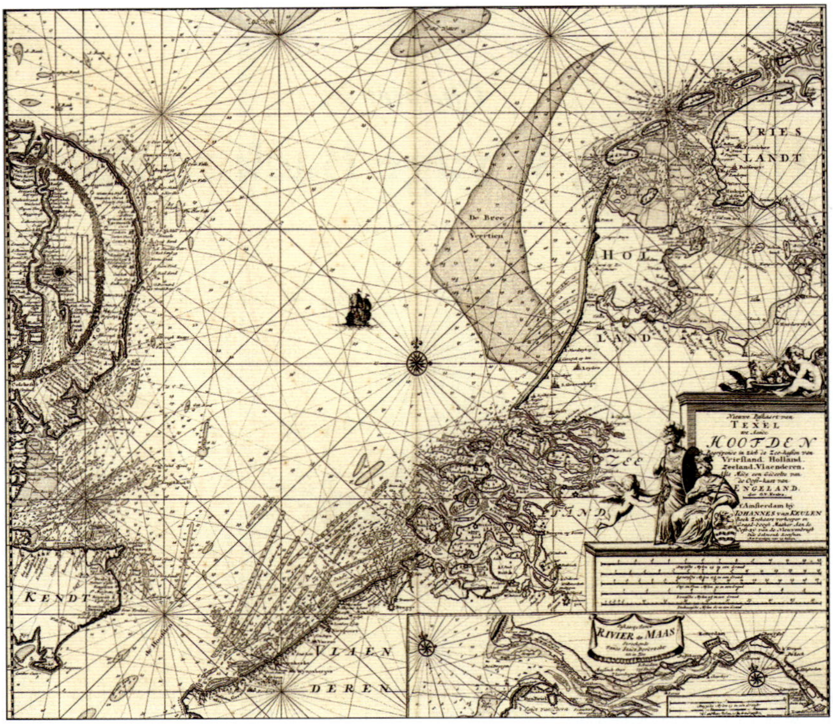

Left: as it ventured northwards into the North Sea, the Armada had to take care to avoid running aground. A map from a seventeenth-century book on navigation shows the North Sea and the multitudinous shoals off the Dutch and English coasts.

all. In the event, the sentence was only carried out on one captain, one of two who had led the errant pack. This was the unfortunate Don Cristóbal de Ávila, captain of the *urca, Santa Bárbara*, who on 11 August was hanged from a *patache*'s yardarm – and *pour encourager les autres* the dangling body was sailed around the fleet. The other captain was sent to the galleys. Others were reduced in rank. Another, of whom we shall hear more, Francisco de Cuéllar (then captain of the 530-ton galleon *San Pedro* of the Squadron of Castile), had been sentenced to death. De Cuéllar vehemently protested his innocence, and presented a six-page affidavit in his defence. This saved his life, but he lost his command and on 14 August the Duke appointed another captain to the *San Pedro*. De Cuéllar was placed in the custody of the Judge Advocate General, Martín de Aranda, in the vice-flagship of the Squadron of the Levant, the *nao, Lavia*.

The Armada continued northwards, making the occasional feint at the English fleet, a few kilometres behind them. At around midday on Friday 12 August, the Spanish ships passed abeam of the Firth of Forth. Although worried that the Spanish might reprovision and return southwards, Lord Admiral Howard had no choice but to abandon his watch on the Armada. Most of his fleet had been at sea for only around a fortnight. However, in a navy not known for generosity in providing on-board stores, they had run out of ammunition and victuals. Sickness was now beginning to ravage the English sailors. Howard ordered his fleet to turnabout, and with a final display of bravado, firing off some guns at the enemy, they headed south. To shadow the Spanish as far as the Orkneys and Shetlands, they left behind a 65-ton pinnace of the Navy Royal, the *Advice,* and a caravel owned by Sir

Francis Drake. Drake, in a letter to Walsingham, speculated that the Spanish might go to Norway or Denmark, musing about the help they might get and 'what the King of Spain's hot crowns will do in cold countries for mariners and men'.

The Armada was now faced with a lengthy voyage. Given the lack of food and water, there was no option but to reduce rations. On 13 August the Duke ordered that the daily allowance was to be 225g of bread, half a litre of water and a quarter litre of wine – a debilitating diet that was soon to induce further frailty and sickness. The great shortage of water resulted in an order to dispose of the animals being transported in the Squadron of *Urcas*. The unfortunate mules on board (hundreds had been transported in the *urcas*, intended to pull the artillery train for use during the planned invasion) as well as 40 horses belonging to the Duke and other notables were thrown overboard. One account tells of the crew of a Scottish fishing boat coming upon the desperate animals, swimming far from shore, with their eyes bulging, about to go under.

The Armada had been transporting 40 horses belonging to the Duke of Medina Sidonia as well as hundreds of mules assigned to pull the artillery train. As the Armada headed up the North Sea towards the Fair Isle Channel, it became apparent that was a general shortage of water. The order went out to throw the unfortunate animals overboard. Below: a detail from the Dutch painter Cornelis Claesz van Wieringen's painting 'The Spanish Armada sails off the English coast' shows the animals, thrown overboard, floundering in the sea.

It was time to consider navigational matters. Medina Sidonia offered 2,000 ducats to a French pilot if he would conduct the Armada to Spain. After consultations, the Duke issued specific directions to the fleet: 'The course that shall be held in the return of this army into Spain ... first ... to the North-North-East, until you be found under 61½°; and then to take great heed lest you fall upon the island of Ireland, for fear of the harm that may happen unto you upon that coast. Then parting from these islands, and doubling the Cape in 61½° [north of the Shetlands, just south of the Faroes], you shall run West-South-West until you be found under 58°; and from thence to the South-West to the height of 53° [roughly level with just south of the Aran Islands]; and then to the South-South-West, making to the Cape Finisterre, and so to procure your entrance into the Groyne [Corunna] or to Ferrol, or to any other port of the coast of Galicia'. (This has been taken from a document captured from Armada survivors in Ireland and sent to England. It was translated into English at the time: the last direction of 'South-West-West' is a mistranslation – it should read 'South-South-East').

Into the Atlantic

In the event, the Armada did not sail as far north as under 61½° latitude, nor did it generally follow these directions. On 18 August, as they ran north of the Scottish mainland, taking advantage of a favourable northeast wind, the Spanish fleet turned to sail through the Fair Isle Channel between the Orkney and Shetland Islands (at around 59½°), and headed westwards, entering the Atlantic. Several days earlier they had come across some fishing boats, including one from Southampton. The fishermen later related that the Spanish had bought dried fish from them, paying handsomely, and that 'there were 120 great ships the likes of such as they had never seen before, and many small ones'. The pressing need for the Armada was to gain knowledge of these northern waters and they took on board several of the fishing crew, intending to make use of their local know-how.

Above: the force of the Atlantic. Rough weather at the island of Cape Clear, Co. Cork, the southernmost point of Ireland. A rutter, a navigational guide issued at Lisbon, in the section dealing with Irish waters, gave sailing distances relative to Cape Clear. Many accounts by those on the Armada, who were either shipwrecked on the Irish coast, or just sailed by it, have references to clearing, or seeing 'Cabo Clear'. Yet no Armada ship that we are aware of ever came near that location.

As the Armada sailed west, away from the Shetlands and Orkneys, the climate became truly Atlantic: they encountered poor weather conditions. With visibility so poor as to make it impossible to distinguish one ship from another, the order went out for the ships to form into separate groups. On 21 August the Duke sent one of his officers, Don Baltasar de Zúñiga, in a *patache* to make haste to Spain with a report to the King. The Duke prefaced the bad news by enlisting the aid of the Deity to help him take a more optimistic view: as the enterprise had been so fervently commended to God, the result 'must doubtless be that which will be most advantage to His service, and that of your Majesty'. Medina Sidonia informed the King of the poor state of the fleet and how, as he said, 'I have set my course for Corunna, so as to make the voyage as short as possible'. He continued: 'our provisions are so scanty that, in order to make them and the water last a month, the rations of every person on the fleet … have been reduced; just enough being served out to keep them alive … Your Majesty may imagine what suffering this entails, in the midst of the discomfort of so long a voyage. We have consequently over 3,000 sick, without counting the wounded, who are numerous, on the fleet'. The Duke requested that stores be ready at Corunna to succour the fleet, adding that he had written to the clergy requesting that preparations be made for the reception of the sick.

On 24 August, it was time to review their position and course along Atlantic waters, and the Duke convened a meeting with his naval advisor, Diego Flóres de Valdés, the Accountant-General Coco Calderón and the French pilot (previously promised 2,000 ducats to guide the Armada back to Spain). Those present verified that they were at 58½° latitude (roughly abeam of the northern tip of Stornoway in the Scottish Western Isles). Calderón and the pilot urged that they give a wide berth to the west coast of Ireland. De Valdés was against this proposal, which would result in a longer voyage. However, the Duke (wisely, as it turned out) agreed with the others – and they set course to sail further west. Nevertheless, as they sailed onwards for the next ten days the winds were unfavourable, blowing from the south.

As Calderón wrote: 'we sailed without knowing whither, through constant storms, fogs and squalls'. Amidst the poor weather and visibility, various ships, either individually or in small groups, fell out of station and lost sight of the main fleet. There was great misery: the soldiers and sailors were suffering from the cold of the North Atlantic – the average air temperatures in those climes in September would have been around 11°C colder than those found in Lisbon. It wasn't helped by the fact that there was a 'Little Ice Age' between 1565 and 1720, and during the late sixteenth century average European temperatures had declined by one degree. Amidst the constant storms and downpours, the ships were permeated by damp, and men lay shivering in their wet bunks, suffering from hunger and thirst. Some ships were even lacking firewood, as evidenced in a letter sent some time before by Don Alonso Martínez de Leyva on board the *La Rata* (*Santa María Encoronada*) to his fellow-commander, Admiral-General Juan Martínez de Recalde, as they sailed north by the Firth of Forth. He requested some firewood so that they could make 'some stew for the wounded and sick and warm up the cooking pots for them'.

As it sailed onwards, the Armada's navigation had to depend more on hope than on exact science. Hitherto, the fleet had mainly been able to find its way by navigation in relation to coasts and the North Sea route would have been familiar to Spanish pilots, as traditionally there had been significant trade with the Baltic. During the preparations for the Armada at Lisbon, pilots from Flanders and Germany with knowledge of the North Sea had been engaged. Now, as it ploughed through the North Atlantic, the Armada had to sail through uncharted waters.

As noted in Chapter 2, the fleet had been issued back in Lisbon with a guide to the route it was expected to take. However, the section describing the coast of Ireland had been rudimentary, only amounting to around 1,000 words – it merely described the Irish southern coast, giving sailing distances relative to the island of Cape Clear, the southernmost point of Ireland. Some later accounts by those on the Armada, who were either shipwrecked on the Irish coast, or just sailed by it, have references to clearing, or seeing '*Cabo Clear*' – used when they had sight of any headland on the Irish Atlantic coast. Yet no Armada ship that we know of ever came near Cape Clear. Spanish fishermen had fished for centuries off Ireland's Atlantic coast, but importantly, there is no record of anybody being in the fleet with that specific experience (save Juan Martínez de Recalde, who had the experience of sailing along the Kerry coast in 1580 and, as we shall see in the next chapter, was to ably use this knowledge towards saving his ship, the *San Juan de Portugal*). One account tells that there had been at least eight Irish

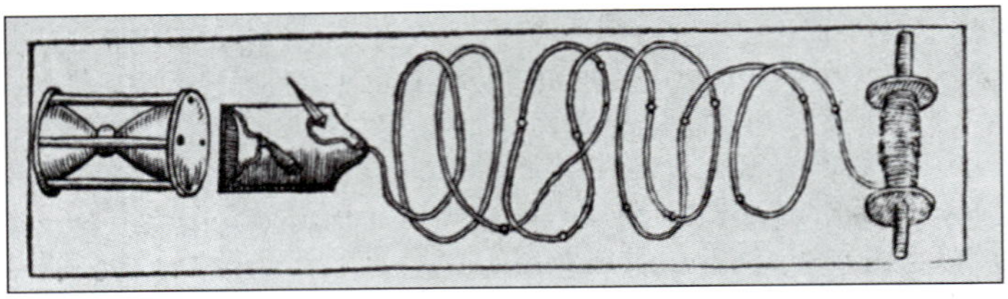

Left: an hourglass with a log and line. The log was dropped overboard and the line was paid out for a set time. Mariners of the sixteenth century used this method to determine the speed of a ship.

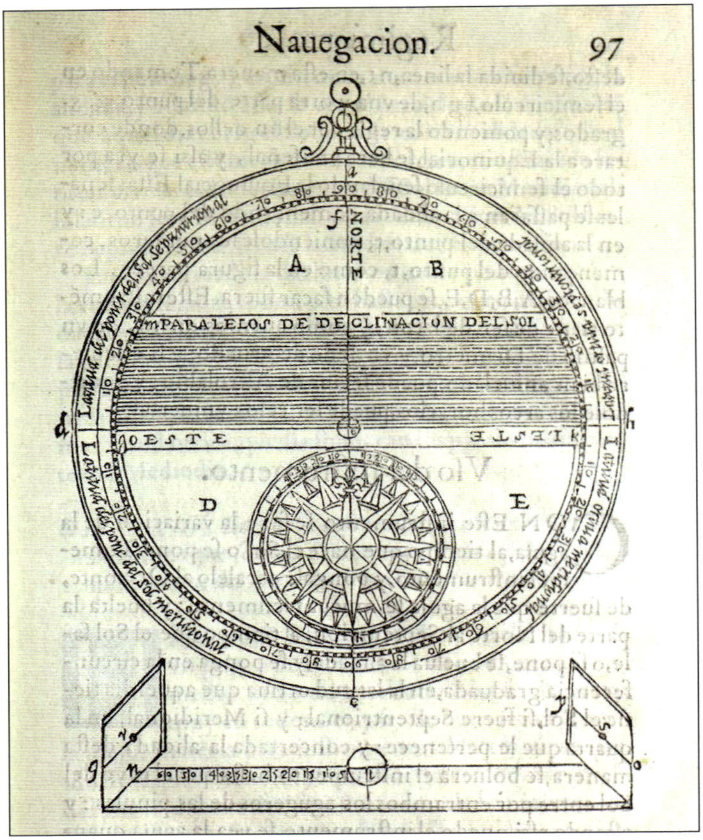

Left: an extract from a sixteenth-century Spanish book on navigation. Mariners of this time could determine their latitude, the position north or south of the equator, measured in degrees, by means of an astrolabe. Using this instrument, they measured the angle of the sun at midday (difficult to do on a heaving deck), and then consulted tables to calculate the latitude. However, there was no method available then to accurately determine longitude.

Left: the remains of a bronze astrolabe, found at the wreck of the 'Girona', in Co. Antrim. It is partitioned in four by bars. The hole in the centre is where the alidade (a bar pivoted so as to swing in a vertical plane to align with a celestial object, allowing measurement of altitude) would have been mounted. The calibrations on the circumference have been eroded.

pilots with the Armada – but there is no information as to whether they possessed any knowledge of these northern waters.

The Uncertain Art of Navigation

Mariners in that era could determine their latitude, the position north or south of the equator, measured in degrees, by means of an astrolabe. Using this instrument, they measured the angle of the sun at midday (difficult to do on a heaving deck), and then consulted tables to calculate the latitude. However, there was no method then available to correctly calculate longitude, the distance west or east of a generally accepted meridian, as to do this one needed an accurate mechanical time-piece. It was to take until the mid-eighteenth century for an accurate marine chronometer to be developed which would allow this precise calculation. During the sixteenth century, as they were going out of the sight of land, mariners endeavoured to establish their east-west position by the technique of calculating speed, using a piece of wood thrown from the ship. The calculated speed could then be used to estimate distance from a known point. The art of navigation in Spain and Portugal, the nations of great oceanic voyages and discovery, was as advanced as it could be. However, due to the limitations of that era, despite great skill on the part of navigators, longitude positions were invariably erroneous. To add to these inaccuracies, there was the effect of currents, a factor known to early navigators, who did not however have systematic methods to calculate the effect of these on navigation. The author Ken Douglas has noted that there are complex flows in the Atlantic around the north and west of Ireland: in addition to the Gulf Stream there are the continental shelf and surface layer currents. In the conditions prevailing in September 1588, Douglas has estimated that the Armada was losing under a knot (1.85 km/hr) in speed, in comparison to the westerly speed the pilots were calculating.

Sailing West

After entering the Atlantic and over nearly two weeks up to 3 September 1588, the Armada fleet sailed west, intending to get well clear of Ireland, and to then turn southwards in the direction of Spain. As noted, the wind was blowing generally from a southerly direction, with the result that the ships had to tack, amidst the stormy conditions, taking a zig-zag path to achieve a westerly course. The effect of the Atlantic currents, little known to the Armada pilots, was that when they thought they had reached their target position well to the west of Ireland, they were actually positioned around 500km further to the east than they had estimated. This ties in with accounts of the Armada voyage, which shows that when those on board, to their surprise, sighted Irish coasts, they had been under the impression that they were around 500km to the west of that point.

On 3 September Medina Sidonia wrote a letter for dispatch to the King: 'By God's mercy, yesterday at noon, the wind shifted to the west, somewhat more in our favour. We were therefore able to sail in a southerly direction, and are now in 58°N'. He prayed that 'God in His mercy will grant us fine weather, so that the Armada may soon enter port; for we are so short of pro-

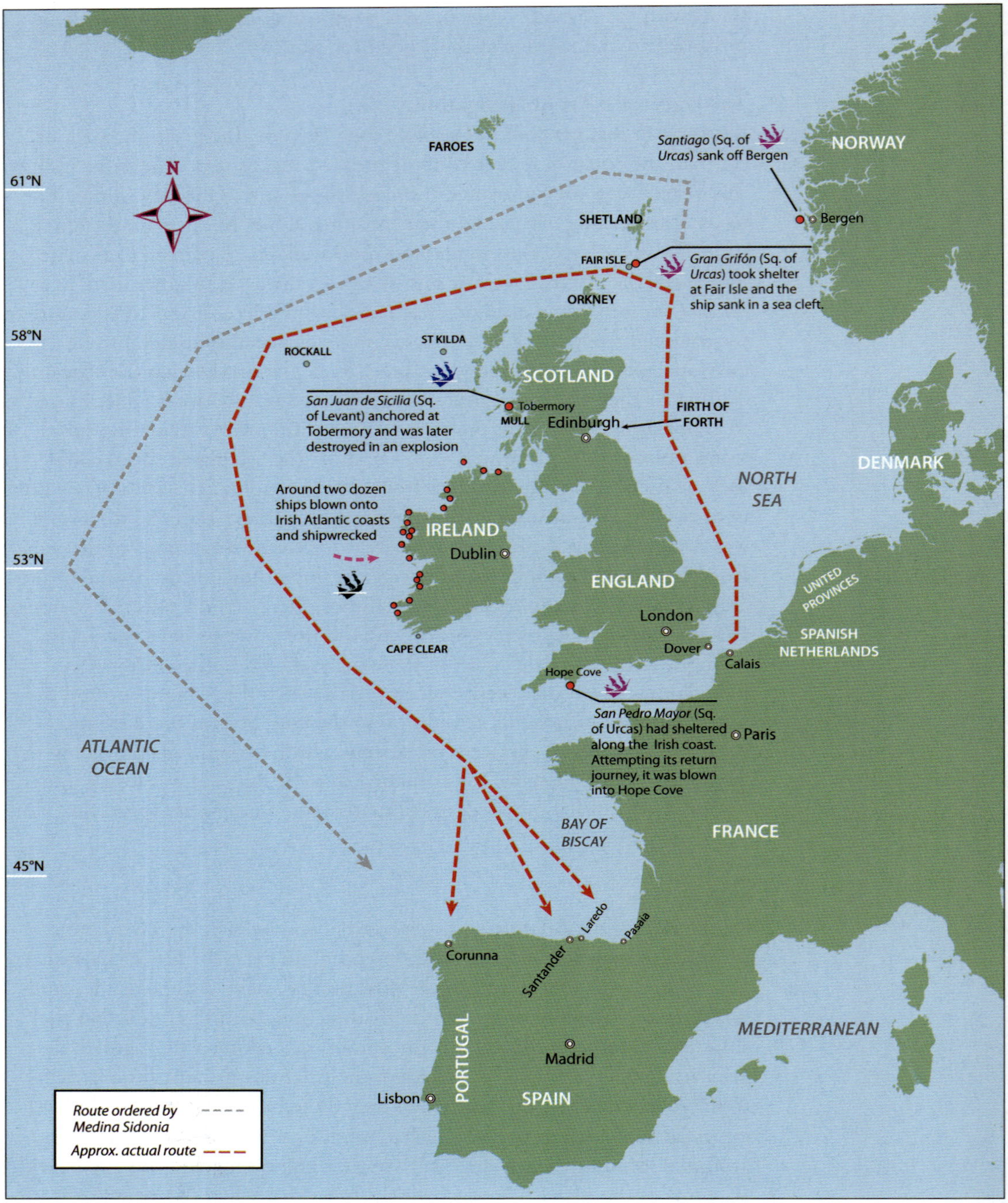

Above: the fraught voyage of the Armada. The route taken from Gravelines back to Spain.

visions that if for our sins we be long delayed, all will be irretrievably lost. There are now a great number of sick and many die'. He related that the fleet was now reduced to 95 ships and that 17 vessels had become detached, including those carrying persons of importance such as Alonso Martínez de Leyva in the *La Rata* and Juan Martínez Recalde in the vice-flagship of the Armada, the *San Juan de Portugal* (who was accompanied by a flotilla of other lost ships). The grim fate of these and the other Armada ships which

Right: a model of the 'San Martín', at the Museo Naval, Cartagena. The flagship of the Duke of Medina Sidonia, it arrived in poor state in the approaches to the harbour of Santander on 21 September 1588. The vessel was soon repaired. During Drake's attack on Galicia and Portugal in 1589, it was on duty protecting ships returning to the Iberian Peninsula. The vessel was also among the Spanish fleet that mustered against Lord Thomas Howard and his ships at the Azores in September 1591.
The 'São Martinho' or 'San Martín' was scrapped in 1593, thus ending the service of 'one of the most celebrated ships in the history of the Portuguese and Spanish navies', as one Spanish account put it.

went adrift on the North Atlantic coasts of Norway, Scotland and Ireland is dealt with in the next chapter.

At last, making headway to Spain

The weather continued to alternate between foul and fair. After 13 September there was a change – favourable winds blew and the battered fleet was able to make headway south towards Spain. They continued to make progress, and by 18 September, what was left of the main fleet (now reduced to 60 sail) had reached a position southwest in the Bay of Biscay, at an estimated latitude of 45°N, around 200km north of Corunna. However, a great storm suddenly blew up (these were the cyclonic conditions which continued north and some days later created the Great Gale which had such a devastating effect along Irish shores). As the Duke wrote a few days later, the tempest was so severe that 'we all expected to perish'. After the storm had abated, there were only 11 ships in sight. With a westerly wind, the Duke and the remaining ships duly set course for Cape Finisterre. At around 2 p.m. on 21 September they spotted land, thinking that they were at the Sisarga islands (just to the west of Corunna). Nevertheless, a caravel which had gone to the shore reported they were actually off Santander: Medina Sidonia and his remaining ships were totally off course, around 400km east of their calculated position. Thus, as we have previously noted, the effect of the complex currents of the Atlantic had disrupted their calculations to establish their east-west position.

As the wind had died down, the *San Martín* could not immediately enter Santander harbour due to contrary currents, and it dropped anchor. Medina Sidonia was weak – he had been severely ill for 25 days. The Duke

Left: an old engraving of Santander.

was a landsman (emphatically so, as he had informed the King the previous February) who had been cooped up on board the flagship for around four months – it is not surprising that he seized the opportunity to go ashore that afternoon. He travelled in a small boat, leaving Diego Flóres de Valdés in charge of the *San Martín*, with orders to have her towed into port. However, a strong south-westerly wind blew up and the flagship was obliged to run, along with 21 other ships, to the nearby harbour at Laredo. Eight ships had already berthed in Santander and the Duke ordered the flagship and other ships to make it to that port when they could. The remains of the Armada fleet began to show up in other northern ports. These included ships of the Guipúzcoan squadron, under Miguel de Oquendo as well as several from the Vizcayan squadron which arrived on 23 September at the sheltered port of Pasaia (near San Sebastián).

One of the stragglers was the 650-ton *San Salvador*, vice-flagship of the *Urca* Squadron, which had lost sight of the main fleet in early September. The journal of the Accountant-General, Coco Calderón, who was on board, gives a flavour of the difficult navigation: 'From 5 to 10 September ... we continued to make for Cape Clear ... On the west coast of Ireland this hulk found herself near an island ... [I] ordered to tack to the northwest, which took her 30 leagues [around 125km] distant, and it is believed that the rest of the Armada will have done the same. On 14 September this hulk was off Cape Clear in 51°N, but did not sight it, and thence set her course for Corunna running south-south-west'. On 21 September the *San Salvador* passed some northbound ships heading towards the Brittany coast, and the

Right: a sixteenth-century hospital. Note, on the bottom left, the women stitching corpses in shrouds. Hospitals across northern Spain were filled by sick sailors and soldiers that came from the returned ships of the Armada.

ship finally arrived in Santander on the night of 23 September. Calderón continued: 'I found the Duke had already arrived, but was very ill, though delighted at our arrival, as he had quite given me up for lost, having left me far to leeward in latitude 58ºN'.

In a Sorry State

The ships of the Armada that returned were in poor state, many with battle damage, several of them showing considerable wear and tear after the battering of the exceptional Atlantic storms. The crews were much reduced, having suffered from battle injuries, hunger, dysentery and disease. Medina Sidonia, in his letters to the King, requested urgent help. Despite the shock over the loss over his great enterprise, Philip (in marked contrast to Queen Elizabeth and the treatment of the sailors of her navy) responded immediately and with generosity to the plight of the Armada survivors.

In a letter of 28 September to the Duke, Philip firstly wished Medina Sidonia a swift recovery to health. He listed the various things that had to be done. These included: the separation of the sick from the healthy; the establishment of hospitals for the sick and wounded to 'provide the best care possible'; and orders for the religious and municipal authorities of Northern Spain to send medicines and doctors as well as the provision of food for the survivors. In the letter, demonstrating his meticulous ability to focus on detail, the King even requested that small ships with provisions be sent out to sea to await the returning Armada vessels and that lanterns be placed at strategic locations to guide them to port. In response to the King's instructions, the bureaucratic sinews of the Spanish state moved into action, drawing down on the deep resources of the kingdom.

One of Philip's emissaries, Don García de Vallejo, soon arrived in Santander and on 4 October, with the cold eye of an accountant, sent a precise and harrowing description to the secretary of the Council of War. There were over 1,000 men sick 'and if the people are not disembarked immediately, so many will burden the hospital', he related. There was no provision for so many patients and the people could not avoid falling ill 'while sleeping in the ships which are full of stench and wretchedness'. There were 7,000 soldiers and sailors to feed and 'it is pitiable to see them'. He urged that the rotten food on the ships be thrown overboard, otherwise someone 'was sure to buy it and grind it up to mix it with the new biscuit, which will be enough to poison all the fleets afloat'.

As noted, Miguel de Oquendo, distinguished naval veteran, had arrived at Pasaia with other ships. On that same day, 23 September, Medina Sidonia had assigned him to take charge of all Armada ships in that port. As it turned out, this appointment was an illusory one as the elderly de Oquendo was dying. He was gravely ill after the harrowing voyage around Britain and Ireland and into the Atlantic. He managed to send some reports to the King (his secretary had to write and sign the last one, on 28 September). De Oquendo died, aged 78, at the beginning of October, as the historian Fernando Duro wrote, 'of grief and sadness, not wanting to see even his wife'. Misfortune continued at Pasaia – on 24 October, the magazine in de Oquendo's flagship, the *Santa Ana*, was ignited by accident, and the ship blew up, according to one account, 'scattering the harbour with corpses'.

De Recalde's Return

We had last seen Juan Martínez de Recalde, Admiral General, in his vice-flagship, the *San Juan de Portugal* on 3 September in northern waters, just after he had separated from the main fleet. His travails along the Irish coast are told in Chapter 5. At the end of September, applying his exceptional seamanship to avoid the reefs and islands, he sailed out of Blasket Sound, Co. Kerry, accompanied by two *pataches*, and, clearing the Irish coast, set sail for Spain. On 7 October, the *San Juan de Portugal* arrived at Corunna.

De Recalde, aged 62, who all through the Armada voyage had been suffering from arthritis, was now seriously ill and in a feeble state, having been confined to his bunk for weeks. All those on board his flotilla of three vessels were starving and suffering from thirst. Of the 661 survivors, around half were sick or much debilitated. Two hundred and thirty men had died during the Armada expedition. Recalde himself expired on 23 October. Before he died he sent letters, along with his diary of the journey, and two letters from Alonso Martínez de Leyva, to the King. In spite of being on his deathbed, de Recalde had Medina Sidonia in his sights. The documents contained sharp criticisms of the Duke. De Recalde, in his letter, made clear that the most important thing was that the errors which had been made in the Armada should not go unpunished because by ignoring them, the same would happen on future occasions. After receiving de Recalde's testimony Philip made a note: 'I have seen all this, although I think it would have been better not to see it because it troubles me so much'.

Loss and Prayers

At the outset of the Armada expedition, the highly respected de Leyva had been designated by the King to take command in the event of Medina Sidonia's death. Over the course of the subsequent events, de Leyva, like de Recalde, had felt that the Duke had ignored his advice. In one of his letters to de Recalde, sent from on board his *La Rata*, he said that he was keeping

The two outstanding commanders of the Armada: Juan Martínez de Recalde (right) and Alonso Martínez de Leyva (below right). Both had been critical of the Duke of Medina Sidonia and considered that he had made tactical errors during the course of the Armada's campaign – and their criticisms were sent to the King. De Recalde died on 23 October 1588, weeks after arriving at Corunna. As it turned out, de Leyva died just five days later, around 1,300km to the north, when the galleass 'Girona', on which he had been travelling, sank off the northern Irish coast.

a record of what had happened and, if he arrived safely, he would immediately set out for the Court, where he would speak the truth. De Leyva was not to get the chance. Shipwrecked twice in Ireland, he found passage at Killybegs, Co. Donegal on the galleass *Girona,* which had been en route to Scotland. At midnight on 28 October the ship was wrecked on the northern Irish coast, and all except a handful of the 1,200 aboard were drowned. Thus, de Leyva died five days after de Recalde. This was not immediately known in Spain: in the following weeks reports filtered in that de Leyva was seen at various Irish locations such as Dursey Head and Mayo. The King still maintained his esteem for de Leyva – earlier, on 29 September, he had written a letter addressed to him, 'when you arrive in port, as I hope you have already done so', to take charge of the soldiers of the Armada, now ashore. On 30 December, Don Agustín de Mexía (*Maestre de Campo*, who with his *Tercio* of Andalucia had sailed in the Armada), wrote from Santander to the King offering to take part in an expedition to rescue de Leyva. As it turned out, the news of the sinking of the *Girona* was then on its way to the King from his ambassador in France, so no rescue attempt was made.

Over the previous months, prayers had been said in churches across Spain for the success of the Armada. On 13 October the request went out from the Escorial to the Spanish bishops that these should cease. Philip explained to them: 'as you know the events of the sea are so varied'. However, he continued: 'Considering the … perilous times in which the entire Armada found itself, battered by a severe and tumultuous storm, a worse outcome could reasonably have been feared'. In consideration of this, he asked for a solemn mass of thanks to be held in their dioceses.

The Survival Rate

The Armada muster of ships that departed from Corunna at the end of July 1588, discounting the diminutive ten *carabelas* and seven *falúas* that accompanied the fleet, added up to 128 vessels. Around 112 had sailed through the Fair Isle Channel. By 20 October, the tally of ships that had returned to Spain amounted to 64. Over the weeks and months that followed, other stragglers reached Spanish ports. It is difficult to be exact about the total, given that the return of some of the smaller vessels, such as the *pataches* and *zabras*, may have been unrecorded. The tally given in that distinguished corpus of work, *La Batalla del Mar Océano*, is that 91 ships eventually made it back to northern Spanish ports. That was a survival rate of 71 per cent, a remarkable achievement, in the circumstances. To give some perspective, it is useful to consider one variable: the weather. If the gales and storms of September 1588 had not been so extreme and unusual, the chances are that there would not have been many (if any) shipwrecks in Scotland or along the Irish coast which would have resulted in a much higher survival rate.

It is a tribute to the Duke, his pilots and mariners, and importantly, to the solid build of Spanish and Portuguese ships, that over two thirds of the fleet managed to return to Spain after encountering such horrendous challenges. The Duke managed to lead a good proportion of the surviving ships, suffering from battle damage and many not built for Atlantic conditions, amidst extreme gales through uncharted waters. Given the vagaries

Right: a replica sixteenth-century nao under construction at the Albaola Itsas Kultur Faktoria, Pasaia, Guipúzcoa. Many of the ships in the Armada were built along the Cantabrian coast: in Cantabria, Vizcaya and Guipúzcoa. As it turned out, most of these sturdy ships enjoyed a good survival rate.

of the art of establishing one's position in that era, it was an incredible feat of navigation to sail thousands of kilometres, battling the wind and waves, all the time trying to avoid the dangerous Irish Atlantic coast. The Levant Squadron had the worst survival rate. Of the eleven ships of this squadron which had set out from Corunna, all but one (the galleon *San Francisco de Florencia*) were cargo vessels, built in and for the Mediterranean. Only three returned – including the *San Francisco*. Of the four vessels in the Squadron of Galleasses that had been built at Naples (disadvantaged by their faulty rudder assembly) only two returned.

And then there was the butcher's bill: given incomplete detail, it is difficult to precisely calculate the number of missing – for example, it took several years for some survivors to reach Spain. From the *Batalla del Mar Océano* documents, it is possible to estimate that, of the around 28,580 soldiers, sailors and others (officials, servants, galley rowers) who left Corunna, the total number of dead or disappeared was around 9,720. The causes were many: being killed or wounded in battle; shipwreck; slaughter in Ireland, or expiring due to hunger, thirst, cold and disease during the long voyage home. The loss was deeply felt in villages and towns across Spain and Portugal, and along the Mediterranean. One account tells of distraught families roving through northern Spanish ports, for months afterwards, searching for their missing soldier or sailor. As we will see in the next chapter, for the deaths in Ireland, an approximate estimate is 5,250. This was due to drowning in shipwrecks on the coast or arising from the extensive and methodical slaughter there. The deaths related to Ireland make up just over half the total estimated losses of the Armada.

Left: gardens in the ducal palace at Sanlúcar de Barrameda. The Duke of Medina Sidonia returned here on 24 October 1588 and was able to settle back to life among his extensive estates. However, he was called back to arms in 1596 when the English once more attacked Cádiz.

Back to Sanlúcar de Barrameda

The man who surely carried in his heart the burden of anguish at the losses soon left the scene. The Duke of Medina Sidonia, on arrival at Santander on 21 September, had been ill for many days. Two days after he stepped ashore, he sent a letter to Philip requesting that he be given permission to return home as he was so sick and weak – if not, 'I will undoubtedly perish in this land if winter comes while I am still here'. To support his case, sick notes from doctors were sent on to the Escorial. Philip, perhaps conscious that he had foisted the position of Armada commander on the Duke against his wishes, acted in a compassionate manner. He allowed Medina Sidonia to depart for his ducal seat at Sanlúcar de Barrameda, and excused him from what would have been the painful duty of reporting personally at the Escorial. On 5 October, having sent a final report to the King on the post-Armada arrangements, Medina Sidonia set out for home, carried in a litter, with an entourage of eleven mules and assorted servants. He maintained a low profile, giving alms to the poor and money to the religious for masses on the way. He arrived at Sanlúcar on 24 October and, amidst the fruit trees and vineyards, was able to settle back to life at his ducal palace, home to his family since the end of the thirteenth century. The Duke regained his health and, as we shall see in Chapter 6, he had the opportunity to rally to Philip's colours once more, in 1596 when the English made their attack on Cádiz.

Chapter 5

Crash onto Cruel Shores

As the Armada sailed west through the Fair Isle Channel on 18 August, four ships, all battle-weary and not suited to Atlantic waters, became separated from the fleet. Three were from the Squadron of *Urcas*: the *Gran Grifón* (650 tons), the *Barca de Amburg* (600 tons) and the *Castillo Negro* (750 tons). The fourth ship, the large *Trinidad Valencera* (1,100 tons) was from the Squadron of the Levant and was leaking, much damaged after the recent battles. This collection of ships spent two weeks trying to set a course to Spain, but was frustrated by the southwest winds. On 31 August, they were somewhere north of Ireland's most northerly point, Malin Head Co. Donegal. The *Barca de Amburg* was leaking like a sieve and, with the pumps clogged, the captain signalled that she was on the point of foundering. Some 100 of the crew were taken aboard the *Trinidad Valencera* and the remaining 80 aboard the *Gran Grifón*. The *Barca de Amburg* sank shortly afterwards. On 2 September, the *Trinidad Valencera* lost sight of the *Gran Grifón* and the *Castillo Negro*. We will look at the wanderings of the *Gran Grifón*, but the *Castillo Negro* was never heard of again and was lost somewhere in northern waters.

The *Gran Grifón*, flagship of the *urcas*, with the squadron commander Juan Gómez de Medina on board, was in bad shape. It had been built in Rostock for the Baltic trade, not for Atlantic storms and definitely not as a gun platform for great naval battles. Despite this, she had fought bravely in the battles in the English Channel and was suffering from battle damage. The vessel was now lost and alone in the North Atlantic, and the captain was desperately trying to tack southwards to home. Next, as they later recounted, they 'discovered the island of Ireland', but the wind blew them from land and they continued to sail south, reaching 54° latitude (roughly abeam of Blacksod Bay). A great storm beset them on 17 September and, as the ship could not withstand any more battering, they decided that they would run with the wind, head north and attempt to reach Norway. During a calm the crew

Left: map of Fair Isle, Scotland. On 28 September the 'Gran Grifón' was blown into the cleft of Stroms Hellier and then sank. Most of the crew survived and managed to eventually reach the Scottish mainland and in time, to the safety of Spanish Flanders.

patched the holes in the ship as best they could, using animal hides and timber boards. On 24 September they saw some Scottish islands, home of '*gente salvaje*' (wild people) as they called them. They continued northeast and, with the water in the hold steadily rising and the pumps now overcome, they decided they had no choice but to head directly for an island. On 27 September, the *Gran Grifón* anchored to the east of Fair Isle, situated between Shetland and Orkney, where, five weeks before, the Armada had sailed past. The following morning, the ship was driven ashore and became jammed into Stroms Hellier, a narrow cleft surrounded by steep cliffs. It was a perilous location, and seven were drowned as she sank. It is thought that many of the crew managed to clamber ashore using the masts resting on the cliffs. Once there, they discovered that there were only a few inhabitants on the 5km-long island, who lived a meagre existence in huts with turf (peat) fires, on a diet mainly of fish. Despite Gómez de Medina paying handsomely for food, there was little to be had. The Spanish resorted to eating everything they could find, including seabirds. By mid-November, the 230 survivors managed to hire boats to take them to Shetland. Weeks later, they reached the Scottish mainland, landing at the village of Anstruther on the shores of the Firth of Forth. We will look at their fate and that of other survivors in Scotland later in this chapter.

The *San Juan de Sicilia* (of the Squadron of Levant, from Ragusa, with the original title of *Brod Martolosi* but given an Italian name to hide her origins from among Ragusa's Ottoman neighbours) was also unable to keep up with the fleet and, amidst the stormy conditions, had separated from it on 18 August. The ship, a veteran of the actions in the Azores in 1582 and 1583, was transporting field artillery and several companies of soldiers, amounting to 267 men. The *San Juan de Sicilia* was much damaged, having collided with another ship during the battle at Gravelines. In addition she had been assailed by English cannon during that battle, with one account saying that 'the portholes were all full of blood' – indeed it probably was due to her solid Ragusan build that she was able to sail at all

Right: a map of the Isle of Mull where on 23 September 1588, the 'San Juan de Sicilia', sailed into Tobermory Bay and dropped anchor. At the beginning of November 1588, the ship, moored in the bay, blew up in a huge explosion, whether due to mischance or by sabotage.

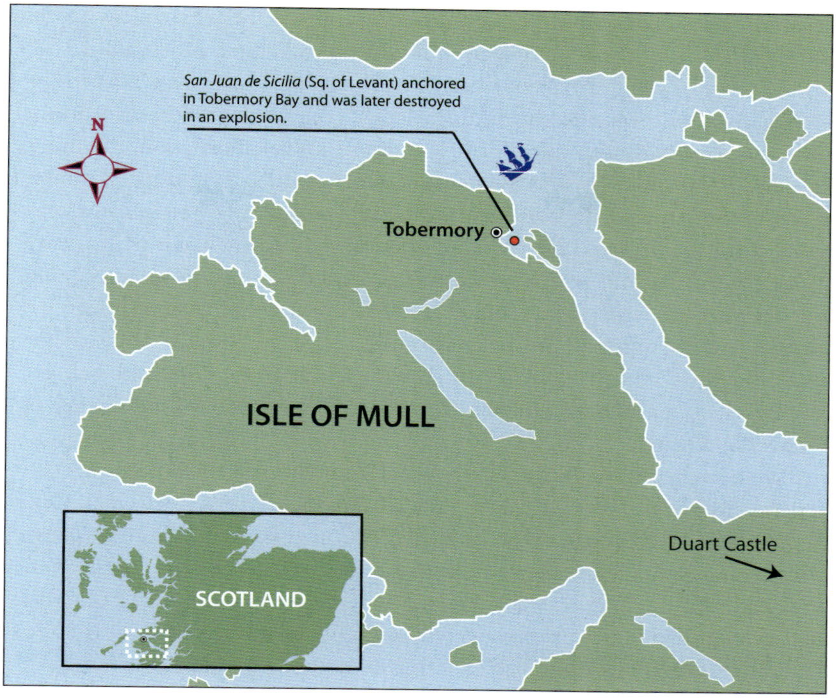

after the damage that was inflicted on her. After more wandering through northern waters, on 23 September the ship sailed into Tobermory Bay, in the Isle of Mull. It was a sheltered harbour and the crew began repairs. The local chieftain, Lachlan Mór Maclean of Duart, made an interesting offer to the captain: if they provided a detachment of troops and some artillery to help settle a feud with neighbouring clans, he would provide assistance. And so, around 100 Spanish soldiers set to and easily defeated Lachlan's enemies across the neighbouring islands. All seemed well until, at the beginning of November 1588, the moored ship and those aboard were blown apart in a huge explosion. The gunpowder had gone up, possibly by accidental ignition, as testified by a survivor, when they were drying gunpowder, rather

Right: Duart Castle on the Isle of Mull, seat of Lachlan Mór Maclean. After the 'San Juan de Sicilia' anchored in Tobermory Bay, the Spaniards obtained help from Lachlan Mór, in return for providing military assistance to defeat his enemies.

than, as some Elizabethan sources implied, sabotage. Fewer than two dozen survived. Most of these succeeded in returning to Spain by the end of 1589.

Another of the strays in northern waters was the ancient *urca*, *Santiago* (600 tons, built in the Netherlands in 1551 – one of the oldest ships in the Armada). She had been transporting mules for the artillery train, the mules' farriers, and – uniquely – was one of the few Armada ships to carry women, wives accompanying their soldier husbands. The *Santiago* had become separated from the fleet and on 18 September she was off the coast of Norway. With the ship's seams widening alarmingly and the pumps were in continuous action they desperately sought shelter. They sailed into a fjord near Bergen and ran aground on rocks. Around half of the roughly 100 survivors were able to reach Lisbon by sea in January 1589. The rest, despite being shipwrecked in Denmark, managed to arrive at the Spanish Netherlands by an overland route.

We have noted the fate of three of the four ships that had become separated from the fleet on 18 August, all save the *Trinidad Valencera*. On 1 September, this ship had taken on board 100 men from the sinking *Barca de Amburg*, and now there were an estimated 510 souls on board. The *Trinidad* (Squadron of the Levant) was a Venetian merchant ship, a veteran of Azores battles, that had been commandeered by the Viceroy of Sicily and had left Palermo for Spain in April 1587. At 1,100 tons, it was one of the largest ships in the Armada. In addition to the normal defensive complement of 42 guns, there were siege cannons in temporary mountings on deck. These comprised three *cañones de batir* (large cannons used to batter down fortifications) that had been cast by the eminent Flemish gun-founder Remigy de Halut, and one large Turkish cannon, probably captured at the Battle of Lepanto. In addition, within the voluminous holds were the carriages with large wheels, the limbers and other accoutrements for these great guns. The siege train was intended to be used against the walls of London or other English fortifications after Parma's army had landed in south-east England.

Don Alonso de Luzón, *Maestre de Campo*, commander of the Naples *tercio*, was in overall charge. Despite being essentially a transport ship, the well-armed *Trinidad* had taken part in the action off Portland Bill and had bravely traded cannonballs with the English at Gravelines, sustaining much damage. Built for trade on the Mediterranean, not for the heavy weather of the Atlantic, it sprang a leak as it sailed in the waters north of Ireland and the pumps were overcome. The north coast of Ireland was sighted. With a heavy gale blowing, and over two metres of water in her hold, it was decided to make for land. The vessel was off the north Donegal coast and the many cliffs in sight did not present an inviting prospect. On 14 September they spotted a bay with a crescent-shaped sandy beach. As the ship sailed in, probably with the intention of beaching close to land, she struck a reef, around 300m off the beach at Kinnagoe Bay, located along the northern coast of the Inishowen Peninsula, Co. Donegal.

Irish Society and the Creeping Colonisation

Before we continue with the Armada shipwrecks and landings in Ireland, it is worth pausing to examine the state of affairs there during the sixteenth

Right: a drawing by Albrecht Dürer, 1521, of soldiers in Ireland: galloglass and kern.

century. As we have seen in Chapter 1, the west coast of Ireland was mainly controlled by Gaelic lords. They and their clans enjoyed a long-established Gaelic society which was bound by ancient laws with a well-developed culture of law, music and poetry. However, it was an isolated culture and very different from that of the more developed mercantile societies of England and the Continent.

There were many contacts between Spain and Ireland during the sixteenth century. Basque fishermen had been sailing for centuries in the rich fishing grounds off the west coast of Ireland, from Cork to Donegal. The Irish fisheries, with their hake, herring and pilchard, were one of the most lucrative locations for the fishermen of northern Spain. During the sixteenth century treaties were made between the Spanish Crown and Irish lords which gave licences to the Spanish to fish in their waters. There was also much trade. In return for hides, leather, salted fish and beef, commodities imported from Spain included wine and finished products like sword blades, managed by merchants in such ports as Galway, Limerick, Cork, Waterford and Dublin. However, with the Tudor expansion of control over Ireland, and particularly with the growth of Anglo-Spanish hostilities from the 1570s, the English tried to restrict this trade and capture it for themselves.

Below: the Lord Deputy, Sir John Perrot's coat of arms at Dublin Castle.

Since the time of Henry VIII, the great initiative to tame the native lords was to 'Tudorise' them. In return for submission to the English sovereign, their rule and lands were confirmed and they received titles. One important objective for the Lord Deputy in Dublin Castle was to extend control amidst the patchwork of lands controlled by the Gaelic lords along the western and northern Atlantic coasts. Ulster was regarded as particularly vulnerable due to the dangerous (in English eyes) influence of Scottish chieftains and their soldiers. The Gaelic lords frequently imported mercenary soldiers from Scotland, to act as their garrison and assist them during their frequent conflicts. These could be the heavier-armed 'galloglasses', or the more lightly-armed 'redshanks'. The arrival of 2,000 redshanks in 1584 to support an offensive by the O'Neills of Tyrone against a rival chief caused

alarm in Dublin Castle. The Lord Deputy, Sir John Perrot, mounted an expedition to the north, but in the event, the redshanks had already withdrawn by the time he arrived. To avert future Scottish intervention and to extend control, Perrot came up with an expedient method: he placed 1,100 soldiers who were to be billeted with local Gaelic lords along the coast of north-east Ulster. Three lieutenancies were assigned to local strongmen, one of whom was Hugh O'Neill, Baron of Dungannon, of the great O'Neill dynasty, who was given charge of the area that was soon to be shired as Counties Armagh and Monaghan.

Above: Kinnagoe Bay on the Inishowen Peninsula, Co. Donegal. On 14 September 1588 the 'Trinidad Valencera' grounded on a reef, to the left, around 300m off the beach.

Grounding at Kinnagoe

Back to Kinnagoe Bay on that gale-blown morning of 14 September 1588, when, seeking safe anchorage, the *Trinidad Valencera* grounded on a reef. She remained upright, with her bow on the rock, with the stern settled into the sand. The commander, Don Alonso de Luzón, led a small group by boat, to land ashore. They were met by a cluster of what he termed 'savage people'. They treated them well, 'until 20 more wild men came unto them, after which time they took away a bag of money containing 1000 reals of [silver] and a cloak … richly laid with gold lace'. Even though both sides subscribed to Catholicism, there ensued a total clash of cultures. Notwithstanding some fishing in Donegal waters by Spanish fishermen, this was likely to be the first encounter by these people with Spaniards. Most initial communication most likely was by using gestures or perhaps Latin. As the Spanish rowboat was damaged, de Luzón hired a local one and within two days most of those aboard had been landed. Despite the wind and waves, some Spaniards stayed aboard, salvaging what they could, alongside locals who were busy plundering this unexpected gift from the sea. Many were drowned when, two days after she grounded, the *Trinidad*, pounded by the waves, suddenly broke apart and sank. Back on land the survivors were starving and managed to buy some local horses and butter, which eclectic fare they consumed.

Hearing that there was a castle to the south of the Inishowen Peninsula about 35km distant, Don Alonso and his men set out for it. The castle belonged to the local lord, who dominated the peninsula, Sir John O'Doherty.

Above: a depiction by Tony Boyle of the 'Trinidad Valencera' stuck on the reef.

He had previously surrendered his traditional lordship to the English and received a regrant of his territory (plus the title). However, he still acknowledged the suzerainty of the regional lord, Sir Hugh O'Donnell (father of Red Hugh O'Donnell, who had been kidnapped by the English in 1587 and brought to Dublin Castle). The Spaniards, like all their fellow Armada survivors, were in the days that followed to enter into the maelstrom created by the curious mix of greed, self-interest and survival adopted by the Gaelic lords along the remote coasts of Ireland, as Tudor control encroached to envelop them.

Three days later, the Trinidad survivors approached Elagh and its castle, which was set on a height, dominating the landscape. A bishop was in residence and apparently said that they could enter the castle, but, as he was fearful of retribution from the English, they were to fire their arquebuses, thus to give the impression abroad that the Spanish had taken the castle by force. As it turned out, the bishop, thought to be the Franciscan, Cornelius O'Devaney, of Down and Connor diocese, was arrested soon after the Armada events. He was released in 1590 and years later, was tried for being implicated in the rebellion of the Earl of Tyrone. In 1612 he was found guilty and was hanged, drawn and quartered in Dublin. (In 1992, this bishop, along with others martyred for their faith, was beatified by Pope John Paul II.) One account, by survivors from the *Trinidad*, Juan de Nova and Francisco de Borja, accused the bishop of deception – that his discharge

Right: Burt Castle, Co. Donegal, where the Hovendens and their men were garrisoned.

Above: *Elagh Castle, Co. Derry. A massacre of many of the survivors of the 'Trinidad Valencera' took place a few kilometres away.*

of an artillery piece was to alert the nearby garrison at Burt Castle – but this is likely to be a misconception in view of the bishop's subsequent activities.

Massacre

There is more clarity about what happened next. The garrison at Burt was under the control of the brothers, Richard and Henry Hovenden, adventurers born in Ireland of English origin. With their deputy, Sergeant-Major John Kelly, they commanded a force of around 200 mercenary soldiers, mostly Irish, composed of horsemen, arqubusiers and bowmen. These were part of the series of northern garrisons that had been assigned by the Lord Deputy to guard against Scottish incursion. The Burt garrison was under the lieutenancy of Hugh O'Neill, Earl of Tyrone, then struggling to gain supremacy over rivals in Ulster. The Hovendens were trusted subordinates, and also happened to be his foster brothers. (O'Neill, after his father's death, had become a ward of the Crown and had been fostered by the Hovenden family, English settlers in the Pale). Alerted to the presence of the Spanish, the Hovendens and their soldiers, carrying the Queen's ensigns, set out on the 10km march towards the Spanish survivors, who were now ensconced in a ruined castle near Elagh. After a roll of drums the parley began. The Hovendens demanded to know: what were they doing in the Queen's dominions? The Spanish explained that they were survivors from a shipwreck and begged to be allowed return on a ship – and they would make payment for this. The reply was that they could not and that they must surrender as prisoners of war. De Luzón refused, and was then threatened that if they didn't surrender immediately, 3,000 English troops would soon arrive and kill them. As night fell, the Hovenden band mounted several attacks. The next morning the drums rolled for yet another parley. Sergeant-Major John Kelly assured the Spanish that if they surrendered, he would escort them to the Queen's governor in Dublin. An ally of O'Neill was also present at the parley. This was Sir Hugh O'Donnell and his formidable Scots wife, Fiona, known as *Iníon Dubh* – as well as seeking opportunities for material gain, they were also interested in being of service to the English cause, so they could secure the release of their son, Red Hugh, then in captivity in Dublin Castle.

As the survivors, de Nova and de Borja later wrote, de Luzón, hearing the offers of mercy and 'seeing that his men were starving and the enemy

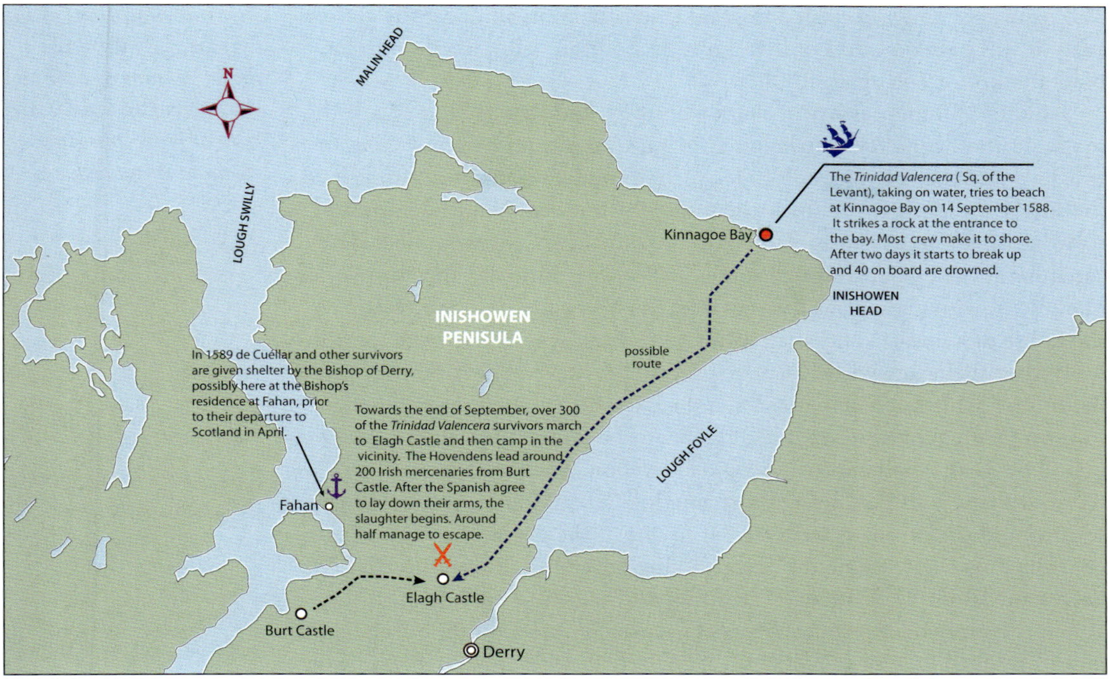

Above: the events in North Donegal after the 'Trinidad Valencera' entered Kinnagoe Bay in September 1588. Francisco de Cuéllar's possible stay at Fahan in 1589 is also noted.

had withdrawn the cattle and supplies, and having no more ammunition for skirmishing, told the enemy that he would surrender the arms honourably if they kept their word and allowed each man to keep his best clothes. They promised and gave their word to do so, and thus they all surrendered their arms'. Next they were 'conveyed …. To the other side of the bog … [and the Hovenden band] fell upon the Spaniards in a body and despoiled them of everything they possessed, leaving them quite naked, and killing those who offered the least resistance'. The Hovendens and their men seized the money, jewels, silver and clothes. No doubt Sir Hugh and his wife claimed their share, and a later account suggests that, as well, they retained a Spanish captain for ransom.

The naked survivors were marched around three kilometres further and were ordered to bivouac in the open for the night, with those worth ransoming, the officers and gentlemen, being separated from the main body. At daybreak, the ordinary sailors and soldiers were marched to an open field, and with the cavalry on one side and the arqubusiers on the other side of them, the Hovenden band set to and up to 300 defenceless men were slaughtered with lance, sword and bullet. It is sobering to remind ourselves that this carnage was carried out by men under the overall control of Hugh O'Neill, Earl of Tyrone, whose name is honoured in Irish history. O'Neill had not been present, but his ally Sir Hugh O'Donnell had been there at the surrender parley. However, O'Neill took great care to advance his position with the English – a few days before the slaughter he had written to the Lord Deputy asking advice on how to deal with the Spaniards. The Hovendens later reported the events near Elagh to the Lord Deputy. Firstly, they stressed the importance of their prisoner, Alonso de Luzón – how he had commanded 30,000 men. They also laid emphasis on their own bravery.

The report certainly succeeded in gaining approbation amongst the authorities – it was passed on to Lord Burghley in London, who noted on it: 'A bold attempt of 140 against 600'.

Around 150 men, many of them wounded, had managed to escape the massacre and flee. They got shelter at Elagh Castle from Bishop O'Devaney. It is recorded that the Bishop of Derry, Redmond O'Gallagher, also helped the survivors. With O'Devaney's help the unwounded Spanish, amounting to around 100, were sent to Scotland. The remainder, the wounded, were cared for at the castle, although some died of their injuries. They were eventually sent, with a guide, as the survivors, de Nova and de Borja, wrote, 'to the house of a savage gentleman called O'Cahan', where they were treated well. After sheltering with O'Cahan's brother for several days they arrived at the impregnable fortress that was Dunluce Castle, situated on a cliff edge, towering high above the sea. Here the Scoto-Irish chief, Sorley Boy McDonnell ('boy' is an Anglicization of *buidhe* – 'yellow,' the colour of his hair) received them with kindness, even arranging Masses for them. Boats were secured and the survivors were ferried to one of the nearest Scottish islands, controlled by clans, where the Scottish king's overall rule was tolerated. The Protestant James VI maintained neutrality during the Anglo-Spanish war. When the survivors from the *Trinidad* eventually reached Edinburgh, King James arranged lodgings for them. Particularly lucky were the 18 who were accommodated in houses of the Catholic nobles, Lord Claude Hamilton and Sir John Seton, who treated them well and arranged for new clothing. (These lords also helped survivors from other Armada ships. In his youth, Seton had attended the Spanish court, and had been inducted as a member of the Order of Santiago). Around a month later, King James ordered that the Spanish be divided up to sail on four Scottish ships that were leaving for France. After bad weather blew some of the ships to the English shore, James intervened and Queen Elizabeth agreed to let the Spanish survivors continue their journey and they reached France safely.

As we have seen, the Hovendens, near Elagh, had separated out those men with ransomable potential before they began slaughtering the rest. These were now marched to the town of Drogheda, around 170km away, with several dying on the way. By November 1588, over 30 *Trinidad* survivors were incarcerated at the Millmount fortification, which sat atop a small hill south of the River Boyne at Drogheda. They made up an eclectic mix: captains, sergeants, drummers, servants, a Portuguese doctor, a Greek, and several Italians. A few died there, but most were ransomed, gaining their liberty by the end of 1589. It proved more complicated for Alonso de Luzón – he was brought to London and had to wait until April 1591 for his freedom, when a ransom payment together with an exchange for a prominent Huguenot, who had been captured in Flanders, was completed.

Hugh O'Neill, Earl of Tyrone, did not forget the Armada events in his territory. In 1594, in a document setting out his grievances to the authorities in Dublin Castle, he noted his achievements – how his foster-brothers, the Hovendens, had killed hundreds of Spaniards, and that he had turned the best men over to the authorities. In turn, he complained that he had received no reward for this.

Right: the locations of the estimated 24 Armada shipwrecks on or close to the coast of Ireland. Each red dot represents an Armada shipwreck.

Castillo Negro
Disappeared, last seen around here
Barca de Amburg
Sank, approximately here
N
TORY ISLAND
MALIN HEAD
KINNAGOE BAY
Trinidad Valencera
RATHLIN ISLAND
Girona
LACADA POINT
DUNLUCE CASTLE
p 200
LOUGH FOYLE
Derry
p 167
Duquesa Santa Ana
p 196
LOUGHROS MORE BAY
Killybegs
DONEGAL BAY
two unknown
ULSTER
Carrickfergus
Juliana
Santa María de Visón
Lavia
STREEDAGH STRAND
Sligo
p 176
BROADHAVEN
p 191
possibly
Ciervo Volante
KILLALA BAY
Ballina
BLACKSOD BAY
La Rata/ Santa María Encoronada
Newry
Dundalk
unknown
San Nicolás Prodaneli
CLEW BAY
CLARE ISLAND
Gran Grin
p 187
Falcón Blanco Mediano
CONNACHT
Drogheda
LEINSTER
DUBLIN
Santa Bárbara
p 205
GALWAY
GALWAY BAY
ARAN ISLANDS
CLIFFS OF MOHER
p 207
San Marcos
San Esteban
Kilkenny
LIMERICK
LOOP HEAD
SHANNON ESTUARY
Anunciada
p 212
Wexford
Nuestra Señora del Socorro
Tralee
p 213
WATERFORD
MUNSTER
Dingle
ría de la Rosa
Fernandome
BLASKET ISLANDS
p 218
possibly Trinidad
CORK
Kinsale
CAPE CLEAR

High Alert

In September 1588, English officials all across Ireland were on high alert for news of Spanish ships and landings. Before describing their treatment of Armada survivors, it is relevant to look at the key figures of the Tudor administration at that time. As we have seen in Chapter 1, English rule had been well established in the Pale (the eastern part of Ireland). To the north, west and south of the country, there was a varied collection of independent Irish lords. As noted, the English administration, seeking to control Ulster, had set up lieutenancies there. In other provinces, to help promote English control, a Presidency of Connaught had been established in 1569, and a similar position in Munster was later put in place. Presiding over this Tudor enterprise was Elizabeth's representative in Ireland, the Lord Deputy, Sir William FitzWilliam. Over the course of his career, FitzWilliam had held many positions of power. Even though he was a Protestant, he had supported the accession of Queen Mary in 1553 over the claims of Lady Jane Grey. On several occasions he had served as lord chief justice in Ireland and in 1572, had been appointed Lord Deputy – not a sought-after position. His first period in this office was not a happy one as it was a time of continual disorder and, suffering from a general shortage of money, he resigned in 1575. Later he was made governor of Fotheringay Castle where Mary, Queen of Scots, was imprisoned and executed. He reputedly had treated her with kindness during that time. In February 1588, at the age of 62, he was called out of retirement and, lured by a higher salary, was reappointed as Lord Deputy.

Richard Bingham

The President (Governor) of Connaught, Sir Richard Bingham, had been born in Dorsetshire in 1528. He was an exemplar of the captain-adventurer of Elizabethan times. Trained as a soldier, he sought military adventures from the beginning and, aged only 19, fought against the Scots. He served with the Spanish army at the Battle of St Quentin in 1557 and also served under Don John of Austria in the Battle of Lepanto in 1571. However, as we will see, this experience of serving alongside Spanish soldiers did not prevent him from directing the widespread slaughter of Armada prisoners. After Anglo-Spanish relations had deteriorated, Bingham fought with the Dutch rebels against the Army of Flanders. It was Ireland which was to offer Bingham real opportunity. As we saw in Chapter 1, in November 1580, Bingham had been Vice-Admiral of the navy warship *Swiftsure*, part of the flotilla engaged in the attack on the Papal forces at Smerwick. He gave a laconic account of the great massacre there, noting that it was carried out by others. In 1584 Bingham was appointed Governor of Connaught and at the same time was knighted by Lord Deputy Perrot. Soon after his appointment he assigned his two brothers to Sligo: George to be in charge of the district and John to be captain of the hundred-strong garrison there. Richard Bingham was strongly of the view that the Irish were treacherous and the best way to deal with them was: 'to keep them under, in such mediocrity, as that by having too little, the country may not be waste, and by having too much the people may not rebell'. In his new position as governor, Bing-

Right: 'the flail of Connaught', Sir Richard Bingham, an exemplar of the Elizabethan captain-adventurer. As President of Connaught, Bingham presided over the slaughter of Armada survivors in his province.

ham took a pro-active role: he managed to increase the flow of tax revenue from the province (a fiscal virtue guaranteed to gladden Elizabeth's heart), and at the same time, ruthlessly suppressing any rebellion by local lords. In September 1586, he led an army against Scottish mercenaries raised by the rebellious Burkes. Bingham was victorious in the battle by the banks of the River Moy. In the rout, around 1,500 of the foe were slain, along with an equal number of women and children. A chronicler of the Bingham family later wrote: 'It must have been a horrid massacre and the heads of the dead were hewn off subsequently'. Bingham has gone down in history as 'the flail of Connaught'.

His bloodthirsty behaviour led to complaints to the then Lord Deputy, Perrot, who relayed these to London, accusing Bingham of cruelty, extortion and disobedience. In July 1587, Queen Elizabeth, hoping that time would heal the differences between Perrot and Bingham, recalled the latter and sent him off once again to the Netherlands, this time to serve with the Earl of Leicester's forces who were supporting the Dutch rebels. Bingham was deeply chagrined at what he saw as his ignominious banishment. However, he was held in high regard in London and after making an appeal to Lord Burghley, he was restored to his position in Ireland, returning there in March 1588, where, as we have seen, the new Lord Deputy, Sir William FitzWilliam had just taken up his post.

It is difficult to find an exact total for the numbers of the English garrison in Ireland during 1588, given that they fluctuated in response to conflicts and there was dependence on subcontracted mercenaries, but one estimate is that in September 1588 it amounted to around 1500. This was clearly wholly inadequate to repel any organised Spanish incursion. Elizabeth was aware of the danger and issued orders to the lieutenants of English counties to be in readiness to march to Ireland within an hour's warning.

'Execute all Spaniards'

When news came of the Armada shipwrecks that were beginning to occur in Ireland, the English administration there took fright. The Lord Deputy responded with severity and issued a commission to his various officials: 'whereas the distressed fleet of the Spaniards, by tempest and contrary winds … [has] been driven upon this coast'. He ordered them to: 'take hulls of ships stores, treasure &c into your hands; and to apprehend and execute all Spaniards found there, of whatever quality soever. Torture may be used in prosecuting this inquiry'. Noteworthy is the admonition to seize the ships and treasure: FitzWilliam was in debt and his entry in the *Dictionary of Irish Biography* observes that 'the uncharacteristic decisiveness he showed in leading his forces to encounter the Spanish Armada survivors would appear to have been due to his eagerness to salvage valuables from the wrecked ships'. Richard Bingham, as news came through of the many Spanish shipwrecks in his territory, issued a proclamation upon 'pain of death', in reference to the Spanish survivors, that: 'every man who had or kept any of them should presently bring them in and deliver them [to officials] and that any man who should detain any of them above four hours after the publication of the said proclamation to be held and reputed as a traitor'.

Tirawly

One of the first off the mark to deal with the Armada survivors was Richard's brother, George who, as Sheriff of Sligo, was based at the castle in Ballymote. On hearing of a large Spanish ship cast ashore at Tirawly (the area extending along the north Mayo coast as far as Killala Bay), he and his soldiers immediately set out for there. A letter, written by the secretary to the Council of Connaught, told how 72 survivors had been taken in by the local chieftain William Burke, who was based near Ballina. These had managed to get ashore but the rest of the ship's company had drowned, save another 80 who, he wrote, had been slain by an axe-wielding galloglass, one Melaghlen McCabb. The opinion of one historian is that it was likely that Burke intervened with his subordinate, McCabb, to stop the butchery. It is assumed that the survivors were subsequently taken prisoner by George Bingham. Details of the ship that was wrecked are vague and no remains have been found: accounts suggest that it was the *Ciervo Volante*, thought to have been blown ashore around 22 September. This was an *urca* of 400 tons built in Germany. It was originally listed as having 39 sailors and 132 soldiers on board at Corunna, and there is no record of it ever returning to Spain.

Three Ships of the Levant

At the beginning of September, three *naos* of the Squadron of the Levant were in trouble off the Irish coast. These were the *Lavia* (728 tons, vice-flagship of the squadron), *Santa María de Visón* (666 tons) and the *Juliana* (860 tons). The *Lavia* had been built in Venice and the other two in various shipyards of the Mediterranean. These vessels were clearly not built for Atlantic service, and after the recent battles and storms, their seams had opened and they were leaking. This trio had become separated from the main fleet after a storm on 2 September, and then had joined up with Don Juan Martínez de Recalde's flotilla of strays. Days later, they lost sight of de Recalde's group, and around 13 September passed by Bloody Foreland headland (north-west Donegal). Next they sailed into Donegal Bay and anchored at the southern end. All three ships were leaking and the *Juliana* in particular was in danger of sinking, being awash.

On board the *Lavia*, under judicial restriction, was one Captain Francisco de Cuéllar, who, weeks before, as noted in Chapter 4, had narrowly avoided execution. Previously he had been captain of the *Don Pedro* and had been condemned to death for not slowing his ship on Medina Sidonia's orders at a crucial stage after the end of the Gravelines battle. He escaped the noose but had been stripped of his command and assigned to the custody of the Judge Advocate General, Don Martín de Aranda, who was aboard the *Lavia*. De Cuéllar was a highly experienced military man – he had begun his career as a soldier on a galleon of the Squadron of the Indies Guard which protected the *flotas* (treasure fleets). Towards the end of 1581, at the age of 24, he had been appointed to a captaincy (commanding both troops and a ship) in a major expedition to the Strait of Magellan, mounted in response to English incursions, with the objective of reasserting Spanish power in the South Atlantic. De Cuéllar was no stranger to military trials. During this expedition, in 1583, there had been an inconclusive battle with English ships at São Vicente (on the coast of Brazil, near present-day São Paulo). In the aftermath, a tribunal of inquiry was held where de Cuéllar and his superior officer exchanged various denunciations. The matter went on to courts of appeal. Their conclusions are lost in the mists of time, but it seems that by the end of 1584, de Cuéllar was vindicated and was free to recommence his career.

History is fortunate that de Cuéllar, after reaching the safety of Antwerp in the Spanish Netherlands, wrote a series of accounts to an important, and most likely noble, friend. De Cuéllar does not lie to his esteemed friend when he recounted that the story might be 'by way of amusement' and, which will 'appear as if taken from some book of chivalry'. The narrative graphically describes his remarkable and adventurous journey, a story that is mostly based on fact and ties in, although many times in a vague way, with the overall geography encountered and the state of affairs then pertaining amongst the Gaelic lordships. It is a fascinating tale, albeit with probable embellishments here and there, and with its accuracy dimmed by time and

distance. Even though the matter is only dealt with in the opening few pages of his narrative, it is thought that the primary reason he wrote this account was to clear his name with regard to Medina Sidonia's tribunal held after the Gravelines battle. He took care to tell how he was 'ignominiously' condemned to death and 'from which Our Lord delivered me'.

Above: with Ben Bulben, part of the Dartry Mountains, in the background to the right, a view of the crescent-shaped Streedagh Strand, Co. Sligo. On 21 September 1588 the 'Lavia', 'Juliana' and the 'Santa María de Visón', of the Squadron of the Levant, were blown by the Great Gale to run aground on the sand, around 100m from the shore.

De Cuéllar tells of their arrival in Donegal Bay, how after a severe storm they were 'forced to make for the land with these three ships, which, as I say, were of the largest size, and to anchor more than half a league from the shore, where we remained for four days without being able to make any provision, nor could it even be made'. There are accounts which indicate that the three ships had made an attempt to sail out: Edward Whyte, clerk of the Connaught Council wrote to his brother that three ships had departed from the harbour of Sligo. George Bingham, Sheriff of Sligo, wrote on 21 September that 'perceiving that the wind changed contrary for the three ships that put out of said bay and blew so strong a gale that they were like to be returned to the same road again'. He noted how 'he made all the haste he could back to attend the landing of the men in those ships or wreck of the same' – we shall soon see Bingham's sanguinary actions at Streedagh Strand.

De Cuéllar does not mention an attempt to sail out, neither does another survivor, the soldier Diego López, from the *Lavia*, who later related in Spain that 'while waiting for the people from the *Juliana* to pass to the other ships, due to [its] deteriorating condition, a great storm struck them all'. López said the storm happened on the eve of 20 September. Several sources say that this occurred on 21 September. In any case, the three ships were anchored at an exposed location somewhere off Streedagh Strand, when, as de Cuéllar recounted: 'There sprang up so great a storm on our beam, with a sea up to the heavens, so that the cables could not hold nor the sails serve us, and we were driven ashore with all three ships upon a beach, covered

with very fine sand, shut in on one side and the other by great rocks'. And thus a great hurricane was being unleashed, heading northeast, as it struck the west coast of Ireland. This was the Great Gale of September 1588. Unlike tropical islands, Ireland with its generally temperate climate normally does not experience many hurricanes, but when they do occur, possibly on a once-in-50-years' basis, they are horrendous and the high winds cause great devastation. Even Sir Richard Bingham, safe on shore, noted: 'there blew a most extreme wind and cruel storm, the like whereof hath not been seen or heard a long time'.

Blown towards Streedagh Strand

Thus the Great Gale blew the *Lavia*, the *Santa María de Visón* and the *Juliana* towards the around-2km-long crescent-shaped beach at Streedagh, in a north-west-facing bay, about 15km north of Sligo town. The three ships, spread out along a distance of around 900m, ran aground on the sand, around 100m from the shore at the western end of the bay. De Cuéllar recorded: 'within the space of an hour all three ships were broken in pieces, so that there did not escape three hundred men, and more than one thousand were drowned, among them many persons of importance, captains, gentlemen, and other officials'. Survivors managed to float towards the beach using barrels or pieces of timber. Amidst the chaos, Don Diego Téllez Enríquez (*Maestre de Campo* of the *tercio* of Sicily) 'took his ship's boat that was decked, and he and the son of the Count of Villa Franca and two other Portuguese gentlemen, with more than sixteen thousand ducats, in jewels and crown-pieces, placed themselves under the deck of the said boat, and gave the order to close and caulk the hatchway … Thereupon more than seventy men, who had remained alive, jumped from the ship to the boat, and while she was making for the land so great a wave washed over her that she sank, and all on deck were swept away. The boat ended upside

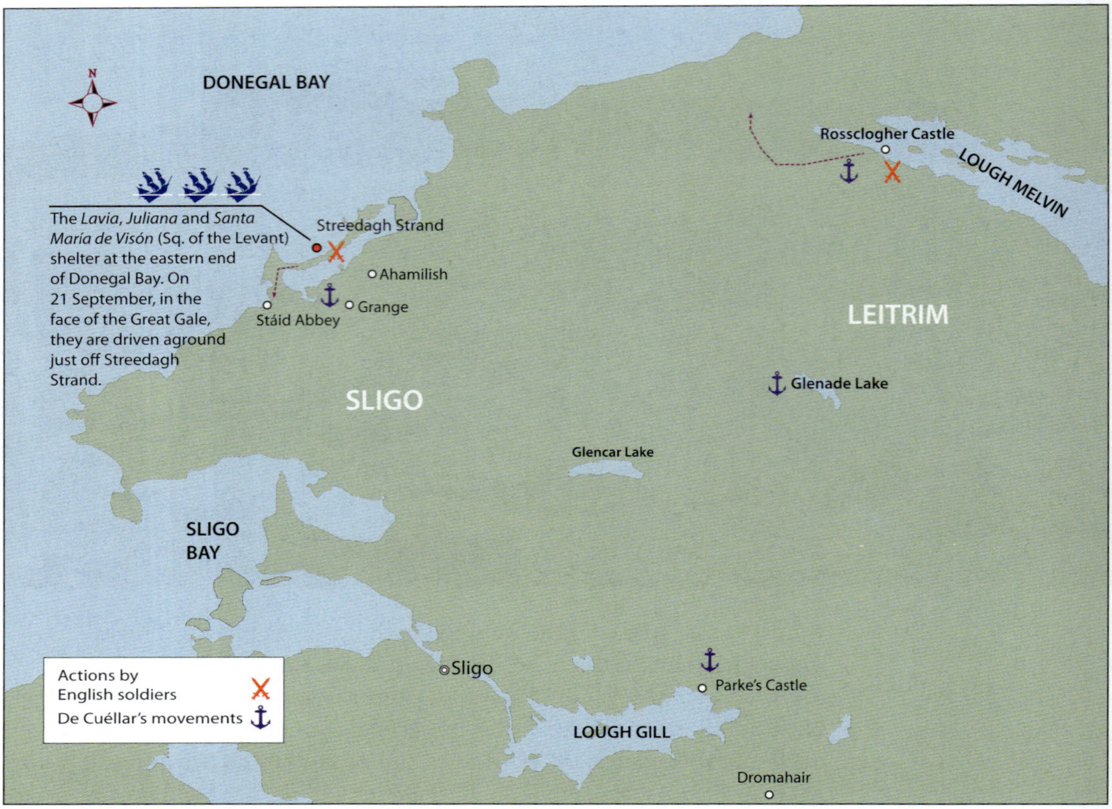

Above: a map of the events at Streedagh Strand and de Cuéllar's wanderings.

down on the beach. Those within the cabin were all dead, save Don Diego'. De Cuéllar continued: 'More than a day and a half after she had grounded, some savages arrived, who turned her up for the purpose of extracting nails or pieces of iron; and, breaking through the deck, they drew out the dead men. Don Diego Enríquez expired in their hands, and they stripped him, and took away the jewels and money'.

De Cuéllar is washed ashore

Still on the *Lavia*, and buffeted by the waves, de Cuéllar, along with his erstwhile warden, the Judge Advocate Martín de Aranda (with his gold coins stitched into his clothes), grabbed a hatch cover. As they threw themselves into the water, a great wave crashed over them. De Cuéllar managed to regain the hatch cover but the unfortunate de Aranda was swept away and sank, weighed down by his gold. The waves cast de Cuéllar onto the beach, where, bloodied and with an injured leg, he saw scenes like something out of Dante's *Inferno*, where the 'savages' as he called them, were busily stripping any survivors of their valuables and clothes.

De Cuéllar managed to slip away from the chaos to a quiet location. Another Spaniard, dazed and naked, joined de Cuéllar. As dusk fell, two locals (one with a large axe) came along and treated them kindly, cutting rushes and grass to cover them, and then 'betook themselves to the shore to plunder and break open money-chests and whatever they might find, at which work more than two thousand savages and Englishmen, who were stationed in garrisons near there, took part'.

It is worth pausing here to analyse the use of the term 'savage' and the attitudes behind this. We have seen how those on the *Gran Grifón* had referred to the inhabitants of the Scottish islands as savage people. Some say that the use of the word has the sense of the nineteenth-century concept of a 'noble savage', or someone living life of goodness and moral superiority in harmony with Nature. However, that was unlikely – there was little nobility to be found on Streedagh Strand that day. De Cuéllar belonged to an officer class in a country which was engaging in vigorous conquest in the Americas and the East Indies. It has been the *modus operandi* for conquering nations, from the Romans onwards, to regard their own culture as superior and deny the human qualities of the natives – a good excuse to conquer and subdue their territory. Spain was the superpower of the time and the Spanish middle class would have entertained metropolitan attitudes towards what they would have regarded as lesser cultures. Indeed, the English then engaged in conquering and colonising Ireland, frequently used the term 'savages' to refer to the local people, all the better to dehumanise them and expel them from their land. (It is ironic that Edmund Spenser, in his racist and genocidal 1596 treatise *View of the State of Ireland*, managed to deride the Spaniards as well. The Irish, he explained 'derive themselves from the Spaniards … but all that is most vaine; for the Spaniard that now is, is come from as rude and savage nations as there may be gathered').

During his expedition along the coast of Brazil some years earlier, de Cuéllar acquired much experience of indigenous people. In any case, in this situation, his use of the word 'savage' was truly heartfelt when referring to these Irish people, who in their frenzied looting, were behaving in a truly savage manner. It was, of course, a colossal clash of cultures. These Irish people were peasants, barefoot and clad in rough garb, such as a *léine*, a long shirt down to the knees, covered by a coarse wool mantle. They lived a subsistence life in the west of Ireland under the fragmented rule of Gaelic lords, where conflict with, and raiding of, neighbouring chiefs was common. There may have been a high level of Gaelic culture such as poetry and music around the fires in the lords' castles, but the ordinary people amidst this rugged territory were living just one step above survival – and were light years away from the mercantile life in continental Europe. It would have been different in the big towns and within the Pale, but for those in the wild and sparsely populated countryside, clothes and weapons were probably more attractive booty than jewels and gold chains. For the inhabitants of the Streedagh hinterland, amidst their drab existence, the sudden appearance of these exotic survivors on the beach was seen as the sea giving up its largesse.

Much of the focus on the archaeology of the Armada to date has been offshore. One wonders where the jewels, gold and other valuables seized from the Armada survivors got to. Are there buried treasure troves still to be found inland from the Armada shipwreck sites, particularly in the Sligo hinterland?

Back in his isolated place of shelter, the exhausted de Cuéllar fell into a deep sleep. At around one in the morning he was woken by the sound of English cavalry riding by. These, an estimated 200 or so, were led by the Sheriff George Bingham. Bingham was returning from the Killala region of Mayo, where he had taken and killed Spanish survivors from a ship (thought to be the *Ciervo Volante*). As we have seen, he had been keeping a close watch on the activities of the three ships and he rushed to the scene. By the time Bingham reached Streedagh there were still around 140 Spaniards by the water's edge, too wounded or weak to leave the beach. Bingham cold-bloodedly ordered his troops to kill them.

As dawn broke, de Cuéllar found that his companion had died. He prudently headed further away from the beach area, now strewn with bodies. De Cuéllar came upon a 'monastery of monks'. There were no monks – it was deserted and had been put to the torch. Within the walls were twelve Spaniards who had been hanged by, as he termed them, the 'Lutheran

Left: a tableau of blood and terror. Streedagh Strand after the arrival of George Bingham and his soldiers.

Above: Stáid Abbey, possibly the location where de Cuéllar found the hanged Spaniards.

English'. The monastery in question has traditionally been considered to be Stáid Abbey (a small building now in ruins) by the coast, a little under two kilometres to the south-west of Streedagh Strand. However a case has been made that the actual location where de Cuéllar found the dozen dead Spaniards was at the church in nearby Ahamlish. Local tradition has it that the church was burnt at the time of the Armada. At the beginning of the nineteenth century, a Protestant church was built on the ruins there.

De Cuéllar, shocked by the scene at the church, 'sallied forth speedily' and entered a wood where he encountered an old woman herding her cows, 'so that the English who had come to stop in her village would not take them' – it seems that Bingham's men had left the beach to continue the hunt further inland. De Cuéllar now limped back to the beach and, amidst

Right: the scene as recounted by de Cuéllar – 'At the dawn of day I began to walk little by little, searching for a monastery of monks that I might repair to it as best I could, the which I arrived at with much trouble and toil, and I found it deserted, and the church and images of the Saints burned and completely ruined, and twelve Spaniards hanging within the church by the act of the English Lutherans'.

Left: the present-day church at Ahamlish, Co. Sligo. Some consider that the original church here was the actual location where de Cuéllar found the hanged bodies.

the looters and hundreds of dead bodies, he came across that of Don Diego Téllez Enríquez, which he buried, with the aid of two other survivors. As four 'savages' accosted them and began to strip them, another, possibly a chieftain, a person with authority, remonstrated and they let them be. The kindly chieftain helped the Spaniards to his village. There two armed young men and a beautiful girl (De Cuéllar had an eye for local beauty) relieved him of the gold chain, coins and relics that he had been hiding amongst his remaining clothes. The maiden, now garlanded with de Cuéllar's relics, sent a boy who gave food and a dressing for his wounds. The boy, seemingly wise beyond his years, then advised de Cuéllar: 'to continue travelling straight towards some mountains that appeared to be about six leagues off, behind which there were good lands belonging to an important savage very friendly to the King of Spain, O'Rourke, and that he gave shelter to, and treated well, all the Spaniards who went to him; and that he had in his village more than 80 of those from the ships …'.

More ordeals in Leitrim

De Cuéllar set off, heading towards the mountains to the north. Next he arrived at a group of huts, where people fed and sheltered him. The following day he hid as a company of English cavalry clattered past, on the search for Armada survivors. Once more he went on his way and then 'there fell in with me more than forty savages on foot … two of those robbers came up to me and gave me six blows of a stick, which bruised my shoulders and arms, and they stripped me of everything that I wore, so as to leave me as naked as when I was born'.

He staggered on, searching for the promised sanctuary of O'Rourke's territory, and came to a lake. It is worthwhile to pause and reflect: de Cuéllar's account is geographically vague and sometimes confusing, which has led to much conjecture about the actual locations. One possibility is that this may have been Glenade Lake in Co. Leitrim. De Cuéllar noted that there were about 30 abandoned huts by the lakeshore and he met three nervous Spaniards here, who had escaped from Bingham's men. Avoiding some locals who were reaping oats, they left and slowly made their way to

Right: Glenade Lake, Co. Leitrim.

another settlement, where at last they received some genuine Gaelic hospitality. They were fed and de Cuéllar's wounds were bound. After resting for some days until he was restored to health, de Cuéllar continued onwards and eventually reached the village, thought to be Dromahair, Co. Leitrim, which was at the centre of Brian O'Rourke's power. It turned out that O'Rourke, the overlord of West Breifne, was away defending his territory from English encroachment. In the village de Cuéllar found 70 naked Spanish survivors, who, in the absence of the chieftain, were being maltreated. He and 20 of the survivors made their way to O'Rourke's house (accounts say that it was the nearby O'Rourke castle, by Lough Gill, now known as Parke's Castle), and begged to be fed.

While there, they heard the welcome news that a large Spanish ship was at the coast, and was taking on board survivors. This was probably the galleass *Girona*, which was then undergoing repairs, anchored in the bay at Killybegs, Co. Donegal, a 75km-march away. De Cuéllar set out for there but did not reach the ship as he met 'many hindrances on the way'. However, his companions did manage to reach Killybegs and sail with the ship. Writing a year later, he was able to gratefully note that 'for me it was an advantage and a mercy which God granted me that I did not arrive at the port'. He was lucky that he didn't actually reach the *Girona* – as we shall see, it sailed out on 26 October, and two days later it was wrecked near the Giant's Causeway; nearly all the 1,200 souls on board were drowned.

By now de Cuéllar was lost. As he wandered on he came across a priest, dressed in ordinary clothes so that he would not be recognised by English soldiers. They were able to converse in Latin. The priest shared his food and directed de Cuéllar in the direction of the castle of 'a wild (or indigenous) gentleman, a very brave soldier and great enemy of the Queen of England'. He duly set out, and after further adventure, reached the seat of Tadgh Óg MacClancy, lord of the Dartry region, an ally of O'Rourke. This was at Rossclogher Castle, situated on a tiny island just off the southern shores of Lough Melvin (between Counties Leitrim and Fermanagh). After his distressing peregrinations, de Cuéllar was now in luck – MacClancy received him courteously: he was given clothes, food and shelter. He spent many

Left: John Derrick's 1581 view of a Lord Deputy setting off from Dublin Castle, with his army. Note the impaled heads at top left. In November 1588, the Lord Deputy, Sir William FitzWilliam, left Dublin at the head of a large force, intending to make a sweep through the north-east, on the hunt for Armada survivors.

weeks recuperating at the castle of his sympathetic and kind host. (Incidentally there was to be retribution later on these lords for their kindness to the castaway Spanish. In 1590, a kinsman led Richard Bingham to Rossclogher where Tadgh Óg MacClancy was captured and, in due course, beheaded. Brian O'Rourke who was also at Rossclogher, managed to make his escape to Scotland. The Scottish Privy Council acceded to an English request and he was handed over and transferred to the Tower of London and was hanged at Tyburn in 1591.)

With his physical condition improving, de Cuéllar was able to note that MacClancy's wife was 'very beautiful in the extreme, and did me much kindness'. He was able to entertain her and her friends with tales about life in Spain – and soon was telling them their fortunes. De Cuéllar was able to take stock and observe the customs of the Gaelic Irish: 'They live in huts made of straw. The men are all large bodied, and of handsome features and limbs; and as active as the roe-deer. They do not eat oftener than once a day, and this is at night; and that which they usually eat is butter with oaten bread. They drink sour milk, for they have no other drink; they don't drink water, although it is the best in the world. On feast days they eat some flesh half-cooked, without bread or salt, as that is their custom. They clothe themselves, according to their habit, with tight trousers and short loose coats of very coarse goat's hair'. He added: '… most of the women are very beautiful, but badly dressed. They do not wear more than a chemise, and a blanket, with which they cover themselves, and a linen cloth, much doubled, over the head, and tied in front. They are great workers and housekeepers, after their fashion. These people call themselves Christians. Mass is said among them, and regulated according to the orders of the Church of Rome'.

His idyll amongst the 'savages' was not to last much longer. News came that the Lord Deputy, Sir William FitzWilliam, had left Dublin in November at the head of a large force. His objective was to make a sweep through the north-west, searching for any Armada survivors being sheltered by the

Right: a depiction of English soldiers arriving at Lough Melvin at the beginning of December 1588, with offshore, Tadgh Óg MacClancy's Rossclogher Castle. De Cuéllar is within, ready to repel attack. He recounted that he and eight companions successfully fended off the siege of the castle by the English army and how the Lord Deputy 'was compelled to depart with his force'.

Gaelic chiefs. FitzWilliam went via Athlone to Sligo, where his force was reinforced by men from the provinces. At the beach at Streedagh he saw the aftermath: 'where, as I heard, lay not long before 1,200, 1,300 of the dead bodies. I rode along upon that strand nearly two miles … there lay as great store of the timber of wrecked ships as was in that place … being … more than would have built five of the greatest ships … and some such masts for bigness and length … I never saw any two could make the like'.

The Battle at Rossclogher

At the beginning of December, the Lord Deputy headed towards Rossclogher. MacClancy, knowing of the fate of anyone found sheltering the Spanish, headed for the hills with his followers and cattle. De Cuéllar requested to stay behind with his eight Spanish companions. Armed with muskets and arquebuses, they built up the castle defences with stones. The island location made the castle more defensible, but de Cuéllar's story perhaps stretches the truth a little – he claims that their heroic little band was able to resist this huge band of professional soldiers. Perhaps in reality the men that besieged Rossclogher formed only a small detachment of the Lord Deputy's forces – FitzWilliam's account does not make any reference to this encounter. A later report from an Irish merchant was received in Santander and referred to a failed attack that the Lord Deputy had made on a chieftain on an island. De Cuéllar recounted that the enemy 'came upon the castle with his forces – about 1,800 men – and observed us from a distance of a mile and a half from it, without being able to approach closer on account of the water which intervened. From thence he exhibited some warnings, and hanged two Spaniards, and did other damages to put us in fear. He demanded many times, by a trumpeter, that we should surrender the castle, and he would spare our lives and give us a pass to Spain … We had been besieged for 17 days, when Our Lord saw fit to succour and deliver us from that enemy by severe storms and great falls of snow, which took place to such an extent that he [the Lord Deputy] was compelled to depart with his force'. After

the English departed, MacClancy returned home and was delighted with the defence of his castle – he was so overjoyed that he offered de Cuéllar his sister's hand in marriage. However, the Spanish captain deduced that MacClancy's 'sole object was to detain us, that we might act as his guard'.

Above: the remains of Rossclogher Castle, on a tiny island in Lough Melvin, which straddles Counties Leitrim and Fermanagh.

To the North and on to Scotland

In any case, de Cuéllar did not want to marry the fair MacClancy girl. What he really wanted was to reach the northern coast where he could secure passage to Scotland. One morning, at the beginning of January 1589, before dawn broke, he and four Spanish companions quietly slipped away. After more adventures, he reached the castle of O'Cahan at Castleroe, west of the River Bann, around 3km south of Coleraine. He had heard that vessels were departing from here for Scotland. O'Cahan did not want to speak to him: 'for, it was said, he had given his word to the great Governor of the Queen not to keep any Spaniard in his territory'. After encountering some English soldiers and managing to give them the slip, he set out in the direction of the Bishop of Derry, 'a very good Christian', who 'was in a castle where the English kept him in banishment and retirement' and who 'went about in the garb of a savage for concealment'. The bishop, Redmond O'Gallagher, had already been active in helping the shipwrecked Spanish: he had visited those at Killybegs and had also given help to survivors from the *Trinidad Valencera*. (O'Gallagher, like others who had helped Armada survivors, came to a sorry end. In 1601 he was captured by English soldiers and immediately put to death).

The bishop helped de Cuéllar and 12 others to find a vessel for their onward journey. After they set sail in what de Cuéllar called a *pobre barca*, or 'modest boat', they were buffeted by storms and eventually landed on a Scottish island, most likely in April 1589. Days later they reached the mainland of Scotland, a neutral country in the Anglo-Spanish conflict. De Cuéllar, who had expectations of good treatment there, was to be let down – for him and his companions hard times ensued. He was unimpressed with James VI, who he feared would hand the Spaniards over to the English: 'the King of Scotland is nobody: nor does he possess the authority or position of a king: and he does not move a step, nor eat a mouthful, that is not by order of the Queen'.

Survivors in Scotland

However, other survivors had found better treatment. As we have seen, some men of the *Trinidad Valencera* had been well received in Scotland by the King and had been lodged with the Catholic nobles, Lord Claude Hamilton and Sir John Seton. Over the months, many Armada survivors made their way to Scotland, a haven that was less than perfect, but clearly better than any alternative. James VI was Protestant, but was trying to follow a middle way, both within his kingdom and in the international sphere. He had many Catholic nobles, as well as many Edinburgh merchants, who were keen to continue their lucrative trade with Spain, so he did not want to offend Philip II. In addition, he had been strongly courted by Spain with offers of great sums of money in return for cooperation. On the other hand, there was a mutual-defence treaty with England in place since 1586. Even though it was only around two years since his mother, Mary, Queen of Scots, was executed by the English, James was careful not to cause Elizabeth displeasure, since his core desire was to gain the English succession. He also had to gauge the reaction of the Scottish Calvinists when they saw these Spanish papists in their streets – de Cuéllar had noted that there were people there 'who called us idolaters and bad Christians, and said a thousand heresies to us'.

As we have seen earlier, around 230 survivors of the *Gran Grifón*, shipwrecked in Fair Isle, had managed to arrive at Anstruther on the Firth of Forth in early December 1588. Their commander, Juan Gómez de Medina, was welcomed by King James, who directed the Provost of Edinburgh to accommodate and feed the Spaniards. Some accounts relate that the English demanded the extradition of Gómez de Medina as well as the handful of Irish notables who had been on board the *Gran Grifón* – a request which spurred Gómez de Medina and his companions to hastily depart for Spain in early 1589 in a ship arranged by the Earl of Bothwell.

By mid-1589 hundreds of Armada survivors were to be seen in the streets of Edinburgh and nearby towns. Clearly this was not well received by the populace, nor by the English, uneasy at the potential of these Spaniards to intrigue and cause trouble. Philip II had been pressing the Duke of Parma to secure the rescue of survivors and, following lengthy negotiations, the arrangements fell into place. Parma was to pay for ships to transport the survivors to Flanders (as well as make a per capita payment which included a charge for their keep). The English had agreed to give a guarantee of safe passage, consequently the ships could sail safely down the North Sea. In August 1589 four ships, chartered from Scottish merchants, left Leith bound for Dunkirk carrying most of the survivors. Among these was Francisco de Cuéllar. His adventures were still not over: bad weather forced the ships into Yarmouth. The Queen's guarantee held, and the ships were allowed to continue their voyage. Approaching Dunkirk, a bevy of Dutch privateers appeared. This was all due to English treachery, according to de Cuéllar, 'for an arrangement had been made with [the Dutch that] they await us at the bar of Dunkirk'. As the Dutch fired their cannons, the Scottish ships made a dash to the safety of the harbour. Running aground, two broke up. Once again, just as at Streedagh, de Cuéllar had to cast himself 'afloat on timbers … I reached the shore in my shirt, without other description of clothing'. And so, after a year packed with danger, privation and adventure, our hero at last reached the safety of Spanish Flanders.

Above: as seen from the slopes of Croagh Patrick, the great sweep of Clew Bay in Co. Mayo, with its more than hundred islands, sunken drumlins, a vestige of the last Ice Age.

Clew Bay

Earlier, at around the same time as the three ships had been swept onto Streedagh in September 1588, Sir Richard Bingham, Governor of Connaught, was receiving a stream of information about other Armada shipwrecks in his territory. He was able to report that there was a 'great ship with 500 men cast away at Inver, the furthest point of 'Irryse' (or the Barony of Erris, a remote part of north-western Co. Mayo). This was in reference to a ship which sank at Corraun to the west of Clew Bay. Most sources conclude that it was the *San Nicolás Prodaneli*. This ship (834 tons) was a *nao* from the Dalmatian Republic of Ragusa (now Dubrovnik in Croatia), captained by Marin Prodanelić, and owned by his family, hence the name. Like the other Ragusan ships in the Armada, it was a veteran of the naval actions in the Azores. The muster taken at Corunna as the Armada departed records that there were 68 seamen and 226 soldiers aboard. The ship had taken full part in the engagements along the English Channel. Separated from the main Armada, it is thought to have been wrecked around 22 September at Toorglass, on the Corraun Peninsula, between Achillbeg and Mulranny. The estimated 80 survivors were unlucky enough to be captured by a detachment under George Bingham. They were all massacred, save around eight, who included the army captains de Zuazo and Riqueleme. Spared also were some Dutch youths who testified that they had been pressed into Spanish service. All of these were marched to Galway, but for them it was only a temporary reprieve. They were killed, after Lord Deputy FitzWilliam, visiting Galway, ordered that all remaining survivors be executed. There are few records of the fate of the *San Nicolás*, but a letter to the brother of the captain, Marin Prodanelić, sent by a Ragusan in London and found in a Dubrovnik archive, tells him that Marin 'perished on the cliffs of Ireland, and of all those that were with him, scarcely a dozen have been saved'.

Below: Ionad Amhairc Armáid na Spáinne (Spanish Armada Viewpoint), located on the Corraun Peninsula, Co. Mayo, near the point where the 'San Nicolás Prodaneli' is thought to have been wrecked. Clare Island can be seen in the background.

The mystery of the ship at Borreis

A letter from a Galway merchant to the Mayor of Waterford told that on 16 September there was 'the arrival of one of the Spanish ships at a place called "Borreis" which is to the northward of Galway 20 leagues, which place belongs to the Earl of Ormond. The same ship is cast upon the shore ... for the most part the men are lost and cast away'. It noted that there were 16 survivors, who were taken into custody by the Earl's tenant. It added: 'the ship was of the burthen of 1,000 tons, and had in her 50 pieces of brass, beside four great cannon, so as the ship is past recovery'. Reflecting

its importance, a copy of the letter was sent to Sir Francis Walsingham in London. Some speculate that the location referred to was Burrishoole in the north-east corner of Clew Bay – in such a situation the ship would have had to navigate through the maze of small islands in the bay and attempted to beach there. Alas, this ship remains a mystery – no remains have been found and all Armada ships of that size, say from 700 tons upwards, have been accounted for.

The *Gran Grín*

Clew Bay in Mayo was the territory of the legendary Grace O'Malley, (Granuaile, head of the O'Malley clan), whose small fleet of ships dominated the west coast of Ireland. The legend runs that in 1593, when she travelled to Elizabeth's court in London, she refused the Queen's offer to make her a countess. In September 1588, it happened that she was not present at her main castle at Clare Island – her acting chieftain there was Dubhdara Rua O'Malley. News came of an Armada shipwreck. This was the huge *nao*, the 1,160-ton *Gran Grín*, of the Vizcayan Squadron. Having lost contact with the Armada fleet, it had anchored off Clare Island. After the Great Gale blew up she was damaged and on 22 September was swept from her mooring to be wrecked at a point thought to be on the south-western shore

Below: the Armada ships that were lost in Clew Bay. Another, the 'San Pedro el Mayor' took shelter in the bay and managed to depart.

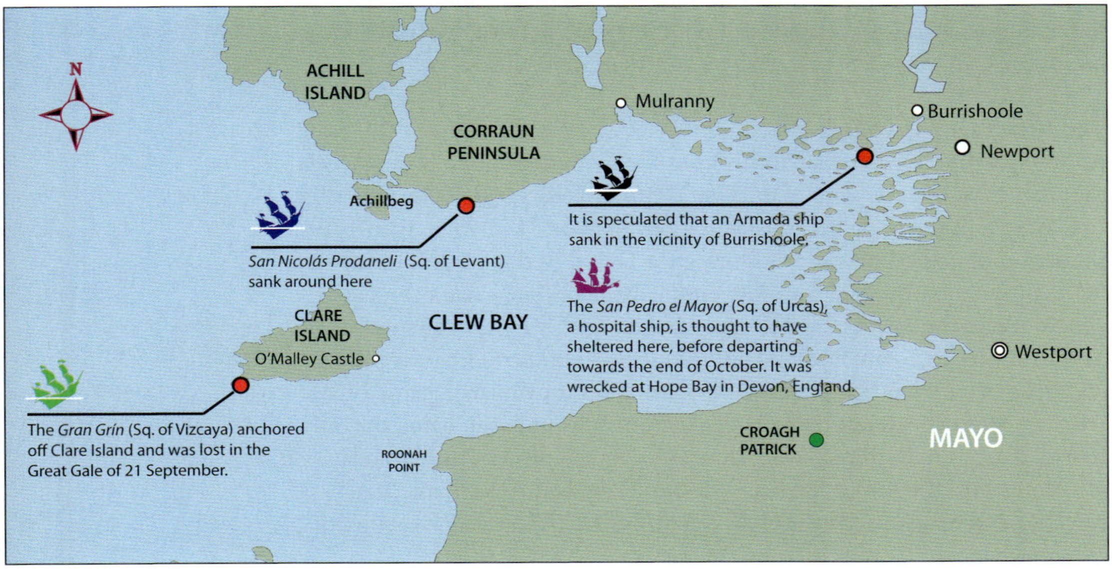

of the island. Around 200 were drowned. The captain, Pedro de Mendoza, managed to land on the island with some survivors. In a report to his brother, Richard, George Bingham recounted that: 'the great ship which was at the Isle of Clear was cast away with 700 men in her and clean sunk to the bottom of the sea, saving 100 men who had landed in the island two days before, the chief of whom was Don Pedro de Mendoza (the captain), as it is said, who perceiving that their ship was lost, would have departed from the island, and carried with them certain boats, belonging to the islanders, and have gone to the other ships which rode before Torrane, but one Dowdary Roe O'Malley, chief of the island, perceiving whereabout they intended to go, called his men together, and put them all to the sword, saving one poor Spaniard and an Irishman of the county of Wexford'. This tale would have been very satisfactory to the Binghams, one where a local Irish chieftain was apparently and very effectively carrying out their mission to slaughter the survivors. However, much was exaggerated: those on board the *Gran Grín* amounted to around 330 men, not 700. O'Malley did kill an estimated 74 of his captives, including Pedro de Mendoza, after they attempted to escape, despite being offered great sums of money by the desperate prisoners. The remaining survivors (estimated at around 36) were handed over to be incarcerated at Galway, where practically all of them were killed.

Above: the O'Malley Castle on Clare Island. On 22 September, the 'Gran Grín' was wrecked on the island. An estimated 74 survivors were put to the sword. The rest were handed over for what turned out to be an equally grim fate at Galway.

The *Urca* that passed by

Another of the stragglers, separated from the main fleet and blown towards the Irish coast, was the *urca, San Pedro el Mayor* (581 tons). A hospital ship, (one of two in the fleet) her muster at Corunna was 34 seamen, with 110 soldiers and medical personnel. During the action in the English Channel many of the wounded from the crippled *San Salvador* had been taken aboard. After the Armada had dropped anchor at Calais on 6 August, some of the officers and seamen of the *San Pedro* deserted, including the pilot and the master, Heinrich Jansen (as a German, he obviously regarded the Armada enterprise as not being his fight). This was unusual, being the only recorded act of cowardice among the sailors and soldiers of the Armada.

Along with the rest of the fleet, the *San Pedro* had circumnavigated England and Scotland. As the crew, in custody in Devon, later recounted,

Above: Hope Cove in Devon, England. The hospital ship 'San Pedro el Mayor' had originally sheltered in Clew Bay in Ireland. It set out for Spain, but after bad weather was driven ashore here, and the crew were taken prisoner. All were ransomed and eventually reached Spain.

they were 'pursued by continual tempests'. In due course, she was swept towards the Irish coast and on 28 September anchored just off the Corraun Peninsula, within sight of the remains of the recently shipwrecked *San Nicolás Prodaneli*. The crew established contact with some locals dressed 'in savage garb', and making rudimentary communication through Latin, they were able to replenish their water barrels. The following day an expedition of ten men was organised to search for provisions. These were unlucky enough to encounter a band of 60 under the command of English captains who stripped them of their clothes and then imprisoned them in a nearby tower. The next day, they were marched out to begin the lengthy journey to Galway. Not long after, a man appeared (who the Spaniards described as 'Tomas Ruiz, an Irish Catholic who has a son in Lisbon') and began negotiation with the English captains for the release of the prisoners. The prospect of large sums of money was enough to persuade the captains to temporarily forget their standing orders to kill all Spanish survivors. A deal was struck for the substantial sum of 2,200 reals for the liberty of four of the Spaniards. The money was collected from the ship at anchor: four prisoners were allowed return to the ship; the other six were left to their grisly fate.

Hope Cove

Despite these travails, the crew managed to acquire some victuals. On 21 October they set sail for Spain, but were forced by a contrary wind to take shelter along the Irish coast for three days. The wind changed and it seemed that this jinxed ship had at last encountered some luck –the favourable wind blew them south to within around 175km of the Spanish coast. Alas, their good fortune proved to be only temporary, and, with their navigation most likely not helped by the absence of the long-deserted master and pilot, the *San Pedro* was blown back on its course. Now running short of food, the crew decided to try and make the coast of Brittany. However, on 6 November 1588, she was driven ashore at Hope Cove, around 7km west of Salcombe in Devon. Just fewer than 200 survivors were able to make it ashore on the lands of Sir William Courtenay. Courtenay, a Catholic, was deputy-lieutenant of Devon and in 1586 his name had been included in a Spanish diplomatic report that was speculating about those amongst the English nobility who would have welcomed an invasion which would depose Elizabeth. Nonetheless, whatever his political beliefs, as we will see, this did not stop Courtenay from behaving with extreme cupidity towards his Spanish prisoners.

The *San Pedro* had lodged on a rock and the local populace surged onto the wreck to seize what they could: in addition to guns and powder, she carried valuable drugs and medicines. The ship finally sank beneath the waves on 15 November. George Cary (another deputy-lieutenant of Devon and a future Lord Deputy of Ireland) was assigned by the Privy Council to recover as much as he could for the Crown: he valued the 'pothecary stuff' at 6,000 ducats, but with water in the upper decks, much had been spoiled. 'The ship, I think will prove of no value … the ordinance is all iron, and no brass …There are no men of account in the ship', he reported, and finished with a request for what, in effect, would be his slaves: 'I would humbly desire the gift of those two Spaniards which I have, not for any profit, but I make trial what skill is in them'. The Council had also assigned Anthony Ashley to cast a cold eye over the survivors and identify those of 'quality and calling'; the rest 'it was thought convenient they should cause them … to be executed, destroyed and dealt withal by martial law, as most pernicious enemies to her Majesty and the Realm'. By the end of November the Privy Council decided to defer the execution of the prisoners. They were billeted across the locality, and the Privy Council ordered that some, who had been patients on board the *San Pedro*, suffering from contagious diseases, be lodged in strict isolation so as not to infect the local populace. There followed much haggling with the Duke of Parma about ransom terms for the Armada prisoners held in England. Eventually, in November 1589 by order of the Queen they were released. However, this did not include the unfortunate 15 prisoners who had been given to Sir William Courtenay for ransom. These had a long stay, as in 1590 Sir William, notwithstanding any sympathy for his fellow Catholics, was seeking the extortionate ransom of 20,000 ducats (estimated to be around three million euros in today's value) – which he then reduced to 12,000 ducats. The desperate prisoners resorted to writing a letter to Elizabeth, which Courtenay intercepted. In retaliation he confined them in Ilton Castle and put them on a bread and water diet – and promptly increased the ransom demand to 25,000 ducats. Eventually, the prisoners were released on some unknown date on terms which included the exchange of English merchants who had been seized as hostages. Sir William had been wildly avaricious – there were generally accepted rates for ransom at the time. For the most part, the English had taken a practical and mathematical approach to ransom: the distinguished prisoner Don Pedro de Valdés, commander of the *Nuestra Señora del Rosario*, wrote a letter of thanks to Walsingham, Elizabeth's principal secretary, in mid-September 1588, as he had been informed that 'her Majesty is pleased to extend to the prisoners ... that they shall be delivered for one month's ransom apiece, according to the rate of their several pay'. The last of the *San Pedro* prisoners to be freed was Lope Ruíz de la Peña, an apothecary, who was only able to depart from George Cary's house in March 1597. Cary had been ordered by the Privy

Council to put him at liberty (in exchange for a relative of Cary's who had been freed in Spain).

Blacksod Bay

Back to the storms on the Irish coast of September 1588. On 17 September, a large Armada ship entered the long and indented Blacksod Bay, Co. Mayo. This was the *Santa María Encoronada* (generally known as *La Rata*, named after its first captain). One of the larger Armada ships, it was an 820-ton *nao* of the Levant Squadron with 35 guns, and thought to have been built in Genoa. The ship had become separated from the main fleet on 21 August and had then been buffeted by storms on 12-13 September. One account tells that the ship had earlier reached the Irish coast and 50 crewmen had been sent ashore to forage for food. However, when more gales blew, the ship was compelled to set sail, leaving the shore party behind. The stranded men managed to make the trek to the north of Ireland and get a ship to Scotland. From there, they were able to get passage on a ship bound for Dunkirk, but were captured by Dutch rebels. They were incarcerated in the castle at Flushing until they gained their liberty in August 1590.

Below: arrivals, a sinking and departures. The events in Blacksod Bay.

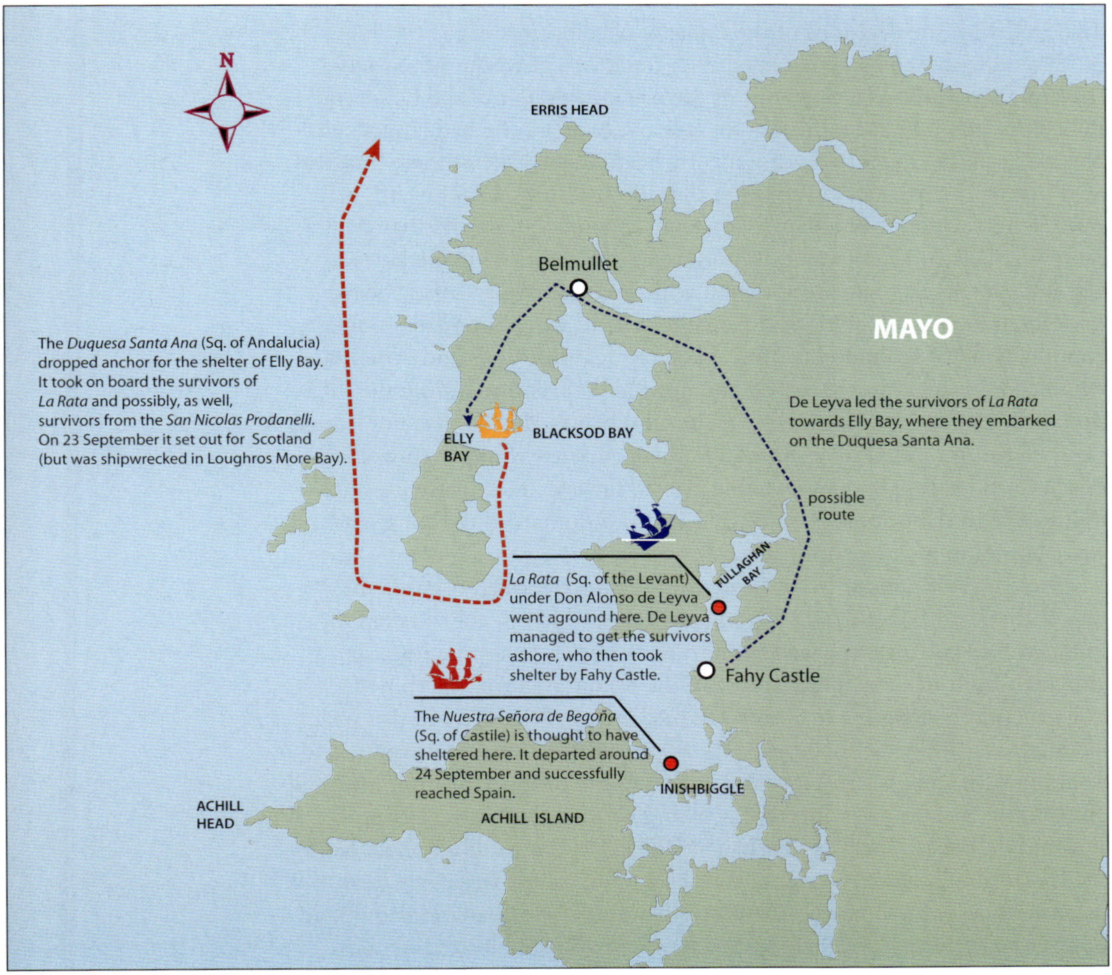

Above: Fahy Castle, near Ballycroy, Co. Mayo. The crew of 'La Rata' came ashore near here and took shelter around the castle.

La Rata was under the command of the distinguished Spanish military leader Don Alonso Martínez de Leyva, of high noble birth, a member of the order of Santiago and Captain General of the Galleys of Sicily and Captain General of the Cavalry of Milan. Even though this commander was only in his mid-thirties, Philip II had judged him to be so capable and trustworthy that he had issued secret orders that de Leyva would take command of the Armada expedition in the event of the Duke of Medina Sidonia's death. Over the course of the Armada, de Leyva had been prominent in the councils of war, where he, along with Juan Martínez de Recalde, had frequently disagreed with the decisions of the Duke of Medina Sidonia.

Several Irishmen had been aboard *La Rata*, two of whom were Maurice and Gerald FitzMaurice, sons of the principal leader of the Desmond Rebellion, James FitzMaurice. As we saw in Chapter 1, he had landed at Smerwick in 1579 and had subsequently been killed. One of these brothers died during the Atlantic voyage after the ship had turned southward. Edward Whyte, clerk of Bingham's Connaught Council, reported that 'Maurice [FitzMaurice], son to arch-traitor James FitzMaurice FitzGerald, was cast into the sea in a fair cypress chest with great solemnity.' Also aboard *La Rata*, in de Leyva's glorious slipstream, was the cream of Spain's noble youth, a band of around 60 young aristocrats, counts, dons and captains, who had been eager to secure honour, fame and adventure during the invasion of England. Along with their plentiful servants, this noble complement would have amounted to around 100. These cosseted young men would not have added much to an invading army. However, their presence was an indulgence to their noble parents, by Medina Sidonia and the King, and was a common practice in those times.

There was no honour or fame on offer as the ship sailed towards the east of Blacksod Bay. *La Rata* was in poor shape – de Leyva had taken the initiative and valiantly engaged in the bloody battles along the English Channel. Built to carry merchandise in the Mediterranean, the ship was not structurally designed to absorb the recoil of artillery. Here in this wide bay there was welcome shelter and the opportunity to carry out repairs and resupply with fresh water. However, after the ship dropped anchor, it turned out that the location was affected by strong rip-tides and it was driven aground on the sandbars of the shallow Tullaghan Bay. A dozen men, led by the Italian ship's master Giovanni Avancini, went ashore in a small boat to reconnoitre – one source says the party abandoned the boat and fled inland to save themselves. Nevertheless, they were seized by the local chieftain

Above: Elly Bay on the Mullet Peninsula, Co. Mayo. The 'Duquesa Santa Ana' had sheltered here from the Great Gale. At the end of September 1588, the ship, laden with survivors from 'La Rata', set out, intending to head for Spain, but was forced by prevailing winds to turn north for Scotland.

Richard Burke, of such ill repute that he was known as 'The Devil's Hook'. Burke had been on his way to plunder the ship. The unfortunate captives were subsequently handed over to the English authorities in Galway where they were put to the sword. In the meantime, with *La Rata* stuck on the sandbars, the crew tried to free it, but to no avail. A decision was taken to evacuate the ship and then set it on fire. Carrying their salvaged valuables, the ship's complement, (estimated at around 400) landed onshore and took what shelter they could at the nearby small Fahy Castle on the coast, near Ballycroy.

Two other ships had also entered Blacksod Bay. One was the *Nuestra Señora de Begoña* (750 tons, Squadron of Castile, 300 men on board at Corunna), which anchored in the bay on around 15 September – the historian Ken Douglas has speculated that this was to the south of the bay near the small island of Inishbiggle. There was time to repair the ship and send boats ashore in search of water and victuals. Sometime during that period, a large party that had gone ashore was captured. Accounts tell that 70 or 80 from the ship were incarcerated in Galway. All but two were executed, one of whom managed to make his escape. The *Nuestra Señora de Begoña* departed around 24 September, having heard news of what had happened to de Leyva and *La Rata* in Blacksod Bay. On route back to Spain, they encountered the galleass *Zúñiga* (in an equally bedraggled state) and finally sailed into the port of Cangas in Galicia, on 10 October, with a complement of 158, around half of those who had set out from Corunna.

The *Duquesa Santa Ana*

Another ship that had entered Blacksod Bay was the *Duquesa Santa Ana*, a 900-ton ship, with a Corunna muster of 272 men. It was part of the Andalucian Squadron, but unlike the rest of this squadron with its sleeker galleons and *naos*, this vessel was an *urca*, broader on the beam and built in Flanders to transport merchandise. It had anchored at Elly Bay, on the Mullet Peninsula. De Leyva and his survivors heard the welcome news that this ship had anchored there. It was around 17km to their north-west, as the crow flies, and they promptly set out for it. Days later, as they arrived, they saw that the crew of the *Duquesa Santa Ana* had fortified a nearby castle at Tiraun, facing out to the broad Atlantic, located on the bleak flat and narrow peninsula. In the meantime, local people had set to on the charred remains of *La Rata* and carried away anything of value. Any shelter was welcome at Tiraun on 21 September when the Great Gale blew up. A few days

later, when conditions were calmer, the men of the Armada trooped aboard the *Duquesa Santa Ana*. As a survivor later testified, the men from de Leyva's ship had brought on board their money, jewels, weapons and armour. Much of this was the visible wealth carried by the young nobles of *La Rata*. This is most likely the reason that there had been such a trove of jewels and gold excavated from the wreck of the *Girona*, on which most of the *La Rata* survivors eventually travelled. And so, crammed on all decks with survivors and its own crew, the *Duquesa Santa Ana* set out on a southwest heading from Blacksod Bay, hoping to return to Spain. However, contrary winds resulted that they could not make any progress. The continuing southerly wind made them decide to change course and head for Scotland. On 29 September, with the ship off the west Donegal coast, they were blown east towards Loughros Point. Gaining some shelter in Loughros More Bay, they dropped anchor. However, as a survivor recounted 'there fell a great storm', the cables snapped and 'struck them upon ground' – on projecting rocks near a great beach.

Above: Loughros More Bay, Co. Donegal. On 29 September the 'Duquesa Santa Ana' was wrecked, blown onto projecting rocks here.

Left: the ruins of O'Boyle's Castle, set on a small island in Kiltooris Lake. Some of the survivors from the 'Duquesa Santa Ana' set up a defensive position here.

Loughros More Bay

Once again, Alonso de Leyva and his men were shipwrecked. Once again, they made their way to land. During the confusion of the ship's grounding, Don Alonso's leg had been injured by a capstan and he had to be carried onshore. Exploring around the isolated countryside, the Spanish found the narrow Kiltooris Lake, around a kilometre inland. Here, on a small island in the lake, while some remained by the wrecked ship, de Leyva ordered the setting up of a defensive position around the ruins of O'Boyle's castle. Adding to their defences were cannons, which they had laboriously manhandled from the *Duquesa*. They were in friendly territory, that of the McSweeny Na Doe clan who gave them assistance. The McSweenys had originally been galloglasses from Scotland, but were now well settled in Donegal. After his run of bad luck, being shipwrecked twice, Don Alonso now encountered what seemed like good fortune – news came that there was a Spanish ship to the south in the bay at Killybegs. After little over a week, the survivors, estimated at around 650, set off on the journey of around 25km southwards to the reported ship, accompanied by the chieftain McSweeny Na Doe. Don Alonso, still immobilised, had to be carried in a litter by four men. The procession included the band of young nobles, clasping their jewels and gold. Traipsing through the boggy Donegal hills, these young men were experiencing a bleak version of 'grand adventure', one that they had not signed up for. As they crested the high ground and began to descend towards McSwyne's Bay, they could see a large vessel at anchor. Closer up, they would have been also able to see the remains of a smaller Armada vessel on the shore, 'brake to pieces', as a spy reported to his English masters. In turn, another ship had sunk just outside the harbour. The names of these two shipwrecked ships are not known.

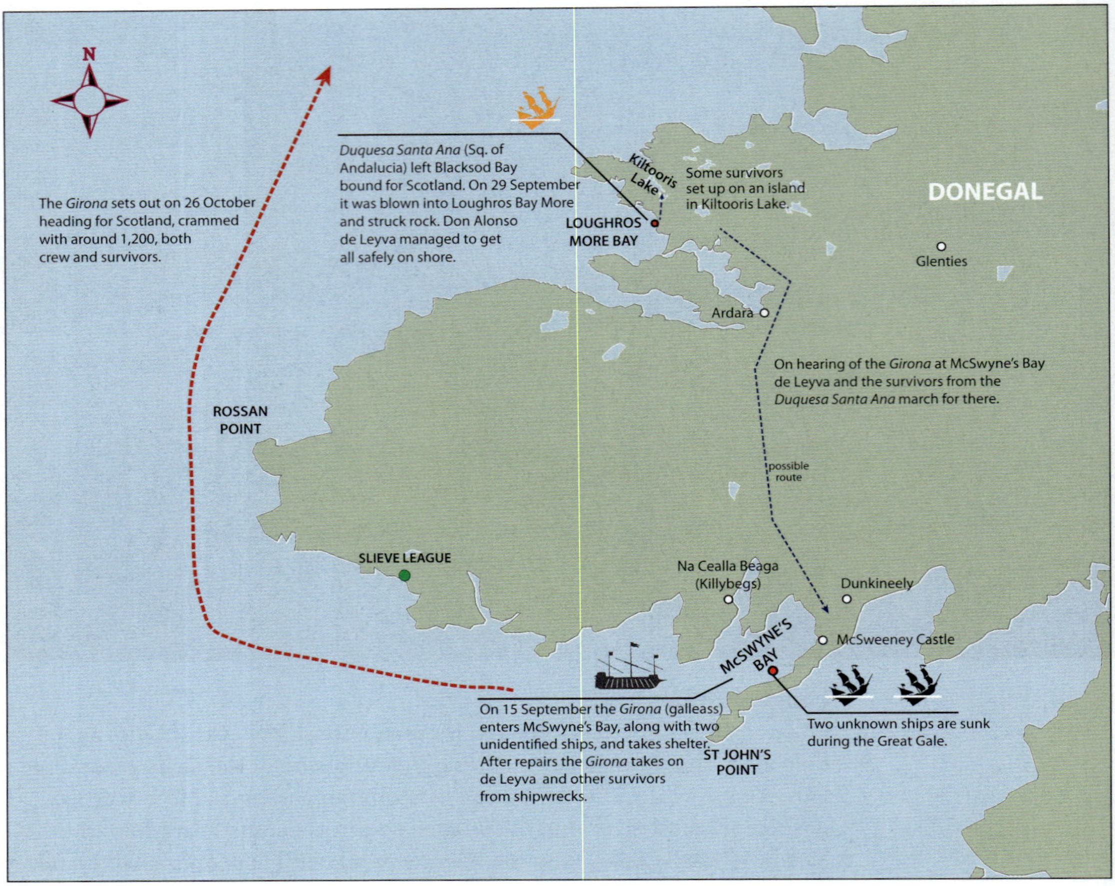

Above: the events at Loughros More and McSwyne's Bays.

McSwyne's Bay

The ship anchored in the bay (some consider that it was actually moored in Killybegs harbour) was the *Girona*, a galleass constructed in the shipyards of Naples around 1584, and with many Italians in the crew. The ship had been named in honour of the Viceroy of the Kingdom of Naples, Pedro Téllez-Girón y de la Cueva. Well armed, with a total of 50 guns, it had fought bravely during the encounters in the English Channel. On 4 August, it had joined in with Alonso de Leyva when he headed to rescue the *Duquesa Santa Ana*, then in danger of being overpowered by the enemy. The galleass, with its high freeboard, was particularly vulnerable to strong winds and at the end of August had become separated from the main fleet. Driven by storms, she had eventually found shelter in McSwyne's Bay. The spy for the English continued with his story: 'the third [ship] being a gally, and sore bruised with the seas, was repaired in the … harbour with some of the planks of the second ship, and the planks of a pinnace which they had of McSweeny'. In addition to being struck by English cannonballs, the *Girona* had been damaged by the recent storms. The repairs took some time and, as noted, they salvaged timber from the other ships. Particular attention was given to the overhaul of the galeass's rudder. When the fleet stopped at Corunna back in June, it had been necessary to strengthen the vessel's rudder.

Above: McSwyne's Bay, with on the right, the McSweeny Castle on St John's Peninsula, around which over a thousand Armada survivors are thought to have sheltered.

The rudders was the weak point of every galleass. These curved components had consistently given trouble all through the Armada voyage – they were especially vulnerable at the bolt in the hinges fixed to the body of the vessel, which allowed the wooden rudder to pivot.

While the work was underway, well over a thousand men, most of the various crews, were camped at a location thought by some to be near a McSweeny castle (this belonged to a different branch – the McSweeny Bannaghs). The castle was at the head of the long narrow peninsula of St John's Point that encircles McSwyne's Bay on the east. Desperate for food, the Spaniards bought up all the available local horses to consume. The McSweenys, despite the danger of English retribution, bravely fed and supported the Spaniards cast ashore on their lands. Feeding such a large number meant that the McSweenys had to use up what was their wealth, namely their cattle. As the countryside was being drained of foodstuffs, another chief in the region complained and asked the Lord Deputy for help in resisting the Spaniards (albeit exaggerating the numbers): 'McSweeny [had] subsisted the 3,000 Spaniards till his country is consumed'. The English administration was alarmed by this great body of Spaniards encamped in Donegal. The sanguinary George Bingham, unlike when he made his brave gallop to Streedagh to put the defenceless survivors of the shipwreck to the sword, now wrote in alarm to his equally sanguinary brother Richard, saying 'The Spaniards will be in Sligo in five days'. Unsurprisingly, Bingham did not set out with his men on the 90km journey to McSwyne's Bay to confront what he thought were thousands of Spaniards. The English need not have

Right: Dunluce Castle, Co. Antrim, home of the chieftain, Sorley Boy McDonnell. After the sinking of the 'Girona', McDonnell helped the few survivors to get passage to Scotland.

Overleaf: wild and dangerous rocks – Lacada Point, Co. Antrim, the narrow reef projecting to the right of centre of the photograph. The 'Girona' struck the reef and broke up.

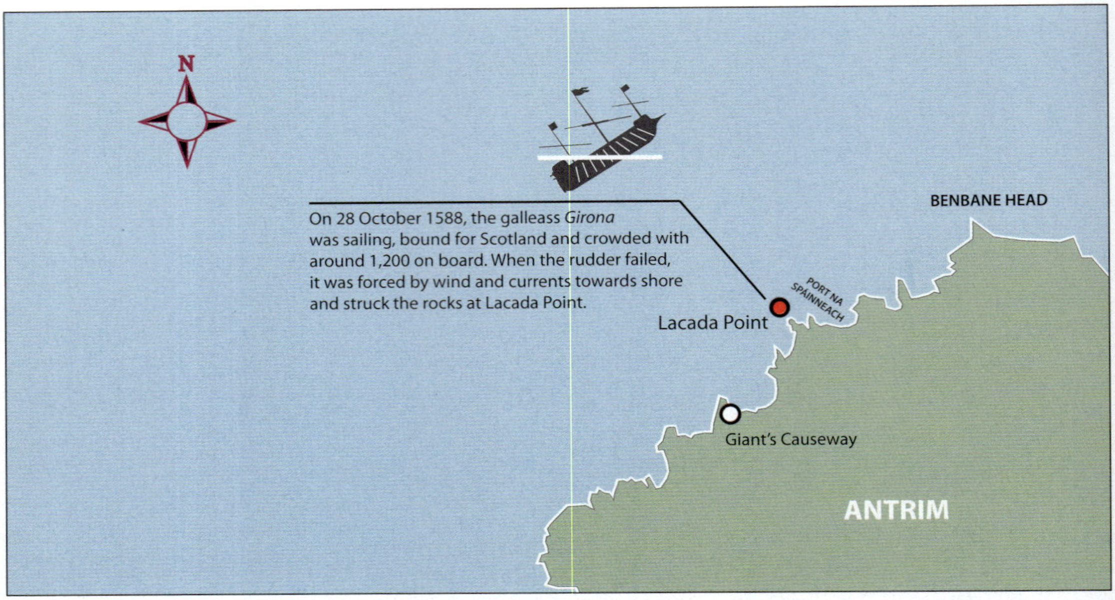

Above: a map of Lacada Point. Of the 1,200 men onboard the 'Girona' only a handful survived. It remains one of the greatest disasters in Irish maritime history.

worried. After the battles along the English Channel, the long voyage and the gales of the Atlantic, none of the Spanish survivors would have remotely considered joining with the local people to resist the English occupation – all they wanted was to reach home as quickly as possible.

After around two weeks, the repairs to the galleass were complete. As the Spanish survivors filed on board, a report from another spy noted that 'the ship cannot receive all'. Space was at a premium and an estimated 200 had to be left behind. Given the quantity of jewels found in the subsequent shipwreck, it would seem certain that all the young nobles managed to get on board – possibly those left behind included some of the convicts and slaves, rowers of the galleass. It is likely that some of those left on shore

Above: a dramatic depiction by Kenneth Riley of the wrecking of the 'Girona'.

made their own way to the north coast to seek passage to Scotland – a wiser choice, as it turned out. Before the ship departed, the grateful Spaniards donated over a dozen butts of sack (fortified white wine) to the McSweenys. They also left behind a great stock of arquebuses and muskets, most likely to free up much-needed space on the ship. And so, on 26 October, the *Girona* departed, with its rudder lashed-up and its decks full to the gills with around 1,200 men, including survivors of multiple shipwrecks. In addition, according to one account, they had sourced three 'skilful pilots for Ireland and one for Scotland'. Their destination was Scotland, which had the benefit of offering a relatively short passage, of around 275km, to the nearest Scottish isles – in comparison to the alternative of sailing for Spain, five times more distant across the open Atlantic. As we have seen, Scotland was nominally neutral in the conflict, albeit ruled by an unsympathetic Protestant king, but infinitely safer for the Spanish than staying in an Ireland under Tudor domination, where it was open season on any Spanish Armada survivors.

Left: St Cuthbert's Church, Dunluce, Co. Antrim. Local tradition says that the dead of the 'Girona' are buried in a mass grave here.

Left: a memorial to the 'Girona' dead at St Cuthbert's Church.

On the right are some of the exquisite jewels recovered during the salvage expeditions in the late 1960s. These decorative items were the property of the officers and young nobles on board the 'Girona', and form part of the Armada exhibition at the Ulster Museum, Belfast, the best display of such artefacts from the 1588 events anywhere in the world.

Right: a salamander pendant, in gold and rubies.

Far right: a gold ring, inscribed 'no tengo mas que darte', or 'I have nothing more to give thee'.

Near right: a gold tooth- and ear-pick, in the shape of a dolphin.

Far right: a cameo in gold, lapis lazuli and pearls. This one of a series of eleven gold frames, six of which retain lapis lazuli cameos.

Near right: the cross of a Knight of the Order of Santiago de Compostela, thought to belong to Don Alonso Martínez de Leyva.

To Lacada Point

The *Girona* sailed west to round Malin Beg, then north-north-east, taking care to maintain adequate sea-room from the sheer cliffs and deep bays of the Donegal coast. Next it set course for Scotland, heading eastwards, with the pilots keeping in sight the coastline on the right. On the night of 28 October, as the *Girona* passed by Dunluce Castle, in north Co. Antrim, she was observed sailing close to shore. Around midnight, as she sailed on, passing the Giant's Causeway, it is thought that the improvised rudder snapped. The *Girona* was swept towards the shore by wind and currents. Most likely, the crew tried to avert disaster by dropping an anchor. The ship swung, turning to a westerly direction. The bow struck the tip of Lacada Point, to the north-east of Giant's Causeway (Lacada comes from the Irish *leac fhada*, or long slab). This long stone reef, projecting below steep cliffs, proved treacherous. The ship broke up, with most of it sinking into deep water to the east of the rock projection. Apart from a handful of survivors (accounts vary, telling of between five and nine), all aboard perished, including the group of young nobles and the illustrious military commander Alonso Martínez de Leyva. Those on deck may have been smashed onto the rocks; those in the decks below would have drowned immediately as the ship sank rapidly. With around 1,200 lives lost, it was the greatest maritime disaster in Irish history up to 1915, when the *Lusitania* sank with around the same loss of life.

The chieftain, Sorley Boy McDonnell at his Dunluce Castle, just as he had earlier done with those from the *Trinidad Valencera*, gave shelter to the few survivors of the *Girona*. (There was a little recompense for Sorley Boy. The English were maintaining a close eye on him and one of their informers, reporting the shipwreck, noted that he 'had taken up sundry butts of wine for his use' from the wreckage.) McDonnell arranged boats so that the survivors could make their way to Scotland and thence back to Spain. One was captured by the English – there is a reference in a letter of July 1589 to an unnamed man who, having escaped the *Girona* wreck, was then in captivity in Drogheda prison.

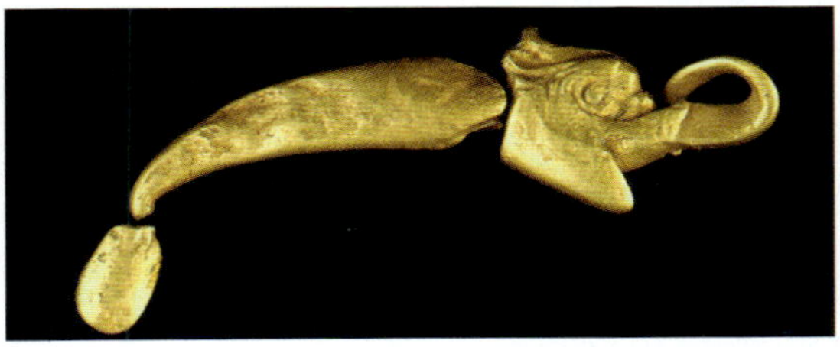

The informer's report on the butts of wine at Dunluce had also noted that '260 dead bodies were driven to the shore'. Local tradition says that most of the dead were buried in a mass grave in a plot of land at the cemetery of St Cuthbert's Church, less than a half kilometre south of the castle. The wreck of the *Girona* was an enormous tragedy, but we are lucky that in 1967 the remains of the ship were discovered by Robert Sténuit, a Belgian diver. The pieces recovered from the galleass are now on display in the Ulster Museum in Belfast. This, the best exhibition of artefacts from the Spanish Armada in the world, has at its core a display of exquisite jewels and gold, much of which belonged to the band of young noblemen who went on board *La Rata* at Lisbon and who, at the end of May 1588, had sailed out with Alonso Martínez de Leyva in search of adventure and glory.

Right: a map of the shipwrecks on the Connemara coast of Galway.

The *Urca* near Inishbofin

The Galway coast also had its share of Armada wrecks. One ship had anchored near Inishbofin Island and then on 25 September was blown onto rocks. This was the *Falcón Blanco Mediano* ('Mediano' to distinguish it from another vessel in the Squadron of *Urcas*, the larger *Falcón Blanco Mayor*), with around 80 on board. At 300 tons, it was a relatively small *urca*, of Dutch or German origin. It is not known where exactly the ship went aground. One tradition has it that it was wrecked at the island of Davillaun, to the east of the larger Inishbofin Island, but the author Niall Fallon stated that the logical site for the wreck is a reef just to the northwest of Freaghillaun South Island, at the entrance to Ballinakill Harbour, near Clifden. This area was within Sir Murrough-na-dTuagh O'Flaherty's territory, Iar-Connaught, which encompassed most of Connemara, then at the fringes of the ever-spreading zone of English control. An unknown number of survivors of the *Falcón Blanco*, including the army captain, Don Luis de Córdoba, were taken captive by the chieftain's men. O'Flaherty had been knighted in 1585 and obviously had a well-developed sense of self-preservation, as he took the decision to march the Spanish survivors to Galway, where they were handed over to meet their doom.

An *Urca* at Dúirling na Spáinneach

An English account tells of other ships in the area: there were 'seen within ten leagues of Galway two ships, and are at anchor these two days a seaward of the island of Arran'. One of these is thought to have been swept onto the rocks at the location now known as Dúirling na Spáinneach, translated roughly as 'pebbled beach of the Spaniards', close to Mace Head (near Carna, Co. Galway). It was originally speculated that it was the *nao*, *La Concepción Menor (Delcano)*, but there are records that this ship returned on 23 September to Laredo in northern Spain. The historian Pedro Luis Chinchilla has recently identified the ship as the *urca, Santa Bárbara* (370 tons, with 50 men on board) – a ship for which there are no records of its return. We have seen in Chapter 4, that on 11 August the unfortunate captain of the ship, Cristóbal de Ávila, had been publicly hanged as punishment for disobeying the orders of the Duke of Medina Sidonia. It is likely that the *Santa Bárbara* was shipwrecked here as there is evidence that survivors of

Right: rough terrain – the mass of large granite stones, rolled smooth by the sea at Dúirling na Spáinneach. The 'Santa Bárbara' is thought to have crashed onto the rocks here.

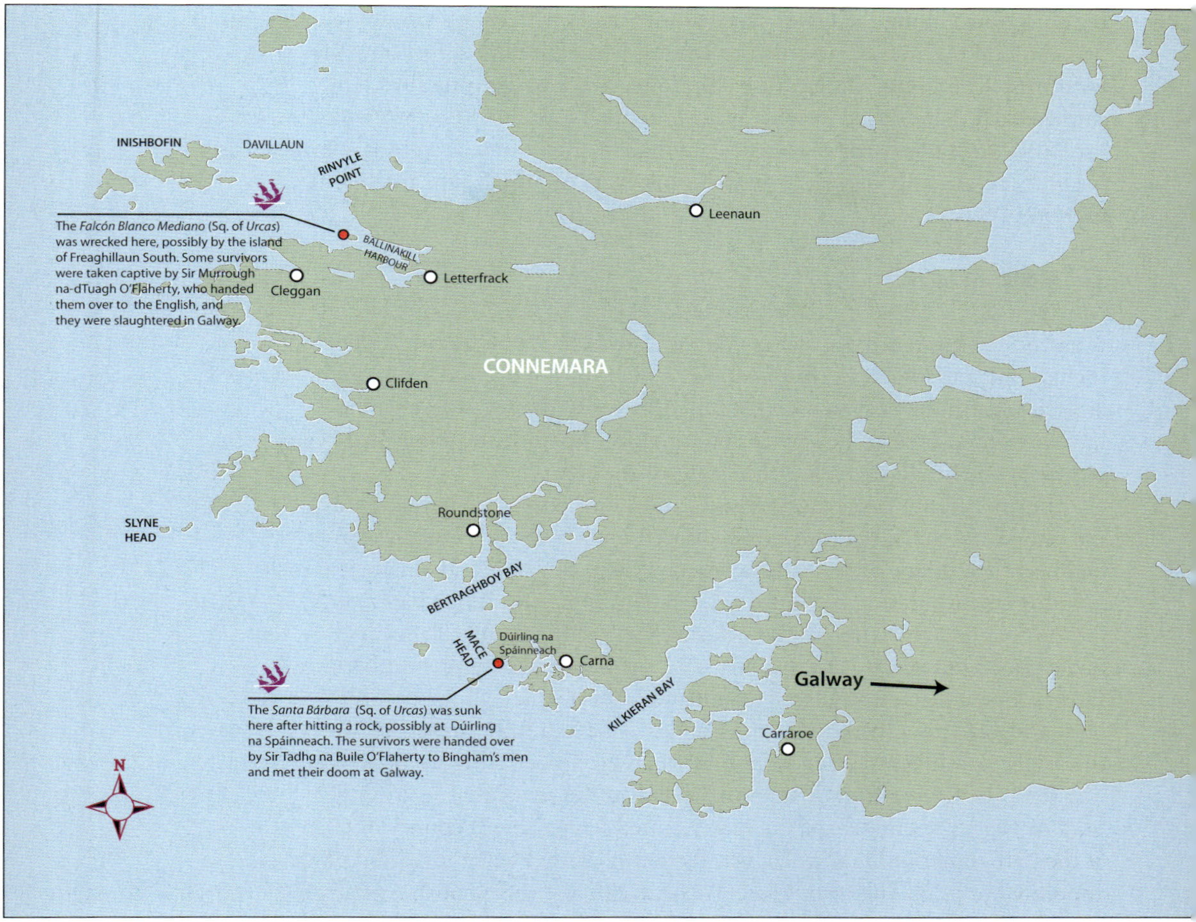
INISHBOFIN
DAVILLAUN
RINVYLE POINT
The Falcón Blanco Mediano (Sq. of Urcas) was wrecked here, possibly by the island of Freaghillaun South. Some survivors were taken captive by Sir Murrough na-dTuagh O'Flaherty, who handed them over to the English, and they were slaughtered in Galway.
BALLINAKILL HARBOUR
Leenaun
Letterfrack
Cleggan
CONNEMARA
Clifden
SLYNE HEAD
Roundstone
BERTRAGHBOY BAY
MACE HEAD
Dúirling na Spáinneach
Carna
Galway
KILKIERAN BAY
Carraroe
The Santa Bárbara (Sq. of Urcas) was sunk here after hitting a rock, possibly at Dúirling na Spáinneach. The survivors were handed over by Sir Tadhg na Buile O'Flaherty to Bingham's men and met their doom at Galway.
N

the ship were among the list of those unfortunates who were slain in Galway. An oral tradition in the district around Mace Head recounts how the local people had lured the Spanish ship to its wreck by lighting fires. The shipwrecked men landed in what was Sir Tadhg na Buile O'Flaherty's territory. (*Na Buile* means 'of the anger'.) Tadhg was afraid of losing his lands or his life, and cravenly handed over these survivors to Sir Richard Bingham's men in Galway.

The Coast of Clare

Moving south along the Atlantic shores, we come to the coast of Clare. It is not quite as indented as that of Mayo, Galway or Donegal, but it does include the remarkable Cliffs of Moher, which run for around 14km and, at their maximum, soar to a height of 210m above the sea. These would have presented a fearsome spectacle to the three Spanish ships that had been blown by the heavy gales to within sight of the coast.

The Sheriff of Clare, one Boetius Clancy, now enters the Armada story. He came from a distinguished and cultured branch of the Clancys, who had been hereditary Brehons (legal learned men) of Thomond, an ancient kingdom incorporating present-day Clare and Limerick. These had maintained the great law school of Knockfinn, Co. Clare. Sheriff Clancy had had a good education; as well as Irish, he was fluent in English and Latin. However, as a history of Clare recounts: 'Boetius Clancy … forsook his faith and gave his adherence to the English' – he had fully engaged with the Tudor administration in Ireland, with an eye to bettering his prospects. The rewards flowing from his new masters had the result that in 1585 he became the representative of the newly-shired (constituted) county of Clare at the parliament in Dublin. He was further rewarded when in 1588 he was appointed as High Sheriff of Clare. As news came of the Spanish Armada in September 1588, Clancy kept a sharp lookout for the Queen's enemies from his castle at Knockfinn, located close to the coast. The Sheriff was able to report to Sir Richard Bingham that 'Last night two ships were seen about the islands of Arran, and it is thought that more sails were seen westward from the islands'. One of these vessels was the *Zúñiga* (500 tons, a galleass, sister ship of the *Girona* and, like it, constructed in Naples around 1584). Having lost sight of the main fleet on 2 September, it had been blown towards the Irish coast. The *Zúñiga* had suffered the curse of the Armada galleasses: the rudder was giving trouble, in this case, the pivot had broken, and the vessel was unable to steer. On 15 September it passed to the south of the Cliffs of Moher and managed to arrive in Liscannor Bay, one of the few locations that gave a modicum of shelter along that stretch of coast. Clancy recounted that it 'is anchored in an unusual harbour, about a mile westward from one of Sir Turlough O'Brien's houses called Liscannor'. Sir Turlough O'Brien was a local lord with a castle in Ennistymon and, like Clancy, was fully within the English camp, having been knighted by Elizabeth in 1583. The description suggests that the ship may have moored at the small indentation in Liscannor Bay, to the west of Liscannor, called Coolrone Cove, where a waterfall descends the cliffs onto a rocky beach. In his message to Bingham

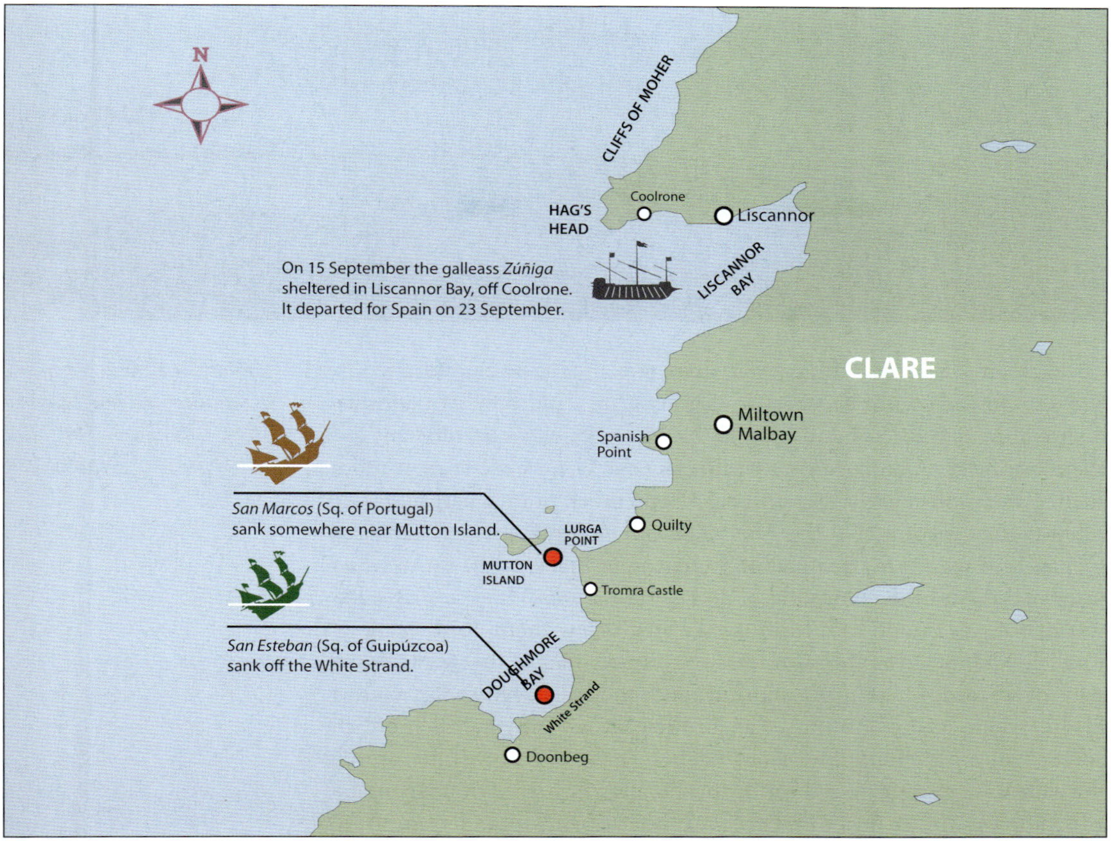

Above: two shipwrecks, one departure – the Armada events on the west coast of Clare.

Clancy had added: 'I do here watch … and shall continue … and as I shall learn I will advertise your worship'.

As the captain of the soldiers on board, Juan de Saavedra, later related, those on board were in dire straits and 'nearly 80 of our soldiers and convicts [the rowers] died of hunger and thirst'. However, he continued, they were in unpromising territory as 'the inhabitants are rustic savages, devoted to England, with a few officials amongst them'. He had come to that conclusion after unsuccessful attempts to obtain food and water. The first boat sent ashore was burned by adherents of the Sheriff. A second boat was sent, along with Pietro Baptista, purser of the *Zúñiga*, where they purported to be merchants and offered money for water and victuals. All was to no avail – such was Boetius Clancy's watchful eye that the locals were terrified to sell anything to the Spaniards. Some of the boat party were seized, including Baptista. The latter, from Naples, could speak Latin and was later interrogated by Sir Turlough O'Brien's brother, Daniel, the (Protestant) Bishop of Killaloe. Baptista's fluency must have pleased the Bishop, for he kept the Italian in his service, thus saving his life. It was at this time that the English authorities came into possession of a copy of the sailing instructions for the return to Spain issued by the Duke of Medina Sidonia (Chapter 4), which document was attached to a letter from Richard Bingham to the Lord Deputy at the end of September – it had been confiscated from one of the prisoners captured from the *Zúñiga*.

Above: the view from Doonbeg at Doughmore Bay, Co. Clare. The 'San Esteban' was shipwrecked here.

Back on the galleass things were desperate and, as de Saavedra reported, 'we were forced by our necessity to take up arms', and they sent another boat and managed to obtain supplies by force, which were sufficient to last them until early October. After weathering the Great Gale at their moored shelter, the *Zuñiga* left for Spain on 23 September. Somewhere along the way they encountered the *Nuestra Señora de Begoña,* which had also managed to set out for Spain after sheltering in Blacksod Bay, and which informed them of the wrecking of de Leyva's *La Rata.* The *Zuñiga* sailed south, but was caught by a furious gale which blew them north as far as the English Channel. The ship was leaking and they had to throw two heavy guns overboard. Once again, short of food, they managed to limp into Le Havre, where it took months to repair the galleass. When at the port, the convict rowers attempted repeated escapes. A run of bad weather prevented the galleass's attempts to sail for Spain. Finally, the arrival of a favourable wind allowed the *Zúñiga* to set sail and she reached Santander on 30 August 1589.

The *San Esteban* and *San Marcos*

Further down the Clare coast, Nicholas Cahane, the coroner for Thomond, noted in a letter to the Mayor of Limerick: 'God hath cast to the coast of Donbegg a great ship from St Sebastians, wherein were 300 men all drowned, but three score or thereabouts; another great ship cast in at I Breckane and lost'. Ibrickane is the barony that encompasses the Clare coast south of Liscannor Bay as far as Kilkee. (For these officials, service in the English administration was above all for self-advancement – Cahane ended his letter by asking to be recommended to the Lord Deputy's favour.) The ship from San Sebastián was a *nao* of the Guipúzcoan Squadron, the 736-ton *San Esteban,* whose muster at Corunna had been 73 seamen and 201 soldiers. There is no shelter along that part of the Clare coast and the ship was blown by the Great Gale to founder in Doughmore Bay, near Doonbeg, at a location thought to be the White Strand. Most of those aboard drowned, save approximately 68 who managed to wade ashore. They were not to survive for long, as they were soon taken into custody by a group of officials of the district, in the service of the Queen. The chances are that these Spaniards were greater in number than this miscellaneous group of locals. However, like other survivors from the Armada shipwrecks on the Irish coast, these bedraggled, starving, weary men, ashore in a strange and,

Above: Lurga Point, with Mutton Island in the background. The 'San Marcos' was wrecked off here.

for them a savage land, were in no condition to offer resistance to what were in most cases smaller bands of armed men.

The other ship off the Clare coast is thought to have been the 790-ton galleon of the Portuguese Squadron, the *San Marcos*, constructed in Portugal around 1585 and which had seen service in the Azores. With 33 cannon, it had fought bravely in the encounters with the English fleet, and had closely supported the *San Martín* flagship during the Gravelines battle, being badly damaged in the process. There had been around 360 men aboard at Corunna and the vessel was under the command of the Marqués de Peñafiel. It had become separated from the main fleet around 26 August. It is probable that it was one of the ships that Boetius Clancy had reported seeing off the Aran Islands. On 18 September, Sir Turlough O'Brien, the local lord, reported that a ship was at Tromra, in Ibracane (south of Quilty). It is probable that the *San Marcos*, on its way back to Spain, had sought safe haven along the Clare coast, which offered no shelter from the Great Gale surging in from the west. The ship was swept onto a reef, believed to be between Mutton Island and Lurga Point. Pummelled by the heavy waves, the great ship broke up on the rocks. All aboard were drowned except four men, who were immediately captured by one of Cahane's underlings, one George Cusack.

The grim fate at Cnoc an Chrochaire

The survivors of the *San Esteban* and *San Marcos* had run out of luck by falling into the hands of Boetius Clancy and his associates. As the antiquarian Thomas Johnson Westropp observed, '[Clancy] gathered a large levy of natives at Liscannor to repel and execute any Spaniards landing from the Armada and carried out Bingham's orders relentlessly'. These soldiers and sailors of the Armada, an estimated 72, were marched to a hill which was subsequently called *Cnoc an Chrochaire* – 'Hangman's Hill' and hanged. It is likely that they were buried at an adjacent location. The actual site of the hangings has not been identified. A likely supposition is that the men had been killed close to where they had been sequestered. However, there are several castles in the general vicinity of the wrecks that had been owned by Clancy and O'Brien, and thus were locations suitable to corral the prisoners prior to execution. Niall Fallon wrote that the executions happened on a hill close to Spanish Point – there is also in the locality a place known as *Tuama na Spáinneach* (The Tomb of the Spaniards). Ken Douglas, in his book, says

Left: a memorial at Spanish Point, Co. Clare, with the insignia of a galleon.

that the survivors were hanged on a hill near Miltown Malbay where the Convent School now stands. The debate continues: one hypothesis is that the survivors had been incarcerated at a castle owned by Clancy at Caherush (around 4km from Lurga Point), from where they were marched a short distance for execution to what was once a hill known as Cnoc an Chrochaire. The hill has disappeared – the sand was excavated and the location is now within the grounds of the Spanish Point Golf Club. Whatever discussion there may be about possible locations, the essential point to remember is that scores of Armada survivors were cold-bloodedly slain and then buried during that gale-swept September of 1588 in that part of Co. Clare. The hanging was presided over by Clancy, attended by Sir Turlough O'Brien, a Captain Mordaunt and other officials in English service – as well as a group of locals. Only one of those from the *San Esteban* survived the slaughter, albeit only for a short time. This was Francisco Marín Centeno, who had been the captain of a company of soldiers on board. He was transferred to the infamous Galway prison, presumably due to his potential for ransom – alas, he was not to secure redemption and was killed.

In the immediate aftermath of the shipwrecks of 1588, there were only a few mentions of items salvaged from the wrecked Armada ships in Ireland. This is in contrast to the abundance of Armada artefacts that were discovered during the twentieth century: particularly those at Lacada Point, Kinnagoe Bay, Blasket Sound and Streedagh. (In England there were only three Spanish ships captured or recovered during 1588, but there exists a veritable forest of timber objects in that country, all claimed to have come from Armada vessels).

After the sinking of the *Girona* an informer's report noted that the wine butts from the vessel were being enjoyed by Sorley Boy McDonnell. At the beginning of 1589, a letter from the Lord Deputy to the Privy Council, referring to strengthening fortifications of towns, mentions two brass and two iron cannon, located in Sligo and Galway, that had been recovered

Right: the Armada Table, said to have been made for Boetius Clancy, using carvings and timber salvaged from Armada ships.

from the Spanish wrecks – other cannons from the *Duquesa Santa Ana* were found on an island in Kiltooris Lake, Co. Donegal. However in Clare, since the time of the Armada, there have been quite a number of items that were claimed to have come from the Spanish ships. Amongst these was a carved mahogany door said to be from an Armada vessel, which, interestingly, had seen duty as a henhouse door in a Clare farm. There are references in folk tradition to other relics, now long disappeared, found in the county: cannonballs, swords and parts of masts. The most famous relic is the rectangular refectory 'Armada Table', partly composed of tropical wood, which came to prominence when it was auctioned in Dublin in 2018, achieving over a third of a million euros. Boetius Clancy is reputed to have salvaged timber and decorations (including heraldic figures taken from the stern of one of the ships) from one of the nearby wrecks and had the table made from these – Clancy later gifted it to the O'Briens of Lemenagh.

The Shannon Estuary

A few days before, another group of Armada ships were adrift, buffeted by the Atlantic storms. For them, the wide Shannon Estuary was to offer welcome shelter. On 15 September this flotilla sailed into the entrance of the estuary. As always, sharp eyes were observing on behalf of their English masters. Nicholas Cahane, coroner for Thomond, reported to his superior, Boetius Clancy, that ships from Flanders and Spain 'have arrived before

Right: Carrigaholt Castle, Co. Clare. On 14 September a flotilla of Armada ships sailed into the Shannon Estuary and moored opposite here.

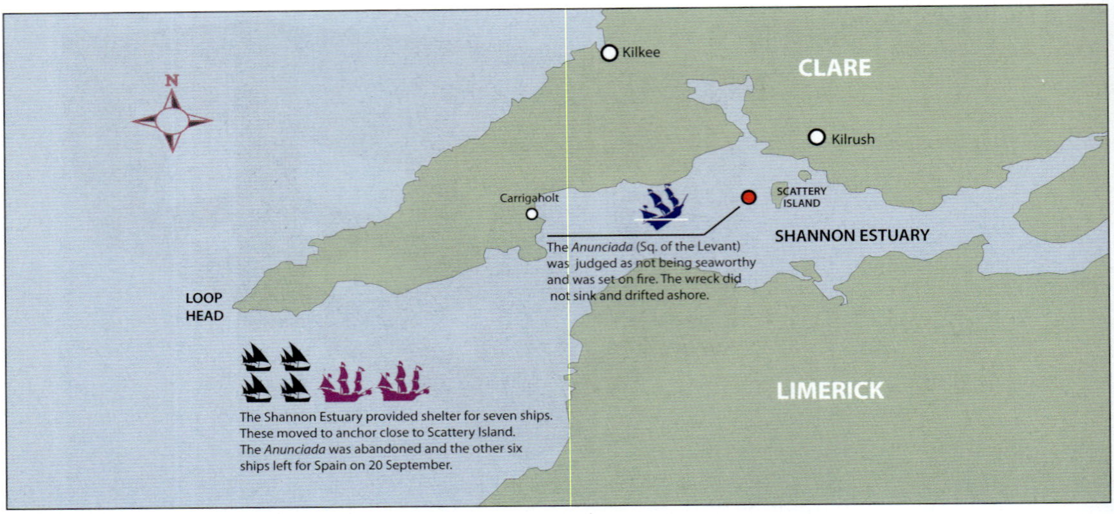

Above: the actions of the flotilla that entered the Shannon Estuary.

Carg-e-colle' (this was Carrigaholt, around 16km east of Loop Head). The 703-ton *nao Anunciada* (original name, *Presveta Anuncijata*, from Ragusa, a veteran of the Azores naval actions and assigned to the Levant Squadron), and a cluster of other vessels, had become separated from the fleet towards the end of August. As well as the *Anunciada*, the group included the small *urca, Caridad* and the four *pataches: Nuestra Señora de Begoña* (not to be confused with the ship of the same name, the *nao* of the Castilian squadron which had entered Blacksod Bay and managed to return to Spain); *San Gerónimo* and two vessels named *La Concepción*, one captained by Francisco de Lastero, the other by Sancho de Carasa. The following day another Armada vessel joined them. This was the *Barca de Danzig*, an *urca*, 450 tons, of German construction, now in poor condition. The flotilla now moved towards a better anchorage. They sailed further up the estuary and moored near Scattery Island, just off the town of Kilrush – Nicholas Cahane owned the castle on the island. Desperately short of supplies, they sent a boat to shore, at a location thought to be near Kilrush. The men of the expedition were confronted by a band led by Cahane, who could speak some Spanish. After an initial desultory exchange where the Spaniards explained that they were from the King of Spain's army, they gave up and decided to return to their ship. However there was a severe shortage of water and a further excursion was mounted. As reported later by Richard Bingham, their desperation was such that they offered a butt of wine in return for one of water and, being rebuffed, even offered one of their ships with all its munitions.

After being in the thick of the fighting in the English Channel and having been buffeted in the Atlantic, the *Anunciada* was in dire straits. She had sprung leaks which the carpenters of the flotilla had tried to seal, but with no success. Being clearly unfit to make the long voyage back to Spain, the decision was taken to abandon her. The captain and owner, Stefan Ivelja, 80 sailors and 180 soldiers, together with a substantial amount of victuals, guns and munition that she had been transporting, were transferred to the *Barca de Danzig* and the *pataches*. The *Anunciada* was then set on fire. As the flotilla departed on an easterly wind on 20 September, a relieved Cahane was able to report: 'God be praised, these seven ships are gone, but one ship that they have burned and let her go to the shore.' Most of the flotilla reached ports in northern Spain at the beginning of October. The battered *Barca de Danzig* arrived at Gijón in mid-October, and after being unloaded, sank the following month.

A *patache* in Tralee Bay

Around five days earlier, a little over 40km to the southwest, a *patache*, holed and leaking, sailed towards Tralee Bay seeking shelter. There are no details of its actual name, but by a process of identifying *pataches* for which there is no record of having returned to Spain, coupled with reference to the size of crew, it is thought that this was the *Nuestra Señora del Socorro* (a *patache* of 75 tons attached to the Squadron of Castile which had departed Corunna with 35 men on board). At the northern entrance to the bay, the vessel, with its small draught, was able to navigate the narrow and shallow channel between Fenit Island and the mainland, which gave entrance to the tidal inlet of Barrow Harbour. Three of the crew swam ashore, most likely in search of food and water, and they were soon apprehended. Lady Margaret Denny, who was living at Carrignafeela Castle, to the east of Tralee, sent out soldiers from the small English garrison at Tralee, and on 17 September the others on board yielded themselves to the Queen's mercy upon promise of their lives and beached the vessel. Lady Margaret was wife of Sir Edward Denny, the undertaker of the district (i.e. a person granted land in a plantation, with an obligation to defend and plant it with English settlers) who we have previously encountered in Chapter 1 at Smerwick. At the time when his wife was taking charge of the Spanish prisoners, Denny was away in Cork at a commission which was determining land disputes.

Below: map of Tralee Bay. On 17 September the crew of the patache yielded themselves to the Queen's mercy upon promise of their lives and beached the vessel. Nonetheless the prisoners were hanged.

The Dennys were an interesting couple. Edward was an English adventurer, living in Kerry at the far west of the Tudor frontierland that was Ire-

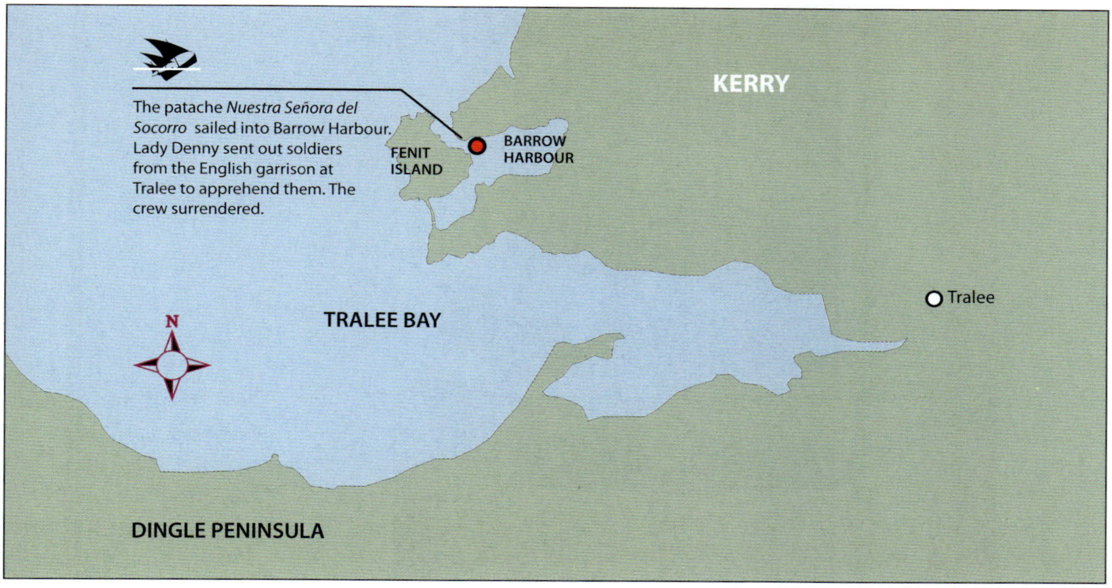

land, a country which offered a mixture of danger, plunder and significant opportunities for advancement. The young Denny had started out by dabbling in privateering. In 1578 he sailed with his cousins Humphrey Gilbert and Walter Raleigh in a flotilla of ships, under a charter from the Queen, on a mission to set up a colony in the Americas – the ill-equipped expedition proved to be a failure. However, opportunity beckoned when in July 1580, Raleigh and Denny were sent to Ireland to help put down the Desmond Rebellion. In November of that year, Denny led his company of 100 men in the assault at Smerwick on the Pope's Italian and Spanish soldiers, where he had been to the fore in directing the slaughter of the 600 who had surrendered. In January 1581, he led an expedition against the rebellious O'Tooles

Above: Barrow Harbour, Fenit, Co. Kerry.

Left: cruelty and avarice obviously paid. The elaborate tomb of Sir Edward and Lady Margaret Denny at Waltham Abbey, Essex, England.

in the Wicklow Mountains – he brought back the head of Garret O'Toole to a grateful Queen. In 1583, now a favourite at court, he married Margaret Edgecumbe, of a prominent family and one of Elizabeth's maids of honour. Reward came four years later when he was assigned 6,000 acres of rich land around Tralee, confiscated from the Earl of Desmond.

A report sent on 19 September to Sir Francis Walsingham told of the 24 who had been captured at Tralee (including two servants of the Duke of Medina Sidonia and two very young boys) and ran: 'They were all of Castile and Biscay … they had lost the Duke [of Medina Sidonia] by tempestuous weather about 18 days since …'. The next part of the captive's story could equally apply to all the other ships blown towards Ireland: '[They] fell with the coast of Ireland, not knowing where they were, but resolved to return for Spain, but that were kept back by contrary winds'. Next, in a desperate attempt to save their lives 'three of them offered ransoms for their lives, promising that they should find friends in Waterford to redeem them, whose names they could not tell'. Waterford was the second city for trade in Ireland and many merchants there imported wine from Spain. In any case it was to no avail – the report laconically records that the Spaniards 'were executed here for that there was no safe keeping for them'.

The killings may have been ordered by the formidable Lady Margaret, although a report sent to Spain at the beginning October by a Genoese spy in London implies that the slaughter was directed by Denny, who most likely had returned hot-foot to Tralee. The report told how the Spaniards 'were hanged by a Captain Denny, on account of some special hatred he bore against Spaniards, in consequence of his once having had a colonel for a prisoner of his in Ireland'. This refers to the aftermath of Smerwick, when as his share, Denny had been assigned the ransom amount for an Italian colonel. However, Don Bernardino de Mendoza, then Spanish ambassador to London, had instead arranged for the colonel's escape. Denied his ransom money, Denny supposedly had vowed vengeance on Spaniards. Perhaps it was jealousy at Denny's good fortune which propelled his neighbouring undertaker in Kerry, Sir William Herbert, to write to Lord Burghley in June 1589 in reference to the Dennys helping themselves to plunder from the Armada, with the complaint that 'Her Majesty and not Sir Edward Denny, is entitled to have the Duke of Medina Sidonia's goods, worth £2,000, if not more'.

Into Blasket Sound

Just around 60km to the southwest, on 15 September, two great ships of the Armada, accompanied by a *patache*, had reached the Kerry coast, just off the Dingle Peninsula. In the afternoon, from the west, they navigated through a narrow channel amidst a complex mix of islands, rocks and reefs, just to the north of the Great Blasket Island. With a keel depth of over 6m, it was possible that the larger ship might have scraped the sea floor. The ships reached their goal, the deep-water Blasket Sound and dropped anchor off the White Strand of Great Blasket Island. The anchorage provided shelter in good weather conditions, but not, as we shall see, when a great storm blew up.

The leading ship was the vice-flagship of the entire Armada, the great galleon, *San Juan de Portugal* (1,050 tons, Squadron of Portugal, with a Corunna muster of 522 men), commanded by Juan Martínez de Recalde, Admiral-General of the Armada. The other was the *nao, San Juan de Bautista* (vice-flagship of the Squadron of Castile, 750 tons, with nearly 300 men on board). The paymaster of the Castile squadron, Marcos de Aramburu, was in charge of the *nao*. Fortunately he has left a detailed account of his dramatic Armada experiences. The accompanying *patache* was the *San Esteban* of the Squadron of Vizcaya (78 tons).

In his narrative, de Aramburu related that by the end of August, his ship, the *San Juan de Bautista*, far to the north-west of Ireland, had lost sight of the main fleet. They soon came upon the *nao, Trinidad* (872 tons of the Castile Squadron), and both ships continued, tacking southwards towards Spain as best they could, amongst the variable winds and on occasion losing sight of each other. On 9 September, de Aramburu estimated that they were just over 400km west of Ireland, at 54°N (abeam of Achill Island). As has been noted, sixteenth-century navigation for latitude was inaccurate. Their calculation was wildly wrong as, at daybreak on 11 Septem-

Above: a westerly view of the Blasket Islands from the side of Mount Eagle. Blasket Sound is the stretch of water that lies between the mainland shore and the Great Blasket Island (in the centre). Dunmore Head is to the left. The gaggle of small reefs and islands to the right of the Great Blasket Island make for difficult navigation into the Sound. On 15 September 1588, de Recalde skilfully led his flotilla through these obstacles to gain the relative shelter of the Sound.

ber, the coast of Ireland came into sight. The following day, a heavy storm blew up, and by midnight they had lost sight of the *Trinidad*. The ship and its crew never returned to Spain and it is speculated that the *Trinidad* sank somewhere near Valentia Island, Co. Kerry. In 1845 a mariner's astrolabe was found on the island, which is presumed to have come from one of the Armada ships.

The *San Juan de Bautista* continued sailing as best she could in a southerly direction amidst changeable winds. On 14 September they saw a large ship and a *patache* in the distance. The next day, as they saw some islands, they were able to catch up. The large ship was the *San Juan de Portugal*, and the *patache* was the *San Esteban*. As has been noted, Juan Martínez de Recalde skilfully led the way and navigated the flotilla through the scatter of islands, past the small Begenish Island to reach Blasket Sound. He had left his bed to do this, being gravely ill from repeated bouts of malaria. A Scottish seaman, who had been captured as they sailed past Scotland, was on board the *San Esteban*, and is said to have assisted in the navigation. However, it was fortuitous that eight years earlier, Recalde had sailed along this very coast when, as part of the ill-fated expedition of 1580, he had led the flotilla that transported the Pope's troops from Spain to Smerwick – a mere 16km sailing distance from Blasket Sound. It is known that he had reconnoitred the coastline and probably was aware of the safe anchorage offered there.

Soon after dropping anchor, a small boat was sent ashore in search of food and water. The party included a Fleming, a Burgundian and a Scotsman (whose Scottish Gaelic would have had similarities to the language of the locals), with a letter for the local governor, with the information that they were merchants bound for Flanders; they had been driven to the Kerry coast by a great storm, and they were willing to pay for fresh supplies. The ruse did not succeed and the eight crew were taken into custody. James Trant, from nearby Dingle (who represented the area in the Parliament in Dublin), had by now alerted the English authorities of the arrival of the ships.

The crewmen taken prisoner were subsequently interrogated – they told of the galleon's difficult encounters in the English Channel and the gruelling journey around Scotland. They revealed the woeful conditions on board the *San Juan de Portugal*: they only had 25 pipes of wine left; their water was foul and stank and there was little bread. One claimed that four or five men were dying each day and that 180 on board had died of the 'sickness' – by comparison, only 20 had died during the fighting in the Channel. Another of the prisoners related that the great ship was now in a wretched state, being much shot through: 'the [main] mast is so weak, by reason of the shot in it, as they dare not abide any storm'.

During the great flight from the fireships at Calais on the night of 7 August many ships had cut their anchor cables. Thus the first order of business on 16 September at Blasket Sound was a swap of suitable anchors: the *San Juan de Portugal* handed over two cables and an anchor to de Aramburu's *San Juan de Bautista*; receiving in exchange a large anchor more suitable for the galleon.

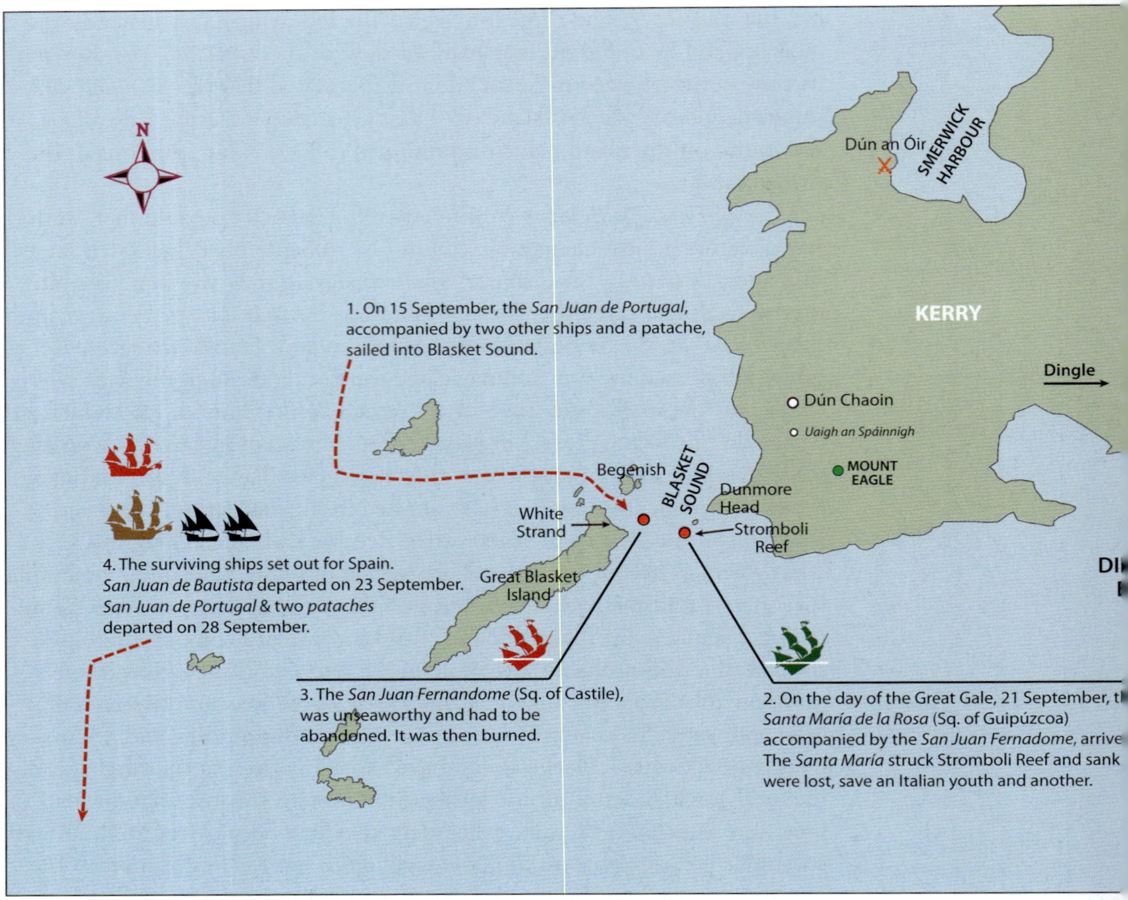

Above: the events at Blasket Sound in September 1588.

The following day, a party of 50 soldiers was dispatched to seek water and victuals, as well as to discover what had happened to the first boat sent out. Approaching the coast, the company was thwarted from landing by the 'wild cliffs' lashed by heavy seas. They gave up the attempt when they saw 100 English soldiers carrying a white standard with a red cross marching along the cliffs. It was clear that the 200 soldiers and 50 cavalry, dispatched by Elizabeth's officials to Dingle, had arrived.

Marcos de Aramburu continued his account, telling how the men of the *San Juan de Portugal* eventually managed, with great difficulty, to obtain some water – probably from springs on one of the Blasket Islands. There is a source of spring water on the Great Blasket and two other islands – it was safer to forage there than on the mainland, now crowded with English soldiers.

The Great Gale blows

Six days after dropping anchor things suddenly got worse for the Spanish flotilla when, on the morning of 21 September, the Great Gale began – blowing 'from the west with a most terrible fury'. Despite the previous exchange of anchors, de Recalde's *San Juan de Portugal* dragged her anchor in the hurricane winds and collided with de Aramburu's *San Juan de*

Bautista, shattering their rear lantern and destroying the rigging of their mizzen mast. Order was re-established when a new anchor was dropped to arrest the *San Juan de Portugal.* As the gale raged, another ship arrived at midday. It was the *nao, Santa María de la Rosa* (956 tons, of the Squadron of Guipúzcoa, built at Pasaia) buffeted by the gale and desperately seeking shelter. The *Santa María* entered the Blasket Sound from the north-west, via a wider entrance close to the mainland, and firing cannon to signal her distress. With the sails in tatters she dropped her only anchor. Two hours later, as the tide turned, she began to swing on the anchor, and was dragged along by tide and wind to within two cable lengths from de Aramburu's ship. The crew of the *Santa María* desperately tried to hoist the only functional remaining sail, the fore mainsail, but suddenly she sank with all on board being drowned, save two – her Corunna muster had been 85 sailors and 238 soldiers. As was revealed in the diving expedition of 1968, when the wreck was discovered, the ship's middle had struck the Stromboli Reef, (to the south-west of Dunmore Head), whose rocks are less than two metres below the surface, so named because HMS *Stromboli* struck it around the middle of the nineteenth century.

The Lost Prince

There were only two survivors. One was a Genoese youth called Giovanni Manona who was washed up naked on a beach, clinging to some timber planks from the ship – and who was promptly taken prisoner. The other was a Diego Sarmiento, whose name appeared in a list of those later slain at Galway. Manona, interrogated in Kerry, had much to disclose. In a series of interrogations he told how he and his father, from Genoa, had embarked on the *Santa María* at Lisbon, where his father had been appointed pilot. Those on board the ship obviously were in a high state of panic and confusion amidst the storm in Blasket Sound, as the youth told how, when the ship hit the rocks, one of the army officers on board killed his father, the pilot, accusing him of treason. Manona went on to tell them that the ship had been hit four times in the Channel battles and there had been deaths on board, both from combat and disease. He told of those on board, of the captain and officers, as well as the presence of two Irish captains. Inaccurately, he claimed that the commander of their squadron, Don Miguel de Oquendo, had been on their ship. Manona added that there had also been three chests on board, with 15,000 ducats in gold coin and the same in silver. This drew their attention, but what particularly intrigued his interrogators was his disclosure that the Prince of Ascoli had been on board the *Santa María* and had drowned. The Prince in question was Don António Luis de Leyva, (a cousin of Alonso Martínez de Leyva, commander of *La Rata*). At the time he was widely thought to be have been King Philip II's illegitimate son, arising from an encounter with one Doña Eufrasia de Guzmán, a lady-in-waiting to Philip's sister, Princess Juana. In one account, Doña Eufrasia was subsequently encouraged by the King to marry the then Prince of Ascoli, whose title would have passed to the young man in due course. (A recent biographer of Philip II considers the liaison with Doña Eufrasia to be implausible.)

Above: Dunmore Head on the left, with the Great Blasket Island in the background and Blasket Sound in mid-picture. The 'Santa María de la Rosa' sank at Stromboli Reef, just off the series of rocks to the upper left of the Head.

The young Italian prisoner continued with his explanation: the Prince, who had been aboard Medina Sidonia's flagship, the *San Martín*, had been ashore at Calais when the great panic broke out amongst the Armada after the fireships drifted there, and boarded the *Santa María* in the aftermath. This was news of such importance to his captors that he was called for another interrogation. The youth gave a detailed description of the Prince, how he, aged 28 years, was tall, thin and had a short beard. He enhanced his tale by informing them how the elegantly-clad Prince had been dressed in a white satin doublet and had stockings of russet silk. In any era, there has been nothing like a bit of salacious royal gossip. Thus, the death of an illegitimate son of Philip II in an Armada shipwreck was indeed explosive news for those back in London – the story featured in many of the reports sent by officials, and prompted Lord Burghley, Elizabeth's chief advisor, when he saw Ascoli's name on a list of the gentleman adventurers who had travelled with the Armada, to annotate it: 'The king of Spayne's bastard'.

A local legend in the Dún Chaoin area runs that a corpse, dressed in fine clothes and boots adorned with gold, was found washed ashore, and that the body was bound with sheets and buried with dignity. Various local references over the following centuries say that the Prince of Ascoli was buried at Dún Chaoin graveyard and that the bodies of the crew of the *Santa María*, washed ashore, were buried there as well. Another local story relates that the prince was buried at *Teampall Mhóire* (a pre-Christian and later Christian burial site –'Temple of Mór', so called from a legend about the goddess Mór, whose temple and grave were held to have been here). Ascoli's grave is supposed to be here at a spot known as *Uaigh an Spáinnigh* ('the grave of the Spaniard'), marked by a prominent pillar stone, set in a small sloping triangular field, in Baile Bhiocáire townland, on the lower slopes of Mount Eagle, overlooking the Blasket Sound.

However, this is not true. Yes, the bodies of the drowned men from the *Santa María* would have been buried locally. It is highly probable that the local people found a body, clad in finery, one of the officers aboard the ship, such as the army captains Lope Ochoa de la Vega or Cristobal de Rivero – or perhaps there had been a few gentleman adventurers on board. The local tradition regarding the Prince, appealing though it is, is not correct. He had not been on board the *Santa María* and had survived the Armada events. As he explained in a letter of 12 August to Philip (the very fact that a young prince could write directly to the King gives a little substance to the proposition that he was Philip's son), he had left the *San Martín* during the fireship attack at Calais on the night of 7 August, having being assigned by Medina Sidonia to broadcast his orders to the other ships. In the melee that followed, Ascoli became surrounded by English ships, and then a gale blew. He managed to reach Calais and from there travelled to the headquarters of the Duke of Parma. He found the Duke and begged 'leave to return to the Armada. This he refused to allow'. He ended the letter with 'my only wish is to be in some place where I may serve your Majesty and do my duty in a manner worthy of my birth'. Ascoli's account and presence are confirmed in other references, principally a contemporaneous letter from the Duke to the King.

The highly coloured details included in the account given by Giovanni Manona are most likely due to the terrified youth telling his captors what he suspected they wanted to know. Seeing their reaction at the news of chests of money, the presence of de Oquendo and particularly that of the prince, he must have decided to embellish the tales – he could have seen the Prince of Ascoli (who as the supposed bastard son of the King would have carried a certain notoriety amongst the sailors and soldiers of the Armada) at Lisbon or during later events. It was in Manona's interest to curry favour and attempt to forestall what he knew was his impending execution. The accuracy of the interrogation was not helped by the self-styled interpreter, one David Gwynn, referred to by the historian Garret Mattingly as 'an imaginative Welshman', who claimed he been a convict rower (he most likely had been captured as a pirate) on board the Armada galley *Bazana* which had run aground at Bayonne. Gwynn alleged that he had led a revolt of the galley slaves and then made his escape. (Some versions of the story say that it was on the galley *Diana*, but this had sailed back to Galicia, arriving on 24 July.) In any event, Gwynn somehow had made his way to Ireland just at the time of the Armada shipwrecks. Shortly after completing his duties in Kerry, the Welshman went to Drogheda to act as interpreter during the interrogations of the Armada prisoners there. Gwynn was a charlatan of doubtful veracity. At the end of October 1588 his venality was such that the Lord Deputy wrote to the Privy Council complaining about Gwynn's 'lewd and undutiful behaviour', and requesting 'the most severe punishment' due to his 'embezzling ... such chains, gold and money as he took from the Spanish prisoners'.

Arrival and Departure

Back to the Great Gale blowing across the Blasket Sound on 21 September. Just after the sinking of the *Santa María,* a *patache* of the Squadron of Vizcaya, *La Isabela*, commanded by Miguel de Ariníbar, arrived. At four that afternoon, the *nao, San Juan Fernandome* (650 tons, Squadron of Castile) also sailed in and dropped anchor. The *nao* had sustained serious storm damage – her mainmast was gone and the fore-sail was ripped to pieces. Having been in the thick of the Channel battles, she had also been damaged by cannon fire. It was obvious that the *nao's* situation was hopeless, so the next day it was arranged that the men on board be divided between de

Left: cross-slab at Teampall Mhóire, an ancient burial ground, near Dún Chaoin, Co. Kerry. It contains a possible prehistoric tomb and, reputedly, Uaigh an Spáinnigh *(the grave of the Spaniard) the grave of the Prince of Ascoli, alleged son of Philip II, supposedly drowned in Blasket Sound. However, in reality, the Prince became separated from the Armada when the fire ships attacked off Calais, and eventually made his way to Dunkirk.*

Aramburu's *San Juan de Bautista* and the two *pataches*, while the guns and powder were be transferred to the *San Juan de Portugal.* De Recalde gave permission to depart to de Aramburu, whose ship was short of supplies, and the *San Juan de Bautista* set out on 23 September on a light easterly wind. Their return to Spain was fraught and they experienced many storms. On 14 October, the ship, weather-beaten and damaged, finally arrived at Santander and de Aramburu gratefully noted that they had anchored in safety, for which we have 'to give thanks to Our Lord'.

In Blasket Sound, on 26 September, de Recalde having salvaged what he could of the cannons of the *San Juan Fernandome*, amidst the heavy seas, ordered the damaged ship to be burned. On the night of 28 September, Recalde set out for Spain in the *San Juan de Portugal*, accompanied by the *pataches*, *San Esteban* and *La Isabela*. On 7 October, Recalde, despite his galleon being badly damaged and almost unnavigable, managed to reach Corunna, along with the *pataches*. As has been noted in Chapter 4, de Recalde on arrival, sent off documents to the King that were critical of Medina Sidonia. However, desperately ill and worn out after the travails along the English Channel and the Irish coast, he knew he was reaching the end. In a letter to Don Andrés de Alba, the secretary of the Council of War, he despairingly wrote: 'Tomorrow I want to confine myself in a cell of the Franciscan monastery and if I die there it will be less trouble to bury me'. Juan Martínez de Recalde, Admiral-General, second in command of the Armada, great mariner of Spain, died on 23 October, just two weeks after arriving in port.

Slaughter at Galway

We have previously seen that the Elizabethan authorities in Ireland had ordered the elimination of all Armada survivors. Lord Deputy William FitzWilliam had issued a general commission to his Governors stating that it was their duty to apprehend and kill the castaway Spaniards and, as already evidenced, this had been complied with, from Kerry all the way to Derry. Many of the killings were carried out spontaneously in the vicinity of the shipwrecks, but it was the city of Galway which emerged as the central killing ground, where the Spanish were killed in an organised, almost industrial manner, under the directions of Sir Richard Bingham. Bingham was President of Connaught and in September 1588, as news came of the Armada's proximity, he had issued a proclamation in Connaught that 'upon pain of death' captured Spanish were to be handed over to his officials. The elimination of the perceived Spanish threat was of great importance to him, as he had few troops, and could only exercise patchy control over his province. Bingham was in a high state of alert for any news of Spanish incursion, and on 24 September, hearing that 1,400 Spaniards were intending to set themselves up in west Mayo, he set out for the county from his headquarters in Athlone Castle. Amidst the febrile atmosphere, he next heard that these had sailed onwards so he now headed for Galway, reaching there on 1 October. Some Spanish survivors had already been brought to the city; others were being handed over by the timorous Irish chieftains, fearful of Bingham's retribution if they didn't. Sir Tadhg na Buile O'Flaherty brought the survivors of the *Santa Bárbara* to the city and handed them over. The other O'Flaherty, Sir Murrough-na-dTuagh, brought in those survivors from the *Falcón Blanco Mediano*, wrecked in Iar-Connacht.

From the time of the Hiberno-Normans, Galway had been fortified and surrounded by walls. In a sign of the precariousness of the times, the walls built on the sea side were intended to prevent any sea-borne incursions from Munster, while those on the landward side were to guard against invasion from inland. Within the city's protective walls, trade continued to grow and the prosperity attracted English settlers. Galway's merchants exported local produce sourced from the nearby chiefdoms and, in turn, they imported commodities from abroad (the principal import being wine from France and Spain). By the sixteenth century, Galway had developed to be one of the primary trade emporia of the Tudor domain in both Ireland and England. Such was the city's affluence that the people of Limerick, jealous of their rival's good fortune, sent an allegation to Henry VIII that Galway had 'degenerated into the manner and customs of the Irish'. Henry responded in 1536 with instructions that the inhabitants should use the 'English order, habit and language'. In 1579, in recognition of their loyalty, Elizabeth granted the city a charter, giving generous privileges. Galway was one of England's principal strategic outposts in Ireland – it was essentially an English city, set at the edge of Gaelic Connemara.

The prison at Galway became the holding area for the Spanish survivors mainly gathered from Connaught. Passing within its grim walls were the soldiers and sailors rounded up from a variety of ships: *La Rata, Nuestra Señora de Begoña, Ciervo Volante, San Nicolás Prodaneli, Gran Grín, Santa Bárbara, Santa María de la Rosa* and the *Falcón Blanco Mediano*. Bingham, whose well-earned epithet as the 'flail of Connaught' has echoed down the centuries, ordered all to be killed. Amidst the savagery, there was calculation – people of nobility or high rank were spared (offering the opportunity for lucrative ransom) while the rank and file were executed. The most senior of the prisoners allowed to live was Don Luis de Córdoba, brother of the Marquis de Ayamonte, who had been called from Sicily by Philip II to take part in the Armada. He had managed to come ashore from the *Falcón Blanco*

Left: a memorial at Forthill Cemetery, Galway City, to the Armada survivors who were slain in 1588 and buried in the cemetery.
It translates (in Spanish): 'The Order of Old Tercio of the Mar Oceano (i.e. the Atlantic), to the soldiers and sailors of the Great Armada, here devoutly interred by the people of Galway in 1588. Many they rest in peace. 22nd June 1988.' (In Irish): 'May they be at the right hand of God.'

Mediano, on which he had command of 100 soldiers. Don Luis, when interrogated, had taken care to tell that his eldest brother was a gentleman of 1,000 ducats per annum – and he was spared. We later hear of Don Luis in June 1590 in London along with Don Alonso de Luzón (of the *Trinidad Valencera*) and others. After protracted negotiations, these men eventually secured their release. Other prisoners spared were from the *San Nicolás Prodaneli*: the captains Gabriel de Zuazo and Alonso Riqueleme as well as some Dutch youths. However, for these it was only a temporary stay of execution. After Lord Deputy FitzWilliam breezed into Galway, he ordered that any remaining survivors be executed.

Bingham personally oversaw the executions, assigning several of his henchmen, including John Byrte, Captain Nathaniel Smythe and Robert Fowley, to arrange the slaughter. Around 9 October, more than 300 prisoners were led to St Augustine's monastery on a hill, then located outside the city. One account tells that the Augustinian friars gave spiritual comfort to the condemned men, exhorting them to meet death bravely. Watched by the people of Galway, the unfortunate men of the Armada were put to the sword. Butchering so many was evidently a tiring process. The *Calendar of State Papers for Ireland* for that period notes that Bingham 'having made a clear despatch of [the Spanish prisoners], both within the town and in the country, he rested Sunday all day, giving thanks to Almighty God for Her Majesty's most happy success in that action, and our deliverance from such dangerous enemies'.

Many were interred in a mass grave at Forthill Cemetery, then associated with the monastery. The matrons of Galway are reputed to have made shrouds for the bodies, in an effort to give them some final dignity. The story of this slaughter resonated for years. In time the news reached Rome and the Papal authorities, who took a charitable view – in a December 1590 report by the (Protestant) Archbishop of Cashel on 'Popish activities' in Ireland, there was reference to one James O'Cleary, a priest who came from Rome, who 'brought a dispensation for the town of Galway for the killing of the holy Spaniards'.

Right: the attendance at the Church of San Agustín in Córdoba at a Mass for the soul of Don António de Ulloa y Sandoval. A series of Masses was held here in March 2024 in accordance with Don António's wishes as expressed in his last will and testament, written over 435 years before at Galway, just before he was beheaded.

Don António de Ulloa y Sandoval

One of the most poignant of all the extensive documentation on the Armada held in the Spanish State Archives, Archivo General de Simancas, is the last will and testament of Don António de Ulloa y Sandoval. He, a survivor from one of the Armada shipwrecks on the west coast, had been imprisoned at Galway and was then put to the sword. An ensign of the *tercios,* Baltasar López de Arbol, who was in the prison at Millmount in Drogheda, had subsequently received the document from an English captain, who made this rare humanitarian gesture. López de Arbol sent the de Ulloa document, along with an account of the situation in Ireland, to Spain, conveyed there by two Catholics: the Irishman, John Stanley, and an Englishman, Richard Hulton.

In the testament, written just as he awaited the axeman at Galway, Don António wrote requesting that many Masses be said for his soul in the churches of his locality and that 100 ducats be given to his cousin Andrés. Harrowingly, he finished the document with a few hastily scribbled words, trailing off in mid-sentence, that 'the executioner does not give me any more time to ...'.

In his missive that accompanied the testament, López de Arbol said that de Ulloa was a native of Toro (Zamora province). However, recent research by the historian Pedro Luis Chinchilla of ArmadaInvencible.org has established that he came from Cordóba, thus allowing identification of the churches and shrines where de Ulloa had requested Masses to be said. Finally, and 435 years later, in March 2024 a series of Masses were said at the Church of San Agustín in Córdoba, in accordance with the last wishes of António de Ulloa y Sandoval.

Above: one of a series of woodcuts by John Derrick, dating from 1581, which shows how savagery was abroad in Ireland under Tudor domination during the late sixteenth century. It depicts the triumphant return of English soldiers from an expedition. In the background they are dragging prisoners and herding plundered cattle with, to the left, a prisoner is being beheaded. The foremost soldier of the band carries a decapitated head by the hair. Two more heads impaled on swords are held up in triumph.

Why the Savagery in Ireland?

Why was such wholesale slaughter by the English authorities carried out in Ireland? In England and the Netherlands, by contrast, the treatment of Armada survivors was infinitely more lenient. As already mentioned, only one Armada vessel was shipwrecked in England, namely the *San Pedro el Mayor* which was driven ashore at Devon. The 158 survivors were not executed (although this was initially considered) and were eventually repatriated. Neither were the crews of the ships captured during the initial battle in the English Channel. The over 390 men of the *Nuestra Señora del Rosario* (which surrendered to Sir Francis Drake on 1 August 1588) were imprisoned in various English locations under harsh conditions and in February 1590 were allowed to return to Spain. The ship's officers received courteous treatment. The commander Don Pedro de Valdés and two senior officers were lodged in comfortable quarters. After negotiations, in February 1593 they were allowed to go to Flanders. A ransom of £3,350 was paid for de Valdés, plus £900 for each of his companions. The sum of £400 per annum for their keep was added, part of which was claimed by Drake. The *nao, San Salvador,* had been captured in the English Channel following the explosion of 31 July , and was towed to an English port. Fewer than 20 of the badly injured men left on board survived and these were repatriated in early 1590.

In Holland, around 300 prisoners had been taken from the *San Mateo* which on 10 August 1588 had surrendered after a fierce battle between Ostend and Sluys – although the Dutch, amidst the fury of battle, had thrown some of the crew overboard. Around 40 were captured from the *San Felipe* which ran aground on a beach between Nieuport and Ostend, as well as another 21 from a *patache*, *San António de Padua*, lost near Ostend. For the Dutch, the immediate reaction to taking Spanish prisoners was not a knee-jerk one to put them to the sword; rather it was to consult with the English. Prince Maurice of Nassau, Stadtholder of the Dutch Republic, sent a letter in early August 1588 to Sir Francis Walsingham, Elizabeth's principal secretary, giving a description of the prisoners from the captured Armada ships, and he asked to 'advertise me of her Majesty's pleasure'. In the event, none were executed, and all were eventually ransomed and liberated.

There were several underlying reasons for what was, in comparison to elsewhere, the savagery in Ireland. The first was that the senior English administrators on the island felt distinctly vulnerable – they had an army that rarely exceeded 1,500. The Gaelic chieftains, who dominated the Atlantic coasts were, in English eyes, only half-tamed, prone to rebellion, and Catholic to boot. This was a great incentive to rapidly minimise the risk that Spanish soldiers ashore would ally with the Irish. Another reason was that life was cheap along the frontiers of Elizabeth's Ireland: we have already seen in Chapter 1 how the technique of issuing a commission with the power to execute any 'malefactors' without trial was a particularly effective (and inexpensive) method to subdue revolt or disorder. However, one key reason must lie in the character of the Queen's men in Ireland. Ireland was the Tudor Wild West; it provided opportunities for adventurers at all levels, whether it was a settler, a captain or an administrator (sometimes these three roles were combined). It was a location where Englishmen developed techniques of bloody subjugation and settlement which was to stand them in good stead later on when the colonisation of North America began. Opportunities for advancement had attracted ruthless men to take up the reins of power. These ranged from the Lord Deputy, Sir William FitzWilliam (who felt a need to rapidly gain wealth), to Sir Richard Bingham (who, in his career had experience of directing great slaughter). These and the numerous captain-adventurers operated in the harsh and unforgiving environment of Ireland, where any dissent was soon stamped out in blood, but where the potential for reward was great.

The killings in Ireland, under instructions sent out by Bingham and FitzWilliam, were very much a local initiative – these had not been sanctioned from England. Indeed, a missive was issued by the Privy Council to FitzWilliam on 28 September on how to treat Spanish prisoners: 'whereas Her Majesty hath been lately informed ... that certain of the Spanish ships being driven upon the coasts of [Ireland] ... and whereas of occasion aforesaid it must needs fall out that diverse Spanish prisoners are taken, their Lordships pleasure is that great care be had of their safe custody and keeping in some convenient place…'. FitzWilliam soon felt the disapproval emanating at high level from England, arising from the executions. He wrote to Lord Burghley (Elizabeth's Treasurer and chief advisor) on 11 October, asking him to intervene with 'Her Majesty in his behalf, if any seek to move her against him for clearing the country of Spaniards'. The more politically sensitive FitzWilliam had changed his tune, as when he wrote to the Privy Council on 22 October, advising them of his intention to proceed against the Spaniards in O'Donnell's country, he added that his aim was 'of offering mercy to such as shall submit'.

However, Sir Richard Bingham had no shame and was of a freer, more buccaneering spirit than the Lord Deputy; he felt that he could broadcast the news of his slaughter of a large number of the Queen's enemies without fear of reprimand. On 13 December 1588, as the Armada events had

Left: over a thousand crosses. An aerial view of the 2023 commemoration held at Streedagh Strand, Co. Sligo, by Spanish Armada Ireland in memory of the Spaniards who died in 1588.

begun to die down (and the bodies of the executed Spaniards lay in their cold graves), he wrote to Elizabeth to proudly advise her that: 'The men of the [Spanish] ships all perished, save 1,100 or more who were put to the sword'. Not forgetting the potential for lucrative ransom, he told of setting aside 'the officers or gentlemen of quality to the number of 50'. He gave the impression that he had been merciful with these men, while implying that, by contrast, FitzWilliam had been bloodthirsty (and wasteful of ransom money), as he noted: 'These gentlemen were spared till the Lord Deputy sent me special direction to see them executed.' He ended on a self-congratulatory note, emphasising how the whole exercise did not require extra cost, a topic dear to Elizabeth's heart: 'Thus was the province quickly got rid of these distressed enemies … without … any extraordinary charge to your Majesty'.

The losses in Ireland

How many soldiers and sailors from the Armada were lost in Ireland? Estimates of the numbers have oscillated over time and allowances have to be made for inaccuracies of that period. At the end of September 1588, in a letter to Sir Francis Walsingham, Sir George Carew (then Master of the Ordinance in Ireland) estimated that some 5,000 or 6,000 perished 'in this land by sword and sea', of whom 'very near 3,000 were slain'. The author Niall Fallon made an approximate estimate that of the 6,000 men on board the ships lost in Ireland, around 750 managed to eventually return to Spain. He calculated that around 3,750 had been drowned or killed in the Irish shipwrecks, and that approximately 1,500 men were slain by English forces or their proxies. This gives a total figure of around 5,250 men from the Spanish Armada who lost their lives in Ireland.

Chapter 6

Aftermath

After 21 July 1588, when the Armada had departed from Corunna, a period of relative calm descended on the Escorial. With the Enterprise of England underway, it was a respite for Philip, no longer having to send messages ordering all concerned to make haste and sail for England. The first real information to arrive was a report of 7 August from Dieppe in northern France, telling that there had been the sounds of a great battle, more than 2,000 cannon shots, and that it was a victory for the Spanish. However, distressing news arrived on the night of 31 August in a dispatch from Bernardino de Mendoza, Philip's ambassador in France, informing him that the Armada had failed to join up with Parma's forces. The King's secretary tried to alleviate the heartache that he was feeling, sending him a note that invoked God's will: 'The pain and the doubt are great, but how much greater is the mercy of God … but in his secret judgements … such a great work cannot remain without great [Heavenly] reward'.

In the light of such bad news, there was nothing the King and his advisors, impotent in their chambers, could do, except identify alternatives as to what the Duke of Medina Sidonia might be able to do now, such as the possibility that the Armada could take refuge in Scotland, allying with Catholics there, or landing at Waterford in Ireland – and in either instance, launching an attack on England the following year. Alas, these were just paper exercises, as the Duke was incommunicado, fully engaged in leading the Armada through the storms of the north Atlantic and back to Spain. On 3 September information arrived with details of the Armada's journey up towards Scotland. The King's response was: 'I hope that God has not allowed so much wickedness, for the whole thing has been done for His service'.

As the days and weeks passed, small pieces of information, some contradictory, reached the Court. On 24 September, Don Baltazar de Zúñiga arrived, having made his way down the Atlantic in a fast *patache* carrying a dispatch from the Duke of Medina Sidonia. In this, written a month before, the Duke told of the sorry situation of the fleet north of the British Isles and how he had set his course for Corunna. As it happens, the Duke had actually arrived at Santander the previous day, and more concrete and timely news began to reach the Escorial on a regular basis. Philip then sprang into action, ordering succour for the survivors on the Armada ships as they began to arrive in the northern ports. As we saw, in mid-October the King sent a letter to the bishops of Spain asking them to cease the prayers for the Armada.

There was to be no succour from the Pope, particularly in the temporal sense – the prospects of getting any money from the Pontiff had vanished. The Spanish ambassador, Count de Olivares, wrote to the King on 9 October: 'We shall get nothing from the Pope. It is impossible to imagine how openly he has shown his selfishness and bad disposition on this occasion'. By early November, as the full extent of the losses became clearer, Philip fell into a depression. He unburdened his heart to Mateo Váquez saying that soon he would find himself in such a state 'that we shall yearn that we had never been born … And if God does not send a miracle … I hope to die and go to Him before this happens …'.

The failure of the principal objective of the Armada and the loss of many ships and men were grievously wounding to Spain, but no territory had been lost. The situation was similar to that referred to by the Ottoman Grand Vizier Mehmet Sokullu, when he addressed a Venetian emissary in 1571, contrasting the Battle of Lepanto (a Christian naval victory) with the Ottoman seizure of the last Venetian fortress in Cyprus some months earlier: 'You come to see how we bear our tribulations. But I would have you know the differences between your loss and ours. In wresting Cyprus from you, we divested you of an arm; in vanquishing our fleet, you have only shaved our beard. An arm when cut off cannot grow again; but a shorn beard will grow all the better for the razor'.

Philip II moves on

It helped that the King still ruled over an empire of overwhelming might. He also possessed qualities of inner strength and a deep belief in God's will – Philip was now able to move on. In mid-November he requested that the Council of State advise him on the policy that should be pursued, taking account of the Armada debacle. The council duly reported that it was too costly to adopt a defensive stance in relation to the English enemy and it was better to mount a new expedition. While the Spanish Empire verged had paused repayments on loans at times, it had infinitely deeper resources than that of England and was able to shrug off the material loss of around 30 per cent of the Armada fleet (and the necessity to repair many of the surviving vessels) – it helped that most of the galleons had survived, with many of the losses being in merchant vessels. Philip pondered deeply and continued to analyse the underlying problems that had plagued the expedition. He noted: the bad coordination; the absence of a deep-water Channel port; the difficulties along the Dutch coast; and, not least, the need to have better ships and guns with improved range. The Venetian ambassador reported that the King 'feels the blemish on the Spanish name and declares

Right: at the Escorial, statues of the family of Philip II at his tomb, completed by the Italian sculptor Pompeo Leoni in 1598. It comprises the King kneeling at a prie-dieu with three of his four wives (Anne of Austria, Isabella of Valois and María of Portugal). At the rear, his son, Don Carlos, kneels between them.

The power of prayer to the Almighty along with an inner strength helped Philip recover after the failure of the 'Enterprise of England'. He soon recovered his old energy and in December 1588 asked the Cortes of Castile for funds to mount a new expedition against the English.

that with a prudent and valiant commander, they can still regain the honour they have lost'.

The King regained his old energy and in December 1588 asked the Cortes of Castile for funds to mount a new expedition against the English. Philip in his message to the Cortes, justified the future expenditure that he had requested by explaining that it was required 'since we need to provide what we lack, and embark upon an offensive war'. The King stated said that the Armada had cost 10 million ducats, and that he thought the future expenditure would be no less. In the opinion of one Spanish economic historian, Philip, who had long experience of negotiating with a reluctant Cortes, endeavouring to get them to increase taxes, had grossly inflated the cost of the Armada as a device to get them to raise even more taxes. At the same time he painted the picture of a monarchy and country in peril. In the event, the Cortes rallied to the flag and in 1590 a new tax was agreed which would contribute eight million ducats over a period of six years, for 'the defence of the faith and of [Philip's] realms'.

The number of ships owned by the Crown in the Armada of 1588 had been relatively small – mainly the galleons of Portugal and those of the Indies fleet, as well as the galleasses and galleys. Philip set in place a major ship-building programme and, in addition, measures for the production of improved cannon – gunnery schools were also set up. The highly effective shipyards along the north coast of Spain were geared up. New ships were laid down including 12 large warships of an improved design (dubbed 'the Twelve Apostles'). A programme was instituted to refurbish those ships of the recently-returned Armada that were salvageable. By 1591, 21 newly-built galleons had been commissioned. These joined the warships involved in the quotidian but hugely important business of escorting the treasure fleet from the Americas.

Left: the great library at the Escorial, where Philip II, a passionate collector of books, manuscripts and works of art, could find solace.

Philip had other issues to contend with. He had to deal with instability at the heart of his kingdom. There were disputes with the Cortes of Aragón, asserting the *fueros* (rights) that had been in force since the time of the uniting of the kingdoms by his great-grandparents, Ferdinand and Isabel. With Aragón in uproar, Philip had to send in his army in October 1591. The revolt was stamped out and Spanish unity was maintained. However, the economy of Spain and its territories had been suffering from underlying structural problems which disimproved as the sixteenth century progressed. In the Americas there had been epidemics, notably one in 1576-9 among the Indians, which had decimated the native population. This in turn severely impeded the output of the mines and agricultural production in the new estates, the *latifundios*. At the same time, as the colonists developed self-sufficiency in basic products, merchants in Seville found it difficult to sell their goods. Economic performance varied by region. The growth of Madrid led to economic expansion across New Castile. Trade in coastal regions grew, while it fell in the interior. The expulsion of the highly productive *Moriscos* from the Kingdom of Granada in 1570 had led to a drop in agricultural output in that territory, as well as that from associated sectors like sugar and silk production. Despite the constant flow of wealth from the Americas, there had been huge expenditure on the various wars. There was little state funding for public works, such as improving irrigation and communications (roads, bridges and canals). The overall financial situation had deteriorated. Philip's previous debt defaults had been sustainable. However, following the high spike in expenditure due to the Armada and other military campaigns, even the silver remittances could not save the Spanish treasury and Philip was forced to sign yet another decree that suspended payment to bankers in November 1596. However, despite many problems, over the entire sixteenth century, output per capita in Spain managed to grow marginally, while that of England remained static.

Spain's Golden Age, a blossoming in architecture, art and literature, continued through the sixteenth century. One of Spain's greatest writers, Lope de Vega (above), had served on board de Recalde's 'San Juan de Portugal' during its epic Armada voyage and had sailed all along the Irish coast.

Nevertheless there was a flourishing: it was a Golden Age in many areas of Spanish life. Architecture, art and literature blossomed. Foremost among the many examples of great buildings was the impressive Escorial. However the immense construction cost for this had placed a burden on the treasury. Some of the greatest painters of the age were creating a distinctive Spanish style of painting – including El Greco and, later, Velázquez and Murillo. Literature thrived – two of the most outstanding writers had connection with the Armada: Miguel de Cervantes had roamed the Andalucian roads seeking supplies for the fleet gathering at Lisbon, and the poet and playwright Lope de Vega had served on board de Recalde's *San Juan de Portugal* during its long and fraught Armada voyage along the Irish coast. There were also innovations in the sciences in such fields as astronomy, navigation, medicine and botany.

That other European great power, France, continued to be a strategic threat to Spain. King Henry III ruled an unstable country, divided between the fervent Protestant Huguenots and the equally assertive Catholic Holy League, led by the powerful Duke of Guise. The Duke was assassinated in December 1588 by order of Henry III – who was assassinated eight months later, to be succeeded by the Protestant Henry of Navarre. The new regime was unacceptable to Philip and he ordered the Duke of Parma to divert from his Dutch campaign in the Netherlands and give support to the Holy League. Parma, displeased to be once again distracted from what he regarded as his primary mission, invaded France at the end of July 1590 and entered Paris in triumph in September. Just a month later a Spanish expeditionary force landed in Brittany to join with French Catholic forces and remained there until 1598. Parma, who had returned to the Netherlands, was soon forced to go back to France to lift Henry of Navarre's siege of Rouen. In late November 1592, Parma once again returned to the Netherlands in poor health and he died, aged 47, the following month. By now Spanish power in the Netherlands had been weakened: the army of the Dutch United Provinces, profiting from the Duke of Parma's absence in France, had enjoyed a string of successes.

What happened in England?

There was an understandable boost to English morale after it became evident that the immediate Spanish threat had been overcome. A thanksgiving service was held on 18 September 1588 in St Paul's Cathedral, where Spanish banners seized in battle were put on display. Services were held all over England giving thanks. Portraits of a victorious Elizabeth were common. One, known as the 'Armada' portrait, shows the Queen in her new exalted status, now empress of the world, with one hand on a globe. To her left is a depiction of a Channel battle and on the right, the shipwreck of Spanish ships.

Up to recent times the perception in Britain has been that the Armada events were a glorious triumph, with Drake and his navy decisively smashing the Armada fleet. However the facts had not been allowed to intrude: in reality Elizabeth had just had a lucky escape; just one Spanish ship had been directly sunk by English cannon fire and the majority of the Armada

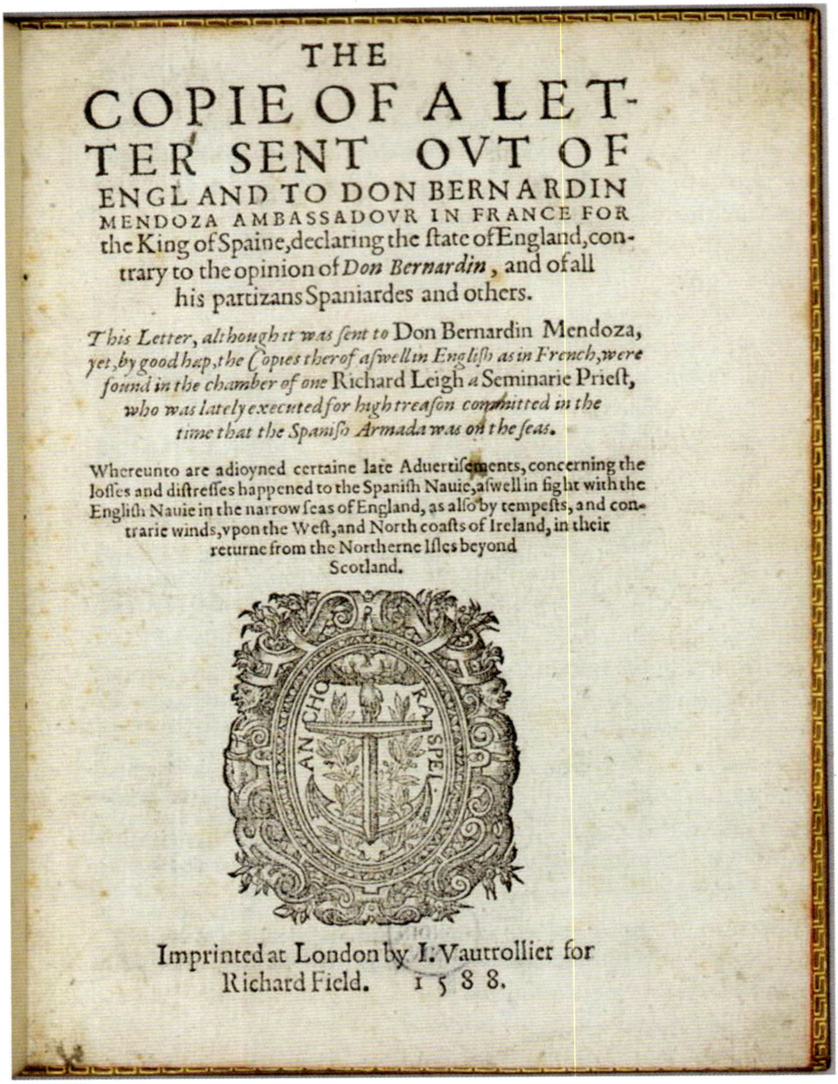

THE COPIE OF A LETTER SENT OVT OF ENGLAND TO DON BERNARDIN MENDOZA AMBASSADOVR IN FRANCE FOR the King of Spaine, declaring the ſtate of England, contrary to the opinion of *Don Bernardin*, and of all his partizans Spaniardes and others.

This Letter, although it was ſent to Don Bernardin Mendoza, *yet, by good hap, the Copies therof aſwell in Engliſh as in French, were found in the chamber of one* Richard Leigh *a* Seminarie Prieſt, *who was lately executed for high treaſon committed in the time that the Spaniſh Armada was on the ſeas.*

Whereunto are adioyned certaine late Aduertiſements, concerning the loſſes and diſtreſſes happened to the Spaniſh Nauie, aſwell in fight with the Engliſh Nauie in the narrow ſeas of England, as alſo by tempeſts, and contrarie winds, vpon the Weſt, and North coaſts of Ireland, in their returne from the Northerne Iſles beyond Scotland.

Imprinted at London by I. Vautrollier for Richard Field. 1588.

Left: utter forgery. 'The copie of a letter sent ... to Don Bernardin Mendoza' (1588), purporting to be from an English Jesuit. It was written by William Cecil, Baron Burghley, Elizabeth I's principal advisor. The intention was to spread the news about the failure of the Armada and to dissuade English Catholics from supporting the Spanish cause and Cardinal Allen's call to overthrow Elizabeth and her regime.

ships lost had been blown by exceptionally great gales onto Atlantic rocks. In the aftermath, there was much exaggeration and dissimulation. One of the most egregious examples occurred in August 1588, when Lord Burghley (Lord Chancellor and Elizabeth's principal advisor), forged a letter that was claimed to have been seized from an English Jesuit (recently executed for treason) and destined for Don Bernardino de Mendoza, the Spanish Ambassador in France. It was originally intended to be a refutation of a call for the liberation of the English people from the yoke of heresy that had been made by the English Cardinal, William Allen. The document purported to rebuke de Mendoza for all his confident promises, which had come to naught. It emphasised Spanish losses and outlined Philip II's 'unjust' reasons for attacking England. Published as a pamphlet, its purpose was to spread the news of the defeat of the Armada and at the same time to dissuade English Catholics from supporting the Spanish cause. Additional details were added

First-class propaganda. These medals (above) were struck in the Netherlands to celebrate the failure of the Spanish Armada. The underlying message was that there was divine approval for the Protestant cause. Top left: a fleet is shown on a stormy sea, with the Latin inscription telling that God blew and they were scattered. Top right: this medal shows the Pope, Philip II and clerics, seated and blindfolded. Their feet are kicking in vain against a bed of spikes. Scorning their aspirations, the inscription above them reads: 'O blind minds of men, O blind souls'. That on the border says 'It is hard to kick against the pricks'.

to later versions of the letter as news arrived of the Armada losses along the Irish coast, and it was first published in Paris in 1588, with the additional aim of discrediting Ambassador de Mendoza (then busy in France supporting the forces of the Duke of Guise and his Holy League against King Henry III). As pointed out in research by the historian Pedro Luis Chinchilla, it appears that the first use of the adjective 'Invincible' to describe the Armada was in a subsequent translation of the document into Italian by the Florentine Petruccio Ubaldini (who also had put together a brief history of the Armada events as told by Lord Admiral Howard). The term, hugely sarcastic in the context of what actually transpired, was never used in Spain at the time. The term may subsequently have fallen into disuse but it was used in the titles of books by Spanish historians from the late nineteenth century onwards (Cesáreo Fernández Duro and Enrique Herrera Oria). The use of 'Invincible' as an ironic term to describe the Armada is still in current use.

Back in 1588, Dutch Protestants in the Netherlands rejoiced just as much as their English coreligionists at the defeat of their common enemy. A set of commemorative medals struck there pointed out whose side God was on, implying that in effect it was a Protestant wind that had confounded the Spanish fleet. One medal depicted a fleet on a stormy sea with the Latin inscription *Flavit et Dissipati Sunt* which can be translated as '[God] blew and they were scattered'. It is significant that the Armada events occurred just as printing technology was gaining its stride. The invention of the printing press allowed the mass distribution of printed material, which in turn allowed the transmission of information across borders. With relatively high levels of literacy in their towns and cities, the printing revolution had taken root in England and the Netherlands, where books, pamphlets and periodicals were issued proclaiming their great triumph of 1588. The failure of the Armada was presented as an overwhelming defeat by plucky (and Protestant) England over a despotic Spain, brimming with the fanaticism of the Inquisition, and inflicting cruelties during its colonisation of the Americas. This demonisation of Spain (called the '*Leyenda Negra*' or 'Black Legend' in that country) has continued over the centuries and traces persist to this day in the Anglophone world.

The Armada events did not turn out well for English Catholics. At the beginning of her reign, Elizabeth had treated Catholics with a light touch – hoping that, over time, they would switch their allegiance from Rome. This did not come about and over time repressive laws were put in place, including the obligation that Catholics attend Church of England services; those who refused to attend were called 'recusants' and had to pay a fine for their obstinacy. Lists of recusants were compiled in each county and they were kept under surveillance. The position of Catholics in England disimproved due to many causes including: the flight of the cream of English Catholic academics and clerics to the Continent; the establishment of colleges there to train young Englishmen; the failed uprising of the Northern Catholic nobles in 1569; the Queen's excommunication by the Pope in 1570 and the many plots against her life, with the object of her replacement by the Catholic Mary Queen of Scots. After 1585, if a priest was arrested and found to have been recently ordained abroad, he was deemed a traitor and executed. Even though there were references to around one third of the English having Catholic sympathies during that era, the Spanish leadership, in planning for an invasion, placed little store on English Catholics being of any significant benefit to an invading army. As war broke out with Spain, some English Catholics had conflicting loyalties – some wanted to fight for England and Elizabeth, but were disappointed when they were not allowed. In early 1588, as rumours of invasion intensified, an order went out to 'cause the most obstinate and noted [recusant] persons to be committed to such prysons as are fittest for their safe keeping'. In the aftermath of the Armada, Elizabeth and her courtiers took an even darker view and looked at English Catholics as a potential fifth column, and even more stringent laws were introduced. In 1593, a 'statute of confinement' was introduced, which decreed that recusants were not permitted to travel further than five miles from their residence without a permit. Around 130 Catholic priests were executed for treason over the course of Elizabeth's reign.

The rhetoric had been great in England about a prodigious Protestant victory, but behind the grandiloquence lay the fact that, unlike the continental great powers, England was small, lacking great landmasses with vast resources of agriculture, forests and mines – or even, with the exception of the even smaller Ireland, any overseas territories. England was a diminutive economic entity from which to extract the revenue to pay for Elizabeth's ambitious policies. Despite the structural weaknesses, Elizabeth's Lord Chancellor, Burghley, had diligently tried to balance the royal books. The rolling Tudor colonisation of Ireland was the most expensive enterprise. By March 1588, this Irish money sink had cost £940,000 since the beginning of her reign; the campaign in the Netherlands, since 1585, had cost £340,000. Against these costs, the outlay for repelling the Armada, with £393,000 disbursed on the navy in the year up to the end of October 1588, (not including the expense of mobilising the land forces) was good value, considering the alternatives.

The English coffers were bare after the Armada events, and Burghley desperately looked around for new finance. A forced loan of £50,000 was raised from merchant companies in London; in December 1588, instruc-

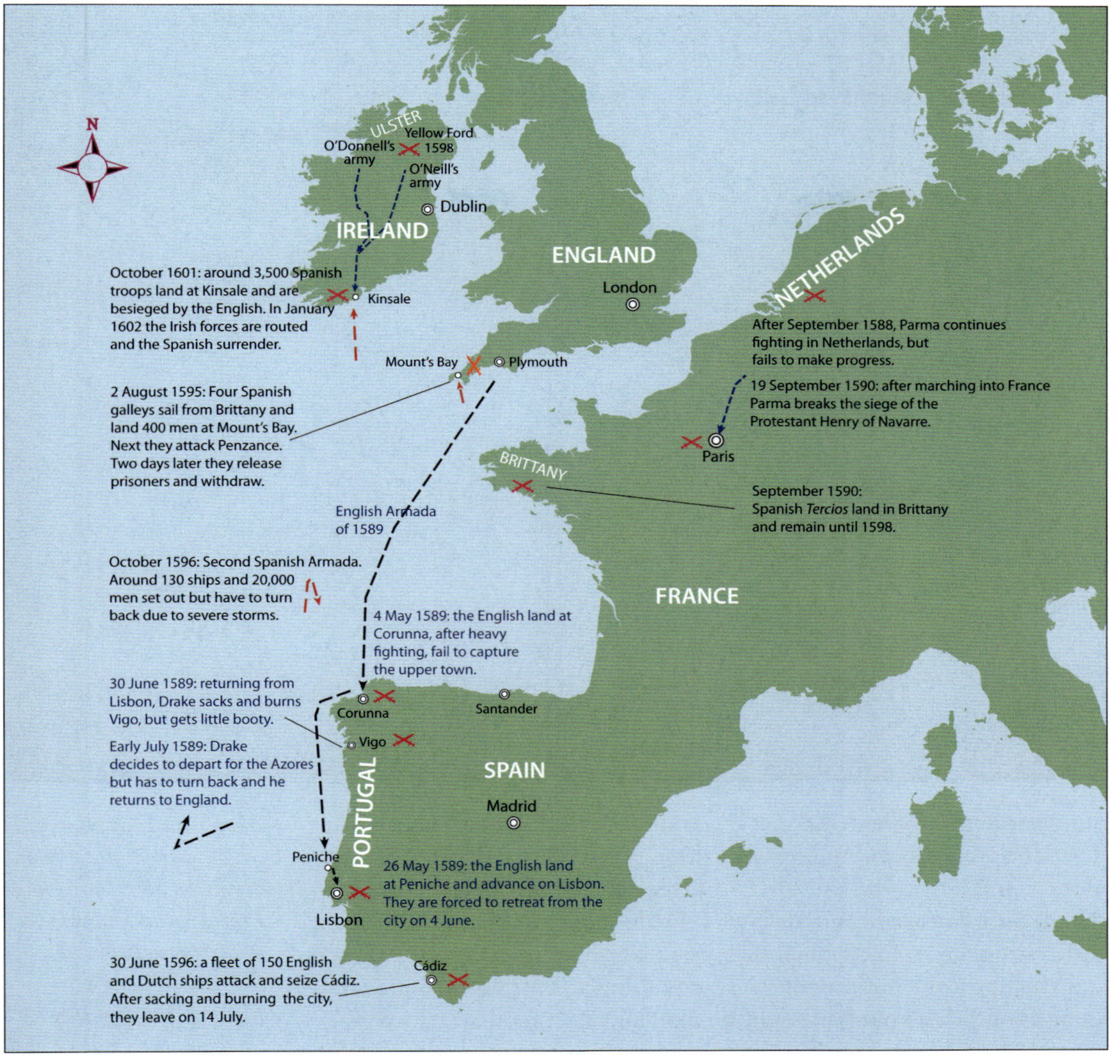

Above: there were many reverberations across Europe in the years after the Armada of 1588 until the signing of the Treaty of London in August 1604, which brought the Anglo-Spanish War to an end.

tions were sent to the lord lieutenant of the counties that they should obtain loans from prominent men in their locality. In the end, Crown lands were required to be sold. Showing the disparity in financial strengths between Spain and England, the sums here pale in comparison to the eight million ducats that the Cortes of Castile voted through for Philip at the end of 1588.

It was not surprising that, immediately after the repelling of the Armada, the concept of raising plunder on the high seas began to be discussed in English circles. It was a beautifully simple solution: send an expedition to seize the Spanish treasure fleet as it made its annual voyage from the Indies to Cádiz. At a stroke this would solve Elizabeth's fiscal woes and also inflict a further humiliating defeat on her Spanish foe. In the first week of September 1588, Sir Francis Drake was informed of the Queen's desire for 'intercepting of the King's treasure from the Indies'. However, as plans were developed, it soon became apparent that the English fleet was in need

of urgent refurbishment and that it was too late to seize that year's treasure fleet. The proposals for raiding went through several iterations, each version more complex than the last. On 21 October the Queen issued a commission to Sir John Norris and Sir Francis Drake authorising them to 'invade and destroy the … forces of all such persons as have this last year … sought and attempted the invasion of the realm of England'. It was intended to be an invasion carried out on the cheap, more privateering than state enterprise, with Elizabeth contributing a fraction of the total costs – and the majority being provided by financiers in London and elsewhere. The Spanish soon received intelligence of the fitting out of 'a great fleet with 15,000 men'. Equally, the English were aware that ships of the returned Armada were being refurbished in northern Spanish ports, with the bulk of these at Santander. Bernardino de Mendoza, ambassador in Paris, was able to report to the King that when Queen Elizabeth had heard about this she vowed that 'she would give your Majesty plenty to do before you could repair damages or turn around'. The English made contacts with the Sultan of Morocco, to secure his assistance for the planned expedition, but these came to nought. In February 1589 Elizabeth issued orders for what had by now developed into a multi-stage operation: Drake and Norris were to sail along the northern Spanish coast, destroying the surviving Armada ships and then to set out for the Azores and seize the islands, all the better to intercept the yearly treasure fleet. Only after destroying the King's ships should they proceed to placing the Portuguese pretender, Dom António (a man of great persistence,

Above: an English manuscript map (it dates from around 1589 and is now in the Kraus Collection of Sir Francis Drake, Library of Congress – the map was possibly prepared for Drake's attack). It shows Santander (left) and Corunna and Ferrol harbours (right). Elizabeth had assigned Drake to attack Santander and destroy the Spanish ships being repaired there after the Armada. In the event, hearing that Corunna harbour was replete with 200 merchant ships, the veteran privateer decided to attack there instead.

Above: the San Antón Castle in Corunna Harbour.

who hadn't gone away after his defeat at Terceira in 1583), on the throne at Lisbon. This declaration of what were three separate objectives, complicating the mission, laid the seeds for what turned out to be a disaster.

The English Armada sails out

Eventually the expedition sailed on 28 April 1589. It comprised over 180 ships, some veterans of the Channel encounters with the Armada. However, as there were smaller vessels (including 60 Dutch flyboats impressed to act as troop carriers), the total tonnage was significantly smaller than that of Philip's Armada of less than a year before. Despite being financed in the most economical way, this was an expedition on a grand scale – the best estimate is that 27,700 soldiers and sailors had embarked (more or less the same number as the Spanish Armada). The preparation and provisioning had been somewhat shambolic and the expedition did not obtain the siege artillery which had been promised (Elizabeth had baulked at the cost of this). Drake had sworn to obey the Queen's orders before he started, but once on the high seas he changed his mind. He cited contrary winds which prevented him from sailing to Santander and, also, the dangers for the flyboats 'among the rocks and on that broken coast'. Most likely, he was also deterred by the difficulty of attacking the well-fortified Santander harbour. Drake had heard of '200 sail of ships of divers nations at [Corunna] … with store of munition, masts … and other provisions for the enemy'. Thus he decided to head for the less fortified port of Corunna. Not for the first time with Drake, a primary English strategic objective (in this case, destroying the surviving ships of the Armada) was overridden by his desire for immediate plunder. On 4 May 1589, Drake and what a historian has called 'his joint-stock Armada' dropped anchor off Corunna. There was complete surprise ashore – the governor, the Marquis of Cerralbo, was attending to private business and very few of the town garrison were in place. A great bonfire was lit at the Tower of Hercules to raise the alarm in the port, which was defended by regular soldiers and a militia that totalled around 1,200

Left: a painting of local heroine María Pita, depicting her in action against the English at Corunna. In 1589, after her husband, an army captain, had been killed in the fighting with the force attacking the upper town, Pita killed an English ensign and seized his lance and banner. María next stood atop the city wall, waving the banner, shouting 'whoever has honour, follow me'. In the face of the increased Spanish resistance, the English soldiers had to retreat.

men. In the afternoon when a favourable wind blew up, the English fleet entered the harbour, as the guns of San Antón Castle opened up. As the English sailed closer, alas there was no sign of the fabled 200 merchant ships, ripe for the plucking. There were just a few vessels, survivors of the Armada: an 870 ton *nao*, *San Bartolomé* (her culverins had previously been transferred to the castle), the *urca, Sansón*, laden with pikes and firearms, and the two galleys, *Diana* and *Princesa*. Drake would have recognised, from the Channel battles, the galleon, *San Juan de Portugal*, which was in the harbour undergoing major repairs after its Armada travails. Don Martín de Bertendona, former commander of the Levant Squadron, was on board. As we have seen, the *San Juan* had been the flagship of the Admiral-General Don Juan Martínez de Recalde, who had died soon after arriving in Corunna in October 1588.

As the English fleet sailed in, they kept to the east of the harbour, out of effective range of the guns of San Antón Castle and the Spanish ships, which, despite being lightly manned, had opened up with whatever guns they had aboard. Using over a dozen small boats, and still out of range of the castle, the English began to land troops on a beach to the south-west of the harbour. Several days of fighting followed and the English forces, led by Sir John Norris, managed to seize much of the lower town. When the galleys made an attempt to intercept the invasion launches, the English opened fire with demi-culverins they had brought ashore – a barrage of such intensity that the captains of the galleys decided to sail to the safety of nearby Ferrol. Martín de Bertendona later called for the captains to be given exemplary punishment. Fire was also directed at the *San Juan*, which was damaged. Bertendona ordered the galleon to be abandoned and set on fire, but to leave some barrels of gunpowder in place. When around fifteen English soldiers charged on board to seize the ship's banners, they went up with the ship. The *San Bartolomé* was scuttled and the *Sansón*, abandoned, was burned. Despite bombarding the walls of the fortified upper town, Norris's men failed to take it. The troops roamed about pillaging lower Corunna. They came upon great wine cellars and many became hopelessly drunk.

The siege of the upper town continued, and an unsuccessful attempt was made to mine a corner tower of the fortified walls. The fierce assault continued and on 14 May, after her husband, an army captain, had been killed in the fighting, a doughty local woman, María Pita, killed an English ensign and seized his lance and banner. In this tale of heroism, María stood atop the wall, waving the banner, shouting 'whoever has honour, follow me' – and in the face of the now-increased Spanish resistance, the English soldiers had to retreat.

The English had been roaming the countryside, looting and laying waste. On 16 May Norris set out from the town with 7,000 troops. At a bridge outside Corunna, Puente de Burgos, he repulsed a counterattack by hastily-raised Spanish levies who had marched to relieve the port. However, with their siege not going anywhere, it was time for the English to leave. On 19 May, after setting fire to the lower town, the expeditionary force re-embarked and set sail. Martin Hume, the English nineteenth-century historian, noted sourly that 'Drake's sole reason for going to Corunna at all against his mistress' orders was to satisfy with loot the mutinous rabble on board his ships'.

Despite having confirmed from interrogation of prisoners that Santander was crowded with Philip's ships, and even though there was a favourable westerly wind which would have blown them there, the English Armada now headed south. As one English account put it 'their [Drake and Norris's] belief that the better part of the King's fleet was in Lisbon was little more than wishful thinking'. Back in London, when the Queen heard of the expedition's action at Corunna, she vented her fury: 'they went to places more for profit than for service'. Days later she sent a missive to the two commanders: it reminded them of their repeated promises 'that [their] first and principal action should be to take and distress the King of Spain's navy and ships where they lay', and that they must 'accomplish it before [their] return'. Unaware of the Queen's sharp rebuke that was on its way by fast boat, Drake and Norris decided to make a landing at Peniche in Portugal, around 80km north of Lisbon. The intention was to rally support for Dom António (who was accompanying the expedition) while on the march to the capital. Drake was also to make a coordinated attack on Lisbon by sea. As they sailed southwards, all was not going well – the ranks on board were now becoming depleted by sickness, referred to in one British account as 'bred of orgies in the Corunna wine cellars and infection from the rotting clothes and baggage of the 1588 Armada' that they had looted. On 26 May, the soldiers made a landing on the beach at Peniche, overcoming fierce resistance. The Portuguese commander of the local fortress agreed to surrender to Dom António, who, escorted by his personal guard, entered the fortification, issuing a proclamation that he was King of Portugal. Two days later, Norris led his men out on the march for Lisbon, while Drake sailed south. In Lisbon, as the alarming news of the great invasion spread, many citizens fled with their possessions, while the defending forces made preparations. Finally, Norris's weary army arrived before the walls of the city,

Left: the rowing bays of a replica galley on display at the Museu Marítim de Barcelona. Spanish galleys defended Lisbon Harbour when the English attacked in 1589. The galleys gave chase after the English fleet sailed out of Cascais and destroyed several English ships. Around six other vessels were damaged, and around 150 English prisoners were taken.

having just fended off a lightning attack by the Spanish. In the meantime, Drake's fleet had appeared off the coast. The English ships did not enter Lisbon harbour, which was guarded by 12 galleys (under Alonso de Bazán, general of the galleys, younger brother of the illustrious naval commander Álvaro de Bazán, Marquis of Santa Cruz, who had died in early 1588). Instead the English fleet moored at the mouth of the Tagus estuary, just out of cannon range of Cascais Castle. The English army, though more numerous than the defenders, engaged in repeated skirmishes, but, hampered by having no siege artillery (as we have seen, Elizabeth had refused to finance this), made no progress. Several days passed as they fruitlessly awaited the Portuguese uprising that had been promised by Dom António. On the night of 4 June Norris gave up, and withdrew, leading his forces through the darkness for the 20km along the estuary towards Cascais, under attack from land and sea. The following day, Spanish units on the outskirts of Lisbon pounced on the English columns. Don Sancho Bravo y Arce and his cavalry struck and killed hundreds, seizing two banners.

As the historian Martin Hume recounted, Drake had not been idle: 'if [he] would not burn the Spanish fleet on this occasion, he was always a splendid hand at plundering merchantmen, and during the six days that his fleet lay before Cascais, he scoured the sea for miles around in search of prizes, taking around 40 German hulks loaded with Spanish merchandise'.

Norris and his men reached Cascais, having suffered severe casualties. With Spanish and Portuguese forces assembling to complete the siege of their emplacement, the English were short of food, having received nothing from Drake's fleet. In one account, they were forced to eat their horses and other animals. Having failed in all their objectives, it was time to depart and go aboard the fleet. On 15 June, as they withdrew, Norris's soldiers blew up part of Cascais Castle and sacked the town, desecrating churches. The following day, the small vessel carrying Elizabeth's missive reached the

Below: on display at Sigüenza Cathedral, what is known as the 'flag of Francis Drake' – an English infantry banner, made of silk taffeta, one of two flags captured by Don Sancho Bravo y Arce from Sir John Norris's troops as they withdrew from Lisbon to Cascais.

English fleet at anchor and Drake and Norris had to absorb the castigation therein. On 18 June the English ships departed from the Lisbon approaches on a westerly wind with the presumed intention of capturing the Azores. As they sailed out, Spanish galleys followed in pursuit. The following day, in a calm, the galleys came into their own. Using their powerful long-range guns mounted on the prow, they were able to sail and manoeuvre at speed and blast the English fleet, which dispersed. Accounts vary but one Spanish historian says that between three and five English ships (of middling tonnage, like most in the fleet) were destroyed and around six others were damaged, with around 150 English prisoners taken. Days later, at Peniche, a Spanish column arrived at the town as the English garrison of 500 were embarking on small vessels, and managed to kill or capture most of them.

Drake had changed his mind about the Azores and had turned back. His fleet appeared off the coast of Peniche on 23 June, but there was nobody left to rescue. Contrary winds blew up and over the next ten days the English fleet was scattered and blown northwards. Those aboard were weakened by hunger and disease and, as the historian Martin Hume describes it 'the men died, and were thrown overboard by the hundred from scurvy, starvation and wounds'. Amidst the variable winds, Drake decided on 29 June to anchor in the estuary of Vigo in Galicia. The next day, the English soldiers attacked the town, seeking victuals and fresh water, while at the same time indulging in the usual looting. A history of Vigo relates that many of 'the English who landed brought with them an epidemic of … typhus and plague which they had contracted …'. Militia were gathered from Galicia and Portugal. Just as these were arriving, the English re-embarked, having set the town on fire, and on 2 July their fleet departed. The winds were still fickle and it was decided that Drake and twenty of the fittest ships would head for the Azores in search of the Indies treasure fleet, while the rest, under Norris, would return to England. A southerly wind blew, scattering the fleet, and all had no option but to follow Drake in his *Revenge*, now leaking badly, back to England. Several ships were lost on the return journey. Two others were captured by Spanish warships, which had set out from the Cantabrian coast. From the middle of July what was left of the English Armada straggled home in small groups. The ships were full of sick and dying men. English and continental sources tell of the losses ranging between, variously, 11,000 and 16,000. One Spanish historian has claimed that, because of the magnitude of losses, the debacle of Drake and Norris's expedition represents the worst naval catastrophe in the history of England. In comparison with the Spanish Armada of 1588, the death rate of upwards of 11,000 exceeds that of the Spanish. It is difficult to estimate the loss of ships, as some of the Dutch flyboats returned home and there are few meticulous records of the English ships, unlike those kept in Spain relating to their fleet. One estimate puts the English losses at 70 ships which, if correct, is around 39 per cent – a significantly higher rate of attrition than the 29 per cent ship losses of the Spanish Armada of the previous year.

And what were the gains? None of the objectives of the expedition were even remotely achieved. The plunder from the expedition amounted to 150 brass cannon seized at Corunna, and £30,000 realised from the sale of the cargoes of the German ships seized near Lisbon – the vessels themselves had to be given back to their (neutral) owners. The surviving soldiers were immediately discharged from service, and in July, fearful of the spread of disease, a government decree barred anyone who had served in the expedition to come 'within the Court's gates'. Drake and Norris suffered over the following years from Elizabeth's disfavour.

The death of Hawkins and Drake

Elizabeth and her ships remained in attack mode. In April 1591, Lord Thomas Howard, Earl of Suffolk (and kinsman of Lord Charles Howard of Effingham, Admiral of the English fleet in 1588), led a squadron made up of the Queen's warships and armed merchantmen to the Azores in another attempt to capture the treasure *flotas*. However, Philip's naval power was resurgent due to the ongoing Spanish shipbuilding programme. The English fleet reached the Azores and, having missed one of the *flotas*, had moored off the island of Flores, awaiting the next one. They sighted a large Spanish fleet in the distance, then discovered to their horror that it was not a treasure convoy but a large force made up of 17 galleons, a mixed batch of *naos*, *pataches* and smaller vessels. Howard's ships managed to make their escape, all save the *Revenge* (Drake's former flagship). The commander, Sir Richard Grenville, put up a heroic fight for twelve hours until, with most of the crew killed, he surrendered, dying of his wounds two days later.

There was a constant stream of English expeditions seeking fortune on the Spanish Main. One of the most significant was the 1595 voyage, when the veteran privateers Sir Francis Drake and his second-cousin, Sir John Hawkins ventured out, once again intending to plunder Spanish settlements and treasure. Once more the venture was sanctioned by Elizabeth, under the usual arrangement, namely her promised share of the spoils. The overall objective was to seize Panama. Nevertheless, when news came that the flagship of the treasure *flota*, the *Nuestra Señora de la Begoña* (a namesake of the

Left: the burial of Sir Francis Drake at sea in January 1596, off the coast of Puerto Bello (now Panama). This is one of four bronze relief plaques on the base of the Drake statue at Tavistock, Devon.

Armada *nao* of 1588), laden with two and a half million silver pesos, had been damaged by a hurricane and was sheltering in the harbour of San Juan de Puerto Rico, they decided to head there. However, as the English ships neared the coast of Puerto Rico, the voyage proved to be John Hawkins's last – the venerable senior Admiralty official and privateer fell ill and died, aged 62. Ominously for the English, five *galizabras,* a new, well-armed and fast, medium-sized warship, had been summoned from Spain. They arrived, and along with shore artillery, saw off the English flotilla, which then headed for the mainland. After making unsuccessful attacks along the Colombian coast, the English headed for Panama. It proved to be Drake's last escapade also. The impulsive, piratical, cunning and brave English adventurer died of cholera, aged 56, off the coast of Puerto Bello at the end of January 1596.

The 1596 attack on Cádiz

The port of Cádiz, from where the *naos* and galleons departed for the Indies, had – infamously – been sacked by Drake in 1587. To English eyes, it was once again time to sack this tempting harbour. In June 1596 a fleet of 150 Dutch and English ships set out from Plymouth, under overall command of Admiral Lord Charles Howard, Earl of Effingham (who had been in charge of the English fleet in 1588). By month's end they reached the port, which was packed with around 45 ships as well as 18 galleys. A fierce assault began and the Spanish ships made a retreat to the inner bay. As the English ships gained the upper hand, several of the Spanish ships ran aground and were set on fire by their crew to prevent capture. Two large galleons were boarded and taken over. Next, thousands of Dutch and English soldiers flooded ashore and quickly gained control of the lightly-defended city. There were occasional skirmishes on the outskirts, but not enough to stop the occupiers from engaging in a two week-long sack and pillage of the rich city. As well as merchandise, clothes and jewels, they took everything they could carry,

Right: a French engraving depicting the attack on Cádiz in 1596.

Above: the tightly packed houses of present-day Cádiz. At the end of June 1596, a fleet led by Admiral Lord Charles Howard attacked the city and port. Two weeks of sack and pillage followed.

including bells, doors and windows. In the midst of the mayhem, the nobles of the city were seized and held for a ransom of 120,000 ducats.

It was not the Duke of Medina Sidonia's finest hour. He had left Sanlúcar de Barrameda, arriving at the outskirts of Cádiz early on in the events. In the manner of an efficient project manager, the Duke then devoted his time to rounding up troops to defend the surrounding towns and cities, However, in this instance, he did not display the fire and initiative of a true military commander and launch an attack to drive the English and Dutch from Cádiz. So, after their uninterrupted two weeks of looting, the marauders departed in mid-July, taking away two galleons as they set the city on fire. One estimate put the loss of the merchant fleet alone at four million ducats. The English fleet paused at Faro (Portugal) to sack and burn it before returning to Plymouth. One story, most probably apocryphal, is that the copious quantities of looted *vino de Jerez* that the English had brought home from Cádiz were the reason for the appreciation and popularity of sherry that subsequently developed in England. In Spain, many were not impressed by Medina Sidonia's tardiness and inability to expel the English, including Cervantes, who wrote the acerbic sonnet '*A la entrada del Duque de Medina en Cádiz*', part of which, in translation, ran:

'The earth trembled and the sky darkened,
Threatening total ruin,
And into Cádiz, with great dignity,
With the Earl already departed, boldly
The great Duke of Medina entered triumphantly'.

Second Spanish Armada

By now, the constant English raids on Spanish ships and possessions had become a recurring fact of life – one estimate is that there had been over 100 English privateering expeditions every year since 1588. However, the new and audacious sack of Cádiz, touching the core of economic life, as well as the indignity of a flagrant rampage in the most important Spanish port, outraged Philip II. He issued orders for a new sea-borne assault on England, now known as the second Spanish Armada. The power of the Spanish state swung into action once again. A multitude of ships, from galleons to *zabras*, were assembled at Lisbon, Seville and Vigo. In October 1596 the fleet sailed, with the objective of aiding the rebellion in Ireland against Tudor rule, which would result in the diversion of English forces from France and the Netherlands. As we have seen, the Spanish had earlier established toeholds in France as part of the conflict with the Protestant Henry IV of

France. As the Armada sailed north towards Brittany, history repeated itself: the fleet of 120 ships was hit by a fierce storm off Cape Finisterre. Many ships were lost and the rest had to return to port.

Indefatigable, Philip dispatched yet another Armada, a year later, the third such. In October 1597, 136 ships set out with the principal objective of landing at Falmouth in Cornwall and establishing a foothold there. For the third time, God (obviously proving himself by now to be a dyed-in-the-wool Protestant!) blew once again and a gale sank dozens of vessels as they reached within 50km south-west of their planned destination. Once again the Armada had to return to port. Once again, Philip had to receive the bitter news of the failure. By now he was ageing and feeble – he retreated to his quarters in the Escorial and on 13 September 1598, died after months of stoically bearing debilitating illness.

O'Neill turns to open rebellion

Over these years, Ireland had been the victim of the continuing Tudor conquest. It was inevitable that it became intertwined with the Anglo-Spanish War. Nevertheless, after the wrecking of the Armada ships along the Atlantic coast and the bloody elimination of survivors in 1588, the danger of a Spanish landing in Ireland had been eliminated for the time being. The following years were relatively quiet, although vengeance was visited on those Gaelic lords who had given assistance to Spanish survivors.

Below: a shield with the insignia of the House of Medina Sidonia at the ducal palace in Sanlúcar de Barrameda in Andalucia.

Hugh O'Neill, Earl of Tyrone, had played a less than heroic role in the 1588 Armada events, when he acted in the English interest. As we have seen in Chapter 5, mercenaries under his overall control had moved to intercept survivors of the *Trinidad Valencera* on the Inishowen Peninsula. Led by O'Neill's foster brothers, the Hovendens, they massacred hundreds of these. O'Neill's early life had been complicated, resulting in competing allegiances. After his father, an O'Neill lord, was murdered, the young O'Neill, a ward of the Crown, had been fostered by the Hovendens, an English settler family at Balgriffin, near Dublin. The intention was to turn him into an English gentleman. He was introduced to Court in London and attended Parliament in Dublin, and thus was seen, in English eyes, to have been converted into a modern 'civilised' Gaelic lord. His conversion appeared to be successful after he returned to Ulster, where he operated as a counterbalance to the other lords of Ulster and generally acted in the English interest. As noted, in 1588 he played an indirect part in eliminating Spanish survivors of the Armada shipwrecks.

The English desired to extend and deepen their control over Ulster, where they had the least influence. However, having ruthlessly eliminated other claimants to the O'Neill lands, Hugh O'Neill now began to regard the creeping English expansion with alarm. As O'Neill became more powerful, Elizabeth refused to grant him more authority. The die for rebellion was cast. O'Neill began to strengthen his alliances with other Ulster lords. The English garrison in Ireland was small and in November 1594, anticipating the coming storm, Elizabeth decided to redeploy 2,000 soldiers from the English expedition in Brittany to Ireland – they arrived the following March. O'Neill made some attacks against the Crown in west Ulster, using proxies. In February 1595, he made his first direct move when his brother attacked an English outpost by the River Blackwater in County Armagh. This represented the start of the Nine Years' War. O'Neill was soon proclaimed a traitor by the English and in the following May he led his army to bloodily defeat an English army at Clontibret, in Co. Monaghan. The fame of the Irish rebel grew – English veterans of the continental wars soon compared his military skills with those of the Duke of Parma. There was alarm in London and in Dublin Castle when letters to Philip II from O'Neill seeking assistance were captured in September 1595 – they even included an offer to grant the kingdom of Ireland to the Spanish king. The contacts continued and in May 1596 Spanish envoys arrived. One of these, Alonso Cobos, reminded his Gaelic hosts of their presumed Iberian origins: 'that their … original ancestors came out of Biskay' – the legend that the Gaels of Ireland were descended from the Milesians of Galicia. The Irish sent back with Cobos a request for 1,000 Spanish soldiers. Nevertheless, the Earl of Tyrone, always adept at looking out for his own interests, continued to negotiate with the English at the same time as he was conferring with the Spanish. O'Neill, who had charmed Elizabeth when he met her at Court in 1587, proved to be an even better expert in dissembling than the Queen herself. However, by now the English realised that it was to be assuredly war with O'Neill and his confederates who by now were posing a serious threat to their rule in Ireland. In August 1598, O'Neill had another victory against a large English force, again near the River Blackwater, a renowned event known as the Battle of the Yellow Ford. O'Neill's mobile and well-trained soldiers routed the English infantry and cavalry, killing 1,500. After this victory, previously neutral lords threw their lot in with the rebel confederation; the English had now to send large reinforcements to Ireland. O'Neill made an attempt to gain the support of the Old English (descendants of English settlers, many still Catholic) in the Pale, which turned out to be unsuccessful. He later toured Munster, seeking to expand his rebellion.

Philip III accedes to the throne

In September 1598, after his father's death, Philip III, aged only 20, succeeded to the Spanish throne. Although inheriting a large burden of debt, he sought to maintain the empire and repel external threats. In the new monarch's eyes, Ireland was useful as a pawn in the Imperial game; it was England's 'Netherlands'. By tying down English forces there, he saw that Elizabeth would be under severe pressure and thus more likely to negotiate. There was also the hope that success in Ireland might even open up the conquest of England, as the old couplet ran:

'He who would England win
In Ireland must begin'.

Senior Irish clerics lobbied strenuously with the Pope in Rome and the King in Madrid for Spanish intervention. These appeals and O'Neill's direct pleas for help were heeded. In 1599 a consignment of arms and ammunition was shipped to Killybegs in Co. Donegal and in April 1600, a further batch of 1,000 arquebuses with ammunition was landed there. After some hesitation, it was decided to send a Spanish expeditionary force to Ireland. In the summer of 1601 preparations started for this, a new Armada. Once more, orders went out across the Iberian Peninsula: soldiers were marshalled; transport ships, warships and supplies arrived at Lisbon. However, the treasury was bare. Only 4,430 troops were marshalled, as against the intended 6,000.

Spanish troops land at Kinsale

On 2 September 1601, a fleet of 33 ships sailed out from Lisbon, destined for Ireland. The troops were under the command of, Don Juan del Águila, a veteran of Flanders, Brittany and the brief 1595 Spanish incursion at Cornwall. However, with what seemed the habitual ill-luck of Armada expeditions, they encountered a fierce Atlantic storm. Some of the vessels were driven back; the remaining fleet was blown towards Kinsale, where the Spanish forces, now reduced to around 3,300, landed on 1 October. The new Lord Deputy, Charles Blount, Baron Mountjoy, responded rapidly and immediately headed for Cork with a small detachment, ordering his main force to follow. Moving towards Kinsale, he circled the town and sealed off the Spanish army, occupying the forts around the harbour. Hugh O'Neill's response was tardy – his preference was to remain in Ulster and defend his domains, which had earlier come under attack from forces sent out by the pro-active Mountjoy. Three weeks after the landing, O'Neill reluctantly set

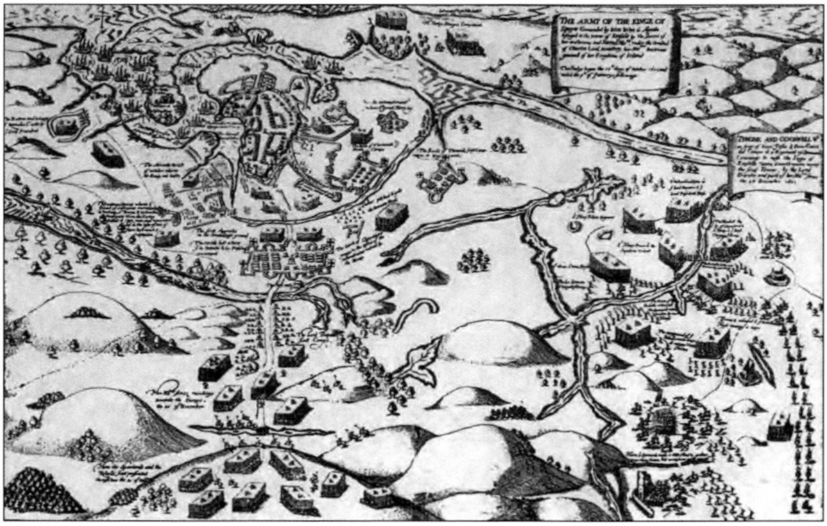

Right: an illustration of the Battle of Kinsale. The victory by the English army here in January 1602 meant the end of the Ulster rebellion.

Above: stamps issued by An Post, with original illustrations by artist Seán Ó Brógáin, to commemorate the 'Flight of the Earls'. (Reproduced by kind permission of An Post ©). The stamps feature Hugh O'Neill, Earl of Tyrone, and Rory O'Donnell, Earl of Tyrconnell, as they prepare to sail out of Rathmullan, Co. Donegal. This event marked the end of the power of the Gaelic lords and signalled the success of the nearly century-long Tudor conquest of Ireland.

out for Kinsale, along with his ally, Red Hugh O'Donnell. With a combined force of around 12,000 men they marched quickly south, arriving at the end of December. The Irish forces set up camp to the west of Innishannon, a village around 12km north-west of Kinsale. Mountjoy's camp was located between the Irish position and that of del Águila in Kinsale. The battle began on 3 January 1602, as the Irish infantry and cavalry moved towards English lines. After some back-and-forth manoeuvres between the forces, the English cavalry made a countercharge. The Irish ranks broke up in disorder and were routed. A small Spanish detachment that had been stationed with O'Neill's men put up a brave fight. English accounts claim that 1,200 Irish were killed in the battle. This unambiguous defeat meant the end of the Ulster rebellion. One of the great imponderables is what might have happened, thus affecting the course of Irish history, if del Águila and his men had emerged from Kinsale to join the battle. The arrangements that had been made between O'Neill and del Águila are unclear. In the aftermath, the latter claimed that he had heard the firing but feared that it was an English ruse to draw him out. On 12 January del Águila surrendered to Mountjoy and he and his men were allowed to return to Spain.

The Ulster leaders withdrew north, losing many as they retreated along the freezing terrain. Hugh O'Donnell immediately departed to Spain, where he died in September 1602, and is buried at Valladolid. As his followers and confederates submitted to the English, O'Neill retreated to the woods of Tyrone. He held out there until on 30 March 1603 he surrendered to the Crown. Unbeknownst to him, the elderly Elizabeth had died a week before. Remarkably, the terms of surrender as set out in the Treaty of Mellifont were generous: O'Neill and other Ulster lords received pardons and retained their estates. It was a close call for Tudor England. Elizabeth's expenditure on her army in Ireland over her reign since October 1595 had amounted to a staggering £1,845,000 – the Nine Years' War had nearly bankrupted her impecunious exchequer.

Peace arrives

Peace was breaking out all over: the Anglo-Spanish War ended in August 1604, when the Treaty of London was signed, with an agreement on a cessation of hostilities between Spain and England. However, the conflict in the Netherlands ground on until the 1648 Peace of Westphalia; Protestant Holland in the meantime grew and blossomed, and was to go on to develop its own maritime empire.

In Ireland, a new Lord Deputy began to encroach on the privileges of O'Neill and his fellow lords. Unhappy with the gradual loss of his power and with a reduced income, he decided to go into exile. In September 1607, O'Neill, together with other Ulster lords, departed from Rathmullan on Lough Swilly for exile on the Continent. O'Neill died in Rome in 1616. This departure of the lords, known as the 'Flight of the Earls', marked the end of the power of the Gaelic lords and signalled the success of the nearly century-long Tudor conquest of Ireland. Thus, although unsuccessful in the earlier attempts to colonise North America, England at last was able to implement the colonisation of Ireland. The way was clear for the government-

Below: the delegates meet. The Anglo-Spanish War ended in August 1604 when the Treaty of London was signed, with an agreement on a cessation of hostilities between Spain and England.

Philip II died in September 1598 after a debilitating illness. In this painting (left) made nearly 50 years later, Bartolomé Estebán Murillo depicts the friar Julián of Alcalá directing the attention of the figures around him to a miraculous apparition in the distance – angels welcoming King Philip II of Spain into heaven.

planned and large-scale plantation of Ulster to proceed. This involved the confiscation of land by the English Crown and plantation with Protestant settlers from Scotland in this, the most Gaelic of Irish provinces.

The historian J.H. Elliot wrote that 'Ireland, like the reconquered Kingdom of Granada [for the Spanish], was both kingdom and colony, and like Andalucia, constituted a useful testing-ground of empire'. From the sixteenth century onwards, Ireland was to provide England with useful practical experience in a more efficient form of the dark art of colonisation: subjugation of the natives, their dispersal or elimination, confiscation of land and the administrative procedures for settlement.

Over the course of the seventeenth century, with expertise in colonisation methods, the Jacobean English were able to commence the establishment of stable and enduring colonies in the New World. This dynamic was to continue and, supported by a Royal Navy, newly ocean-going and increasing in size and power, the (now) British Empire expanded all over the globe during the following centuries, covering a quarter of the world's land mass at its peak ('the Empire on which the sun never sets'). It is ironic that in 1588, there had been an attempted, but failed, assault on England (then a minor power in European terms), by Spain, the superpower of the age, ruled by Philip II, whose worldwide domains were also known as '*el imperio donde nunca se pone el sol*'.

Appendix A

Guns and Ships

Manufacture of Artillery

Making cannon during the sixteenth century was a highly skilled and intricate process. These were cast in clay moulds, muzzle up. A core (strengthened by an iron bar) had been inserted. Great skill had to be used to ensure that core's centreline was in line with that of the barrel. Vents were included at various points to allow the air to escape while the molten metal was carefully poured in from the top. After the metal had cooled, the gun was extracted from the mould and cleaned. Next a touchhole was drilled. The barrel would be sounded by hitting it with a hammer to see if the metal had a sound ring, indicating that it was free of small cavities or cracks.

Gun-founders were allowed some indulgence in placing ornamentation on the cannon, with decoration of the surface and the lifting handles. Coats of arms and the mark of the gun-founder could be added, as could dates, and the weight of the gun. English guns (in line with Protestant taste) tended to be less ornate.

During the sixteenth century guns were made of either iron or bronze. Iron ore was more readily available than the components of bronze: copper and tin. Iron guns were cheaper (only around one-third of the cost) than bronze pieces – although more care had to be given during production. However, artillery made of bronze had many advantages. Bronze guns were not liable to corrosion or cracking like iron ones, and lasted longer. A bronze gun might fail by bulging or deformation at the muzzle, but an iron gun could simply suddenly explode, thus with potentially catastrophic results for the gun crew.

In Philip II's time external threats had multiplied: the war in Spanish Netherlands; the conflict with the Turks and culminating in the Battle of Lepanto and the attacks by privateers on the treasure *flotas*. Thus there was a

Right: at work in a sixteenth-century cannon foundry in the Low Countries. The molten bronze flows into a gun mould, submerged vertically in the floor, On the right, the artist has added a scene depicting what the cannons could do.

huge demand for guns from whatever source. Málaga was a key location in providing cannon to face the challenge of the Ottomans across the Mediterranean and in 1499 a cannon foundry and school of artillery had been founded there. Málaga also had important gunpowder factories – others were located in Burgos and Cartagena. A new and more efficient variant of gunpowder had been developed by the mid-sixteenth century: 'corned' powder, which provided greater energy for a given weight.

At the same time, the *Reales Atarazanas* (Royal Shipyards) of Barcelona produced guns and naval ships (mainly galleys). In Seville, the *Casa de Contratación* procured cannon for the needs of the Atlantic fleet, and in 1575 it established an artillery school. A private foundry was established in Seville in 1565, to supply cannon for the treasure fleet and the colonies. It was set up by the son of Bartolomé Morel, the master bell-founder, whose masterpiece is a bronze statue of a woman representing the triumph of faith that crowns the Giralda, the bell-tower (a former minaret) of Seville Cathedral.

Most cannon in Spain were made in bronze during the sixteenth century. However in the Basque provinces, there was developing expertise in iron founding. Iron cannonballs had been made from locally sourced iron. In 1578, with the assistance of iron founders from Flanders, the manufacture of iron cannon began there. Within the Spanish domains, the Netherlands was the centre of advanced industries. A royal foundry had been established in 1520 at Malines (Mechelen), just south of Antwerp. Remigy de Halut was the master founder there who cast bronze cannon for the Spanish Crown, producing 270 highly ornamented artillery pieces over the period 1538 to 1556. His guns can be seen in museums worldwide, recovered from sunken Spanish ships. Fine examples from the Armada can be seen in the

Left: the roof of the 'Real Fábrica de Artillería', Seville. In 1565 it commenced as a private foundry, using the expertise in bronze casting of the Morel family, to supply cannon for the treasure fleet and the colonies.

Above: a view of an artillery siege train. Everything had to be transported on the ships in the Armada for the planned battles in England: the guns, dismantled gun carriages, shot and powder, mules and muleteers.

Ulster Museum in Belfast and the National Museum of Ireland at Collins Barracks in Dublin.

In the latter part of the sixteenth century there was a chronic shortage of cannon in Spain. Royal armourers had to resort to buying some cannon from foreign sources. Hostility between England and Spain resulted in an official ban on trade; however some English cast-iron guns were acquired illegally for the Spanish army in Flanders. A huge variety of land and naval artillery was gathered from all over the Spanish Empire for the Armada. There were also pieces from the Italian states and Ragusa (Dubrovnik), together with guns from France, the Baltic states, and as we have seen, England. There were also pieces captured in battle – one of the guns found on the *Trinidad Valencera* wreck was of Turkish origin (as was a gun from the Streedagh wrecks) and are thought to have been captured at Lepanto. Training of artillerymen (both for land and sea) was seen as important and by 1575 there were schools of artillery in Barcelona, Málaga, Seville, Gibraltar and Cartagena.

Early English guns had been made of wrought iron, sometimes with rings placed at intervals along the barrels to increase strength. Equally, in the early days, gunpowder had to be imported. It was only in 1561 that the English became self-sufficient in saltpetre, the important ingredient in gunpowder. The first casting of bronze cannon in England was in 1529. Initially, the copper had to be imported. England became self-sufficient when copper was mined in Cumbria in 1566. There was a big iron-founding industry in the Weald, to the south of London. The forests there were a source of charcoal, local streams provided power for the ironworks, and it turned out that the local iron ore was suited for the casting of guns. With state support and foreign expertise, the foundries of the Weald began to produce many small and medium-sized cannon, gaining a good reputation for quality. They were relatively cheap and, as time went on, became easily affordable for any self-respecting English privateer. The foundries were relatively close together, and this led to an element of standardisation which, as we can see during the Armada events, gave advantage in the management of supply of shot for large fleets.

Left: on display on a replica gun carriage at the Tower Museum in Derry, a heavy 'cañón de batir' (cast by Remigy de Halut, in Malines, just south of Antwerp) recovered from the 'Trinidad Valencera'. This gun was be used in the siege train that was intended to attack the walls of London and other English cities after the Spanish army landed.

Artillery at Sea

The Spanish carried many siege guns on board, some of very heavy calibre. However, it is not entirely clear how many of these were stowed for transportation, or how many were actually deployed as part of the ship's armament – probably few, if any. Around 60 per cent of the cannon carried in the Spanish Armada were bronze. A late-sixteenth-century inventory of the guns of Elizabeth's Navy Royal showed a predominance of bronze at 80 per cent.

As noted, the cannon for the Spanish Armada were procured from Spain, Flanders, the Mediterranean and beyond. Coming from such a wide variety of locations, they were cast to different standards and a under a diversity of nomenclature. Thus it was a quartermaster's nightmare in Lisbon, trying to procure shot that fitted the cannon for the fleet, particularly as this was on such a grand scale. As to the English fleet, given that their guns were sourced mainly from England, there was a certain element of standardisation. It is also likely that captains and officers of the private merchantmen (cum privateers) would have procured their shot and powder on an individual basis, and thus were able to ensure that these were fit for purpose. However, given the parsimony of the Queen's treasury, the English fleet that was assembled to repel the Armada was short of powder and shot.

Artillery at sea during the sixteenth century was a capricious weapon. Firing cannon on a ship was not very accurate. It was hard to aim accurately and hit an enemy vessel from a ship's deck pitching in three dimensions. In addition, there was a short gap in time from the decision to fire, to the actual firing of the gun. A linstock (a staff with a fork at one end to hold a slow match, blown to make it glow) was used for ignition. As the rest of the gun crew stood back, the gunner, at the side of the gun, would place the glowing tip against the priming powder and the gun would detonate – the small interval involved added to the difficulty of hitting a target.

A cannon ball loses velocity at longer distances. Thus, to seriously damage ships (to cause major damage, such as piercing the hull, or destroying masts) what was needed were guns, employed at relatively close quarters, with the ability to hurl shot of a significant size and adequate velocity. Analysis by Dr I.A.A. Thompson has shown that the Spanish had many more light guns, useful for anti-personnel purposes or for destroying rigging. In

Right: dolphins. The decorative handles on the 'cañón de batir' by the master founder, Remigy de Halut, now to be seen at the Tower Museum in Derry.

addition, he determined that the English fleet carried 251 guns firing balls of 16 pounds (7.3kg) and upwards. This was around double that carried by the Armada in that category, which totalled 126 guns. However, it is not quite as simple as that. Research by the historian A. L. Goméz Beltrán has shown that it was difficult to compare like for like, as guns such as the culebrins and cannons of each side had different characteristics. There are also other considerations which affect efficiency, such as which deck the artillery pieces were placed on. There is also the tactical efficiency in the use of the guns. The game-changing Armada battle was that off Gravelines. In the next paragraphs we will look at the different tactics of the opposing sides, which gave different results.

We turn to the much-analysed issue of comparative rates of fire by the respective fleets. Over the course of the battles along the Channel and at Gravelines, some eyewitnesses estimated that the English gunners were able to discharge guns at several times the rate of their Spanish counterparts. Much has been made of the presumed disadvantage arising from moving around the two-wheeled Spanish gun carriages – with a supposed lesser rate of fire. By contrast the English used shorter four-wheeled gun-carriages. However, Goméz Beltrán has shown, using a cross-sectional diagram, that there was ample space to manoeuvre these on the gun decks of large galleons such as the *San Martín*, even though the Spanish gun-carriages were around 90cm longer than the English equivalent.

The problem of overheating is thought to have been the underlying cause for the lesser rate of Spanish fire. Guns of that era overheated after sustained action – the effect of overheating on a brass culverin is that it would begin to deform. The gunners, whether by touching the barrel or looking at the colour of the metal, could assess the condition of their gun and would desist from firing, probably after three or so shots. Remedies included waiting for the gun to cool down, covering the gun with wet blankets or sheepskins, or dousing with vinegar. All of this took time, and the gunner had to ensure that the inside of the barrel was dry before he charged the gun again. This phenomenon affected the Spanish gun crews, particularly on the fateful day of Monday August 8, in that most important encounter off Gravelines – during that fierce battle which raged for

around eight hours. With their ships scattered after the fireship scare, the Armada had now fallen out of its defensive formation, and was scattered. The English squadrons fell upon the rearguard, led by Medina Sidonia in the *San Martín*. The English now enjoyed a large preponderance in numbers. Groups of English ships were able to target an isolated vessel and then swoop in and fire their guns at close quarters. Next they wheeled around and, after an interval, returned to fire once more. The key thing was that by means of this tactic, the English gunners had an interlude when their guns could cool down. (However, by this scattershot approach they were rapidly running down their munition stores.) The gunners on board an individual Spanish ship in the rearguard, at the centre of the maelstrom, did not have the luxury of this interval. They had to do their best and try to return fire at the enemy ships in a measured and targeted way as they sped by. Nevertheless they would have to pace themselves to avoid the guns overheating. Thus the reason for a lesser rate of fire could have been down to the vagaries of metallurgy, set against the conditions of how these battles unfolded.

Above: in the Museo Naval in Madrid, a Spanish demi-culverin.

Left: a representation of an English cannon, on a four-wheeled gun-carriage. This was relatively compact.

Left:, the arrangement of the Spanish two-wheeled carriage was around 90cm longer. Nevertheless, given the space available on the decks of the larger Spanish galleons, this did not make much difference to the rate of fire. However the time needed to let the guns cool did affect the Spanish rate of fire in light of the way the battle at Gravelines evolved.

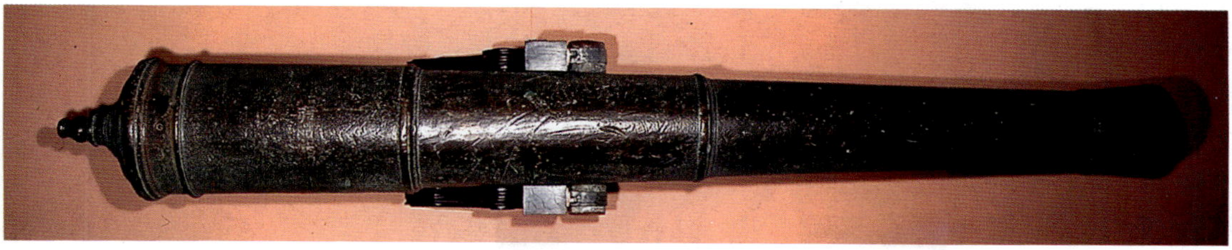

Above: also in the Museo Naval, Madrid, an English demi-culverin.

Overleaf: on display in the Museu Marítim de Barcelona, a full-size replica of the Royal Galley, flagship of Don John of Austria in the Battle of Lepanto in 1571. The original was built in Barcelona at the Royal Shipyard in 1568 and was the largest galley of its time. It was 60 metres long and weighed around 240 tons empty. It was equipped with three heavy and six light artillery pieces and was propelled by a total of 240 rowers.
Spain's principal naval might, a large fleet of galleys, was concentrated in the Mediterranean up to around the 1570s. After that date, there was an increasing focus on the Atlantic and ocean-going naos and galleons were constructed to add to the naval units already there.

Types of Gun

There was an almost unlimited diversity of gun types in 1588, both Spanish and English – and each nation used differing specifications for their respective categories. This is brief generic list of some types.

Type	***Length***	***Shot***	***Description***
Demi Cannon	*3-3.7m*	*13-17kg, iron*	*Firing at ranges between 300m and 1,600m.*
Culverin	*3.5-4m*	*7-9kg, iron*	*Long relative to its bore. Firing at ranges between 250m and 2,300m.*
Demi-Culverin	*3-3.6m*	*4-5.5kg, iron*	*Firing at ranges between 250m and 2,300m.*
Saker	*2-2.5m*	*2-3.5kg, iron*	*Firing at ranges between 300m and 1,600m.*
Falcon Pedrero	*2-2.5m*	*0.75-1kg, stone*	*Anti-personnel.*

Spanish Ships

During the first part of Philip II's reign the principal strategic threat was in the Mediterranean, from the Ottoman Empire. This was countered by maintenance of a navy made up of well over a hundred galleys, operating from Spain's eastern coasts to Italy and beyond. (The galleys were constructed in the shipyards of Barcelona, Naples and Sicily.) However, from 1580 onwards, as the Ottoman threat receded, the focus was now on the Atlantic. Spanish naval strength there had evolved from the 1520s onwards in response to changing strategic threats, including the various wars with France. A *Guardacostas de Andalucía,* whose remit extended as far as the Azores, was in place under that name up to 1562. With the accelerated growth of French, Dutch and English privateers preying on Spanish shipping and coasts, there was need for an increased royal naval presence on the high seas. In 1570 a fleet, the *Armada Real de la Carrera de las Indias,* was established to protect the route to the Indies. It consisted of 12 small galleons, built in Bilbao. Following Philip's succession to the Portuguese throne in 1580, there was the acquisition of the excellent Portuguese Atlantic galleons, and to these were added Cantabrian-built ships to form the *Armada del Mar Océano.*

La galera: una màquina per dominar la Mediterrània
La galera: una máquina creada para dominar el Mediterráneo
The galley: a machine for ruling the Mediterranean
A bord la galera: una vida difícil

Santander
Guarnizo
Castro
Urdiales
Bilbao
Pasaia
San Sebastián
FRANCE
CANTABRIA
VIZCAYA
GUIPÚZCOA

Left: it could be said Spanish ships had hearts of oak – the necessary 'quercus robur' oak was readily available in the forests along the Cantabrian coast: in the (present-day) Basque provinces of Guipúzcoa, Vizcaya and the autonomous community of Cantabria. A large proportion of the galleons, naos, and smaller craft like pataches in the Spanish Armada was constructed in the shipyards that proliferated along here.

Left: an eighteenth-century sailing ship is moored at the entrance to Pasaia Harbour, near Donostia/San Sebastián. In the 1580s several naos of the Guipúzcoa Squadron were constructed here.

Spanish shipbuilding flourished during the sixteenth century along the Cantabrian coast, generally from Santander to the French border, a location blessed with abundant forests and iron. Over this period, approaching 90 per cent of the ships which left Seville and Cádiz were built in this region. At an early stage in his reign, Philip took steps to promote and expand naval construction along these coasts. In 1563 he appointed Cristóbal de Barros, a man of great experience in nautical matters, as custodian and administrator of funds which were to be given as interest-free loans to shipyard enterprises. There were other incentives, such as an exemption from the *alcabala* sales tax on materials used for shipbuilding. De Barros continued all though Philip's reign to initiate, manage and monitor the construction of ships for Crown use, and to certify their completion. As years went by, with the Azores under threat and with privateers ranging along the Atlantic, Philip decided to accelerate the programme of naval construction, ordering new ships and guns. From 1582, the shipyards of Cantabria, Vizcaya and Guipúzcoa intensified their construction of ships, supported by royal funds. The new ships were constructed to the specifications of the Crown – the King had previously called together the most prominent experts in shipbuilding, naval captains and experts, including Juan Martínez de Recalde, to discuss and establish the optimum design of warships. During the first half of the century, Álvaro Bazán the Elder (father of the Marquis of Santa Cruz) and Pedro Méndez de Avilés, had been innovators in warship design, drawing on their vast naval experience.

Seminal books on navigation and construction of ships were the *Itinerario de navegación de los mares y tierras occidentales* by Juan Escalante y Mendoza, based on his quarter-century of experience sailing with the *flota*

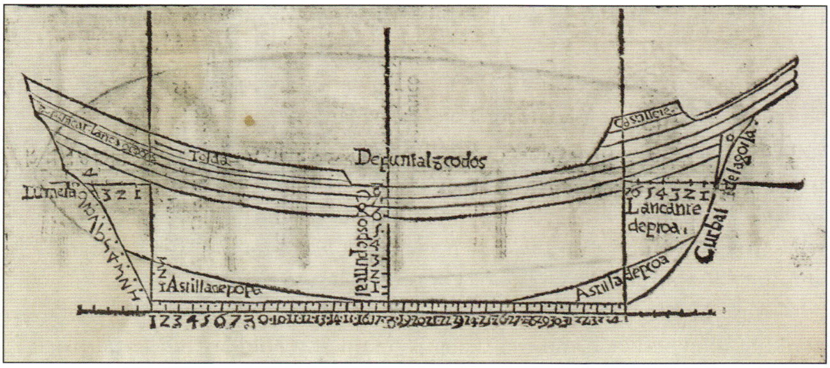

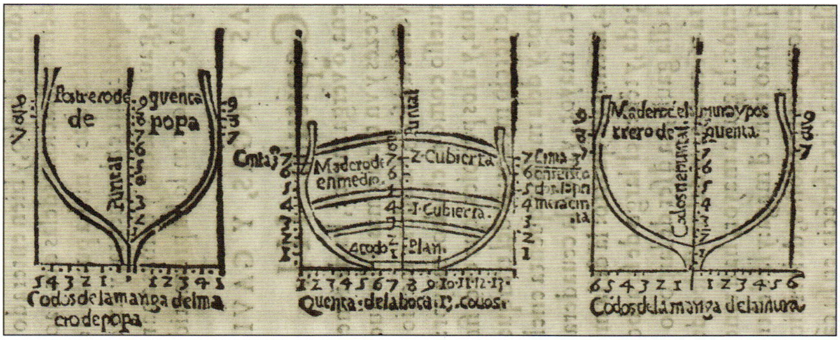

Right: seminal Spanish books on the construction of advanced ships suitable for the oceans were published from 1575 onwards. Master carpenters were now able to set out their ships using these publications. Here we see plans for construction of a Spanish nao of around 150 tons. These are taken from the book by Diego García de Palacio (from Santander) 'Instrucción Náutica, para el buen uso y regimiento de las Naos', published in Mexico in 1587.

Above: the structure takes shape, at the beginning of the construction a replica of a 1565 nao at the Albaola Itsas Kultur Faktoria, Pasaia.

of the Indies (published in 1575) and the *Instrucción Náutica, para el buen uso y regimiento de las Naos* by Diego García de Palacio, published in Mexico in 1587. As the shipbuilding programmes progressed, there was a gradual evolution: the ships became progressively larger and with a greater length in relation to the beam, resulting in faster speeds. The stern and forecastles were reduced in height, and with better arrangements of masts, the ships became more agile and manoeuvrable.

Ever since man made his first tentative voyage in a coracle, the entire northern Spanish coast had been steeped in maritime activities. Some parts of the hinterland were relatively unproductive and this had led the inhabitants to turn their face to the sea. Fishermen from these coasts sailed out to rich and faraway Atlantic fishing grounds, such as those off Ireland and Newfoundland. The ports along the coast became entrepots for goods between Spain and northern Europe. To service this sea trade and fishing, there has always been a tradition of shipbuilding. Various shipyards along the river inlets and harbours were engaged in building fishing vessels and merchant ships, and now, during the second half of the sixteenth century, warships for the Crown.

A typical shipyard would have a slipway and structures for storage of wood and naval fittings. The keel would be laid on a cradle placed on the slipway, a large flat space with a small gradient. Master carpenters would travel to the forests with patterns of the structural members and identify suitable trees. The oaks were cut in winter and, according to tradition, only when the moon was in wane, when the effect was thought to reduce the amount of sap in the tree. The oak was then left to dry and season.

Construction would commence with the master carpenters, keen of eye, working to experience and mathematical tables, would lay out patterns, allowing them to mark and cut the wood with accuracy. It all began with the keel, which formed the basic length of the ship. The stem and stern timbers would be attached. The ribs would be placed, and thus a skeleton of the ship was formed. Next came thick horizontal planks, laid end to end, and which formed the ship's hull. Timber knees were fixed to the ribs to support the deck beams and deck planks. An inner skin, again of timber planking, was attached to the structural ribs. As the ship reached completion, caulkers, working on the outside of the hull, plugged gaps with oakum and tar. Various protective treatments, including mixtures of tar, were painted on the hull below the waterline. It was important to install the delicate mechanism of the rudder correctly, and this was connected by hinges to the

Above: constructing the inner part of the nao at the Albaola Itsas Kultur Faktoria.

sternpost. When the bulk of the ship was completed, it was time to launch the vessel. Retaining pieces were removed and, using manpower and sometimes teams of oxen, the ship was pulled into the water. Once in the water, the various masts were lowered into place, to be secured by stays. Next came the sails and rigging made of hemp or esparto. Finally the cabins, bulkheads and other fitments were completed. It could take well over a year to complete a galleon.

The forests of Cantabria and the Basque provinces were conveniently close to the shipyards. Pedunculate oak (*Quercus robur*) was the most suitable wood for the structural parts of a ship (the keel, frames and sternpost). As well as oak, pine and larch could be used for planks and curved pieces. A long, tall fir tree was ideal for a mast. Beech could be used for oars and rudders, due to its resistance to rotting. Some of the larger main pieces were crafted in the forest and then transported to the shipyard, sometimes loaded onto boats in adjacent rivers. Otherwise, oxen and carts were used to move the wood. An enormous amount of timber was required for a large galleon – one estimate is that a 560-ton galleon required about 900 oak trees. However, there was invariably a shortage of timber – in northern Spain there was also competing demand for timber destined for charcoal to power the artillery foundries and the many factories making small arms. Thus with shortages of timber, priority was given to shipbuilding needs. In the time of Charles V, an order was issued to increase the number of trees that were reserved for naval construction. In turn, Philip took particular interest in making sure that this strategic material was readily available for the construction of his fleet of warships. He instructed Cristóbal de Barros to make sure there was compliance with his edict that a specified quantity of oak be planted annually, within two leagues from the coast, in the ship-building regions of northern Spain.

It was during the Enterprise of England, in the battles along the English Channel, that the Spanish ships were fully put to their mettle. And it was during the Battle of Gravelines on 8 August that the fighting reached its highest intensity. After the fireship attack of the night before, the Armada had lost its tight defensive formation and was scattered. As noted, the English fleet then swarmed on the individual ships of the rearguard and poured cannon fire at relatively close distances. Yet, despite this concentrated fire, the English only managed to directly sink one ship, while two others, badly damaged in the fighting, foundered on the Flanders coast shortly afterwards.

So, what were the elements that allowed the Spanish (and Portuguese) ships to withstand this pounding? Firstly there was the excellence of the well-chosen and properly-aged wood from the Cantabrian Mountains (and the forests of Portugal). The ship layout and plans, based on centuries of experience, and with recent design upgrades from experienced mariners like Juan Martínez de Recalde, were excellent. Then there was the highly skilled assembly, led by the master carpenters. Within the overall design and assembly a high factor of safety for each ship was plainly built in. This was borne out by the fact that most of the Armada ships built in the Iberian Peninsula were generally able to stand up to the exceptional structural demands placed on them, whether due to cannon fire, artillery recoil or, particularly, as when they sailed along the west coast of Ireland, the intense unseasonal gales.

English Ships

In 1546, Henry VIII, with the principal threat being from the French, established the Navy Royal (the ships were his personal property, not that of the state). Significantly, he also set up an administration to manage the construction, repair and supply of the fleet. On Henry's death the treasury was empty, due to his various wars as well as arising from his expenditure on the navy. When Elizabeth ascended the throne, much needed to be done. There was a growing awareness that it was going to be maritime power, as opposed to a land army, which would defend England against external threats. Parliament voted more money for the navy, and expenditure was increased. From 1570 onwards a series of new warships were constructed for the royal fleet.

Most shipbuilding was concentrated in the south of England. Many of the larger ships were built in and around London, with some at Bristol. The principal locations for building navy ships were Deptford and Chatham dockyards. As in Spain, oak was the prized timber used for ships. The navy had first call on timber from the royal parks and woods – there were also regulations giving priority for timber used in naval construction. Other shipbuilding materials like masts, tar, canvas and cordage were sourced from the Baltic.

The privateer John Hawkins, appointed Treasurer of the Navy in 1578, is credited with the improvements in English naval construction, although the naval historian Nicholas Rodger has written that Hawkins 'had reservations about the new ships built in this decade [the 1570s]'. Accounts say that the move to develop faster warships was part of a general western European trend, from Denmark down to Spain. Irrespective of who was the source, the general tendency then was to lengthen ships and reduce the height of the traditional ship castles at front and back.

Matthew Baker had been appointed Master Shipmaster at Deptford in 1572 and was reputed to have travelled in the Mediterranean in his youth where he absorbed knowledge of ship design. The techniques were being set

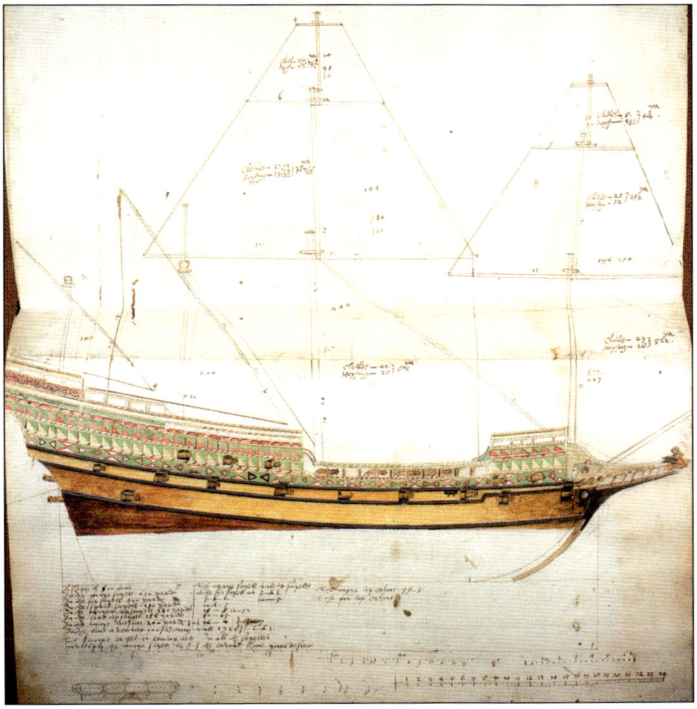

Right: an illustration of the 'Revenge' warship from 'Fragments of Ancient English Shipwrightry', a treatise on ship design by the English Master Shipwright Matthew Baker, thought to have been published around 1586. (By permission of the Master and Fellows, Magdalene College, Cambridge).

down on paper – the Spanish had produced their first book on ship design in 1575. In turn the literate Baker produced a treatise around 1586 on the design of ships, made up of notes and sketches. Over his career he brought a more mathematical approach and designed ships for the new slimmer disposition. Baker is credited with the design of at least 13 royal ships up to 1588. Wealthy investors, building their ships for privateering, also adopted the new ship designs – this resulted in better quality ships being available for the overall English fleet under the public-private arrangements where privately-owned ships were contracted into the English fleet in times of crisis.

In contrast with some ships of the existing Navy Royal, most of the new build of ships were smaller, in the range 400-500 tons. The designs, in line with the general trend, were what was called 'race-built' with the castles fore and aft being lower. These relatively smaller ships were armed with a range of heavy guns, arranged on several gun decks. A benefit of placing guns on lower decks was that the centre of gravity was not too high.

The English navy had been transformed into a force suitable for a defensive war operating in coastal waters. Their ships were not ideal for long-distance cruising as they were crowded and their limited hold space could not accommodate many supplies – over the years when Drake set out on his distant forays, his ships had to stop frequently at ports to obtain victuals and water (usually sourced by pillage). The English ships' abilities were suited for the way the battles turned out in the English Channel and off Gravelines, just a short distance from home ports – although when they were following the Armada up the North Sea, they ran out of victuals after reaching the Firth of Forth.

Ship Types

Galleass	A hybrid of a sailing ship mixed with a galley. These had banks of oars and three masts, with heavy guns in the bow and stern. (In the Armada, 500 tons.)	
Galleon	These were developed from the *nao* design to create ocean-going warships. They were slimmer and lower than a *nao,* to give speed and manoeuvrability. Two specially strengthened decks allowed heavy armament, and there was a gun in the bow. The hull was strongly built, to better stand the rigours of the Atlantic. (In the Armada, 250-1,050 tons.)	
Galley	A shallow-draught vessel propelled by banks of oars on each side, with a large lateen mast and with heavy armament at the bow. Designed for warfare in the Mediterranean. (In the Armada, 100-250 tons.)	
***Nao* (or carrack)**	Capable of sailing the oceans. Incorporated improvements in seaworthiness, stability and speed. Strong and with good cargo capacity, but also carrying defensive artillery. (In the Armada, 300-1,300 tons.)	
***Urca* or hulk**	A round-hulled large merchant ship, with large capacity, from northern Europe. (In the Armada, 200-650 tons.)	

The tender or supply and communications vessels for the Armada, usually fast sailing and with two masts, were the ***pataches*** (between 50-100 tons) and ***zabras*** (40-50 tons). Even smaller vessels were used in the Armada: ***carabelas*** and ***falúas***, lightly manned small craft employed to bring water and victuals to the fleet.

Appendix B

The Fleets

Spanish Armada

Squadron of Portugal *Duke of Medina Sidonia*						
Name	***Type***	***Tons***	***Built***	***No of guns***	***Corunna Muster***	***Outcome***
1. San Martín *Capitana general*	galleon	1,000	Portugal, 1574	50	469	Returned to anchor off Santander, 21 September 1588.
2. San Juan de Portugal *Almiranta general*	galleon	1,050	Oporto, Portugal, 1583-6	58	522	Returned to Corunna. In May 1589, set on fire by its crew during the English attack on the port.
3. San Felipe	galleon	800	Lisbon, Portugal, 1582-3	40	439	Damaged after Gravelines, captured between Nieuport and Ostend and then sank.
4. San Luis	galleon	830	Oporto, Portugal, 1585	38	439	Returned to Santander.
5. San Marcos	galleon	790	Portugal, c.1584	33	386	Wrecked near Mutton Island, Co. Clare, Ireland.
6. San Mateo	galleon	750	Portuguese Goa, c.1579	32	389	After Gravelines, drifts towards Flanders. Captured, it sinks at the approaches to Flushing.
7. Santiago	galleon	520	Lisbon, Portugal, 1581-3	26	387	Returned to Santander.
8. San Bernardo	galleon	352	Unknown	20	236	Returned to Corunna.
9. San Cristóbal	galleon	352	Portugal	24	211	Returned to Santander.
10. Augusta	*zabra*	166	Unknown	14	92	Returned to Laredo.
11. Julia	*zabra*	166	Unknown	16	135	Returned to Santander.
Squadron of Castile *Diego Flóres de Valdés*						
Name	***Type***	***Tons***	***Built***	***No of guns***	***Corunna Muster***	***Outcome***
1. San Cristóbal *Capitana (flagship)*	galleon	700	Guarnizo, Santander, 1583	32	303	Returned to Santander.
2. San Juan Bautista *Almiranta (vice-flagship)*	galleon	750	Cantabria, c.1585	24	296	Returned to Santander.

3. San Medel y San Celedón	galleon	530	Guarnizo, 1584	19	272	Returned to Laredo.
4. San Juan Menor	galleon	530	Guarnizo, 1584	21	284	Returned to Laredo.
5. Santiago Mayor	galleon	530	Guarnizo, 1584	22	293	Returned to Laredo.
6. Asunción	galleon	530	Guarnizo, 1584	22	240	Returned to Santander.
7. San Felipe y Santiago	galleon	530	Guarnizo, 1584	22	234	Returned to Santander.
8. San Pedro	galleon	530	Guarnizo, 1584	26	274	Returned to Santander.
9. Nuestra Señora del Barrio	galleon	530	Cantabria, 1583	21	277	Returned to Santander.
10. Santa Ana	galleon	250	France, 1581	14	153	Returned to Laredo.
11. Nuestra Señora de Begoña	*nao*	750	Cantabria, 1585	24	300	Returned to Cangas (Galicia).
12. Trinidad	*nao*	872	Cantabria, c. early 1580s	24	241	Lost off Ireland in September 1588 – at a location thought to be near Valentia Island, Co. Kerry.
13. Santa Catalina	*nao*	882	Cantabria, c.1586	19	320	Returned to Santander.
14. San Juan Fernandome	*nao*	650	Cantabria, c.1586	24	240	Burned in Blasket Sound, Co. Kerry on 26 September, 1588.
15. Nuestra Señora del Socorro	*patache*	75	Cantabria, c.1586	6	35	Thought to have been lost in Barrow Harbour, Tralee Bay, Co. Kerry, Ireland.
16. San Antonio de Padua	*patache*	75	Cantabria, c.1586	6	46	Captured near Blakenburg, in Flanders, after the Gravelines battle.
Squadron of Vizcaya *Juan Martínez de Recalde*						
Name	***Type***	***Tons***	***Built***	***No of guns***	***Corunna Muster***	***Outcome***
1. Santa Ana *Capitana*	*nao*	798	Cantabria, 1586	30	384	Entered the harbour of le Havre, France.
2. Santiago *Almiranta*	*nao*	666	Cantabria, 1585	25	312	Returned to Pasaia.
3. Gran Grín	*nao*	1,160	Unknown	28	336	Wrecked near the southwest of Clare Island, Clew Bay, Co. Mayo, Ireland.
4. Santa María de Montemayor	*nao*	707	Ragusa, 1578	18	202	Returned to Santander.

5. María Juan	*nao*	665	Cantabria, 1585	24	306	Badly damaged in the Battle of Gravelines, it sunk in the aftermath – it was the only Armada ship to be directly sunk by cannon fire.
6. Magdalena	*nao*	530	England, unknown date	18	244	Returned to Pasaia, Guipúzcoa.
7. Manuela	*nao*	520	England, 1580	12	163	Returned to Santander.
8. Nuestra Señora de la Concepción mayor, de Zubelzu	*nao*	468	Cantabria, 1585	16	219	Returned to Pasaia.
9. La Concepción menor de Juan Delcano	*nao*	418	Cantabria, 1585	18	225	Returned to Laredo.
10. San Juan Bautista	*nao*	350	Pasaia, Guipúzcoa, 1586	18	190	Returned to Santander.
11. La María de Suso	*patache*	96	Cantabria, c.1581	6	45	Returned to Santander.
12. San Esteban	*patache*	78	Cantabria, 1585	6	35	Returned to Corunna.
13. Isabela	*patache*	71	Cantabria, c.1583	5	53	Returned to Corunna.
14. La María de Aguirre	*patache*	70	England, unknown date	6	44	Returned to Santander.
Squadron of Andalucia *Pedro de Valdés*						
Name	***Type***	***Tons***	***Built***	***No of guns***	***Corunna Muster***	***Outcome***
1. Nuestra Señora del Rosario *Capitana*	*nao*	1,150	Ribadeo, 1586	46	359	Surrendered to Drake in the English Channel on 1 August 1588 and sent into Torbay.
2. San Francisco *Almiranta*	*nao*	915	Cantabria, 1584	22	323	Returned to Santander.
3. San Juan Bautista	galleon	810	Thought to be Cantabria, 1580	32	333	Returned to Santander.
4. Duquesa Santa Ana	*nao*	900	Flanders	23	272	Wrecked at Loughros More Bay, Co. Donegal, Ireland.
5. La Concepción Retana	*nao*	862	Thought to be Cantabria, 1580	21	260	Returned to Laredo.
6. San Bartolomé	*nao*	876	Cantabria, before 1583	28	240	Returned to Corunna.
7. Santa Catalina	*nao*	730	Probably Cantabria, 1584	24	289	Returned to Laredo.

8. Santa María de Juncal	*nao*	730	Cantabria, 1584	18	287	Returned to Santander.
9. Santa Trinidad	*nao*	650	Unknown, of old construction	13	210	Returned to Santander.
10. San Juan de Gargarín	*nao*	569	Probably Cantabria, 1586	16	203	Returned to Santander.
11. Espíritu Santo	*patache*	70	Castro Urdiales, Cantabria, 1585	8	33	Returned to Santander.
Squadron of Guipúzcoa *Miguel de Oquendo*						
Name	***Type***	***Tons***	***Built***	***No of guns***	***Corunna Muster***	***Outcome***
1. Santa Ana *Capitana*	*nao*	1,200	Cantabria, 1586	47	400	Returned to Pasaia, 23 September. Blew up a month later.
2. San Salvador *Almiranta primera*	*nao*	958	Pasaia, 1586	25	371	Blew up in the English Channel. Captured and taken into Weymouth.
3. Nuestra Señora de la Rosa (or Santa María de la Rosa) *Almiranta segunda*	*nao*	956	Pasaia, 1586	26	323	Wrecked on Stromboli Reef at Blasket Sound, Co. Kerry, Ireland, 21 September 1588.
4. San Esteban	*nao*	736	Cantabria, 1586	26	274	Wrecked at Doughmore Bay, Co. Clare, Ireland.
5. Santa Cruz	*nao*	680	Cantabria	18	165	Returned to Santander.
6. Santa Marta	*nao*	548	San Sebastian, 1586	20	239	Returned to Pasaia.
7. Santa Bárbara	*nao*	525	Cantabria, 1586	25	182	Returned to Pasaia.
8. San Buenaventura	*nao*	379	Cantabria, before 1582	21	212	Returned to Pasaia.
9. María San Juan	*nao*	291	Pasaia, 1578	12	135	Returned to Lisbon.
10. Doncella	*urca*	500	Germany, unknown date	16	141	Returned to Santander
11. San Bernabé	*patache*	69	Cantabria, c.1586	9	34	Returned to Pasaia.
12. La Asunción	*patache*	60	Castro Urdiales, c.1586	9	34	Returned to Santander.
13. La Magadalena	pinnace	50	Cantabria, c.1586	1	14	Returned to Ribadeo.
14. Nuestra Señora de Guadalupe	pinnace	50	Cantabria, 1586	1	12	Went to Calais and then returned to Spain.

Squadron of the Levant *Martín de Bertendona*						
Name	***Type***	***Tons***	***Built***	***No of guns***	***Corunna Muster***	***Outcome***
1. Regazona *Capitana*	*nao*	1,294	Venice	32	371	Returned to Muros (Galicia).
2. Lavia *Almiranta*	*nao*	728	Venice	25	302	Wrecked at Streedagh Strand, Co. Sligo, Ireland.
3. Trinidad Valencera	*nao*	1,100	Venice	42	413	Wrecked at Kinnagoe Bay, Inishowen Peninsula, Co. Donegal, Ireland.
4. San Francisco de Florencia	galleon	961	Tyrrhenian coast, Italy	51	383	Returned to Santander.
5. La Rata/Santa María Encoronada	*nao*	820	Genoa	35	448	Grounded and set alight at Tullaghan Bar in Blacksod Bay, Co. Mayo, Ireland.
6. Juliana/ Santa María, Santiago y Santa Clara	*nao*	860	Possibly Mataró (Catalonia) or Ragusa, 1571	32	412	Wrecked at Streedagh Strand, Co. Sligo, Ireland.
7. La Trinidad/La Santísima Trinidad de Escala	*nao*	900	Tyrrhenian coast, sometime in the 1550s.	19	408	Returned to Santander.
8. San Nicolás Prodaneli	*nao*	834	Ragusa	26	294	Wrecked in Clew Bay off the Corraun Peninsula, Co. Mayo, Ireland.
9. San Juan de Sicilia/ Santa María de Gracia y San Juan Bautista	*nao*	800	Ragusa, before 1582	26	320	Blew up in Tobermory Bay, Isle of Mull, Scotland.
10. Anunciada/Ntra. Sra. de la Anunciada	*nao*	703	Ragusa	23	266	Entered the Shannon Estuary. Burnt by her crew.
11. Santa María de Visón	*nao*	666	Tyrrhenian coast	18	325	Wrecked at Streedagh Strand, Co. Sligo, Ireland.
Squadron of *Urcas* *Juan Gómez de Medina*						
Name	***Type***	***Tons***	***Built***	***No of guns***	***Corunna Muster***	***Outcome***
1. El Gran Grifón *Capitana*	*urca*	650	Rostock	38	279	Wrecked at Stroms Hellier, Fair Isle, Scotland.

2. San Salvador *Almiranta*	*urca*	650	Germany, 1565	30	271	*Contador General* Pedro Coco Calderón's ship. Returned to Santander.
3. Castillo Negro	*urca*	750	Flanders	27	203	Disappeared in Atlantic, north of Ireland.
4. San Pedro el Mayor	*urca*	581	Germany, 1567	29	144	Hospital ship. Sailed into Clew Bay in Ireland and, returning to Spain, was blown back and wrecked at Hope Cove, Devon, England.
5. Barca de Amburg	*urca*	600	Germany, 1567	23	287	Sank, north of Malin Head, Ireland.
6. Barca de Danzig	*urca*	450	Germany, 1572	20	178	Entered Shannon Estuary. Returned to Gijón.
7. Santiago	*urca*	600	Netherlands, 1551	19	65, plus wives	Carried horse, mules, farriers and soldier's wives. Sank near Bergen, Norway.
8. Falcón Blanco Mayor	*urca*	500	Germany, 1587	16	216	Returned to Ribadeo.
9. Sansón	*urca*	500	Emden, Germany	18	215	Returned to Corunna. In 1589, was burned during the English attack on the port.
10. San Pedro el Menor	*urca*	500	Probably Germany, 1587	18	198	Sank in Morbihan, Brittany.
11. El Ciervo Volante	*urca*	400	Germany	18	171	Wrecked, possibly at Killala Bay, Co. Mayo, Ireland.
12. San Andrés	*urca*	400	Possibly England	14	65	Returned to Santander.
13. Gato	*urca*	400	Possibly Flanders	8	71, plus wives	Carried horses, mules and soldier's wives. Returned to Santander.
14. Falcón Blanco Mediano	*urca*	300	Germany or Netherlands, 1564	16	80	Wrecked on rocks at entrance to Ballinakill Harbour, Co. Galway.
15. Casa de Paz chica	*urca*	350	Baltic, 1560	18	175	Returned to Santander.
16. Santa Bárbara	*urca*	370	Flanders, 1559	10	50	Captain de Ávila hanged after Gravelines. The ship is thought to have been wrecked near Mace Head, Co. Galway, Ireland.
17. La Paloma Blanca	*urca*	250	Flanders	12	97	Returned to Ribadeo.
18. Esayas	*urca*	280	Germany, 1542	4	47	Returned to Santander.
19. San Gabriel	*urca*	280	Flanders, 1561	4	47	Returned to Santander.
20. El Perro Marino	*urca*	200	Flanders	8	98	Returned to Laredo.
21. La Ventura	*urca*	160	Flanders	4	64	Returned to Santander.
22. Casa de Paz grande	*urca*	650	c.1572	26	221	Returned to Laredo.
23. David chico	*urca*	450	1563	7	74	Damaged, so didn't sail and remained at port.

Squadron of *Pataches and Zabras* *Agustín de Ojeda*						
Name	***Type***	***Tons***	***Built***	***No of guns***	***Corunna Muster***	***Outcome***
1. Nuestra Señora del Pilar Zaragoza *Capitana*	*nao*	305	Cantabria, at Castro Urdiales, near Bilbao. c.1584	11	173	Returned to Laredo.
2. La Caridad, inglesa	*nao*	180	England	15	80	Was in Shannon Estuary. Returned to Santander.
3. San Andrés, escocés	*urqueta*	150	Dundee, Scotland	12	65	Returned to Pasaia.
4. El Santo Crucifijo	*patache*	150	Cantabria, c.1583	8	64	Returned to Laredo.
5. Concepción de Lastero	*patache*	75	Castro Urdiales	6	18	Was in Shannon Estuary. Returned to Castro Urdiales.
6. Concepción de Carasa	*patache*	70	Castro Urdiales	5	39	Returned to Castro Urdiales.
7. Nuestra Señora de la Fresneda	*patache*	58	Cantabria	–	20	Returned to Santander.
8. Concepción de Castro	*patache*	60	Castro Urdiales	10	19	Returned to Santander.
9. Nuestra Señora de Guadalupe	*patache*	100	Castro Urdiales	9	49	Returned to Santander.
10. Nuestra Señora de Begoña	*patache*	64	Cantabria	4	23	Was in Shannon Estuary. Returned to Santander.
11. Concepción de Capitillo	*patache*	60	Cantabria	2	38	Returned to Santander.
12. Nuestra Señora de Gracia	*patache*	57	Santander	5	43	Sent to assist galleys. Went to San Sebastián.
13. Nuestra Señora del Puerto	*patache*	55	Santoña, Cantabria	8	55	Returned to Santander.
14. San Gerónimo	*patache*	55	Castro Urdiales	4	40	Entered Shannon Estuary. Returned to Santander.
15. San Juan de Carasa	*zabra*	50	Castro Urdiales	2	52	Returned to Santander.
16. Trinidad	*zabra*	40	Castro Urdiales	2	24	Returned to Santander.
17. Santa Catalina	*zabra*	50	Castro Urdiales	4	20	Thought to have carried dispatches to the Duke of Parma. In November 1588 was in Santander.
18. Concepción de Valmaseda	*zabra*	50	Castro Urdiales	2	32	Returned early, to Burela, Galicia on 2 August 1588.
19. Nuestra Señora de Castro	*zabra*	50	Castro Urdiales	2	18	Sank due to a storm after returning, just off Spanish coast.

20. San Andrés	*zabra*	40	Castro Urdiales	2	17	Returned to Santander.
21. La Asunción	*zabra*	50	Castro Urdiales	2	18	Returned to Santander.
22. San Francisco	*patache*	86	Castro Urdiales	4	57	Remained in Corunna.
23. Concepción de Somarriva	*zabra*	50	Castro Urdiales	4	18	Lost in Danish or Norwegian waters, after Gravelines.
Squadron of Galleasses *Hugo de Moncada*						
Name	***Type***	***Tons***	***Built***	***No of guns***	***Corunna Muster***	***Outcome***
1. San Lorenzo *Capitana*	galleass	500	Naples, c.1583	50	368, plus rowers	Grounded at Calais after the Battle of Gravelines.
2. Napolitana *Patrona*	galleass	500	Naples, c.1583	50	321, plus rowers	Returned to Laredo.
3. Zúñiga	galleass	500	Naples, c.1584	50	298, plus rowers	On return sheltered in Le Havre. Returned to Spain in August 1589.
4. Girona	galleass	500	Naples, c.1584	50	349, plus rowers	Smashed onto Lacada Point, Co. Antrim, Ireland. Practically all of the 1,200 aboard were drowned.
Squadron of Galleys *Diego de Medrano*						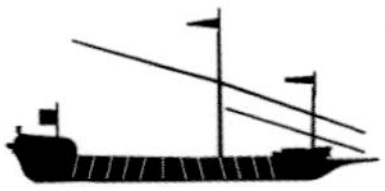
Name	***Type***	***Tons***	***Built at***	***No of guns***	***Corunna Muster***	***Outcome***
1. Esphera *Capitana*	galley		Naples, 1576	5	109, plus rowers	Sailed to Bayonne. Returned to Fuenterrabía, then San Sebastián.
2. Diana *Patrona*	galley		Barcelona, 1571	5	79, plus rowers	Returned to Viveiro, 24 July. Rowers mutiny.
3. Princesa	galley		Barcelona, 1571	5	81, plus rowers	Blown by winds to a Brittany harbour. Returned to Pasaia.
4. Bazana	galley		Naples, 1574	5	72, plus rowers	Ran aground at the approaches to the harbour at Bayonne. The rowers desert. Returned to Fuenterrabía.

Note: Spanish tonnages given in the sixteenth century were established using complicated calculations related to the cargo-carrying capacity of the vessel. The tons given in this table for ships of the Armada are those presented as *toneladas* in pages 151-359, *La Batalla del Mar Océano, Vol V.*

English Fleet

Navy Royal			
Name	***Type***	***Tons***	***Detail***
Ark Royal	galleon	720	Lord Admiral Howard's flagship.
Revenge	galleon	628	Sir Francis Drake, commander. Captured by Spanish off Azores in 1591 and sank days later.
Rainbow	galleon	512	Lord Henry Seymour, commander.
Triumph	galleon	988	Sir Martin Frobisher, commander. Rebuilt 1578.
White Bear	galleon	972	
Elizabeth Jonas	galleon	912	
Victory	galleon	753	Sir John Hawkins, commander.
Mary Rose	galleon	613	
Vanguard	galleon	599	Sir William Wynter, commander.
Elizabeth Bonaventure	galleon	597	
Golden Lion	galleon	561	
Hope	galleon	537	
Dreadnought	galleon	540	
Nonpareil	galleon	507	
Antelope	galleon	455	
Swallow	galleon	443	
Bonavilla	galley	250	
Swiftsure	galleon	384	
Foresight	galleon	392	
Bull	galleass	257	
Aid	galleon	340	
Tiger	galleon	199	
George	hoy (single-masted coastal vessel)	100	
Tramontana	galleon	184	
Scout	galleon	176	
Achates	barque (small three-masted vessel)	139	
Brigantine	small galley	90	
Charles	pinnace	107	
Merlin	pinnace	50	
Moon	pinnace	91	

Spy	pinnace	65	
Advice	pinnace	65	
Sun	pinnace	60	
Cygnet	pinnace	37	
Privately-owned ships			
Name	***Type***	***Tons***	***Detail***
Galleon Leicester	galleon	400	Owned by Earl of Leicester.
Merchant Royal	galleon	400	Owned by Levant Company.
Roebuck	galleon	300	Owned by Sir Walter Raleigh.
Hercules	galleon	300	London
Sampson	galleon	300	
Edward Bonaventure	galleon	300	
Toby		250	London
Golden Noble		250	
Galleon Dudley	galleon	250	Owned by Earl of Leicester.
Centurion		250	London
Samaritan		250	Dartmouth
Minion		230	Bristol
Violet		220	London
Susan Parnell		220	London
Mayflower		200	London
Minion		200	London
Ascencion		200	London
Primrose		200	London
Margaret and John		200	London
Tiger		200	London
Red Lion		200	London
George Bonaventure		200	London
Griffin		200	
Minion		200	London
Bark Talbot		200	Fireship
Thomas Drake		200	Owned by Sir Francis Drake, fireship.
Spark		200	
Hopewell		200	
Virgin God save Her		200	
Hope Hawkins		200	
Edward		186	Maldon
Gift of God		180	London

Anne Frances		180	Under Lord Howard, paid for by the Queen.
Bark Potts		180	London
Hope		180	Fireship, Plymouth
Solomon		170	London
Bark Burr		160	London
Brave		160	London
Bark St Leger		160	
Bark Mannington		160	
Royal Defence		160	London
Vineyard		160	London
Nightingale		160	
Daniel		160	Newcastle
Bark Bond		150	Fireship
Bark Bonner		150	
Bark Hawkins		150	
John Trelawney		150	
Galleon Hutchins		150	Newcastle
Bark Lamb		150	Newcastle
Marigold		150	Aldeburgh
Grace		150	Great Yarmouth
Mayflower		150	
Cure's Ship		150	Fireship
Frances		140	Fowey
Golden Lion		140	London
Thomas Bonaventure		140	London
Samuel		140	London
Bear Yonge		140	Fireship
White Lion		140	
Crescent		140	Dartmouth
William		140	
Richard Duffield		140	
Mary Rose		140	
William		140	Ipswich
Bartholomew		130	Topsham
Unicorn		130	Bristol
John		130	Barnstable
Katharine		125	Ipswich
George Noble		120	London
Toby		120	London
Antelope		120	London
Prudence		120	Leigh, Essex

Primrose		120	Harwich
Elizabeth		120	Dover
Elizabeth		120	Leigh
Angel		120	Fireship, Southampton
Golden Ryall		120	Weymouth
William		120	Plymouth
Elizabeth Bonaventure		120	
Bearsabe		120	
Solomon		120	
Jewel		110	Leigh
Salamander		110	Leigh
Dolphin		110	Leigh
Rose		110	Topsham
Robin		110	
Anthony		100	London
Rose Lion		100	Leigh
Pansy		100	London
Jane Bonaventure		100	London
Galleon		100	Weymouth
Grace of Apsam		100	
Pelican		100	
Pearl		100	
Marigold		100	
Jonas		100	
Plus around 75 ships under 100 tons			

Note: tonnages were calculated differently in England during the sixteenth century. These given here for the English fleet are broadly as per the 'tons and tonnages' listing (considered best comparable to Spanish figures), as presented in pages 400-404, *La Batalla del Mar Océano, Vol V.* Other information has been sourced from the *Armada, 1588-1988*, ed., M. Rodríguez-Salgado, Penguin Books, 1988 and *Armada*, C. Martin, G. Parker, Yale University Press, 2022.

Image Credits

Images on the specified pages are courtesy and copyright of the following (abbreviations for top, bottom, left, middle, right, respectively, are: t, b, l, m, r):

Alamy: (IanDagnall Computing) 71, (North Wind Picture Archives) 95, (incamerastock) 112l, (Hilary Morgan) 112r, (digital image library), 129; Albaola Itsas Kultur Faktoria, Pasaia: 262b, 264, 265; Alejandro Chinchilla: 4, 224; An Post (artist Seán Ó Brógáin): 250; Author's collection: 18, 50, 68, 99, 148t, 148m, 171, 182, 197b, 226, 249; Biblioteca Nacional de España: 74, 144, 255, 263; Biblioteca Nacional Digital de Portugal: 101; Clark Art Institute, Williamstown, Massachusetts: 252; Geograph.org.uk: St Faith's church in Gaywood, C17 painting (detail), cc-by-sa/2.0, © Evelyn Simak, geograph.org.uk/p/2019526 – 138, Denny Monument, cc-by-sa/2.0, © Richard Croft, geograph.org.uk/p/1032693 – 214b; Germanisches Nationalmuseum, Digitale Bibliothek: 109; Helene Brennan, www.helene-brennan.com: 216; James Adam & Sons, Dublin: 211t; Kronos Servicios de Restauración & Sigüenza Catedral (foto Lidia Santalices): 242b; Library of Congress: 36, 43, 62, 123, 152, 234, 235, 238; Mar Villalba, www.miruta.es: 254; Master and Fellows of Magdalene College, Cambridge: 267; Metropolitan Museum of Art (The Elisha Whittelsey Collection): 116; Michael B. Barry: 8, 14 (National Museum of Ireland, Collins Barracks), 19, 22, 30 (M. Guillén), 49, 51, 67, 85-86, 158, 247 (Fundación Casa Medina Sidonia), 91, 111, 114, 118-119, 131, 146, 150, 151 (Museo Naval, Cartagena), 157 (Albaola Itsas Kultur Faktoria), 160, 161t, 163b, 164, 165b, 166, 167, 169, 174-175, 176, 178t-179t, 180, 181, 184, 186b, 186t-187t, 187b, 188, 191, 192, 193, 194b, 194t-195t, 196, 197t, 198-199, 200, 202, 205, 207, 208, 209, 210, 211b, 212, 213, 214t-215t, 218, 220, 222, 225, 237, 239, 242t, 246-247, 260-261, 262t; Michael Harpur, www.eoceanic.com: 189; Museo Naval, Madrid: 26, 110, 130, 258t, 259t; Museum de Lakenhal, Leiden: 133; National Gallery of Art, Washington DC: 98, 128, 253; National Maritime Museum, Greenwich: 47; Patrimonio Nacional: Real Monasterio de San Lorenzo de El Escorial, 19007034: 231; Rijksmuseum: RP-P-OB-78 – 25, BI-1895-3811-44 – 34, BVB01-BDH19769PK – 37, RP-P-2009-765 – 39, W_SK-A-1068 – 40, RP-P-OB-79.992 – 59, RP-P-OB-80.052 – 89, RP-P-AO-15-65A-2 – 90, RP-P-OB-104.113 – 92, SK-A-1629– 121 (and 145b), RP-P-OB-78.747 – 125, RP-P-OB-80.068 – 132, RP-P-1982-1001 – 134, RP-P-OB-48.300 – 141, 245; Seán Ó Brógáin (seanobrogain@yahoo.ie) and Macha Media: 178b, 179b, 183; www.spanisharmadaireland.com: 228; Tower Museum, Derry (DCSDC Museum and Heritage Service): (Tony Boyle) 165t, 256, 257; Turismo de Galicia: 108; Ulster Museum (National Museums NI): 148b, (Kenneth Riley) 201, 203; Universiteitsbibliotheek Gent: 17, 97; Veronica Barry: 11, 65, 103, 143, 159, 229, 258m, 258b, 268.

Wikimedia Commons – 16th century etching of a hall in the Hôtel-Dieu, unknown author, http://www.mja.com.au/public/issues/177_11_021202/dec10354_fm.html#i1067496, Bajor kifli: 153; Álvaro de Bazán, Museo Naval Madrid, de Rafael Tegeo, Own photograph of the original painting, Dominio público, 56https://commons.wikimedia.org/w/index.php?curid=25875810: 56; Anthony, Prior of Crato, by Unknown author, Unknown source, Public Domain, https://commons.wikimedia.org/w/index.php?curid=17293880, Lumastan: 54; AtaqueDrakes.jpg Par Auteur inconnu – [1] Ayuntamiento de San Fernando, Cádiz, Domaine public, https://commons.wikimedia.org/w/index.php?curid=2544862: 81; Burial of Drake, by Lobsterthermidor at en.wikipedia, Own work transferred from en.wikipedia, CC0, https://commons.wikimedia.org/w/index.php?curid=17875836: 244; By Albrecht Dürer, http://moghroith.blogspot.com/2012/12/in-company-of-kern-flying-enemy.html, Public Domain, https://commons.wikimedia.org/w/index.php?curid=30887836: 163t; By Antonis Mor, Hispanic Society, Public Domain, http://hispanicsociety.emuseum.com/objects/2631/fernando-alvarez-de-toledo-third-duke-of-alba: 27; By Hans Eworth - https://www.flickr.com/photos/60861613@N00/3956264299/; original is in the Bedford Collection, Woburn Abbey, England; published between pages 220 and 221 in Porter, Linda (2007) Mary Tudor: The First Queen. London: Little, Brown. ISBN 0749909826: 12; By Original: Biblioteca Nacional de LisboaPhoto: User: Joserebelo, Biblioteca Nacional de Lisboa, Public Domain, https://commons.wikimedia.org/w/index.php?curid=472967: 33; By Otto van Veen, 3. meisterdrucke.es/impresion-art%C3%ADstica/Otto-van-Veen/961276/Retrato-del-condottiero-Alejandro-(Alessandro)-Farnesio1 & 2. Not provided by uploaders, Public Domain, https://commons.wikimedia.org/w/index.php?curid=288720, Ecummenic: 58; By Steven van der Meulen, https://waddesdon.org.uk/the-collection/item/?id=3289, Public Domain, https://commons.wikimedia.org/w/index.php?curid=1583840: 60; By Titian; direct link to the image: (converted in JPG before upload), National Museum of Capodimonte, Naples, Google Arts & Culture asset ID: egG5dtLApoTuPA: 23; By Xauxa Håkan Svensson, Own work, CC BY-SA 3.0, https://commons.wikimedia.org/w/index.php?curid=1597402: 232; De Bernardino de Escalante (fl. 1577) http://cvc.cervantes.es/obref/china/era_moderna.htm, Dominio público, https://commons.wikimedia.org/w/index.php?curid=15412490: 75; De Leyva, de El Greco, Web Gallery of Art (Montreal Museum of Fine Arts), Imagen Info about artwork, Dominio público, https://commons.wikimedia.org/w/index.php?curid=15461899, JarektUploadBot: 155b; Departure of fleet from Lisbon harbour, engraving from c.1592 by Theodor de Bry illustration in "America Tertia Pars". Location: Service Historique de la Marine, Vincennes, Walrasiad: 76; Di Filippo Bellini, 2021 Stamps: Vatican City (Pope Sixtus V), Philatelic Pursuits, Pubblico dominio, (Musée national du château de Pau) https://commons.wikimedia.org/w/index.php?curid=115273568: 69; Disembarkation of the Spanish troops in the Terceiras islands, Afresco de Niccolò Granello, Sala de las Batallas, Monasterio de San Lorenzo de El Escorial,Antgb~commonswiki: 57; Duart castle, by Philippe Giabbanelli – Own work, CC BY-SA 3.0, https://commons.wikimedia.org/w/index.php?curid=11875873, 161b; El Escorial, view from the north-west, Volodymyr Vlasenko, 29; Elizabeth I of England, the Armada Portrait, Woburn Abbey, formerly attributed to George Gower, http://www.luminarium.org/renlit/elizarmada.jpg, Public Domain, https://commons.wikimedia.org/w/index.php?curid=28313, Shakko: 139; Giorgio-vasari-battle-of-lepanto.jpg, Palazzo Apostolico, Rome, Alonso de Mendoza: 31; https://en.wikipedia.org/wiki/Image:The_Brewer_designed_and_engraved_in_the_Sixteenth._Century_by_J_Amman.png: 77; Juan Martinez de Recalde, de desconocido, http://www.foromaritimovasco.com/documentos/barlovento/JUAN%20MARTINEZ%20DE%20RECALDE.PDF, Dominio público, https://commons.wikimedia.org/w/index.php?curid=17625157, Harrias: 155t; Lisbon in 1572, Civitates orbis terrarum, Georg Braun and Franz Hogenberg: 105; Lope de Vega, (Museo Lázaro Galdiano), Atribuido a Eugenio Cajés [2], Dominio público, https://commons.wikimedia.org/w/index.php?curid=947123: 233; Maria Pita, de Arturo Fernández Cersa 1866-1937, Patrimonio Artístico Municipal da Coruña, Dominio público, https://commons.wikimedia.org/w/index.php?curid=68762943: 240; Mary, Queen of Scots, After Rowland Lockey, Public domain, via Wikimedia Commons, Government Art Collection (UK): 35; Portrait of Queen Elizabeth I, Nicholas Hilliard, Walker Art Gallery, Google art project, DcoetzeeBot: 20; Route of Francis Drake's circumnavigation of the globe 1577-1580 By unattributed, Christie's, Public Domain, https://commons.wikimedia.org/w/index.php?curid=41611127: 44; The Harbour in Amsterdam, Schloss Schleissheim, PD-Art: Hendrick Cornelisz Vroom, Rlbberlin: 93; The Somerset House Conference, 1604, by Juan Pantoja de la Cruz, National Maritime Museum, Public Domain, https://commons.wikimedia.org/w/index.php?curid=758485, Alonso de Mendoza: 251; The Surrender of Pedro de Valdés, by John Seymour Lucas https://i.pinimg.com/originals/f9/2b/a6/f92ba6183c04aa0149d234c13af08a25.jpg, Public Domain, https://commons.wikimedia.org/w/index.php?curid=130133167, National Trust at Buckland Abbey: 117; Torre de Belém at 2009-06-06.jpg, Bert K. from Roermond, Netherlands: 106; Unknown author, Mary, Queen of Scots, was executed on 8 February 1587 at Fotheringay Castle, National Portrait Gallery of Scotland, Dencey: 64; Virrey Diego Carrillo de Mendoza, Museo Nacional de Historia, de Pintor no identificado, Bicentenario México, Dominio público, https://commons.wikimedia.org/w/index.php?curid=8773040: 135.

Every effort has been made to establish copyright, but if a copyright holder wishes to bring an error or omission to the notice of the publishers, then an appropriate acknowledgement will be made in any subsequent edition.

Glossary

Almiranta	The flagship of the second in command of a Spanish fleet or squadron.
Arquebus	A matchlock gun, equipped with a trigger, of various lengths and weights.
Asiento	Contract with foreign bankers, a form of short-term debt in sixteenth-century Spain.
Astrolabe	An instrument used in navigation for calculating latitude.
Broadside	The simultaneous firing of the guns mounted on one side of a ship.
Capitana	The flagship of the Admiral or commanding officer of a Spanish fleet or squadron.
Caulking	The act of making seams watertight; usually by a mixture of pitch and oakum.
Compass	An instrument with a magnetic needle pointing north, which allows a course to be set.
Ducat	A Spanish unit of currency (generally corresponding to a gold escudo). In the sixteenth century four ducats were roughly equivalent to one English pound sterling.
Enterprise of England	A term used in the late sixteenth century in Spanish circles to describe a plan to invade England and depose Queen Elizabeth I.
Flota	A merchant fleet – a term used to describe the Spanish treasure fleets from the Indies.
Galloglass	Elite, heavily-armed mercenary from Scotland, contracted by Irish lords. The name comes from the Gaelic: *gall* and *óglach*: 'foreign young warrior'.
Great Gale	A term used by the author Ken Douglas to describe the unseasonal hurricane (or tropical cyclone, with winds exceeding 120km/h) that blew in the North Atlantic and hit the west coast of Ireland on 21 September 1588, as an eyewitness wrote: 'with a most terrible fury'.
Juro	A form of long-term domestic debt, usually a perpetual annuity, in widespread use in sixteenth-century Spain.
Kerns	Lightly-armed Irish soldiers.
Latitude	A point on a line around the earth parallel to the equator.
League	A measure of distance. A Spanish naval league of the sixteenth century was 4.18km. An English league was 4.83km.
Letters of Marque	A government licence that authorized a private entity to attack and capture enemy vessels – a practice that was widely interpreted and much abused by French, Dutch and English privateers during the sixteenth century.
Longitude	A point on a line drawn between the North and South Poles, giving an east-west direction.
Maestre de Campo	The commanding officer of a *tercio*, roughly equivalent to a modern colonel.
Morisco	An Iberian Muslim who became a baptised Christian, living under Christian rule.
Musket	A long-barrelled matchlock gun.
Navy Royal	The assembly of Queen's ships in the Kingdom of England, Elizabeth's standing navy during the second half of the sixteenth century. The forerunner of the British Royal Navy.
Plantation	Part of the colonisation of Ireland, where the country became a 'laboratory for empire'. From the mid-sixteenth century onwards, English administrators confiscated the lands of the Gaelic lords and then planted these with loyal English and, later, Scottish settlers.
Privateer	A state-sponsored pirate, also 'corsair'.
Race built	A sixteenth-century term to describe a ship built with a greater length in relation to the beam, with relatively lower fore- and stern-castles.
Redshanks	Lightly-armed Scottish mercenaries contracted to fight in Ireland during the sixteenth century by Irish lords.
Rutter	A route map and guide used by mariners.
Shot	A projectile fired from a large gun.
States-General	Originally the assembly of all the provinces of the Burgundian Netherlands. In 1579, during the Dutch Revolt, the States-General split and the northern States-General declared that Philip II no longer had authority over them.
Stern-castle	A platform, built on the stern of a ship, which could be used for defence or boarding .
Tercio	An infantry unit in Spanish service of up to 3,000 men.
Weather gauge	To gain this position, windward to other ships, gave advantage in battle.

Bibliography

Principal Libraries, Museums & Archives consulted:
Albaola Itsas Kultur Faktoria, Pasaia, Guipúzcoa; Archivos, Fundación Casa Medina Sidonia, Sanlúcar de Barrameda; Library of Congress, Washington; Biblioteca Nacional de España, Madrid; Archivo General de Simancas; British National Archives, Kew; National Archives of Ireland, Dublin; National Maritime Museum, Greenwich; National Library of Ireland, Dublin; National Museum of Ireland, Dublin; Museos Naval, Madrid and Cartagena; Inishowen Maritime Museum, Greencastle, Co. Donegal; Spanish Armada Visitor Centre, Grange, Co. Sligo; Tower Museum, Derry, Trinity College Library, Dublin; Ulster Museum, Belfast.

Periodicals:
General Irish, Spanish and British newspapers
History Ireland
The Irish Sword
Revista de Historia Naval

Websites
www.armadainvencible.org
www.spanisharmadaireland.com
www.dbe.rah.es

Books:
Ackroyd, P., *The Tudors*, Macmillan, London, 2012.
Allingham, H, *Captain Cuellar's Adventures in Connacht & Ulster*, Project Gutenburg.
Atherton, D., *La Trinidad Valencera*, Great Sea Books, 2013.
Atherton, D., *The Spanish Armada in County Donegal*, Inishowen Maritime Museum, 2023.
Bagwell, R., *Ireland under the Tudors*, Longmans, Green, London, 1885.
Bicheno, H., *Elizabeth's Sea Dogs*, Adlard Coles, London, 2014.
Brewer, J, Bullen, W., (ed.), *Calendar of the Carew Manuscripts*, Longmans, Green, London, 1868.
Canny, N., *Making Ireland British 1580-1650*, Oxford University Press, 2003.
Canny, N., *The Elizabethan Conquest of Ireland*, The Harvester Press, Sussex, 1976.
Casado Soto, J., *Los Barcos Españoles del siglo XVI y la Gran Armada de 1588*, Editorial San Martín, Madrid, 1988.
Chinchilla, P., *Los Prisioneros de La Armada Invencible: La historia nunca contada sobre los capturados de la Gran Armada Española de 1588*, Ediciones B, Barcelona, 2023.
Connolly, S., *Contested Island: Ireland 1460-1630*, Oxford University Press, 2009.
Coote, S., *Drake*, Simon & Schuster, London, 2003.
Corbett, J., *Drake and the Tudor Navy*, Longmans, Green, London, 1917.
Cordero Bravo, J., Hernandez Asencio, R., *Operación Gran Armada: La Logística Invencible*, Ediciones Díaz de Santos, Madrid, 2011.
De Courcy Ireland, J., *Ireland and the Irish in Maritime History*, The Glendale Press, Dún Laoghaire, 1986.
Dietz, F., *English Public Finance 1485-1641*, Routledge, London, 1964.
Douglas, K., *The Downfall of the Spanish Armada in Ireland*, Gill & Macmillan, Dublin, 2010.
Elliot, J, *Europe Divided, 1559-1598*, Fontana, London, 1968.
Elliot, J., *Empires of the Atlantic World: Britain and Spain in America 1492-1830*, Yale University Press, London, 2020.
Elliot, J., *Imperial Spain 1469-1716*, Penguin Books, London, 2002.
Fallon, N., *The Armada in Ireland*, Wesleyan University Press, Connecticut, 1978.
Fernández Duro, C, *La Armada Invencible, (Vols 1 & 2)* Real Academia de la Historia, Madrid, 1884.
Fernández-Armesto, F., *The Spanish Armada, the Experience of War in 1588*, Oxford University Press, 1989.
Flanagan, L., *Irish Wrecks of the Spanish Armada*, Country House, Dublin, 1995.
Frost, J., *The history and topography of the county of Clare*, Sealy, Dublin, 1893.
Froude, J., *English Seamen in the Sixteenth Century*, Charles Scribner, New York, 1895.
Froude, J., *The Spanish Story of the Armada*, Longmans, Green, London, 1892.
Gallagher, P., Cruickshank, D., ed., *God's Obvious Design, Papers for the Spanish Armada Symposium, Sligo, 1988*, Tamesis Books, London, 1990.
Garcia Hernan, E., *Irlanda y el Rey Prudente*, Laberinto, Madrid, 2003.
Gómez Beltrán, A., *Felipe II y el Mito de la Armada Invencible*, Ediciones Platea, Málaga, 2022.
Gómez Beltrán, A., *Islas Terceiras, Batalla Naval de San Miguel*, Salamina Serie Naval, Málaga, 2017.
Gómez Beltrán, A., *La Invencible y su Leyenda Negra, Del Fracasa Inglés en la 'Derrota' de la Armada Española*, Arin Ediciones, Benalmádena, 2013.
Gorrochategui Santos, L., *The English Armada, the Greatest Naval Disaster in English History*, Bloomsbury, London, 2018.

Gracia Rivas, M., *La Sanidad en la Jornada de Inglaterra*, Editorial Naval, Madrid.
Guilmartin, J., *Galleons and Galleys*, Cassell, London, 2002.
Hamilton, H., ed., *Calendar of State Papers, Ireland, Elizabeth, August 1588 – September 1592*, Her Majesty's Public Record Office, London, 1885.
Hanson, N., *The Confident Hope of a Miracle, the True History of the Spanish Armada*, Doubleday, London, 2003.
Hardiman, J., *The History of the Town and County of Galway*, Folds and Co., Dublin 1820.
Herrera Oria, E., *La Armada Invencible (1587-1589)*, Archivo Histórico Español, Madrid, 1929.
Herrera Oria, H., *Historia de España y de Sus Indias*, Academia de Estudios Histórico-Sociales de Valladolid, 1929.
Hibbert, C., *The Virgin Queen*, Viking, London, 1990.
Hume, M., (ed.) *Calendar of Letters and State Papers relating to English Affairs belonging to the Archives of Simancas, Vol. I, Elizabeth, 1587-1603*, Her Majesty's Stationery Office, London.
Hume, M., *The Year after the Armada and other Historical Studies*, The Macmillan Co., New York, 1896.
Hutchinson, R., *The Spanish Armada*, Hachette, London, 2013.
Kamen, H., *Imagining Spain, Historical Myth & National Identity*, Yale University Press, London, 2008.
Kelleher, C., *The Spanish Armada Wrecks in Streedagh, Co. Sligo*, Heritage Guide No 79. Archaeology Ireland, Wordwell, Dublin, 2017.
Kelly, F., *Captain Francisco de Cuéllar*, Four Courts Press, Dublin, 2020.
Kennedy, P., *The Rise and Fall of British Naval Mastery*, Penguin Random House, London, 2017.
Knox, H., *The History of the County of Mayo*, Hodges Figgis, Dublin, 1908.
Lardas, M., *Spanish Galleon vs English Galleon*, Osprey Publishing Oxford, 2020.
Laughton, J., *State Papers relating to the Defeat of the Spanish Armada, (Vol 1 &2)*, Navy Records Society, London, 1894.
Lemon, R., (ed.), *Calendar of State Papers, Domestic Series of the Reign of Elizabeth, 1581-1590*, Longmans, Green, London 1865.
Lennon, C., *Sixteenth-Century Ireland, the Incomplete Conquest*, Gill & Macmillan, Dublin, 1994.
Losada, J., *Los Generales de Flandes*, la Esfera de los Libros, Madrid, 2009.
MacCaffrey, W., *Elizabeth I*, Hodder & Stoughton, London, 1993.
Martin, C., *Full Fathom Five, Wrecks of the Spanish Armada*, Chatto & Windus, London, 1975.
Martin, C., Parker, P., *The Spanish Armada*, Gild Publishing, London, 1988.
Martin, C., Parker, P., *Armada*, Yale University Press, London, 2022.
Martin, P., *Spanish Armada Prisoners*, Exeter Maritime Studies, 1988.
Mattingly, G., *The Defeat of the Spanish Armada*, Jonathan Cape, London, 1983.
McCalmont, R., *Memoirs of the Binghams*, Spottiswode, London, 1915.
Morgan, H, *The Battle of Kinsale*, Wordwell, Dublin, 2004.
Morgan, H., *Tyrone's Rebellion*, The Boydell Press, Suffolk, 1999.
Morris, T., *Europe and England in the Sixteenth Century*, Routledge, London, 1998.
Notario Lopéz, I., *The Spanish Tercios*, 1536-1704, Osprey Publishing, Oxford, 2013
Ó Tuathaigh, G., *The Massacre at Dún an Óir*, 1580, Cló Dhuibhne, Kerry, 1980.
O'Brien, D., *History of the O'Briens*, 1949.
O'Neill, T., *Merchants and Mariners in Medieval Ireland*, Irish Academic Press, Dublin, 1987.
O'Rahilly, A., *The Massacre at Smerwick*, Cork University Press, 1938.
Parker, G., *Imprudent King, a New Life of Philip II*, Yale University Press, London, 2015.
Parker, G., *The Army of Flanders and the Spanish Road*, Cambridge University Press, 1972.
Parker, G., *The Dutch Revolt*, Penguin Books, London, 1985.
Parker, G., *The Grand Strategy of Philip II*, Yale University Press, New Haven, 2000.
Pelayo, J., *La Empresa de Inglaterra*, Spain, 2019.
Prescott, H., *Mary Tudo*r, Orion Books, London, 2003.
Riaño Lozano, F., *Los medios navales de Alejandro Farnesio, 1587-1588*, Ministerio de Defensa, Madrid, 1999.
Rodríguez-Salgado, M., Armada 1588-1988, the Official Catalogue, Penguin Books, London, 1988.
Sanz Camañes, P., *Los ecos de la Armada*, Silex, Madrid, 2012.
Stapleton, J., *The Spanish Armada 1588, the Journey of Francisco de Cuéllar*, de Cuéllar Project Committee, 2001.
Tellechea Idogoras, J., *Otra Cara de la Invencible, la Participacion Vasca*, Sociedad Guipúzcoana de Ediciones y Publicaciones, San Sebastián, 1988.
Various ed., *La Batalla del Mar Océano (Vols. 1 to 5)*, Ministerio de Defensa – Armada Española, Madrid, 2015.
Various, ed., *La Gran Armada, Simposio Hispano-Británico Londres, Junio, 1988, Madrid Noviembre 1988*, Instituto de Historia y Cultura Naval, Madrid, 1989.
Various, ed. *The Spanish Armada of 1588 and the English Counter Armada of 1589*, Proceedings, Cartagena, Ministerio de Cultura y Deporte, Madrid, 2021.
Rodger, N., *The Safeguard of the Sea: A Naval History of Britain: 660-1649*, W. W. Norton & Company, New York, 1999.
Wernham, R., *The Expedition of Sir John Norris and Sir Francis Drake to Spain and Portugal, 1589*, Temple Smith, 1988.
Whitelock, A., *Mary Tudor, England's First Queen*, Bloombury Publishing, London, 2009.
Wilson, A., *The Elizabethans*, Hutchinson, London, 2011.

Index

P

R

S

T

U

V

W

Y

Z

Books by Michael B. Barry

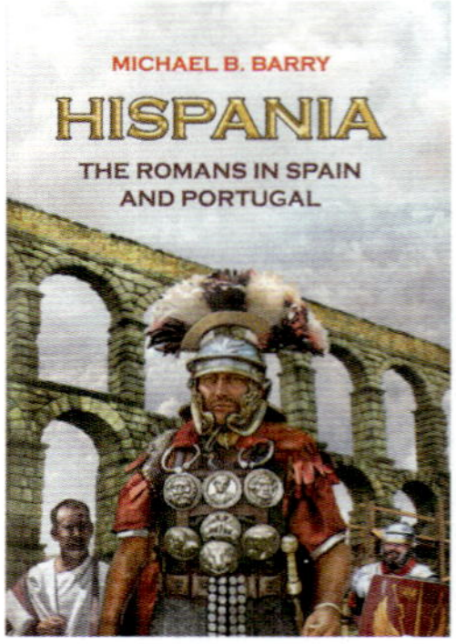

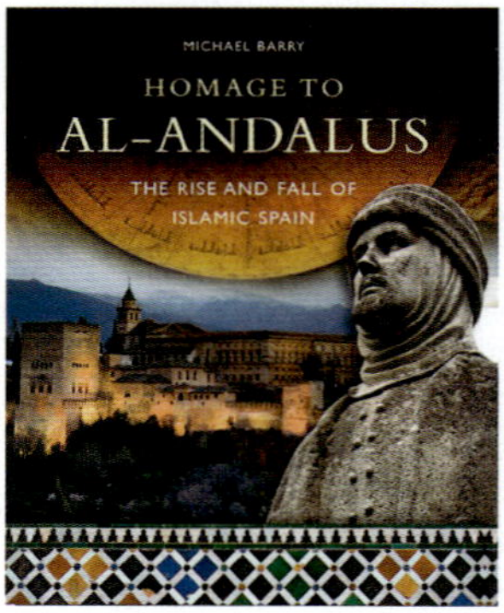

Hispania, the Romans in Spain and Portugal

The landing by Roman soldiers on the Iberian Peninsula in 218 BC, in what they called Hispania heralded a conquest which took two centuries to complete. As the peninsula's riches flowed back to Rome, Hispania developed into the most favoured of all the Empire's provinces. In this masterly book, Michael B. Barry, using a wealth of full-colour images and maps, tells the story of the six centuries of the Roman presence in Spain and Portugal.

Homage to al-Andalus, the Rise and Fall of Islamic Spain

The Iberian Peninsula was conquered by Islamic forces in 711 AD and the Islamic presence continued for 900 years. The rule by (what has been termed) the Moors left an indelible stamp such as the wonders of the Alhambra and the Great Mosque of Córdoba. This richly illustrated book tells the story of al-Andalus, its rise to splendour and sophistication and its decline.

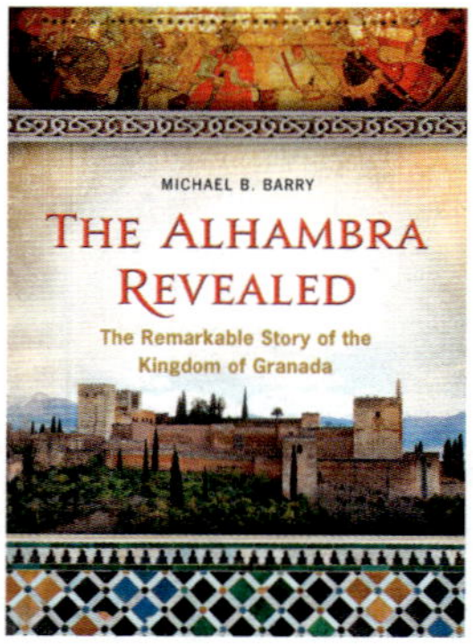

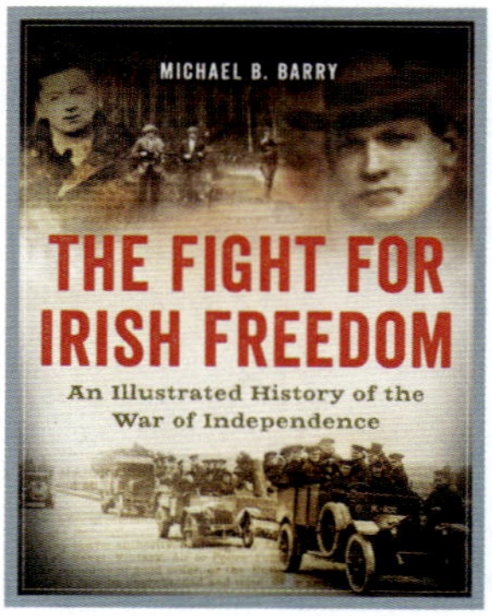

The Alhambra Revealed, the Remarkable Story of the Kingdom of Granada

The Alhambra is one of the world's great monuments. Within this palace complex is an array of buildings which contains outstanding examples of Islamic architecture. Richly illustrated, this book is essential not only for those visiting the Alhambra, but also for those who wish to explore the history of the Kingdom of Granada.

The Fight for Irish Freedom, an Illustrated History of the War of Independence

From 1919 onwards, the IRA, using guerrilla tactics attacked the Crown forces. By mid-1921, with casualties rising, the British opted for a truce. This was followed by the Anglo-Irish Treaty. This essential book brings the War of Independence alive. The activities of the IRA and the Crown forces are set out in this book, supported by incisive text, as well as maps of key engagements.

Available in eBook or print on **amazon**